Fresh Ecocritical Voices in African Literatures and Cultures

Fresh Ecocritical Voices in African Literatures and Cultures

Edited by
Chinonye C. Ekwueme-Ugwu
Joyce Onoromhenre Agofure
Nsah Mala

SPEARS BOOKS
Denver, Colorado

SPEARS BOOKS
An Imprint of Spears Media Press LLC
7830 W. Alameda Ave, Suite 103-247
Denver, CO 80226
United States of America

First Published in the United States of America in 2025 by Spears Books
www.spearsbooks.org
info@spearsmedia.com
Information on this title: https://bit.ly/3VnBuLl

© 2025 Chinonye C. Ekwueme-Ugwu, Joyce Onoromhenre Agofure & Nsah Mala
All rights reserved.

No part of this publication may be reproduced, distributed, or transmitted in any form or by any means, including photocopying, recording, or other electronic or mechanical methods, without the prior written permission of the publisher, except in the case of brief quotations embodied in critical reviews and certain other noncommercial uses permitted by copyright law. For permission requests, write to the publisher, addressed "Attention: Permissions Coordinator," at the above address.

ISBN: 9781957296647 (Paperback)
ISBN: 9781957296654 (eBook)

Spears Media Press has no responsibility for the persistence or accuracy of urls for external or third-party internet websites referred to in this publication, and does not guarantee that any content on such websites is, or will remain, accurate or appropriate.

Designed and typeset by Spears Media Press LLC
Cover design: D. Kambem

Distributed globally by African Books Collective (ABC)
www.africanbookscollective.com

To all lovers of environmental studies in literature

Contents

Foreword   xi
Acknowledgments   xv

1. Introduction: On Fresh Ecocritical Voices in African Literatures and Cultures   1
   Chinonye Ekwueme-Ugwu, Joyce Agofure, & Nsah Mala

PART ONE: ECOCRITICAL DIALOGUES ACROSS BORDERS: ANGLOPHONE & FRANCOPHONE AFRICA, BRITAIN, AND JAPAN

2. Exploring African Ecocriticism in Three African Literary Texts   19
   Joyce Onoromhenre Agofure & Ezekiel Solomon Akuso

3. Resisting Anthropocentrism: Reading Deep Ecology in Selected Poems of Alice Oswald and Nol Alembong   35
   Mary Louisa Lum

4. That All May Be Green: Investigating Three Francophone African Narratives as Ecomedia   51
   Eunice E. Omonzejie

5. Rhinos, Rangers, and (Eco) Returns in Contemporary South African Literature   69
   Beverley Jane Cornelius & Jean Rossmann

6. Eco-activism, Eco-disasters, and Vulnerability in Niyi Osundare's "Our Earth Will Not Die" and Kinno Yukie's "God"   87
   Sunday Olaoluwagbamila Dawodu & Gracious Ojiebun

7. Place and Socio-natural Environment in the Poetry of Akachi
   Adimora-Ezeigbo & Warsan Shire   103
   Deborah Chinonyerem Uzoma

8. Environmental Degradation: Interrogating Triggers
   and Paradigms in Select African Imaginaries   115
   Victory Ogochukwu Okpala, Ezinwanyi Edikanabasi Adam, &
   Arinze Thankgod Okpala

PART TWO: ECOCRITICAL ISSUES FROM NIGERIAN ART, LITERATURE, THEATRE AND ORATURE

9. Outrage and Marginal Communities: Postcolonial
   and Ecocritical Meditations on Jerry Buhari's
   Landscapes of the Soul (1993-2022)   131
   Dominic James Aboi

10. Art and Society: An Ecocritical Reading of Aliyu Kamal's
    Fire in My Backyard and EE Sule's Makwala   153
    Abubakar Shehu Usman

11. Towards Harmonious African Ecosystems: Estrangement
    and Resilience in Ibirawi Ikiriko and Nnimmo Bassey's
    Poetry Collections   167
    Abundance Amamchukwu

12. Theatrical Design, Environment, and Children's
    Theatre Practice in the ABU Studio Theatre   179
    Franklin Zaure

13. Greg Mbaijiorgu's Wake Up Everyone and the Scourge
    of Climate Change on Food Security   199
    Hameed Olutoba Lawal & Tijime Justin Awuawuer

14. The Nigerian Creative Writer and Ecocritical Challenges in the 21st Century: An Appraisal of Adamu Kyuka Usman's Death of Eternity   215
    Suleiman A. Jaji

15. Folktale as a Pedagogical Agent for Social Justice: An Ecocritical Perspective   233
    Tayo Olubunmi Agboola

PART THREE: ECOCRITICISM AND ENVIRONMENTAL COMMUNICATION FROM CAMEROON AND NIGERIA

16. Language Framing of Climate Change and Ecocritical Consciousness in Nigerian Newspapers   251
    Zulfaa Yushau-Waziri

17. Archeological Alternatives: Towards Africa's Eco-cultural Sustainability   277
    Arthur Nebengou Njume Ndeley

PART FOUR: NEW DIRECTIONS IN AFRICAN ECOCRITICISM: EMPIRICAL & OTHER GESTURES

18. Experimenting with Empirical Ecocriticism: Author and Ecological Imaginaries beyond the Text   293
    Chinonye Ekwueme-Ugwu & Chiamaka Ugoka

19. Three Cameroonians on the Futures of African Ecocriticisms: Interviews with Nnane Ntube, Ekpe Inyang, and Nji Tem   311
    Nsah Mala

Contributors   323
Index   329

List of Figures

Figure 9.1. "Soft Landscape with Two Soft Elements," Acrylic on paper, Jerry Buhari, 15x22 inches, 2007.	136
Figure 9.2. "The Landscapes of the Soul," Watercolor on paper, 6.4x9 inches, Jerry Buhari, 2005.	142
Figure 9.3. "Anthills of Nsukka," Watercolor on paper, 9x13 inches, Jerry Buhari, 2008-2009.	143
Figure 9.4. "Warm Spillage," Mixed media on paper, 11x18 inches, Jerry Buhari, 2016.	145
Figure 9.5. "Dark Melting Planet," Mixed media on paper, 14x14.6 inches, Jerry Buhari, 2016.	147
Figures 9.6. & 9.7. Figure 9.6. (L) "Soft Masquerades Pretending to be Iroko Trees," Acrylic on Canvas, 36.2x60.2 inches, Jerry Buhari, 2022, and Figure 9.7. (R) "Landscapes of Angels and Devourers," Acrylic on canvas, 35.8x58.3 inches, Jerry Buhari, 2020-2022.	148
Figure 12.1. & Figure 12.2. Images of the Studio Theatre (A.B.U. Studio Theatre) (Drama Village)	189
Figure 12.3. & Figure 12.4. Inside the Studio Theatre (A.B.U. Studio Theatre)	189
Figure 12.5. Inside the Studio Theatre	190
Figure 12.6. & Figure 12.7. Picture of plants shared with the children	190
Figure 12.8. Image of children given plants to plant in their communities	191

Foreword

In 2015, when Swarnalatha Rangarajan, Vidya Sarveswaran, and I coedited the volume *Ecocriticism of the Global South*, one of our stated goals was to bring forth the hitherto silenced voices of environmental scholars from developing nations worldwide, including those in Africa. To some extent, these voices were already percolating in Amazonia, Eastern Europe, and South Asia. This is how we knew that we could find more such scholars if we made an effort to look for them and welcome their perspectives into the global conversation about the state of the Earth and how we might make good use of literature and the arts to mobilize vital public discussions about mitigating anthropogenic damage and looking toward a more sustainable future for human beings and the more-than-human world.

As the editors of this new book have carefully enumerated, a decade after the appearance of *Ecocriticism of the Global South*, there is now an abundance of ecocritical writing about African environmental culture, just as there has been a surge of eloquent and engaging ecocritical work in many other regions of the Global South. This is a reason for both celebration and continued vigilance. Many of the commentators on African environmental literature are citizens of the Global North, despite their expertise in African studies, or they are African ex-pats, living in Europe or America. For those who believe ecocriticism, and the environmental humanities more broadly, are essential contributors to energetic and hard-hitting discussions of serious issues in society, from habitat destruction to public health crises, it is particularly important that these conversations take place not only in the rarefied realm of international scholarly conferences and publications but in classrooms and websites and newspapers, even in the homes and streets, within the regions of the world directly affected by ongoing environmental degradation. For this reason, home-grown ecocritical voices and perspectives, such as those offered in this book, are of special value.

What happens in Africa—what is *currently* happening in Africa—matters. It is essential to acknowledge the profound impact of social and environmental upheaval in various regions of the African continent. To borrow a phrase from the American social movement Black Lives Matter, we could say that *African Lives Matter*. This means people's lives throughout the African continent, from North to South, East to West. This means the livability of urban and rural environments, ranging from the ever-expanding Sahara Desert to the lush and mountainous Congo. This means the viability of animal species and the health of river and forest ecosystems across the continent as well. What is happening in Africa, a quarter-century into the new millennium, is not only significant within Africa but also a model—perhaps even a warning—for the rest of the world. If we care about our own backyards in North and South America, Europe, and Asia—everywhere!—we should be paying attention to the situation in Africa vis-à-vis environmental destruction.

According to the website Earth.org, which tracks environmental health worldwide, Africa is facing multiple crises in 2024, including rising atmospheric CO_2 levels, biosystem viability issues, the mass extinction of threatened species, and severe pollution problems. As is the case in many other parts of the world, from Borneo and peninsular Malaysia to the Amazon in South America, deforestation is one of the most pressing problems in Africa. Much of this results from land clearing for agricultural productivity in countries such as Côte d'Ivoire, Ghana, Nigeria, and Cameroon. Who would have thought that one of the world's guilty pleasures—cocoa consumption—might be implicated in increased susceptibility to flooding and the removal of a vital carbon sponge needed to fight global climate change? Even as African forests are being felled, the expansion of the oil and gas industry in Nigeria and South Africa is contributing to worsening air pollution that, as documented in a 2019 study by the National Aeronautics and Space Agency (NASA) in the United States, contributes to nearly 800,000 premature deaths per year in Africa. In other words, more and more toxic emissions are being released in Africa, while there are fewer and fewer forests to help absorb these emissions and prevent dangerous ecological and public health consequences. The oil and gas industry is also responsible for destructive oil spills, with approximately 240,000 barrels of oil leaked into the Niger

Delta each year, which is a specific case of water pollution, one of the key African ecological crises identified on the Earth.org website. All of these problems have profound implications for human well-being in Africa and globally, as well as for ecological health and biodiversity in Africa.

The articles collected in this new book are responses to the rich and insightful environmental texts being created by African writers and artists, which are in turn responses to the environmental and social conditions in specific African places and communities. These articles insightfully clarify the range of human responses to ecological crisis, from precarity to resilience. While some chapters highlight the artistic sophistication of African environmental culture, the book's trajectory moves toward a final section devoted to ecocultural sustainability and practical ecocriticism—in other words, toward engagement with the serious and worrisome issues of today and the anticipated future.

For readers who understand that African lives matter and ecocriticism matters, this is a valuable and exciting volume—a much-needed contribution to the ongoing efforts of artists, journalists, scientists, and scholars to make a positive difference for society and the planet.

Scott Slovic, Professor Emeritus
Oregon Research Institute & the University of Idaho

Acknowledgments

As three editors from diverse African backgrounds, we extend our heartfelt gratitude to Professor Scott Slovic, a doyen of environmental literary discourse and scholarship. His steadfast support and inspiring guidance were pivotal in realizing this book project, forming a solid foundation for our collaborative efforts. Slovic's extensive knowledge and critical insights into ecocriticism have not only enriched our understanding but have also encouraged us to articulate a vision that is inclusive and reflective of the diverse ecological narratives present across our African continent.

We also acknowledge the significant contributions of existing works in the field of African ecocriticism. The scholarship surrounding this discipline has evolved significantly, moving beyond a narrow focus on environmental justice to encompass a broader spectrum of themes, including indigenous ecology, climate fiction, and the complex interrelations between human and nonhuman entities. This expansion reflects a growing recognition of the diverse narratives that shape African literature and its engagement with ecological issues. As we delve into these themes, we are reminded that literature serves as a powerful medium through which ecological awareness can be fostered, allowing for a deeper understanding of the interconnectedness of all life forms.

Remarkably, the pioneering efforts of scholars such as William Slaymaker, Byron Caminero-Santangelo, Cajetan Iheka, Stephanie Newell, Ogaga Okuyade, Étienne-Marie Lassi, Eunice Ngongkum, Sule Egya, Alembong, and many others have highlighted the shifting geography of African ecocriticism. Their works emphasize foundational roots while also pointing toward innovative studies that challenge traditional paradigms. In addition to these scholarly contributions, we acknowledge the activism of figures such as Wangari Maathai and Ken Saro-Wiwa. Their legacies continue to inspire contemporary discourse on environmentalism in Africa. Maathai's Green Belt Movement exemplifies grassroots activism aimed at combating deforestation and promoting sustainable land use, while Saro-Wiwa's poignant critiques of oil exploitation in Nigeria highlight the urgent need for environmental justice. Their commitment to ecological justice serves as a poignant reminder of the vital role literature plays in advocating for sustainable practices and raising awareness about environmental degradation.

As we embark on this journey through our collaborative research, the diversity of voices represented in this volume is a testament to the richness of African literature and its engagement with ecological themes. From established scholars to emerging voices, each contributor has offered invaluable insights that reflect the multifaceted relationship between culture and environment. Your willingness to share your research, experiences, and creative expressions has not only elevated the quality of this work but has also fostered a collaborative spirit that is vital for advancing the field.

By knitting together these diverse threads, we aim to contribute meaningfully to the ongoing conversation surrounding ecology and literature in Africa, ultimately enriching our understanding of how these interactions shape cultural identities and environmental futures in the 21st century.

Chinonye Ekwueme-Ugwu, Joyce Agofure, & Nsah Mala

CHAPTER ONE

Introduction
On Fresh Ecocritical Voices in African Literatures and Cultures

Chinonye Ekwueme-Ugwu, Joyce Agofure, & Nsah Mala

Beyond the Western philosophical ecocritical boundaries, the postcolonial African perspectives to literary environmentalism opened up by the continent's environmentalist authors and critics, at home and in the diaspora, including Rob Nixon, Byron Caminero-Santangelo, Anthony Vital, Cajetan Iheka, Ogaga Okuyade, Étienne-Marie Lassi, Eunice Ngongkum, Sule Egya, Kenneth Nsah (aka Nsah Mala), F. Fiona Moolla, Evan Maina Mwangi, Makuchi Nfa-Abbenyi, Toyin Falola and Emily Brownell, and many others created the ripple effects of broadening and deepening the African literary environmentalist frontiers. Yet few opportunities exist for ventilating the views of the highly disadvantaged mass of African ecocriticism scholars and writers based on the continent, whose voices and experimentations are often invalidated by the lack of acceptance and publication opportunities, thus remaining stunted--with a few notable exceptions (e.g., see Ngongkum 2017; Egya 2020; Alembong et al. 2015). Against this backdrop, this volume seeks to provide one such opportunity to advance the growing field of literature, culture, and the natural environment in postcolonial African scholarship.

The initial postcolonial ideological deflation of William Slaymaker's (2001) rather hasty assumptions on the ecocritical credibility of African literature sparked off several divergent other postcolonial socio-political and economic reactions to the environmentalist question in the continental literatures, continuously regenerating and growing into an army of African literary scholars and critics seeking vistas for airing

INTRODUCTION

their environmentalist viewpoints; thus rendering inviolable the task of making audible as many silenced voices as possible.

The above concern and the desire to "rethink thinking"[1] as it were, on the ecocriticism of the region, from its inception at the turn of the twenty-first century to its present, informed the panel proposal for the 9th European Conference of African Studies, ECAS. The panel call for papers, following the acceptance of the proposal, attracted an enormous number of ecocritical African and pro-Africanist voices from different regions of the continent and beyond, including the USA and Europe. The disparate conditions of Africa, with the rest of the world, are encapsulated in the thematic concerns of the proposal, expressed as follows:

> Africa's relationship with the rest of the world–Europe and America, especially – has been one of the struggles between predator and prey, exploiter and exploited, with the African environment as a battleground. On the other hand, global attention has, in this 21st century, been increasingly focused on the best options for humanity's enjoyment of the preponderant gains of advancements in science and technology, while at the same time reducing, to the barest, human actions that create pollution, climate and biodiversity crises. To the global West, whose authors and critics are at the forefront of environmental criticism and advocacy, this seems logical. However, environmental criticism and advocacy from the largely underdeveloped countries of the Global South apparently contradicts those of the industrialized West, as theoretical and methodological stances from the two blocs reveal. Leveraging an extant body of environmental literature and criticisms from Africa, and the African diaspora, this panel seeks to explore ecocriticism in African Literature - past, present, and future. It will evaluate, from a postcolonial viewpoint, the position of African ecocritics. It will evaluate what critics have been up to, since the turn of the twenty-first

---

1   Steven Van Wolputte et al. 2022. "The Aftermath – What Future for African Studies (in Europe?). A View from Behind the Scenes of ECAS9."

century, when the first paper on ecocriticism by an African appeared in an international journal, on the subject of literature and environment. It will evaluate convergences and divergences in the theoretical and methodological views from various African and African diaspora ecocritics, environmentally conscious authors - poets, playwrights/dramatists, novelists, writers of short stories, and critics, in African literature of the 20th and 21st centuries.[2]

Thus, with the aim, partly, to interrogate the extant body of literature and criticisms of African literature, discussants were expected to offer new, more viable ways of rethinking the past and present and proposing a viable future for the sustainability of environmental consciousness within the ambits of Africa's postcolonial socio-political, economic and environmentalist experiences. The objective was to discover fresh perspectives to existing voices through which the environment in the continental literatures and criticism may be approached with "environment" as the general term for the physical surroundings, as well as the psychosomatic, socio-economic, and political conditions that shape and are shaped by the African spatial and other ecological issues.

However, diplomatic, financial, and other constraints limited the physical participation of many who submitted their papers to the panel. Very credible authors, scholars, and researchers who indicated an interest in participating in the conference but were thus hindered were encouraged to submit their works that address ecocriticism from the African ecological viewpoints (past and present) in fresh ways and provide recommendations for the future. The hope was also to comprehend representations of pre-colonial African ecosystems in their natural state; the socio-cultural, political, and economic indicators that condition present ecological injustices that African and postcolonial ecocritics and writers explore in their works, and to tender prognostic insights towards the reclamation of lost African environmental histories. Accordingly, this volume incorporates some views from the papers presented at the

---

2 See abstract describing the theme of the panel, culled from <https://nomadit.co.uk/conference/ecas2023/p/12443> accessed on 10 September 2024.

conference and other fresh ideas that could not be presented, but are nonetheless relevant to initiating multidisciplinary conversations on the wide-ranging meditations and critical insights regarding African literatures and cultures of the environment in the twenty-first century.

PERSPECTIVES IN POSTCOLONIAL AFRICAN ECOCRITICISM(S)

We recognize the significant contributions of existing works in the field of African ecocriticism. Notably, *African Literature: An Anthology of Criticism and Theory* by Tejumola Olaniyan and Ato Quayson stands out as a key anthology that consolidates essential texts in African literary theory and criticism. This collection not only deepens the understanding of African literary traditions but also encourages the ongoing development of African literary criticism. It serves as a crucial resource for anyone interested in the complexities of African literature and its critical discourse, weaving together a rich tapestry of voices and perspectives that highlight the multifaceted nature of African literary expression. By incorporating, moreover, four ecocritical views of Africa from William Slaymaker, Rob Nixon, Byron Caminero-Santangelo, and Juliana Makuchi Nfa-Abbenyi, the anthology arguably ushered into the annals of African literatures the environmentalist questions that form the bedrock of the current postcolonial ecocritical advocacies.

Toyin Falola and Emily Brownell's *Landscape, Environment and Technology in Colonial and Postcolonial Africa* investigates two essential categories of knowledge production related to Africa during colonial and postcolonial periods: "environment" and "landscape". Discussions about African environments often portray Africans as the primary agents of land degradation, attributing this to a lack of knowledge and technological resources. To enhance the understanding of these categories and explore how they have been constructed and utilized to shape colonial and postcolonial narratives, this volume examines the concept of the "technological pastoral." By critically engaging with these themes, it advocates for a reevaluation of narratives, promoting a fair representation of Africa that acknowledges the complexities of its environments and the diverse experiences of its inhabitants.

Byron Caminero-Santangelo and Garth Myers, in *Environment at the*

Margins, bring together literary and environmental studies in a robust interdisciplinary dialogue, challenging prevailing ideas about nature, conservation, and development in Africa, while exploring alternative narratives from writers and environmental thinkers.[3] The essays in their volume integrate scholarship from geography, anthropology, and environmental history with African and colonial literatures, fostering a rich literary analysis. In doing so, *Environment at the Margins* posits the potential for an ecocriticism that transcends limiting and marginalizing visions of Africa.

Okuyade Ogaga offers critical insights into the representations of the relationship between humans and the environment in contemporary African literature.[4] The book examines how various literary works articulate connections between human experiences and ecological concerns, emphasizing the need for a harmonious relationship between humanity and nature. It aims to go beyond thematic analysis to explore literature's ethical and activist roles, addressing ecological imbalances across the continent. Ogaga's work encourages African scholars and students to engage with ecocriticism in a way that underscores the urgency of environmental issues within their cultural contexts, thus enriching the discourse surrounding African literatures and cultures.

Dustin Crowley's Africa's *Narrative Geographies* delves into the complex literary landscapes of Africa, introducing innovative approaches to understanding the geographies depicted in African literatures.[5] By employing frameworks from cultural geography and political ecology, Crowley emphasizes the interplay between literature and geography, highlighting how narratives are shaped by socio-political contexts. Through a critical examination of various texts, the book seeks to uncover how African writers express their experiences and perspectives on their environments, revealing the complexities of their lived realities. This

---

3 Byron Caminero-Santangelo and Garth Myers, eds. 2011. *Environment at the Margins: Literary and Environmental Studies in Africa*. Athens: Ohio University Press.

4 Ogaga Okuyade. 2013. *Eco-critical Literature: Regreening African Landscapes*. New York: African Heritage Press.

5 Dustin Crowley. 2015. *Africa's Narrative Geographies: Charting the Intersections of Geocriticism and Postcolonial Studies*. London: Palgrave Macmillan.

interdisciplinary approach enriches the understanding of African literatures while contributing to broader discussions about environmental justice and the socio-political dimensions of place.

F. Fiona Molla's, in the edited volume *Natures of Africa,* explores the intersections between ecocriticism and animal studies, providing a nuanced understanding of cultural representations of nature.[6] The book examines how contemporary African literature reflects and shapes perceptions of the natural world and its inhabitants, emphasizing the intricate relationships between humans, animals, and the environment. The contributors argue that these representations are deeply embedded in cultural, social, and political contexts, influencing societal engagement with ecological issues. By integrating animal studies into ecocritical discourse, they broaden the scope of environmental literature, allowing for a more inclusive exploration of ecological themes across various cultural forms. In one of the chapters of the book, Chengyi Coral Wu investigates various literary works that depict the intricate dynamics of human-nature relationships, emphasizing how these texts reflect the realities of environmental degradation and the resilience of affected communities.[7] Wu highlights the importance of recognizing local ecological knowledge and practices woven into African narratives. By advocating for a more inclusive ecocritical approach, she emphasizes African literature's diverse voices and experiences. Her chapter also examines the aesthetic dimensions of environmental literature, analyzing how literary techniques enhance the representation of ecological themes and deepen readers' engagement with pressing environmental issues.

Meanwhile, Byron Caminero-Santangelo, in his 2016 monograph, investigates the African environmental literary tradition through a diverse array of texts, highlighting their ecological themes and local significance.[8]

---

6   F. Fiona, Molla, ed. 2016. *Natures of Africa: Ecocriticism and Animal Studies in Contemporary Cultural Forms.* Johannesburg: Wits University Press.
7   Chengyi Coral Wu. 2016. "Towards an Ecocriticism in Africa: Literary Aesthetics in African Environmental Literature." Molla Fiona F. *Natures of Africa: Ecocriticism and Animal Studies in Contemporary Cultural Forms.* Johannesburg: Wits University Press.
8   Byron Caminero-Santangelo. 2016. *Different Shades of Green: African Literature, Environmental Justice, and Political Ecology.* New York: University of Virginia Press.

His approach, termed "postcolonial regional particularism," advocates for understanding narratives as intricately tied to specific locales and local concerns, especially regarding environmental justice struggles. He includes memoirs, political texts, and contemporary literature, expanding the definition of environmentally relevant literature and enriching the understanding of how environmental issues intersect with African social and political realities.

Moradewun Adejunmobi and Carli Coetzee's *Routledge Handbook of African Literature* is a comprehensive resource that consolidates studies of African literary texts through various contemporary approaches.[9] This anthology incorporates frameworks from queer theory, eco-criticism, food studies, and network theory alongside traditional discussions of postcolonial politics. It is organized into seven distinct sections, facilitating a multifaceted exploration of themes and fostering interdisciplinary dialogue.

Ernest N. Emenyonu, Cajetan Iheka, and Stephanie Newell's special issue, *Environmental Transformations: African Literature Today,* investigates the literary strategies employed by African writers to articulate the effects of climate change and environmental transformation.[10] They affirm that the geography of African ecocriticism has shifted significantly, highlighting the expanding scope of ecocriticism in Africa. This exploration is crucial in the context of African literatures, where writers often engage deeply with pressing environmental issues and the socio-political dynamics shaping their narratives. This critical lens enriches the discourse surrounding environmental literatures and positions African voices at the forefront of global conversations about climate change and sustainability.

Sule E. Egya's *Nature, Environment and Activism in Nigerian Literature* focuses on the Nigerian context within postcolonial ecocriticism, analyzing the textual strategies and historical aspects that inform ecological themes in contemporary literature.[11] By emphasizing nature, environment,

---

9   Moradewun Adejunmobi and Carli Coetzee, eds. 2019. *Routledge Handbook of African Literature*. London: Routledge.
10 Ernest N. Emenyonu, Cajetan Iheka, and Stephenie Newell, eds. 2020. *Special Issue Environmental Transformations: African Literature Today*. New York: Boydell and Brewer.
11 Sule E. Egya. 2020. *Nature, Environment, and Activism in Nigerian Literature*.

and activism, the author reorients African ecocriticism, highlighting an eco-social perspective that distinguishes Nigerian environmental writing from that of other African countries. This study illustrates how Nigerian authors connect with their communities' natural landscapes while addressing ecological issues through indigenous literary techniques.

In addition, Cajetan Iheka's *Naturalizing Africa* emphasizes the connection between ecological violence and postcolonial narratives, showcasing the agency of African voices in resisting environmental degradation.[12] Iheka explores the complex relationships between humans and their environments, particularly in the context of postcolonial struggles, illustrating how narratives articulate the lived experiences of communities facing environmental crises. This work underscores the critical role of African literature in framing ecological concerns as integral to postcolonial identity and agency. Furthermore, Cajetan Iheka's *African Ecomedia* presents a profound exploration of the intricate relationship between media production and environmental impact across the African continent.[13] By examining diverse visual media forms, including film, photography, and sculpture, Iheka offers a multifaceted perspective on the socio-ecological costs associated with media technologies. His approach acknowledges the resourcefulness of African media makers, recognizing their potential to use visual media as a platform for raising awareness and catalyzing change. This profound perspective challenges simplistic narratives that depict Africa solely as a victim of environmental exploitation, instead positioning the continent's artists and filmmakers as active agents in confronting these complex issues.

Kenneth Toah Nsah (aka Nsah Mala), in his award-winning doctoral thesis, examines how English and French African literary texts– poems, plays, and novels– can help in addressing climate change and ecological concerns and thus contribute to saving the Congo Basin, which is the

---

London: Routledge.

12 Cajetan Iheka. 2018. *Naturalizing Africa: Ecological Violence, Agency, and Postcolonial Resistance in African Literature.* Cambridge: Cambridge University Press.

13 Cajetan Iheka. 2021. *African Ecomedia: Network Forms, Planetary Politics.* Durham, NC: Duke University Press.

second largest tropical rainforest in the world.[14] In terms of place-based African ecocriticism, Nsah moves beyond the centrism of the Niger Delta to foreground the Congo Basin as another geopolitical spot of global importance in terms of biodiversity, climate mitigation, minerals, and sustainable development amidst forces of injustice and green colonialism. Relatedly, Nsah Mala and Nicki Hitchcott, in a recently edited volume, engage with a wide variety of ecologically-attuned texts such as film, comics, zines, novels, poems, etc., from the postcolonial Francophone world of the Global South, including numerous contributions from Africa.[15] For instance, their volume presents ecocritical discussions of topics in Africa such as nuclear pollution and waste, critical plant studies, and pandemics, among others.

These foundational works significantly enhance the discourse on African ecocriticism, emphasizing the necessity of examining the connections between colonial encounters, resource extraction, and ecological destruction in African contexts. They affirm that any critique of postcolonialism must engage with ecocritical frameworks, validating the assertion that literature can play a vital role in advancing environmental awareness and advocating for sustainable practices.

FRESH ECOCRITICAL VOICES IN AFRICAN LITERATURES AND CULTURES

Our volume significantly adds to the existing body of literature by underscoring the enduring importance of environmental discourses within African literatures and cultures. While many foundational texts in African ecocriticism focus on established frameworks, this anthology emphasizes the emergence of new perspectives and methodologies that reflect contemporary ecological concerns and cultural contexts. The chapters reveal a complex interplay of historical, environmental, and

---

14 Kenneth Toah Nsah. 2022. "Can Literature Save the Congo Basin? Postcolonial Ecocriticism and Environmental Literary Activism". Aarhus University, PhD Thesis. This won the 2022 Prize for Francophone Theses in Foresight and Futures Studies from Fondation 2100 (France) and Agence Universitaire de la Francophonie (AUF).

15 Nsah Mala and Nicki Hitchcott, eds. (2025). *Ecotexts in the Postcolonial Francosphere*. Liverpool: Liverpool University Press.

socio-ecological viewpoints, illuminating the historical legacies of colonialism that shape contemporary ecological challenges while advocating for sustainable practices and environmental justice to address critical socio-environmental issues.

Furthermore, one notable aspect of the book is the commitment to amplifying diverse voices and experiences within contemporary African literatures. Integrating a wide range of cultural-literary forms and genres fosters a more inclusive understanding of how ecological themes manifest across different cultural narratives. In addition, the anthology addresses the interconnectedness of environmental issues with socio-political dynamics, emphasizing the role of literature as a tool for activism and social change. These diverse viewpoints highlight the pressing need for ongoing exploration of environmental themes and ecological scholarship in literature from and about the region, serving as a vital means to inspire efforts toward ecological restoration and sustainability in Africa and beyond. Thus, *Fresh Ecocritical Voices in African Literatures and Cultures* not only builds on the foundational works in the field but also pushes the boundaries of ecocritical scholarship, making it a vital contribution to the ongoing conversation about literature, culture, and the environment in Africa.

Many of the eighteen distinct chapters of the book incorporate ideas about the possibility of mitigating the socio-environmental problems of Africa through environmental "faction" (incorporating the elements of the real with the imagined) and nonfiction, including language and the media, with some questioning the distinction between art and science. Significant new areas relate essentially to approaches, demonstrating how ecocriticism of Africa can and actually does deviate from that of the global North, which has thrived mainly on imaginative writings and criticisms of nature and the natural environment, within the earlier Romantic traditions, the non-fiction Nature-Writing practices of English and North American poetics, and more recently cli-fi. Some contributors to our volume have demonstrated welcome deviations toward conversations on the possibilities of empirical ecocriticism (an emerging branch in the field) and more pragmatic representations of the plight of indigenous African ecosystems, persons, and cultures by ecologically conscious authors and critics. This empirical strand is particularly evident in the chapter by Chinonye Ekwueme-Ugwu and Chiamaka Ugoka.

CHAPTERS IN BRIEF

The chapters open with an introduction by the editors aimed at clarifying the background, discussing basic assumptions, and presenting the aims and objectives of the book. This is followed by Joyce Onoromhenre Agofure and Ezekiel Solomon Akuso's delineation of ecocriticism in African literatures from its diverse postcolonial viewpoints, since the turn of the 21st century, to the discovery of African ecocriticism as a distinct sub-field of global ecocriticism that stresses the embeddedness of the environmentalist consciousness, with cultures that defy any treatment of the environment as "other." They highlight, especially, African societies' awareness of the environment through their myths, songs, proverbs, taboos, and rituals, demonstrating African environmentalism that perceives the environment as sacred and an essential part of the world balance. Contrasting it with the industrialists' "othering" mentality, their chapter raises important issues regarding African literatures, past, present, and future.

From visual artistic viewpoints, Dominic Aboi explores the beauties and sorrows in diverse African landscapes, such as the one entitled "Ant Hills of Nsukka" or "The Earth Bleeding" in the one entitled "Warm Spillage." These are from Jerry Buhari's collection of paintings entitled *The Landscape of the Soul*, which represents pre- and post-colonial Africa, juxtaposed with present-day realities, a strong message for the future. Aboi decries the state of global environmental politics and their "narratives of colonial enslavement ... as catalysts in forced migrations across diverse demographics." Arguing that Western narratives undermine Africa's sociopolitical and cultural relationships, and put the continent and the world at grave risk, he warns that despite previous and current admonitions against unrestrained exploitation, lack of "political will, and capitalist impulse" have continued to frustrate all moral dispositions towards the physical African environment. Jean Rossmann and Beverley Jane Cornelius, in their exploration of three recent South African literary texts, underscore the representations of "the historical exploitation of, and damage to the region's environment," with a postcolonial elucidation of the reasons for these, and suggestions for fostering future environmental justice. They present fresh perspectives, offering some philosophical reflections on African animist ontology and a new ethics of caring for the environment, with a sense of hopefulness for the future that does not sentimentalize problems or trivialize the multiple cultural and socio-political challenges that must be addressed.

Abundance Chizurum Amamchukwu underscores the connection of environment and cultural nuances with human experiences in Africa, and confronts "ecological estrangement" as a barrier to building a sustainable African future, prioritizing "the harmonious coexistence between humans and the environment." Towards the sustainability of eco-cultural activities in African literature, Arthur Nebengou Njume Ndeley uncovers archaeological approaches towards the preservation of "ancient cultures on taboo, totemism, and magic realism" in selected African narratives, as relevant to environmental protection and the preservation of endangered animals and plant species in Africa. Sunday Dawodu and Gracious Ojiebun underscore the role of ecoactivism in mediating environmental collapse and vulnerability in their cross-border analysis of activism in the poetry of Niyi Osundare and Kinno Yukie as responses to recognized environmental challenges, respectively, in their Nigerian and Japanese settings. By offering a cross-national comparative eco-analysis of disasters, vulnerability, and eco-activism, they achieve a remarkable comparison of the two, showcasing entanglements between ecological issues in Africa and elsewhere in the world. Deborah Uzoma explores the concept of place from the West African and East African perspectives of Akachi Adimora-Ezeigbo and Warsan Shire, respectively, in their poetry collections, and uncovers strong connections of place, gender, and environmental consciousness in the poems. Reacting to the eco-activism movement, Mary Louisa Lum questions the anthropocentric theory that affirms human dominance over the natural world and avers that it breeds environmental exploitation. She also examines the activist tendencies of poems by Alice Oswald and Nol Alembong through a thorough ecological analysis. The Earth-centered viewpoint that both poets promote emphasizes harmony with the natural world. They acknowledge the oneness of humans and nature while addressing postcolonial spatial dynamics, and they call for a change in human perspective towards moral and sustainable behavior. The study aligns with the ideas of George Sessions and Arne Naess by combining deep ecology and romantic philosophy to support de-centering mankind and embracing actual environmental conservation. Like Dawodu and Ojiebun, Lum also highlights interconnections between ecological concerns in Africa and elsewhere on our shared Earth.

Abubakar Shehu Usman underscores the significant role of ecocriticism in art, which he believes could be "used to analyze and understand the complex relationship between humans and the natural world." Eunice Omonzojie, on the other hand, examines the "African traditional and cultural reality of mutuality and inter-subjectivity between humankind and his environment." In her research of Francophone African novels, she underscores the traditional African relationship with the non-human significance towards the preservation of Africa's environment and natural history, and also underscores the multilingualism characteristic of African literatures and cultures. From dramaturgy, Hameed Olutoba Lawal and Tijime Justin Awuawuer highlight some proactive steps that can be taken to combat food insecurity and the devastating effects of climate change in Africa, using Greg Mbajiogu's play *Wake Up Everyone* as an example. On the other hand, Zulfaa Yushau-Waziri examines newspaper framing of climate change from Nigerian national dailies. She underscores the socio-cultural and political influences that shape such framing and concludes that cultural dimensions, power dynamics, and the interplay between global and local perspectives shape media representations of climate change in Nigeria.

Olubunmi Tayo Agboola explores African oral literature and folktales in particular and their contribution to the formation of law and order, including those that guide the relationship between human beings and their environment in ways that guarantee social and ecological justice. In their interrogation of environmental degradation in select African imaginaries, Ezinwayi Adam and Victory Okpala touch on various issues, including authors' commitment to, manifestations and triggers of degradation among the African poor, and which foregrounds ills such as "hunger, unfulfilled promises, neglect, and marginalization." Franklin Pyokpung Zaure's chapter is a reflection on theatre and the environment, with a defense for environmental consciousness through theatre, as well as the deployment of environmentally friendly materials in artistic creations such as props and scenery. This aligns with recent research by

Nsah and co-authors on the slowness in integrating sustainability into contemporary theatre and performance practices in Cameroon.[16] From an ecocritical viewpoint, Suleiman A. Jaji's chapter is an appraisal of the challenges facing the Nigerian writer in the 21st century. He traces environmentalism in literature from historical times to the present and underscores the future benefits of a postcolonial shift towards ecocriticism, provided that the writer can surmount the socio-economic barriers that inhibit creativity. Chinonye Ekwueme-Ugwu and Chiamaka Ugoka's chapter is a gesture in the direction of empirical ecocriticism, integrating discoveries from Aliyu Kamal's novel, *Fire in My Backyard*, with analyses of the author's responses to their interviews on the impact of the natural environment on the author's imagination.[17] Finally, Nsah Mala's chapter, which concludes our volume, consists of an interview with some Cameroonian/African writers and scholars (viz. Nnane Ntube, Ekpe Inyang, and Edwin Nji Tem) on current developments and new or potential directions in African ecocritical writings and scholarship.

Put together, the eco-critical perspectives emerging from *Fresh Ecocritical Voices in African Literatures and Cultures* contribute significantly to the existing body of literature, emphasizing the lasting importance of environmental discourses within African literature. The discussions and narratives embedded in it reveal a complex interplay of historical, environmental, and socio-ecological viewpoints. They not only illuminate the historical legacies of colonialism that have shaped contemporary ecological challenges but also advocate for sustainable practices and environmental justice. By accentuating the interconnectedness of human and environmental health, these scholars and writers amplify marginalized voices and address critical socio-environmental issues. Ultimately, these diverse viewpoints highlight the pressing need for ongoing exploration of environmental themes and expansion of ecological scholarship in the literatures from and about the region of Africa. This exploration, we

---

16   Kenneth T. Nsah, Lisette N. Malung, and Noella M. Ngunyam. 2022. "The Slow Integration of Sustainability into Contemporary Theatre and Performance Practices in Cameroon." *Peripeti*, no. 32, DOI: https://doi.org/10.7146/peri.v19i37.135191

17   The interview technique (as well as field research) is also used by Nsah in his 2022 award-winning doctoral thesis about the Congo Basin.

hope, should serve as a vital means to inspire efforts toward ecological restoration and sustainability in Africa and beyond.

REFERENCES

Adejunmobi, Moradewun and Carli Coetzee, eds. 2019. *Routledge Handbook of African Literature*. London: Routledge.

Alembong, Nol, Oscar C. Labang, and Eunice F. Fombele, eds. 2015. *Ecocultural Perspectives: Literature and Language*. Raytown, MO: Ken Scholars Publishing.

Caminero-Santangelo, Byron. 2016. *Different Shades of Green: African Literature, Environmental Justice, and Political Ecology*. New York: University of Virginia Press.

Caminero-Santangelo, Byron, and Garth Myers. 2011. *Environment at the Margins: Literary and Environmental Studies in Africa*. Athens: Ohio University Press.

Crowley, Dustin. 2015. *Africa's Narrative Geographies: Charting the Intersections of Geocriticism and Postcolonial Studies*. London: Palgrave Macmillan.

Egya, Sule E. 2020. *Nature, Environment, and Activism in Nigerian Literature*. London: Routledge.

Emenyonu, Ernest N., Cajetan Iheka, and Stephenie Newell, eds. 2020. *Special Issue Environmental Transformations: African Literature Today*. New York: Boydell and Brewer.

Falola, Toyin, and Emily Brownell, eds. 2011. *Landscape, Environment, and Technology in Colonial and Postcolonial Africa*. New York: Routledge.

Iheka, Cajetan. 2021. *African Ecomedia: Network Forms, Planetary Politics*. Durham, NC: Duke University Press.

Iheka, Cajetan. 2018. *Naturalizing Africa: Ecological Violence, Agency, and Postcolonial Resistance in African Literature*. Cambridge: Cambridge University Press.

Lassi, Étienne-Marie, ed. 2013. *Aspects écocritique de l'imaginaire africain*. Bamenda: Langaa RPCIG.

Molla, Fiona F., ed. 2016. *Natures of Africa: Ecocriticism and Animal Studies in Contemporary Cultural Forms*. Johannesburg: Wits University Press.

Ngongkum, Eunice. 2017. *Anglophone Cameroon Poetry in the

Environmental Matrix. Lausanne: Peter Lang.

Nsah Mala, and Nicki Hitchcott, eds. 2025. *Ecotexts in the Postcolonial Francosphere*. Liverpool: Liverpool University Press.

Nsah, Kenneth Toah. 2022. "Can Literature Save the Congo Basin? Postcolonial Ecocriticism and Environmental Literary Activism." PhD diss., Aarhus University.

Nsah, Kenneth T., Lisette N. Malung, and Noella M. Ngunyam. 2022. "The Slow Integration of Sustainability into Contemporary Theatre and Performance Practices in Cameroon." *Peripeti* 32. DOI: https://doi.org/10.7146/peri.v19i37.135191

Okuyade, Ogaga, ed. 2013. *Eco-critical Literature: Regreening African Landscapes*. New York: African Heritage Press.

Olaniyan, Tejumola, and Ato Quayson, eds. 2007. *African Literature: An Anthology of Criticism and Theory*. New York: Wiley-Blackwell.

Wu, Chengyi Coral. 2016. "Towards an Ecocriticism in Africa: Literary Aesthetics in African Environmental Literature." In *Natures of Africa: Ecocriticism and Animal Studies in Contemporary Cultural Forms*, edited by Fiona F. Molla. Johannesburg: Wits University Press.

Wolputte, Steven van, Michael Thomas Bollig, Martina Gockel, Clemens Greiner, and Noah Kahindi. 2024. "The Aftermath – What Future for African Studies (in Europe?). A View from Behind the Scenes of ECAS9." *Africa Spectrum* 59, no. 2.

PART ONE

ECOCRITICAL DIALOGUES ACROSS BORDERS: ANGLOPHONE & FRANCOPHONE AFRICA, BRITAIN, AND JAPAN

CHAPTER TWO

Exploring African Ecocriticism in Three African Literary Texts

Joyce Onoromhenre Agofure & Ezekiel Solomon Akuso

INTRODUCTION

Every society's ecological knowledge and culture are the expression of how people live within a given place and space. In this context, the environmental crises of the twenty-first century have given rise to literature that signifies the fragility of the interrelatedness of all life forms; thereby underpinning the frailty of the ecosystem. This development necessitated the emergence of Ecocriticism – an approach that addresses the increasing presence of discourses on the tension between environment, power, and consumerism in the postmodern world. Ecocriticism as a form of literary and cultural critique emerged in North America. It was borne out of a desire to improve how the environment is treated by its human constituents. This idea or movement was advanced through non-fiction and fiction. Ecocriticism entreats humans to examine themselves and the world around them by critiquing how humans interact with, construct, and represent the environment. Thus, Ecocriticism has become a productive field, bringing in new opportunities to articulate the environmental crisis and the future.

Within this context, scholars have argued for African Ecocriticism, which examines imaginative texts, cities, and nature. Nonetheless, indigenous peoples practiced many of its principles before ecocriticism came into the mainstream lexicon. Ecocritical thought is embedded in African beliefs, values, actions, and ways of life such that it is completely inherent or innate. By 'Africans', we mean Africans before Western colonization disturbed and compelled them to engage in undertakings that are un-African. Consequently, this study upholds that African ecocriticism, or environmentalism, in its distinct form, has always existed in the African literary, social, and cultural space. Small wonder, the like of William Slaymaker rejects the romantic aesthetics of the American and British early ecocriticism, especially in their notion of celebrating wilderness and individualism. He puts it that "there is no rush by African literary and cultural critics to adopt ecocriticism or the literature of the environment as these are promulgated from many of the world's metropolitan centers and because they misrepresent the varied landscapes of sub-Saharan Africa… Ecocriticism… appears as another hegemonic discourse from the Metropolitan West."[1] Then, Slaymaker seemed to suggest that "the low visibility of ecolit and ecocrit in recent black African writing is temporary. The green revolution will spread to and through communities of readers and writers of African literature 'echoing' the booming interest."[2] Indeed, in its expansion and shift, ecocriticism is gaining a lot of traction in Africa, as evidenced by the representation of the human and the nonhuman world in African literature as found in the writings of Anthony Vital, Ogaga Okuyade, Cajetan Iheka, Fiona Moolla, and many others. Attesting, Iheka and Newell put it that, "the field is growing rapidly as there is now a rush to adopt ecocriticism in African literary and cultural studies. The fact that Slaymaker's position is now dated is a testament to the growing body of works in African Ecocriticism."[3] This chapter, therefore, adds to existing perceptions that African ecocriticism unveils distinct and complicated past and present, alongside how industrialization and globalization have impacted the African natural world, hence the determination to have a sustainable way of inhabiting a place as captured in African literary efforts.

---

1   William Slaymaker, "Ecoing the Other(s): The Call of Global Green and Black African Responses," in *African Literature: An Anthology of Criticism and Theory*, eds. Tejumola Olaniyan and Ato Quayson (U.S.A: Blackwell Publishing, 2007), 134.
2   Slaymaker, "Ecoing the Other(s)", 139.
3   Cajetan Iheka and Stephanie, Newell, "Introduction: Itineraries of African Ecocriticism and Environmental Transformations in African Literature," *ALT 38* (September 2020): 2.

EXPLICATING AFRICAN ECOCRITICISM / ENVIRONMENTALISM

With the current array of published works on African ecocriticism, it can be said that African ecocriticism, or environmentalism, is a vast and dynamic conversation. African ecocriticism is a literary and cultural approach that recognizes the correlation between the natural and human worlds. It is articulated within the African space based on socio-cultural, political, environmental, colonial, neocolonial, and globalization issues affecting Africa. There have been contentions about ecocritical writings in Africa over the past decades. Caminero-Santangelo once expressed that "there have been little Eco-critical literary writings from Africa" and that rather than environmental issues ... African writers are concerned with primarily addressing political and social issues."[4] Nonetheless, imbued in these socio-political concerns are also vigorous ecological matters. Anyokwu asserts that "contrary to what Western ecocritics hold, [landscape] in traditional African consciousness is not 'other'. Rather, it is apprehended by the people as an object of veneration rather than aesthetic appreciation."[5] African ecocritical ideas abound, which show the harmonious co-existence of African people and the environment.

To elucidate further, the environment is considered Mother Earth in African cosmology. This is evident in African origin, beliefs, ethics, and values closely connected to the forest, its animals, and the land. The uniqueness of land to Africa is that it is a gift from God and ancestors, a source of livelihood that can be cultivated for food, shelter, spirituality, and rituals. For instance, the Igbo and Yoruba, like other ethnic groups in Nigeria, perceive the earth—'ala' and 'Ife' respectively—as the mother earth which sustains all things. The land is esteemed as sacred and not labeled 'other' as often indicated among industrialists, capitalists, and supporters. Instead, it is a vital part of the African traditional world equilibrium. In addition, African environmentalism, according

---

4   Byron Caminero-Santangelo, "In Place: Tourism, Cosmopolitan Bioregionalism, and Zakes Mda's *The Heart of Redness*" in *Postcolonial Ecologies: Literatures of the Environment*, eds. Elizabeth DeLoughrey and George Handley (New York: Oxford University Press, 2011), 7.
5   Christopher, Anyokwu. (2023). "Osundare's Poetry and the Yoruba Worldview." *Purdue*, (December 2). http://docs.lib.purdue.edu/clcweb/vol13/iss1/3/.

to Kelbessa, underlines that "human beings are mere co-occupants of nature with other species, without any heavenly mandate to dominate, subdue or exploit nature. This attitude toward nature is opposed to the mechanistic and anthropocentric outlook initiated by Francis Bacon and René Descartes who perceive humans as privileged members of the ecological community with the moral authority to monopolize nature."[6]

However, African scholars such as Segun Ogungbemi (Nigeria), Godfrey Tangwa (Cameroon), Bujo (Democratic Republic of Congo), Murove (Zimbabwe), and Martin Prozesky (South Africa) have articulated diverse environmental ethical responsibility. Ogungbemi refers to this as ethics of nature-relatedness, and Tangwa describes it as eco-bio-communalism, whereas Bujo calls it African holism. For Ekwealo, African ecocritical ideas "deal with the fundamental principles that govern the relationship between man and the environment based on an African worldview. It has a background belief in the connection of nature, community, and man, from which an ethical relationship is well-defined."[7] Ikuenobe puts it that, "activities that have raised environmental concerns in Africa did not exist before colonialism because Africans had conservationist values, practices, and ways of life. African views and thoughts on ontology, cosmology, medicine, healing, and religious practices support their moral attitudes toward conserving and preserving the environment. Traditional African thought perceives nature as a holistic, interconnected continuum of humans and natural objects that exist in harmony."[8] Also, Ogar and Bassey, write that the "broad-based understanding of our environment as a person, as a subjective base of our action, as the world in which our beings unfold, is the combination of all the facts and relations that go to shape our consciousness."[9] In other words, Africans utilize the cultural norms embedded in taboos and proverbs to promote human forbearance

---

6   Kelbessa Workineh, "Can African Environmental Ethics Contribute to Environmental Policy in Africa? *Environmental Ethics* 36 (2014): 31-61.
7   Ekwealo Chigbo, "Environmental Ethics and Values in the 21st Century: An Africanist Philosophical Analysis", *Journal of African Environmental Ethics and Values*, no 2 (2011): 23-24.
8   Polycarp Ikuenobe, "Traditional African Environmental Ethics and Colonial Legacy", *International Journal of Philosophy and Theology*, 10 (2014): 31.
9   Joseph N. Ogar and Samuel A. Bassey, "African Environmental Ethics" *RAIS Journal for Social Sciences* 1, no 3 (2019):71- 81.

towards plants, animals, mountains, and rivers. Thus, the traditional African ethical perspective on the environment encourages a collective sense of responsibility toward environmental preservation.

Ukpokolo asserts that "the commitment of African people towards environment conservation and wildlife preservation is inculcated in the core being of an African and indigenous knowledge system which is transmitted through taboos, proverbs, clan names, and folklore."[10] African ontology holds that there is no such thing as dead matter since all living things, including grains of sand, exude a life force that can be used by sages, priests, kings, doctors, and artists to help bring the universe to its completion. In other words, naturally, Africans are perceptive to the outside world and the material side of things; that is, they are perceptive of materials, shape, color, weight, and other tangible attributes. Africans have valuable concepts and opinions that can assist humanity in living in harmony with the ecosystem.

Museka and Madondo explain that "African people's ecological intelligence and wisdom are aptly captured in their belief structures, particularly, beliefs in omens, taboos, rituals and the sacred. These beliefs help people to interact with nature virtuously, morally, ethically, and justly, that is, in a way that shows unhu/ubuntu."[11] Soyinka, writes that the notion of time, soul, human wellness, and morality is intertwined to issues of the natural world hence "the African, exist within a cosmic totality and did possess a consciousness in which his earth being, his gravity-bound apprehension of self was inseparable from the entire cosmic phenomenon."[12] However, these cosmic forces differ in their essence, so there exist the divine, celestial, or terrestrial, human, animal, vegetal, and material or mineral forces. The forces, whether in physical or non-physical forms, exist in unity and contribute to harmony. Anything that endangers the African people's natural world violates and jeopardizes their survival and

---

10 Isaac Ukpokolo, *Themes, Issues, and Problems in African Philosophy* (Switzerland: Springer, 2019), 159.
11 Godfrey Museka and Manasa Madondo, "The Quest for Environmental Pedagogy in the African Contexts: Insights from Unhn/Ubuntu Philosophy", *Journal of Ecology and Natural Environment* 4, no. 10 (2012): 258-265.
12 Wole Soyinka, *Myth, Literature, and the African World* (London: Cambridge University Press, 1976), 3.

synchronization with the earth. The land, which will provide food and dignity, is the most important value for colonized people, such as Africans.

Thus, African writers address ecological issues through literature by focusing on environmental consciousness using imageries of the African forest to call for ecological sustainability as seen in Chinua Achebe's classic novel in his criticism of European colonialist exploitation in *Things Fall Apart*. African writers have deliberately portrayed the bizarre onslaught and transformation of their landscapes. They have often used their texts as veritable tools in questioning the moral correctness of such egoistic acts. From the early writers to the contemporary writers, there has been an obvious frowning at such contempt for African terrain. This is because African landscapes are experiencing developments that have deleterious effects on the natural environment, contrary to African practices of environmental preservation. These are some of the concerns that African writers bring to the front burner. Given these delineations, one can contend that the rudiments of ecocriticism have always existed as the focal point in African literary conversations.

AFRICAN ECOCRITICAL CONSCIOUSNESS IN AFRICAN LITERARY TEXTS

The selected literary works of Wangari Maathai from Kenya, Niyi Osundare from Nigeria, and Zakes Mda from South Africa- East, West, and Southern Africa, respectively, justify the fundamental concerns about African ecocriticism. Their works lament the consequences of development, urbanization, exploitation, displacement, and dispossession. These environmental writers reveal the practices of extractive capitalism that lead to detrimental effects on the continent's biodiversity, including water and air pollution, tree felling, and other abusive industrial activities. In *Unbowed: A Memoir*, the activist and writer Wangari Maathai, a co-founder of the grassroots environmental movement, Green Belt Movement, illuminates the "relevance to mobilize Kenyan women to develop tree nurseries and plant trees to combat deforestation as well as resist land grab and plundering of natural resources by the Kenya government and corrupt politicians."[13]

---

13   Caminero-Santangelo, "In Place: Tourism" 148.

In her memoir, Maathai describes the environmental changes after the colonial destruction of the Kenyan landscape. Maathai draws on what Lawrence Buell refers to as an indigene pastoral to give narrative shape to her vision for social and environmental regeneration in Kenya. She laments how "the demonization of Africa's indigenous culture led to the virtual disappearance of the cultivation of many indigenous foods like millet, sorghum… as well as the decimation of wildlife, all in favor of a small variety of cash crops… the loss of indigenous plants and the methods to grow them has contributed not only to food, insecurity but also to malnutrition and reduction of local biodiversity."[14] She uses motifs of indigenous plants in favor of cash crops, loss of wildlife, and trees to raise concern about the problems of exploitation, land-grabbing, dispossession, and starvation experienced by the Kenyan people in her work. "Maathai's writing… the struggle against the environmental implications of modernity's narrative of development and positing alternatives."[15] Maathai's activism stems from the necessity for responsibility and care for life. Her work connects literarily and factually to her distinct regional places and environment. Maathai persistently reminisces about the place she had known and grown up in. She invokes the Kikuyu people's belief in the mutual link between the people, the environment, and the necessity to conserve biodiversity. She elicits, "there was a connection between the fig tree's root system and the underground water reservoirs. The roots burrowed deep into the ground, breaking through the rocks beneath the surface soil and diving into the underground water table."[16]

Maathai bewails the shift away from African environmental knowledge and worldview in the name of progress. In *Unbowed*, she reveals how progress comes to a place at the cost of environmental destruction; hence, the writer opposes multinational corporations and their cohorts. She indicts the capitalist-driven modus of development toward the destruction of Africa's biodiversity:

They eliminated local plants and animals, destroying the natural ecosystem that helped gather and retain water…. Over the subsequent

---

14 Wangari Maathai, *Unbowed: A Memoir* (London: Arrow Books, 2006), 175.
15 Caminero-Santangelo, "In Place: Tourism" 32.
16 Maathai, *Unbowed*, 46

decades, underground water levels decreased markedly, and eventually, rivers and streams either dried up or were greatly reduced.[17]

Using her oeuvres, Maathai maintains that Africa's ecological quandaries stem from the denigration of indigenous cultures by colonialism and the consumerist outlook that supports the commodification of the natural world. Despite the anomaly that her work unveils, her text reinforces the centrality of African ideals as a framework for eco-restoration and regeneration. Her commitment is to mitigate environmental annihilation to improve the well-being of the people.

Similarly, Osundare's poetry opus, *The Eye of the Earth*, is suitably colored by common expressions of traditional life using proverbs and songs, which reflect the worldview of his people. In the collection of poems, the forest, rocks, and rain are deployed as metaphors for the activities associated with the exploitation and veneration of the natural world. Onah explains that "the environmentally-conscious poet uses nature – flora and fauna to establish a sense of local habitation …that consists part of the flesh and blood of his poetry."[18] Therefore, Osundare's collection suggests that a disconnection from the earth and all its undertones has an upsetting impact on his welfare and that of his people. *The Eye of the Earth* opens with the poem "Forest Echoes." The first thing that strikes the poet as he moves into the forest of *Ubo Abusoro* is the desecration of the land and trees by timber vendors he refers to as *agbegilodo*. The poem mourns the pillage activities of these greed-enlivened industrialists in defense of the natural world as the source of sustenance. This divine essence of the landscape functions as the mobilizing impetus for Osundare as he constructs his poem.

This is again evident in the poem "The Rock Rose to Meet Me." Anyokwu asserts that "Osundare's environmentalism turns largely on the overarching centrality of [landscape] to the mechanics and logistics of his verse-making."[19] Osundare idolizes the rock Olosunta. Doki explains that "Osundare celebrates the rocks of Olosunta because they are both

---

17   Maathai, *Unbowed*, 39
18   Godfrey Onah, "The Meaning of Peace in African Traditional Religion and Culture" *Afrikworld*, February 27, 2023.
19   Christopher Anyokwu. "Osundare's Poetry and the Yoruba Worldview." CLCWeb: Comparative Literature and Culture 13, no. 1 (December 2, 2023).

an aspect of physical nature and have a mystic dimension in Ikere Cosmology."[20] Through honoring the rocks of his birthplace, Osundare draws attention to the enduring, substantial elements of nature that serve as enduring markers of space and time. Osundare, in the Preface of *The Eye of the Earth*, regards the rock with the appellation of a reverend entity. He admits: 'The Rock Rose to Meet Me' is a homecoming of a kind, a journey back (and forth) into a receding past that still has a right to live. The rocks celebrated in this section... Occupy a central place in the cosmic consciousness of the Ikere people; they are worshipped and frequently appeased with rare gifts, thunderous drumming, and dancing.[21]

This only explains how the African landscape seems to have much influence on the African people, both at a physical and metaphysical level. Osundare also criticizes Africans for straying away from the initial agrarian practice that characterizes their reverence for their landscape. In "Ours to Plough, not to Plunder," Osundare rebukes Africans for their increasing disregard for their landscape. The poem metaphorically represents the earth and admonishes that one should not take advantage of it, nor should it only be regarded in terms of its 'use value'. He stresses that moderation is required to explore the landscape's resources and that the earth should be treated with the utmost respect. Osundare ends this particular poem the way he starts it. The refrain he employs is a style that suggests the reinforcement of African ecocriticism: the "earth is / ours to work not to waste// ours to man not to maim/ the earth is ours to plough not to plunder."[22] The motifs that run through his collection of poems call for an ecological culture valuable to Africa, in opposition to the capitalist ecological development model.

Moreover, Mda's *Heart of Redness* is pertinent in circumscribing African ecocriticism. The novel centers on oppression, exploitation, colonialism, and apartheid. It switches from the mere depiction of a contemporary Xhosa village to a time in the past in the mid-nineteenth century. It explores the conflict of values between the unbelievers in the characters of Bhonco and Xoliswa and the believers in the characters of

---

20   Niyi Osundare, *The Eye of the Earth* (Ibadan: Heinemann Educational Books, 1996).
21   Osundare, *The Eye of the Earth*, xiii.
22   Osundare, *The Eye of the Earth*, 10.

Zim and Qukezwa. The unbelievers support modernization, urbanization, and development:

> The Unbelievers are moving forward with the times. That is why they support the casino and the water sports paradise that the developers want to build. The Unbelievers stand for civilization. To prove this point, Bhonco has now turned away from beads and has decided to take out the suits that his daughter bought him many years ago from his trunk under the bed. From now on, he will be seen only in suits.[23]

They do not appreciate the worth of their indigenous land. Whereas the believers defend their land as having invaluable worth. It is this collective identity and personality that they wish to protect and preserve from any destructive onslaught. *Heart of Redness* conveys a Xhosa community struggling to preserve their land, Qolorha-by-sea, from manipulation and abusive industrial enterprise into a rich tourist business. Huggan and Tiffin applaud this gesture as "providing viable alternatives to Western ideologies of development."[24]

The novel conveys the struggles and resistance of a local South African community to avoid the environmental destruction of the region by building a casino, game reserves, and tourist development for people who would end up losing their land. Also, the novel captures how the African ecosystem is manipulated by introducing non-native species to kill the local wildlife. Using *Heart of Redness* emphasizes the real meaning of the natural environment, human sensitivity, and the need for ethics of place in the face of external destruction. Thus, "the text's historical memory creates a sense of place, of a rich and unique heritage accrued through time."[25] Mda raises sensitive concerns on African ecocriticism and ethos. His work calls for protecting African ecocritical values and biodiversity even while operating in a global world order. The way Mda presents South Africa artistically highlights the interconnectedness of

---

23 Zake Mda, *The Heart of Redness* (New York, Farrar, Staus and Giroux, 2000), 59.
24 Graham Huggan and Helen Tiffin, *Postcolonial Ecocriticism: Literature, Animals, Environment* (New York: Routledge, 2010), 27.
25 Caminero-Santangelo, "In Place: Tourism", 296.

politics, culture, economy, human connections, nature, and animal habitats as ecological elements that must be brought into harmony to achieve sustainable development.

THINKING AFRICAN ECOCRITICISM FOR A BALANCED FUTURE

Humanity's shared capacity to nurture a sustainable relationship with the natural environment is not being achieved. This is because, as the global system increasingly advances, the environmental significance of place is disregarded. Regions have become susceptible to the impacts of globalization (the process of integrating economies/markets and societies around the world), increasing their consumption pattern, thereby depleting their ecosystems. Real sustainability can be realized through African ecocriticism because every human community exists within a specific region that can maintain that place. Therefore, perceptions of African ecocriticism are a viable way of countering unmanaged exploitation of water, land, wildlife, and their inhabitants. African environmentalism respects husbanding the resources of the land to preserve it for future generations. In this moral scheme, the ethical obligation is not limited to the present generation but also to the future generation. In this fused view of the natural world, the world of the living, the unborn, spirits, the supernatural, and even the dead embody the ecosystem.

On this note, the natural world does not imply the same thing to Africans as to non-Africans. For instance, the historical concept of Classical Greek Humanism emphasizes the inherent superiority of humans over other species and nature and defines humans as rational animals. For Pojman, the Greeks hold that humans, in virtue of their rational capacities, have greater value than any non-rational being, including nature. "Rationality is the key to human superiority over animals."[26] Therefore, having a strong interest in human welfare alone and downplaying the importance of the non-human permits the degradation of the natural world. Also, Cartesian dualism severs humans from non-humans; therefore, it implies that human beings are superior animals on account of

---

26 Louis Pojma, , *Environmental Ethics: Reading in Theory and Application* (Belmont: Wadsworth Publishing Company, 1995), 107-108.

their possession of souls. This ideology spurs humankind to alter the natural environment purely for its interests and needs.

Similarly, the Judeo-Christian concept claims human beings are made in God's image and have a higher place in the 'great chain of being.' Against this backdrop, Lynn White Jr. in "The Historical Roots of Our Ecological Crisis" maintains that "modern science and technology are products of Western culture and because Western culture has Christian attitudes and principles at its roots, nature has no reason for existing except to serve mankind. Thus, Christianity bears a huge burden of guilt for the current ecological crisis."[27] The portion of the Bible most quoted by critics who consider Christianity arrogant toward nature is found in Genesis, Chapter One: "And God created man in His image, in the image of God He created him; male and female he created them. And God blessed them; and God said to them, be fruitful and multiply and fill the earth, and subdue it; and rule over the fish of the sea and the birds of the sky, and over every living thing that moves on the earth."[28] The Christian ideology of humans dominating the natural environment for self-aggrandizement and profit over the ages has supported the persistent exploitation of natural resources.

To put it another way, the 19th-century Industrial Revolution was a crucial component of the capitalist market economy system, which promoted consumerism, ongoing economic expansion, and increasing concentration of income and wealth. This is inevitable because of the "paramount need of those controlling the means of production to maximize profits through improvements in economic efficiency and competitiveness. Signifying the phenomenon of the modern nation-state with its contradictions, banalities, and trauma through urbanization, unequal power, and economic relations."[29] Industrialization minimizes the social controls that protect the environment and treat it as a resource

---

27 Junior Britto, "An Ecocritical Reading of William Wordsworth's Tintern Abbey". *Academic Research International* 2, no. 1 (March 10, 2012): 23.
28 YouVersion Bible, "Genesis 1:27-28," December 23, 2023, https://www.bible.com/bible/compare/GEN.1.27-28/..
29 Tanimu Abubakar, "Nigerian Prose Fiction, Structural Adjustment, and Globalisation" *Gombe Papers on Nigerian Literature: A Journal of the Department of English*, no 1(1995): 43.

or input in production. However, with material ecocriticism and new materialism, the natural world, bodies, and materiality have navigated back into environmental discourses. Africans in the past and present do not see the natural world as other; hence, they bewail the alteration of the people's way of life due to technological advancement and the craze for human development, which compromises the health of local places by multinational corporations for natural resources exploration and exploitation. Thus, despite the destructive ongoing industrial consumerism and over-exploitation in the African everyday way of life, African values persist. African environmental consciousness is still perceptible in African viewpoints, beliefs, customs, and practices about the environment. The likes of Maathai, Mda, Osundare, and other African writers, alongside their texts, accentuate the connection between culture and African ecological knowledge toward socio-environmental justice. Their works amplify African environmental perceptions to communicate environmental disquiets that stem from inherited colonial and postmodern industrial habits.

CONCLUSION

Amidst the rising hyper-trends in environmental crisis due to the craze for accumulation and development, this chapter supports that African ecocriticism is a worthwhile region-centered environmental imagination that can bring about a sustainable environmental prospect. Although the term ecocriticism is a North American response to the modern environmental predicament, African ecocriticism/environmentalism has much to add to a globally sustainable ecosystem in Africa articulated in Nigeria's Niyi Osundare's *The Eye of the Earth*, Kenyan's- Wangari Maathai's *Unbowed: A Memoir*, and South Africa's- Zake Mda's *Heart of Redness*. African ecocriticism pays close attention to the undercurrents between the living and nonliving, human and non-human materialities in Africa. There is therefore a dire necessity to act and exist in an eco-efficient equilibrium amid the whirl of technological advancement and urbanization.

REFERENCES

Adejunmobi, Moradewun and Carli Coetzee, eds. 2019. *Routledge Handbook of African Literature*. London: Routledge.

Abubakar, Tanimu. 1995. "Nigerian Prose Fiction, Structural Adjustment, and Globalisation." *Gombe Papers on Nigerian Literature: A Journal of the Department of English* 1, no. 1: 43.

Alembong, Nol, Oscar C. Labang, and Eunice F. Fombele, eds. 2015. *Ecocultural Perspectives: Literature and Language*. Raytown, MO: Ken Scholars Publishing.

Anyokwu, Christopher. 2023. "Osundare's Poetry and the Yoruba Worldview." *CLCWeb: Comparative Literature and Culture* 13, no. 1.

Britto, Junior. 2012. "An Ecocritical Reading of William Wordsworth's Tintern Abbey." *Academic Research International* 2, no. 1: 23-42.

Caminero-Santangelo, Byron. 2016. *Different Shades of Green: African Literature, Environmental Justice, and Political Ecology*. New York: University of Virginia Press.

Caminero-Santangelo, Byron and Garth Myers. 2011. *Environment at the Margins: Literary and Environmental Studies in Africa*. Athens: Ohio University Press.

Caminero-Santangelo, Byron. 2011. "In Place: Tourism, Cosmopolitan Bioregionalism, and Zakes Mda's *The Heart of Redness*." In *Postcolonial Ecologies: Literatures of the Environment*, edited by Elizabeth DeLoughrey and George Handley. New York: Oxford University Press.

Chigbo, Ekwealo. 2011. "Environmental Ethics and Values in the 21st Century: An Africanist Philosophical Analysis." *Journal of African Environmental Ethics and Values* 2, no. 2: 23-24.

Crowley, Dustin. 2015. *Africa's Narrative Geographies: Charting the Intersections of Geocriticism and Postcolonial Studies*. London: Palgrave Macmillan.

Egya, Sule E. 2020. *Nature, Environment, and Activism in Nigerian Literature*. London: Routledge.

Emenyonu, Ernest N., Cajetan Iheka, and Stephenie Newell, eds. 2020. *Special Issue Environmental Transformations: African Literature Today*. New York: Boydell and Brewer.

Falola, Toyin, and Emily Brownell, eds. 2011. *Landscape, Environment, and Technology in Colonial and Postcolonial Africa*. New York: Routledge.

Huggan, Graham and Helen Tiffin. 2010. *Postcolonial Ecocriticism: Literature, Animals, Environment*. New York: Routledge.

Iheka, Cajetan. 2021. *African Ecomedia: Network Forms, Planetary Politics*. Durham, NC: Duke University Press.

Iheka, Cajetan. 2018. *Naturalizing Africa: Ecological Violence, Agency, and Postcolonial Resistance in African Literature*. Cambridge: Cambridge University Press.

Iheka, Cajetan and Stephanie Newell. 2020. "Introduction: Itineraries of African Ecocriticism and Environmental Transformations in African Literature." *ALT 38* (Environmental Transformations): 1-10.

Ikuenobe, Polycarp. 2014. "Traditional African Environmental Ethics and Colonial Legacy." *International Journal of Philosophy and Theology* 10: 31-21.

Lassi, Étienne-Marie, ed. 2013. *Aspects écocritique de l'imaginaire africain*. Bamenda: Langaa RPCIG.

Maathai, Wangari. 2006. *Unbowed: A Memoir*. London: Arrow Books.

Mda, Zakes. 2000. *The Heart of Redness*. New York, Farrar, Straus and Giroux.

Molla, Fiona F., ed. 2016. *Natures of Africa: Ecocriticism and Animal Studies in Contemporary Cultural Forms*. Johannesburg: Wits University Press.

Museka, Godfrey and M. Munashe Madondo. 2012. "The Quest for Environmental Pedagogy in the African Contexts: Insights from Unhn/Ubuntu Philosophy." *Journal of Ecology and Natural Environment* 4, no. 10: 258-265.

Ngongkum, Eunice. 2017. *Anglophone Cameroon Poetry in the Environmental Matrix*. Lausanne: Peter Lang.

Nsah, Mala and Nicki Hitchcott, eds. 2025. *Ecotexts in the Postcolonial Francosphere*. Liverpool: Liverpool University Press.

Nsah, Kenneth Toah. 2022. "Can Literature Save the Congo Basin? Postcolonial Ecocriticism and Environmental Literary Activism." PhD diss., Aarhus University.

Nsah, Kenneth T., Lisette N. Malung, and Noella M. Ngunyam. 2022. "The Slow Integration of Sustainability into Contemporary Theatre and Performance Practices in Cameroon." *Peripeti* no. 32. DOI: https://doi.org/10.7146/peri.v19i37.135191

Ogar, Joseph Nkang, and S. Akpan Bassey. 2019. "African Environmental Ethics." *RAIS Journal for Social Sciences* 3, no. 1: 71-81.

Okuyade, Ogaga, ed. 2013. *Eco-critical Literature: Regreening African Landscapes*. New York: African Heritage Press.

Olaniyan, Tejumola, and Ato Quayson, eds. 2007. *African Literature: An Anthology of Criticism and Theory*. New York: Wiley-Blackwell.

Onah, Godfrey. 2023. "The Meaning of Peace in African Traditional Religion and Culture." *Afrikworld*, February 27.

Osundare, Niyi. 1996. *The Eye of the Earth*. Ibadan: Heinemann Educational Books.

Pojman, Louis. 1995. *Environmental Ethics: Reading in Theory and Application*. Belmont: Wadsworth Publishing Company.

Slaymaker, William. 2007. "Ecoing the Other(s): The Call of Global Green and Black African Responses." In *African Literature: An Anthology of Criticism and Theory*, edited by Tejumola Olaniyan and Ato Quayson. USA: Blackwell Publishing Limited.

Soyinka, Wole. 1976. *Myth, Literature, and the African World*. London: Cambridge University Press.

Ukpokolo, Isaac. 2017. *Themes, Issues, and Problems in African Philosophy*. Switzerland: Springer.

Wolputte, Steven van, Michael Thomas Bollig, Martina Gockel, Clemens Greiner, and Noah Kahindi. 2024. "The Aftermath – What Future for African Studies (in Europe?). A View From Behind the Scenes of ECAS9." *Africa Spectrum* 59, no. 2

Workineh, Kelbessa. 2014. "Can African Environmental Ethics Contribute to Environmental Policy in Africa?" *Environmental Ethics* 36: 31-61.

Wu, Chengyi Coral. 2016. "Towards an Ecocriticism in Africa: Literary Aesthetics in African Environmental Literature." In *Natures of Africa: Ecocriticism and Animal Studies in Contemporary Cultural Forms*, edited by Fiona F. Molla. Johannesburg: Wits University Press.

YouVersionBible. 2023. Accessed December 23, 2023. https://www.bible.com/bible/compare/GEN.1.27-28/.

CHAPTER THREE

Resisting Anthropocentrism
Reading Deep Ecology in Selected Poems of Alice Oswald and Nol Alembong

Mary Louisa Lum

INTRODUCTION

Ecological consciousness is fundamental in the twenty-first century, especially against the backdrop of harmful human actions that hurt the environment and threaten human well-being. Unfortunately, the anthropocentric viewpoint that centers humanity as the sovereign of the species enhances technocratic societies in the blatant abuse and destruction of the environment. This research is premised on the assumption that Alice Oswald and Nol Alembong utilize their respective poetic works to advocate for the nonhuman species of nature and raise awareness on the need for harmonious coexistence. Also, the study attempts to show that this ecological admiration echoes the romantic veneration of nature. Though Oswald and Alembong emerge from different backgrounds, they are unified in advocating for environmental protection and exposing the devastating consequences of neglecting the ecosystem.

Eco-criticism has increasingly gained appeal as an interdisciplinary theoretical tool because of its impactful role in garnering ecological consciousness. The concepts of deep ecology, propounded by Arne Naess and George Sessions (1984) in the eight ecological principles, are relevant in the analysis of environmental trends in the poetry of Oswald and Alembong. In his attempt to conceptualize deep ecology, Bill Devall (1985) provides evidence by differentiating deep ecology from reformist ecology, which is revolutionary in nature and fights to protect the wilderness. To Devall (1985), deep ecology is radically opposed to the social paradigm, which is the anthropocentric worldview, because it negates elements of nature that are not deemed profitable to human needs. Deep ecology is therefore a reaction to the excesses of blatant human exploitation of nature and its resources without regard for sustainability. Devall's interest in deep ecology derived from the effort to propel the contributions of Arne Naess and George Sessions. Naess (1984) proposes deep ecology as an environmental perspective that encourages humanity to rethink its anthropocentric stance towards nature in order to avert the ecological crisis. In this light, Naess (1984) and George Sessions (1984) posit the eight principles of deep ecology in an effort to reject essentialist perceptions of the environment; and emphasize the right of nature to exist, irrespective of its usefulness to human beings; the need to reduce human population; to ensure sustainability, and the fact that nature does not exist for the benefit of mankind.

By de-centering humanity as the paramount of nature and other species, the scholars challenge the anthropocentric notion of human supremacy in the hierarchy of existence. Alembong's (2017) poems echo the primacy of nature and caution mankind to treat nature reverently, supporting the deep ecology ideology. To this end, Devall and Sessions (1984) posit that:

> Deep ecology goes beyond a limited piecemeal shallow approach to environmental problems and attempts to articulate a comprehensive religious and psychological worldview. The foundations of deep ecology are the basic intuitions and experiencing ourselves and Nature which comprise ecological consciousness... ecological consciousness and deep ecology are in sharp contrast with the dominant worldview of technocratic-industrial societies which regards humans as isolated and fundamentally separate from the rest of nature, as superior to, and in charge of, the rest of creation (310).

It is misguided to condone an anthropocentric view of the world against the evidence of the harm caused to the environment and the negative implications for human survival. Deep ecology does not approve of minimal innovations mainly because they are unsuccessful against the impending threat. The biocentric appeal to respect nonhuman species and curb greed requires repetition, as seen in the poetry of Oswald (2016, 2009, 2002) and Alembong (2017).

Self-realization, as a concept of deep ecology, is ingrained within the poetry of Oswald and Alembong, evident through the concern for human and nonhuman species. Rejecting selfishness and creationist ideas of humanity's superiority is helpful in the journey to self-realization. In this regard, Devall (1985) asserts that deep ecology solidifies the complementary position of human beings within and above nature. The transformation of individual and collective consciousness, as well as social organization, is therefore the only true reform that can enhance humanity's relationship with nature. Alembong (2017) in *Green Call* exposes the ironic behavior of anthropocentric-minded individuals since nature can heal itself from any affliction, but humanity faces extinction.

Another unique way Alembong responds to the deep ecological quest for self-actualization in his poetry is through the revelation of the ritualistic bonds with nature. African traditional religion shares a semblance of pantheism since the gods are believed to be in nature. Adopting Eastern philosophical views of nature credited additional consciousness to humanity's relationship with nature, by deep ecology validating the African religious inclination. In the praxis of post-colonial theory, East refers to non-Western traditions and customs considered exotic by the West. Africa falls within this paradigm wherein its cultures venerate nature and strike a harmonious relationship with the environment. Alembong (2017) as an African folklorist, exemplifies this link within his poetry.

Pantheistic rituals and mythmaking are among the strategies used by the authors under study to establish a kinship with nature. The relationship between deep ecology and the romantic admiration for nature propelled this researcher to find correlations within the selected poems of Oswald (2016, 2009, 2002) and Alembong (2017). The attempt to find the spiritual link with nature is essential for the deep ecology quest; the approach, Naess believes, "resulted from a more sensitive openness to ourselves and nonhuman life around us" (Devall & Sessions 1984, 309). The worship of nature by deep ecological activists has been acknowledged by critics like David Rothenberg, who quotes Bookchin and Foreman's observation that some activists do not seem to understand the unequal "social structures of our culture" (Rothenberg 740).

The poets in context have used their poetry as a vehicle of activism on behalf of the environment, an undertaking which multiple scholars have acknowledged. Critics like Eugene Ngezem (2017), Stella Johnson (2017) and Kenneth Nsah (2017) have commented on Alembong's environmental poetry and their views center on the ways in which the poetry collection *Green Call* ascribes to the conversations regarding humanity's relationship with the environment. Ngezem (2017), in a Foreword to *Green Call*, conjectures that the poet "explores topical and universal concerns about Global Warming/the environment, and displays the fearless passion and spirited wit of a poet scholar" (ix). Apart from remarking on the general subject matter of the collection, Ngezem (2017) further observes that the poet equally makes use of imageries and metaphors that represent "peace, prosperity, progress, purpose, and assorted virtues in a world, which is vainly swimming against safe and fulfilling environmental currents" (x). This current endeavor interrogates the various imageries and metaphors presented within Alembong's *Green Call* in an attempt to situate his environmental activism within the context of deep ecology's philosophical inclinations.

Like Ngezem (2017), Oscar Labang (2012) has also identified the potent use of metaphors in Alembong's poetry, although the latter critic reads these metaphors to support the claim of a political ideology. Labang (2012) captures the metaphor of the forest as a representation of the nation of Cameroon by insisting that "Alembong employs and explores the image of the forest, drawing close association between the making of the forest and the making of Cameroon" (2022, 20). The diversity of critical opinions on the poetry of Nol Alembong demonstrates artistry and suggestiveness.

Stella Johnson (2017) enunciates that Alembong's *Green Call* positions the poet within the construct of green writing and "through the colour green, the poet captures the splendours of natural environment and advocates for global environmental protection, enrichment and sustenance" (2017, ix). By identifying the activist tendencies of the poet, the critic lauds the vigor and freshness that energize the quest for the protection of nature. In addition to the militant stance towards environmental discourse, the romantic and African spiritual connotations are explored.

Moreover, Kenneth Nsah (2017) offers effusive praise to Nol Alembong and his penchant for environmental poetry. Nsah declares: "I salute your poetic artistry, great eco-patriot! Many more critics and researchers, including myself, will continue to feed on this wonderful poetic and intellectual food you are offering us" (CAMLIT@yahoogroups.com 2015[1]). This admiration was in response to the poet's ability to highlight salient issues like environmental consciousness within his poetry. Reading the poetry from a deep ecological standpoint reveals some of these admirable traits and how they can be transmitted into action.

Like Alembong (2017), Oswald (2016, 2009, 2002) has received critical attention from scholars who commend her ecological activism. Hazel Streeter (2021) explores elements of temporality and ecology in the poetry of Alice Oswald and maintains that the poet's uniqueness emerges from showing that time is vital in addressing the ecological crisis. The critic further acknowledges Oswald's advocacy for the nonhuman species as an outstanding trait. Other critics like Rashid (2022), Parham (2012), and Reimann (2018) have analyzed Oswald's poetry from an ecocritical point of view. Though Streeter (2021) takes an ecocritical reading, the focus is on temporal perspectives, while this present effort examines issues of self-realization and biocentrism.

The appreciation of the English landscapes and landmarks is an attribute of Oswald's poetry, scrutinized by Heather Yeung (2021). Pastoral themes are conveyed through the multiplicity of voices that signify the diverse natural genus. Dialogue within the poems is conducted between the persona and the elements of the landscape. Yeung (2021) posits that by giving voice to inanimate features of nature, the poet acts as an activist crusader for the environment. Oswald creates a link with the landscape, both as a beautiful natural phenomenon as well as the mystical prowess of nature. This mystical connection is what the present research reads as romantic inclinations in the poetry. Rowan Middleton has also examined Oswald's celebration of landscapes, as seen in poems like *Dart*.

---

1 The CAMLIT@yahoogroups.com was a creative writing forum that encompassed Cameroon Writers of English Expression at home and in the Diaspora. Nsah Mala had commended the literary contributions of Nol Alembong in 2015; a comment that was included in the blurb of the 2017 publication of *Green Call*.

GREEN: SYMBOL OF HARMONIOUS CO-EXISTENCE

Alembong's *Green Call* denotes the word green as a major motif within the collection. The centrality of this symbol was previously captured by Stella Johnson (2017), who is of the view that "to the poet green is a symbol of vigour, vitality, exuberance, freshness, life, health, rectitude, fertility and the natural world" (2017, ix). Although these surface observations are relevant in an eco-critical reading of these poems, it is necessary to employ a deeper exploration to connect this symbolism to the deep ecological doctrine of the spirituality of ecological consciousness. This spiritual connection can only be achieved when there is harmonious existence between humanity and nature. In the poem "Green, in you I take Refuge", the protective tendencies of nature are espoused:

> Green, in you I take refuge,
> For you are the forest that shelters me;
> So I shall never call you jungle (Alembong 2017, 10).

The persona sees nature as a place of refuge and protection. There is a resolution to honor nature in return for its security and never to be disparaging. Albeit the simplicity of diction that conforms to Wordsworth's dictate that "a poet is a man talking to men" (qtd in Abrams 1995) and should speak in a language that men truly understand, underneath this simplicity is a multiplicity of imagery. The first imagery is in the first line, 'in you I take refuge', suggesting a threat afoot. Green here symbolizes the forest's diversity, a source of natural conservation and nourishment. The imagery invoked by the phrase 'shelters me' continues to show the strong link between the persona and nature and underscores nature as a safe space. In the final line, the imagery of the jungle, along with the use of negation, echoes the technocratic perception of nature as a jungle of resources meant for outlandish exploitation. The persona refuses to promote this view of nature because it will destroy that harmonious possibility of co-existence. Green is further symbolized as a defensive maternal force that ensures the thriving of the offspring. It is the order of things for the mother to shield her infant from all threats, no matter the enormity:

> Green, in you I take refuge,
> For, like the hen her chicks,
> You cover me [by] turning your back on the hawk (2017, 10).

The repetition of 'Green, in you I take refuge' in the first line of the first stanza of the three-stanza poem symbolizes the pertinence of nature from the persona's worldview. It equally establishes the fundamental defensive role nature plays. The symbolism of nature as the hen that safeguards its chicks from predators like the hawk indicates that nature is vital for humanity's well-being, and humankind will perish without its largess. Deep ecologists adhere to the maxim that harm to nature is harm to the self as connoted by Alembong (2017) in "Green, in you I take Refuge." The avian imagery featuring the hen and hawk, the former passive and the latter aggressive, showcases the predatory relationship between human beings and nature when the anthropocentric view abounds.

Humanity can only be in harmony with nature when self-realization is attained. Devall and Sessions (2017) describe this phenomenon as the rejection of the narcissistic ego, acceptance of others and respect for nature. Rejecting individualism, the formation of communal relationships, and respect for the environment illustrate how self-realization as a core value of deep ecology intersects with romanticism and traditional African philosophy. This intersection is made manifest in "Green Call":

> The forest is green when man is green,
> The sky is gray when man burns green,
> Who knew roses could bud the green,
> When roses never look green (Alembong 2017, 15)?

The organic relationship between people and nature is described in images of green. When human beings seek nature's resources to meet their basic needs, there is harmony. In relation to man in the above excerpt, "green" refers to the stage of innocence, wherein humanity is not driven by greed and avarice. It is the stage of romanticism, when nature is revered from a pantheistic worldview. The following line shows the consequences of the breach of the spiritual link, which happens when human actions become destructive towards nature. The imagery of the grey sky implies a lack of rainfall that leads to droughts and, by extension, famine. It is paradoxical that humans who need nature for nourishment still believe they are superior to nature. It is against the understanding that humanity cannot flourish without the bounties of nature that the third ecological principle is outlined, cautioning that "humans have no right to reduce this richness and diversity except to satisfy vital needs" (Devall & Sessions 2017, 314). On this premise, deep ecology encourages a simplistic and organic way of life. The imagery of the rose flower emerging from a green bud continues to show the beauty of nature, while the rhetorical question is intended to encourage humanity to marvel at the wonders of nature.

Following the romantic glorification of nature, the poet champions the virtues of nature, echoing romantic sentiment befitting of Wordsworth. The poet uses repetition to illustrate the relevance of nature:

> Green, green, green as green
> Melon is sweet when green.
> Green, green, green as green.
> Traffic flows when lights are green (Alembong 2017, 15).

The poet's repetition of green is an attempt to raise awareness about the preservation of nature. Melon is used as a synecdoche representing the succulent gifts of nature. Human beings need nourishment such as food, water, and clean air. When humanity respects the first ecology principle that "the well-being and flourishing of human and nonhuman life on earth have value in themselves… these values are independent of the usefulness of the nonhuman world for human purposes" (Devall & Sessions, 1985, 314). The last line of the excerpt dwells on the role of the green traffic light in ensuring traffic circulation. Considering that "Green Call" is the collection's title poem, its message is topical in calling for a change in attitude towards the environment.

Nol Alembong's emphasis on green is also symbolic of the support of the Greenpeace mission and vision, which is focused on protecting the earth to ensure the nurturing of its species and entities. This support of the Greenpeace message is seen when he pays homage to the environmental activists:

> Greens make houses green,
> Greens make man green,
> Greens make life green,
> Greens make vision green (Alembong 2017, 16).

There is the use of anaphora in the four-line stanza with the repetition of the phrase 'Greens make' at the beginning of each line. Repetition is a strategy Alembong employs to campaign on his environmental message. In the first line, the Greens honored include the environmentalists who advocate and build eco-friendly houses. In the second line, the Greens under focus are the activists who encourage fair treatment of the environment, while the third and fourth lines refer to those activists who work to guarantee an eco-friendly future. This homage credits reformist ecologists who believe that environmental reform within the status quo of social organization can adequately derive environmental protection goals. In this light, they advocate for environmentally friendly policies relating to the protection of wildernesses, eco-friendly habitats, recycling, and curbing pollution. Deep ecologists like Naess and Sessions (1984) believe that reformist ecologists have become complacent to political machinations, thus centralizing humanity as the top of the food chain at the detriment of nonhuman species. They desire to see the veneration of nature as the centrality of social organization, not just an afterthought.

The spiritual liaison between humanity and nature advocated by deep ecology resonates in Alembong's "Glory be to Green." The poet adopts the tone of a supplicant who comes to seek nurturing from the fount of nature:

> Glory be to Green
> For all it stands for
> As it was in the beginning,
> And ever shall be
> Till the end of time (Alembong 2017, 19).

The poem's opening mimics the Christian prayer of veneration to the holy trinity that constitutes the supreme deity. Instead of giving glory to the God the Father as in the entreaty, Green is the object of worship, bringing forth pantheistic tendencies that justify the romantic sensibility in the poetry of Alembong. Within pantheism, nature is god and is worshipped profusely, as evident in the poetry of William Wordsworth. Nature is glorified as the first aspect to come into existence and will remain till the end of time. Here, Alembong sustains the evolutionary argument of existence while debunking the creationist logic that centers existence around humankind's superiority over nonhuman species.

Myths and symbols represent the expression of poetry from the viewpoint of Rene Wellek (1990), and these mythical and symbolic elements abound in the poetry of Oswald and Alembong. The former leans on the mythmaking traditions of classical writers, while the latter dwells on using green as the life force. In "Dunt: a poem for a Dried up River," Oswald (2009) invokes the myth of the classical water nymph attempting to rejuvenate a dried-up river. There is the insinuation that the damage is caused by human action, yet:

> Exhausted utterly worn down
> A Roman water nymph made of bone
> Being the last known speaker of her language
> She tries to summon a river out of limestone (Oswald 2009, 39).

A nymph is a nature deity credited with ensuring fertility, fecundity, and water supply. The futility of her effort is manifest in the fact that she has been worn to the bone in the attempt to restart the water flow. Throughout the poem, the persona repeats "try again" to show the nymph's consistency against evident defeat. Ineffectiveness is a metaphor for the irreparable damage done to nature by anthropocentric behavior.

In "Glory be to Green," the persona continues to address nature as a deity that can show the path to illumination. As is customary of Alembong (2017), the poet uses repetition to ingrain the significance of nature to humanity. In the ten subsequent stanzas, the phrase "teach us" is repeated at the beginning of the supplication. The persona takes the role of the chief priest, as evident in the ten invocations that take the place of commandments. The first plea "Green, teach us to live in the light of your radiance" (Alembong 2017, 19) and this relates to co-existence between human and nonhuman species and also correlates to the next which implores "Green, to teach us the will to give freely" (Alembong 2017, 19). Generosity is an attribute that comes from a place of selflessness, while the third supplication, "Green teaches us to be moderate" (Alembong 2017, 19), discourages selfishness. Truth, goodness, fairness, love, and service are virtues extolled by the petitioner in their communion with nature.

EMBRACING BIOCENTRIC EQUALITY

Alice Oswald takes a biocentric perspective in her environmental activism through her representation of the nonhuman aspects of nature. Yeung (2021) and Middleton (2021) opine that the representation of the nonhuman entities through dialogue and the veneration of landscapes render credibility to the ecological crusade. Pinard (2009) suggests that Oswald's special connection with nature is derived from her intuition as a poet gardener. Deep ecologists aver that the intuition of biocentric equality is that all things in the biosphere have an equal right to live and blossom and to reach their own individual forms of unfolding and self-realization within the larger Self-realization (Devall & Sessions 312). Through myths and symbols, Oswald celebrates this biocentric message.

The moon is a marvel to humanity, and many primordial cultures worshipped it as a divinity. In "Full Moon", Oswald metamorphoses into the moon through a dream state in an attempt to experience life from its vantage point. The poem opens thusly:

> Good God!
> What did I dream of last night?
> I dreamt of the moon.
> I woke and found myself still asleep (Oswald 2002, 26).

The opening starts with an interjection, "Good God!" suggesting that the experience is uncanny. It also shows an aspect of excitement for such an otherworldly occurrence. Through the rhetorical question "what did I dream of last night?" the sense of exhilaration is underscored about the uniqueness of the phenomenon. Dreaming of the moon is not uncommon, but what makes this dream different is the fact that it is not really a dream, evident in "I woke and found myself still asleep."

Romantics believe in transcendence through nature, and the childlike desire of the persona to encounter the moon has paid off, leading to the transportation into the metaphysical realm. Like in a fairytale, the persona is transformed into the moon with the ability to feel emotions that have hitherto been impossible to describe:

> It was like this: my face misted up from inside
> And I came and went at will through the peephole.
> had no voice, no mouth, nothing to express my trouble,
> Except my shadows leaning downhill, not quite parallel
> (Oswald 2002, 27).

It is difficult to portray a force of nature, as seen in the above stanza. The moon's intangibility cannot be contained in a physical entity, which explains why the persona becomes immaterial upon metamorphosing into the moon. Being able to float through peepholes and be everywhere are equally powerful feelings, yet there is a sense of sadness in the lack of speech: "I had no voice, no mouth, nothing to express my trouble." The sense of frustration is poignant, for if the moon is a deity that watches over the world, the incapacity of speech becomes a major handicap. Yet the moon has ways of communicating that the untrained human eye might misunderstand, like the way in which a shadow reflects.

Samuel Taylor Coleridge is one of the Romantic poets who celebrate nature's mystical and mysterious status and suggest that human beings can enjoy these attributes through transcendence. Not everyone can benefit from transcendence since it requires following the laws of nature to the letter. Only the innocent/childlike-minded individuals could profit. Oswald (2002) captures this sentiment in addition to the dream or trancelike state that encapsulates the experience of transcendence. The persona continues describing her vision as follows:

> Something needs to be said to describe my moonlight
> Almost frost but softer, almost ash but wholer
> Made almost of water, which has strictly speaking
> No feature, but a kind of counter-light, call it insight

> Like in woods, when they jostle their hooded shapes,
> Their heads congealed together, having murdered each other,
> There are moon-beams, sound-beings, such as deer and half-deer
> Passing through there, whose eyes can pierce through things (Oswald 2002, 28).

The use of the possessive "my moonlight" suggests a metaphorical connotation to the experience of transcendence. The persona attempts to find a tangible likeness for an intangible occurrence, leading to associations that cannot quite capture the magnitude of the feeling. Neither frost nor ash can express the softness of the moonlight. The use of similes is intended to make associations with tangible reality and to render understanding of the phenomenon. The fact that words cannot fully explain the experience further heightens the metaphorical angle of transforming from negative experiences into a dispensation of positivity. The last line of the poem, "Good God! Who have I been last night, gives a clue into the persona's positive rejuvenation. The sense of childlike wonder in the poem echoes the sentiment in Ted Hughes' "Full Moon and Little Frieda."

Biocentric equality relates to recognizing and respecting every aspect of nature, both human and nonhuman, irrespective of value. Oswald embraces the biocentric quest for equality between human and nonhuman species in her poetry by celebrating the marvels of nature, which are often overlooked in humanity's blatant exploitation of nature. The poem "the self-playing Instrument of Water" gives a glimpse into the joyful experience by the persona upon encountering this trend of nature. Like Alembong, Oswald oozes with a sense of wonder akin to Wordsworth's depiction of nature. Music as an artistic persuasion brings joy and solace to many, yet nature offers the same, but very few can recognize its merit. In the opening line, the persona announces the subject matter, "the story of the falling rain." To the mundane mind, the falling of the rain is nothing special, but the manner in which the rain falls "to turn to a leaf and fall again" (Oswald 2002, 41). The music of nature is multifaceted. Music of nature can be witnessed in the unique sounds like "the secret of a summer shower / To steal the light and hide it in a flower" (Oswald 2002, 42). Summer showers sound differently musically to the sound of "water through a plume of grass." Wordsworth also touches on the musicality of nature through birdsong when he compels the reader to "come, hear the woodland linnet/how sweet his music!" (Abrams, 1882).

Paying homage to environmental activists is a tendency both Oswald and Alembong share. The poem "Fox" pays homage to Ted Hughes, an environmental poet activist who advocated for biocentric equality. Both poems describe the fox during their midnight forage. In the silence of the night, the persona is alerted to the fox:

> I heard a cough
> As if a thief was there
> Outside my sleep
> A sharp intake of air
>
> A fox in her fox-fur
> Stepping across
> The grass in her black gloves
> Barked at my house (Oswald 2016, 17).

There is the use of personification when the persona comments on the 'cough' of the fox. Since it is the dead of night, the fear is that 'a thief was there' which brings a sense of fear and insecurity evident through 'a sharp intake of air. It is quite a relief when the source of commotion is revealed to be "a fox in her fox-fur." The magnificence of the fox is manifest in the confident manner that the fox gallivants across the yard in its 'black gloves'. Co-existence between human and nonhuman species can only be attained when habitats are designated for all. Human populations have taken over animal spaces, making it difficult for them to flourish. The persona sees it as an intrusion:

> Just so abrupt and odd
> The way she went
> Hungrily ask
> In the heart's thick accent (Oswald 2016, 17).

In the aforementioned excerpt, the abrupt appearance of the fox seems surreal. The persona exhibits surprise at the intrusion and oddity of the fox appearing outside its habitat, indicating that humans do not respect the boundaries of coexistence. Its hunger is equally evident, which further shows the anthropocentric disrespect of the nonhuman species. The necessity of consciousness among humans regarding the nonhuman species will foster harmony within nature. The persona's reaction also comes from the unconscious arrogance of humankind's claim at the top of the ecosystem; incidentally, the ecologist Aldo Leopold insists that "humans are 'plain citizens' of the biotic community, not lord and master over all other species" (quoted in Devall and Sessions 2017, 312).

CONCLUSION

The foregoing paragraphs attempted to analyze selected poems of Alice Oswald and Nol Alembong from the perspective of deep ecology to show that they are environmental crusaders. Using myths and symbols, the poets justify the need for human beings to protect the nonhuman species as a survival strategy. The veneration of nature that cuts through both poets, points to their romantic inclination. They espouse values of selflessness and respect towards nature as the recipe for harmonious coexistence. The observations gleaned from the poetics of Alembong and Oswald reveal that it is imperative for the human species to become mindful regarding boundaries in order to enhance peaceful coexistence with the nonhuman species. Biocentric equality, therefore, is the attitude to adopt for the sake of cordiality and survival for humanity.

REFERENCES

Alembong, Nol. 2017. *Green Call*. Chennai: Notion Press.

Devall, Bill 1985. The Deep Ecology Movement. *Natural Resources Journal*, edited by Alan Drengson and Yuichi Inoue, 299-322. New York: North Atlantic Books.

Devall, Bill & George Sessions. 2017. Deep Ecology. *The New Environmentalism*, Vol. 8, No 6 (1985): 308-315. DOI:10.4236/ojmh.2912.210001.

Johnson, Stella. 2017. A Review: *Green Call* by Nol Alembong. Chennai: Notions Press.

Labang, Oscar. 2012. The Forest: A Metaphor of the Nation in Nol

Alembong's *Forest Echoes. Imagination: Theorizing the Nation in Anglophone Cameroon*. 20-42. Kansas City: Miraclaire Publishing.

Ngezem, Eugene. 2017. Foreword: *Green Call* by Nol Alembong. Chennai: Notions Press, 2017.

Nsah, Kenneth. 2017. A Review: *Green Call* by Nol Alembong. Chennai: Notions Press.

Oswald, Alice. 2016. *Falling Awake*. London: Penguin Books.

---. 2009. *A Sleepwalk on the Severn*. London: Faber & Faber.

---. 2002. *Dart*. London: Faber & Faber.

Sessions, George. 1987. The Deep Ecology Movement: A Review. *Environmental Review*. Vol 11, no 2. 105-125.

Streeter, Hazel. 2021.Keeping to its Clock': Temporality and Ecology in the Poetry of Alice Oswald. Bristol: Bristol UP.

Rothenberg, David. 2012. Deep Ecology. *Encyclopedia of Applied Ethics*. Vol 19, no 2. 738-744. DOI:10.1016/B978-0-12-373932-2.00352-5.

Yeung, Heather. 2021.Of Lyric Temporality and Materiality: Alice Oswald's Environmental Poetics. *Modern Ecopoetry*. Vol 16.

CHAPTER FOUR

That All May Be Green
Investigating Three Francophone African Narratives as Ecomedia

Eunice E. Omonzejie

INTRODUCTION

Literary discourse of the new millennium is often infused with environmental issues and contributes to the global struggle for the preservation of nature. It divulges how human life is entrenched in non-human life in the world. All ecological criticisms share the fundamental premise that human culture is connected to the physical world, affecting it and being affected by it. Ecocriticism or green studies considers the interconnections between nature and culture, specifically through the cultural artifacts of languages and literature. It must involve a genuine dialogue between ecology and literary theory (Vignola 2022). Glotfelty (1996) argues that as a critical stance, it has one foot in literature and the other on land; as a theoretical discourse, it negotiates between the human and the non-human. Furthermore, for Coupe, it encompasses "the literary *representation* of nature and, just as importantly, the power of literature to inspire its readers to act in *defense* of nature" (2013, 155). Thus, literary ecomedia and zoomedia articulate the dimensions of participation of literary discourse of the new millennium in the ecocentric dialectics of contemporary times.

As literary activists in the global environmental reclamation struggle, contemporary francophone African writers transcribe environmental issues into their narratives by expanding their representation of the world to include the entire ecosphere. They reinforce the African traditional concept of mutuality and inter-subjectivity among all things, which is in tandem with the environmental scientist Barry Commoner's first law of ecology – that "Everything is connected to everything else," and which William Rueckert (cited in Glotfelty and Fromm 1996, 108) emphasizes as a mode of critical inquiry. They seek to attract attention to the non-human world through what Jeffers calls "inhumanism" (i.e., non-human forms: animal and vegetation). The literary authors document and preserve natural history in their works through the aesthetic and thematic focus on the human relationship with the nonhuman world.[1]

Twenty-first-century contemporary African writers (novelists and poets alike) are going green by engaging ecological issues in their narratives: Bessora, Koulsy Lamko, Fatou Diome, Mabanckou, Michèle Rakotoson, Sow Fall, Nadine Gordimer, etc. They foreground inhumanism, and valorize ecophilic cultures in a threatened natural world, and advocate for eco-preservation, eco-equilibrium, and make Afrocentric identity a major subject matter in their narratives.[2] This establishes ecocentric prose narratives of African writers as ecomedia (and zoomedia) – a green campaign communicative form.

The aim of my study, therefore, is to evaluate the textualization structures of the ecocritical interconnectedness in three francophone novels – Koulcy Lamko's *La phalène des collines* [*The moth of the hills*], Aminata Sow Fall's *Douceurs du bercail* [*Comforts of the Fold*] and Alain Mabanckou's *Mémoires de porc-épic* [*Memoirs of a porcupine*] –by exposing the stylistic and thematic foci of the authors in their treatment of environmental issues and their expression of African cultural values, which align with green thinking.

Thus, the ecocentric perspective of my examination will be two-dimensional – zoocritical and ecocritical. On the one hand, my ecocritical approach would involve the application of ecological concepts in restructuring the environmentalist discourses in Lamko's, Sow Fall's, and Mabanckou's narratives, which uphold the conservation of nature and vehemently oppose its degradation. This ecocritical application derives its significance from the reality of the interconnectedness involving man,

---

[1] For further details, see articles by Colette Trout (2020) and Anne Simon (2015).
[2] See ecocriticism studies of African novels by Atilade (2022), Germain (2019), Magdelaine-Andrianjafitrimo (2018), Eya'a Obame (2021), and Bassintsa-Bouesso (2017).

nature, and culture as divulged in the plots of our three selected texts.

My zoocritical study, on the other hand, would reside squarely in the domain of zoopoetics (animal studies in literary expression) – encompassing animal representation, animal subjectivity, and animal rights. I will examine in the three texts, the aspect of animal studies that interrogates man's domination and exploitation of animals, based on the assertion that all beings are sentient, intelligent, communicative, and cultured entities.[3] Both eco-centric perspectives in this paper fully appreciate Glen Love's assertion that:

> the most important function of literature today is to redirect human consciousness to a full consideration of its place in a threatened natural world… Paradoxically, recognizing the primacy of nature and the necessity for a new ethic and aesthetic embracing the human and the natural, these may provide us with our best hope of recovering the lost social role of literary criticism (1996, 237-238).

In performing this social function of literature, the three selected texts of my ecomedia study, landscapes and culture-scapes are valorized as they critique humans' deplorable values and attitudes vis-a-vis the environment, human and non-human nature. The novels explicitly challenge the anthropocentric view of nature, which endorses the supremacy of humans over nature and their right to exploit it for selfish ends. These dual perspectives of ecocriticism and zoocriticism in literary studies entail the consideration of animals as polemical agents that interrogate the human category and the connectedness between humans and animals (Fioritti 2020).

The all-pervasive premise in the narratives of *La phalène des collines*, is that all life forms (human, animal, earth) are essentially equal and interdependent. The novels advocate for the interconnectedness of all factors within the ecosystem–social, political and the phenomena of the natural world. Lamko and Mabanckou's concerns are focused on

---

3   For a broader overview, see studies by Gregory Bateson (1985), Tom Regan (1985), and Huggan & Tiffin (2010).

the exposure of the homophobic, zoophobic, and ecophobic activities of humans, which are detrimental to their natural environment. Sow Fall's environmental representation is in a persuasive style, a passive-aggressive ecophilia–preferring to highlight the positive side of nature, to influence her audience's attitudinal change toward the environment. She focuses on the appreciation of nature, the return to the land, and the immersion in the earth for sustenance and healing. Thus, my three selected francophone novels serve as ecomedia, campaigning for the primacy of nature and advocating the affirmation of African identity through a positive green culture.

THAT ALL MAY BE GREEN: PROCLAIMING THE PRIMACY OF NATURE

The plot of Mabanckou's *Mémoires de porc-épic* is anchored on the traditional belief in parts of Africa that humans possess a spiritual double in the animal kingdom. The novel is the fantastic tale of the life and travails of the eponymous protagonist-narrator who finds itself coerced into servitude as the animal double of a human master, Kibandi. Being under his spiritual subjugation, the porcupine is summoned at will as Kibandi's agent of death to eliminate his enemies using its dangerous spikes. Consequently, ostracized and abandoned by its animal kinfolk, it wallows in total solitude (but for the baobab) at Kibandi's untimely demise.

In valorizing Africa's green landscapes and culture-scapes through character creation, Mabanckou's anthropomorphism—the narrative code of the fable genre of African oral tradition—attributes human characteristics to both animal and plant, making them mouthpieces for the preservation of the natural environment; and to echo the ecologists' appeal for peaceful co-existence amongst all of nature's creatures. His personification of the baobab tree as an interlocutor-character in its own right, makes the whole narration an extended apostrophe where the plant (a potent element of nature) is a living spiritual being. The tree symbolism in African ethos represents the totality of plant life as the life-source of humans, providing for their essential needs of food, shelter, clothing, and medicine.

Native to the Savannah region of Africa, the iconic baobab tree is a magnificent, hardy, and deciduous succulence of great cultural and environmental importance, a powerful symbol of adaptability and transformation. Known as "the Tree of Life," many healing and protective powers are attributed to it, making it an indomitable part of the African landscape and an indispensable component of the life of the people. Melissa Shales emphasizes that:

> The bark and flesh are soft, fibrous and fire-resistant and can be used to weave rope and cloth. Baobab products are also used to make soap, rubber, and glue; while the bark and leaves are harvested for traditional medicine. The baobab is a life-giver for African wildlife, too, often creating its very own ecosystem. It provides food and shelter for a myriad of species, from the tiniest insect to the mighty African elephant (2021).

Thus, as a reflection of the baobab's role in African mythology, in Mabanckou's narrative, Baobab is the sedentary passive interlocutor of the porcupine-narrator. Serving as a traditional spiritual medium to communicate with the ancestors, it is the receptacle of the worries and woes of the animal beings. Thus, the porcupine goes to Baobab to narrate its evil deeds as the "double nuisible" ("the malevolent double") of its human master Kibandi, who compels him to execute vengeance killings of perceived enemies or their intimate relatives (an innocent infant in one instance). Baobab is the confessional figure who imparts forgiveness to the transgressor and infuses rest of mind, even as it is mute. This plant allegory can easily be associated to the important role of the "arbre à palabres" ("the palaver tree") in African tradition, celebrated as a rallying point under which villagers assemble to share their stories, perform rituals and ceremonies, and sort out serious issues concerning their communal life such as governance, disputes and crisis management.

Ecocriticism in Mabanckou's novel also implicates the sketches of the picturesque and serene rural landscapes of the Séképembé and Mossaka communities of the Congo, with particular attention to the diverse specificities of flora and fauna elements of the skies, trees, forests, rivers, hills, birds, etc. The ecological message is underlined by the narrator's direct reference to "green" when describing the habitat of the Baobab tree-character: "tu as de la chance de vivre dans un lieu paradisiaque, tout est vert ici" (*Mémoires de porc-épic* 148). ["you are lucky to live in a heavenly place, here, all is green"]. Baobab stands sentinel over its entire natural environment as "le gardien de la forêt" (149) ["the protector of the forest"]; so, it is portrayed as a total living being which possesses intelligence, integrity and soul, just like humans.

Mémoires de porc-épic exemplifies man's ecophobia through his degradation of the environment. Underlining the man-made conflict between landscape and human lifestyle in contemporary times, the protagonist affirms that several failed attempts are made by some "village fools" to reduce the Baobab to firewood, claiming that it is blocking the horizon and daylight (*Mémoires de porc-épic*, 149). Throughout Lamko's novel, ecocritical pastoral and agrarian depictions are prominent—the celebration of life and liberty through commune with nature: "l'immense parchemin de la poésie pastorale et agraire: celle qui célèbre la nature, la vie; celle qui entonne aussi le refus des lâchetés … les oiseaux pépient liberté » (*La phalène des collines*, 215).

As ecomedia, Sow Fall's, Mabanckou's and Lamko's novels upturn the anthropocentric viewpoint by attributing both intelligence and life-force to animals and vegetation, endowing them with souls and individual traits. The pervasive mode of all three novels is that all life forms should be respected as they are basically equal and interdependent. Thus, flora, fauna, and ecophilic cultures are valorized in the narratives, while the ecophobic, zoophobic, and homophobic ethics of humankind are unequivocally condemned.

At this juncture, it is imperative to point out that my choice of novels for this study covers both spectrums of the ecological polemic—Lamko's and Mabanckou's plots represent the concerns of conservation and constraint by the environmentalists (the light greens); while Sow Fall's narrative is an argument for a complete return to nature as advocated by the deep ecologists (the dark greens). Her explicit campaign is to integrate ecology into cultural identity:

> Le plus dur aujourd'hui est que l'espoir s'en va… Malgré tout je continuerai à prêcher : Aimons notre terre; nous l'arroserons de notre sueur et la creuserons de toutes nos forces,

avec courage. La lumière de notre espérance nous guidera, nous pourrons emprunter les routes du ciel, de la terre et de l'eau sans être chassés comme des parias. Nous ne serons plus des voyageurs sans bagages. Nos mains calleuses en rencontreront d'autres en de chaudes poignées de respect et de dignité partagée… (*Douceurs du bercail,* 88).

[The hardest today is that hope dies … Despite all I will continue to advocate: Let's love our land; we will water it with our sweat and dig into it with all our might, with courage. The light of our expectations will guide us, we can follow the paths of the sky, of the earth and of the sea without being chased away as pariahs. We will no longer be travelers without baggage. Our calloused hands will link with others in warm fists of respect and shared dignity.] (*All translations in this essay are mine.*)

The animal protagonists-narrators in Lamko's *La phalène des collines* and Mabanckou's *Mémoires de porc-épic,* draw attention to the non-human (inhuman) world. Their iconoclastic representations of man in his relationship with nature and culture effectively negate age-long anthropocentric beliefs. They unveil humans possessing inferior intelligence to animals as the despicable devastators and wanton wasters of flora and fauna.

As for Aminata Sow Fall's narrative focus, her earlier novels *Le Jujubier du patriarche* and *L'Appel des arènes* both reflect her ecocritical stance. The former features the jujube tree as a symbolic life-giving plant, just like the baobab, which responds to all the people's needs on issues concerning illness, sterility, and even unemployment. The latter presents nature, the rural environment, the homeland and the home culture as stabilizing life-forces in the affirmation of the identity of the African person. This is inherent in *Douceurs du bercail,* right from the title of Sow Fall's narrative ("comforts of the fold")—a portent of the goodness emanating from communing with kinsfolk and nature. This viewpoint aligns with Rueckert's view that man's homeland is the earth, and nostalgia must pull him back to it for his well-being. Sow Fall's protagonists receive mental and physical healing only after their return, not just to their homeland but to the earth, cultivating and extracting essential elements of food and medicine. Sow Fall's thrust in the novel is the idea of a generous, nourishing and hospitable earth: «l'idée d'une terre généreuse et hospitalière capable de donner plus qu'on lui a offert» (*Douceurs du bercail* 127). Implicating ecofeminism in her narrative, Sow Fall chooses as the focalizer of the eco-centric issues Asta, a strong African woman who effectively leads a predominantly male group of deported emigrants back to earth (their natural condition), where they all find self-realization, cultural identity, and economic and psychological fulfillment. Sow Fall's ecofeminist protagonist advocates against international displacement and champions the campaign for man's intimate interactions with his natural environment.

> Anne mon amie, tu le sais bien mais j'éprouve tant de plaisir à te le répéter: c'est ineffable bonheur de sentir la terre, de communier avec elle quand, de son sein, jaillit la vie, la nourriture qui donne vie et consistance... c'est très profond dans mon cœur... (*Douceurs du bercail* 200).

> [Anne my friend, you know it but I feel so joyous repeating it to you: it is ineffable happiness to feel the earth, to commune with it when, from its bosom, life springs forth, nourishment that gives life and sustenance... it is very profound in my heart...]

Anne considers her two weeks' vacation spent with her friend Asta in Africa, away from her hectic metropolitan hustle, as idyllic and an invigorating health cure: "a été comme une cure ... un bol d'oxygène administré à quelqu'un à bout de souffle. Vraiment." She metaphorically terms it "a bowl of oxygen administered to a breathless person." The various elements of nature perform a stirring symphony to Anne's delight – birds, trees, stream and sunset.

"Ils ont aduré les calories d'oiseaux regagnant leur nid au sommet des arbres, et Anne a savouré jusqu'à l'ivresse les adieux du fleuve au soleil qui s'en va» (*Douceurs du bercail* 178).

Moreover, man's mental composite is psychologically healed by the joy derived from his commune with nature: «Ces bonheurs qui sauvent de la désolation d'un monde de détresse où grondent la misère et l'angoisse » (*Douceurs du bercail* 198). ["These joys that save one from the desolation of a world in distress where misery and anguish groan"]. The primacy of human interaction with nature, is further underscored:

> …cette terre qui cache tant de merveilles en son sein … Mais ce qui sera le plus important … c'est l'ineffable bonheur de sentir la terre, de communiquer avec elle quand, de son sein, jaillit la vie, la nourriture qui donne vie et conscience …(*Douceurs du bercail* 200).

The commune with nature also implies that the homeland should not be abandoned for foreign climes. Sow Fall condemns the idolization and idealization of everything Western because it results in the abandonment of the African soul, the erosion of African cultural values, and the loss of traditional heritage. This is a major worry for Asta, whose son Paapidesires to migrate:

> Je voulais le convaincre que le Paradis n'est pas forcément ailleurs, qu'il y a des tas de jeunes qui partent, se cassent la figure contre le mirage mais persistent à croire à un bonheur qui leur échappe… (*Douceurs du bercail* 201).

Asta claims that decultured migrants in exile wander around like lost souls ["vivoter comme une âme perdue"]. Her humiliation by the French migration officers at the airport and conversations with other deportees precipitate her epiphany on ecological identity, from which she concludes that: "L'alienation est assurément la plus grande mutilation que puisse subir l'homme" ["Alienation is definitely the greatest mutilation that man can experience"]. Only by returning to the homeland can the psychologically mutilated African individual attain spiritual wellness and mental equilibrium. So she commits to advocate against emigration to her family and friends stating that Eldorado is not to be found in migration but in the entrails of the earth: "Quand je sortirais d'ici, je serai plus à l'aise pour dire à mes frères, sœurs, parents et amis, que l'eldorado n'est pas au bout de l'exode mais dans les entrailles de notre terre."

Convinced of this, Asta flees the city, putting behind her negative traveling experiences and a failed love affair, and escapes to the picturesque setting of Naatangué in the hinterland of Senegal, where she builds an idyllic communal life as an ideal world view.

ANIMAL AESTHETICS AND THE CELEBRATION OF AFRICAN TRADITIONAL ETHOS

From time immemorial, African traditional ethos has always conceptualized animals as an essential composite of the physical environment of human societies. Generally, African prose narratives of the 21st century have witnessed an influx of animal characters—a phenomenon, according to Woodward, that is linked to African spirituality and belief systems (Woodward 2008). Hence, they abound in African oral traditions of riddles, songs, chants, proverbs, adages, fables, and folktales replete with moral lessons drawn from the animal world, designed for human consumption and considerations (Doudoroff 1989). It might thus be argued that in environmental literacy campaigns to help readers adapt better to the world, ecomedia and zoomedia have become a potential force of enlightenment and change in public perceptions, attitudes and experiences towards nature and animals.

In full accordance with the theory of green studies that literature has the power to inspire its readers to act in defense of nature (Coupe 2013), I have conceived the ecological construct in the corpus of my study in dual narrative modes: Kate Soper's naturalistic mode and compassionate mode. In *Douceurs du bercail*, Aminata Sow Fall's human protagonist Asta adopts the naturalistic mode for her ecocritical portrayal of the human/nature relationship "in a fairly straightforward way and figure as part of the narrative situation and environment" (Soper 2005, 303). She presents nature in all its glory and goodness through a narrative exploration of its physical beauty, its cultural functionality and its agricultural benefits.

Then, to gain the reader's empathy, the compassionate mode of zoopoetics is more aptly employed by Lamko's and Mabanckou's animal protagonist-narrators as eco-citizens to insidiously render themselves as victims of man's homophobia, ecophobia, and zoophobia. Copiously drawing from the traditional African fable genre, they employ anthropomorphism and zoomorphism to satirize human attitudes and actions through their hypercritical interpretations, offering moral lessons to humankind.

It is not by chance that in the characterization in the two novels, the rodent-protagonist (*Mémoires de porc-épic*) and the insect-protagonist (*La phalène des collines*) are selected from the lower categories of the animal species, to unfavorably project the human species in the eco-social sphere. The two satires seriously challenge the Cartesian disclaimer of the attributes of rationality, consciousness, language, and sentience in the animal species. Aversely, they attempt to validate the Aristotelian philosophy of animals sharing with humans such capacities as desire, pain, and imagination.

In Lamko's and Mabanckou's zoomedia, the animal characters are ascribed the sense of justice, honor, uprightness, and truth; and the animal society is attributed with an organized social structure, adherence to territorial integrity, and environmental consciousness. They are thus in accord with the philosophized claims of the French Renaissance humanists Michel de Montaigne and Pierre Charon that animals had intelligence and superior integrity compared to humans.

Mabanckou's zoocritical stance is underscored by an iconoclastic portrayal of humankind in interference with nature and the environment. The voice of the rodent-protagonist systematically strips away humankind's various hypocritical layers of "civilization" and exposes its savagery (Kibandi's cannibalism and ferocious vindictiveness) against his fellow men, his animal cohabitants of earth and his natural environment.

> les hommes ont tort de se vanter là-dessus, je suis convaincu qu'ils ne naissent pas avec leur intélligence … leur seule consolation sera d'être homme … ce sont tous des crétins, être des hommes est leur dernier argument, or ce n'est pas parce que la mouche vole que cela fera d'elle un oiseau … (*Mémoires de porc-épic* 25-26).

Here, the porcupine denounces the self-arrogated superiority of the human species, asserting that humans are all rogues, bereft of native intelligence, concluding with a proverb reinforcing its view of man as a sub-being: "The fact that a fly flies does not make it a bird."

On its part, *La phalène des collines* features another demonstration of traditional African ethos concerning the human-animal interconnectedness and the probable animal reincarnations in the hereafter. The unnamed local queen protagonist, who is brutally raped and murdered by a priest, immediately transforms into a moth and flits from one location to another to keenly observe and critically narrate the disturbing desecration of her corpse as well as the other viciousness inflicted on her tribespeople during the Rwandan genocide. The moth's raw account serves as Lamko's narrative code for the hypercritical depiction of humankind in its most barbaric mode – recklessly executing rape, torture, mass slaughter, dismemberment, disembowelment, etc. In Lamko's textualization of the human/animal ecological conflict (*Homo sapien* vs *Lepidoptera*, in this case), his deliberate choice of an insect-narrator (a tiny creature) underscores man's meanness in his interactions and activities against human and non-human nature.

Both novels depict man's greed, bloodthirstiness, and quest for power by which he dominates and abuses other humans, animals, and the earth. The often-employed sarcasm of Lamko's moth narrator denigrates human intelligence and exposes human barbarism against fellow humans, stating that humans are adult enough themselves to carve and mutilate each other. « Dans cette sale affaire l'on a tendance à accuser tout le monde sans prendre en compte le fait que les gens sont suffisamment adultes pour s'entrecouper, s'entretailler, tous seuls … » (*La phalène des collines* 95). As for Mabanckou's zoomedia, his porcupine-narrator renders direct condemnation of human violence against man and nature:

> …mes compères écoutaient avec intérêt la caricature que notre gouverneur dressait de l'espèce humaine, celui-ci proclamaient que l'homme était indéfendable… qu'il était la pire des créatures qui puisse exister sur cette terre … puisque les humains nous mènent la vie dure…puisqu'ils sont hostiles et sourds à notre appel à la coexistence pacifique… puisqu'ils ne comprennent pas la nécessité d'une entente qu'après une longue bataille qui les décime, qui laisse des traces indélébiles

dans leur mémoire....(*Mémoires de porc-épic* 69).

[My cronies listened with interest to the caricature that our governor sketched of the human species, he declared that man was indefensible...that he was the worst of all creatures that ever existed on this earth ... because humans make us live hard life ...because they are hostile and deaf to our appeal for peaceful coexistence ... because they do not understand the need for an agreement until after a long battle that decimates them, that leaves indelible traces in their memory...]

In fact, in the narration, the rodent-narrator gains the reader's sympathy by portraying itself as an innocent victim of humankind's evil desires, summoned to become an unwilling agent of death and compelled by the spiritual traditions to do the bidding of its human double.

Lamko and Mabanckou underscore the duality of attributes in the characters of the animal-protagonists and the human antagonists, creating a clear dichotomy of virtues against vices. While the porcupine and moth demonstrate the humaneness, compassion, and unselfishness of the animals, they expound on the hatred and destructiveness of humans.

In the moth's derisive descriptions of the mindless destructiveness of the Rwandan genocide, the human-animal roles are reversed: man becomes the beast in his acts of bestiality and inhumanity through his gluttony, perfidy, foolhardiness and foul character, disfigured by his horns. « Peur de la terre, de sa gloutonnerie, sa perfidie, sa bêtise, sa teigne à la naissance cabossée de ses cornes ... toutes ses vallées et crevasses d'infortune » (*La phalène des collines* 14). Lamko's moth is scathing in its portrayal of man's destructive nature.

> Je ris du territoire des hommes! Un triste tableau d'art soufflé en relief accidenté et tourmenté de sable rouge sang! Cocasse l'homme, surtout quand il se prend pour la plus lumineuse des créatures!

(*La phalène des collines* 19)
[I laugh over man's territory! A sad, blown-up artwork in

rugged and tormented relief of blood-red sand! Comical man, especially when he considers himself as the brightest of creatures!].

Its zoomorphic analogy deliberately places man on the same level as other lower species of the biosphere, an embodiment of all their negative traits. He is thus portrayed as an indiscriminate devourer who avariciously ravages the vegetation, reducing its verdant vibrancy to desolation. The moth's disdain for humankind is evident in its comprehensive and captivating wordplay, rendered pithy with animal epithets:

> C'est dans l'animal qu'il faut creuser pour déterrer les limites de l'homme. L'homme-chenille, lâché sur la toison verte des pâturages et des feuillages, dévore sans retenue jusqu'aux nervures. L'homme-criquet effeuille les épineux, les dénude... L'homme-boa avale le buffle jusqu'à la racine des cornes... L'homme-éléphant...écrase toutes les termitières sur son passage...déracine les bananiers, les plantes de manioc, vide les marigots d'espoir. L'homme-hibou... nocturne... dévoreur-de-visages ! ...hypocrite... L'homme-chat minaude, cache ses travers et ses crottes dans le sable... pour afficher pureté. L'homme-chien...son maitre... lui jette des reliefs... un énorme tas d'arêtes de hareng...se piquant les babines, la langue...lèche le carreau...(*La phalène des collines* 48-49).

> [It's in the animal world that one must dig to unearth man's limits. The caterpillar-man dropped on the green fleece of pastures and foliage, devours without restraint up to the veins. The cricket-man defoliates the thorny bushes ...The boa-man swallows the buffalo...The elephant-man ...crushes all anthills in its path...uproots banana-trees, cassava plants, drains the creeks of hope. The owl-man...devourer of faces!... hypocrite...The cat-man minces, hides its flaws, and litters in the sand...to feign purity. The dog-man...its master...throws him leftovers...a huge pile of herring bones...pricking its chops, its tongue...licks the floor....] (*Emphasis mine*)

It then proceeds to predict apocalyptic devastations on a huge scale when the world would self-destruct into celestial debris and terrestrial shards, if humankind continues in its unreasonableness and to block its heart from even a modicum of affection:

> Je prédis cependant des apocalypses, le choc infernal des débris du ciel et des lambeaux de la terre dans un bain-marie, si la vanité des hommes refuse de se laisser greffer un cœur un peu plus généreux (*La phalène des collines* 15).

The last aspect on the zoomedia narratives of my corpus bears on the homophobic portrayal in Sow Fall's *Douceurs du bercail*. Her zoocritical focus is the exposure of the human-human debasement in a migrant setting, portraying homophobia (more precisely, Afrophobia) –human injustice to humankind with a strong race-specific tincture as it affects African emigrants in Western societies. The novel details the humiliation of the protagonist Asta in the hands of human-animals—French customs officials at the Charles de Gaulle airport in Paris. Spending days in that enclosed space with other African detainees awaiting deportation, she becomes the unwitting recipient of their various tales of Afrophobic dehumanization experienced as emigrants in a foreign land. However, her epiphany-induced conviction in an eco-cultural identity enables Asta to turn the fortunes around for the group; not just by renouncing exile in favor of the African homeland, but by returning to the earth to actively partake of nature's flow of cultural and physical bounties.

CONCLUSION

This chapter derives its significance from the African traditional reality of the interconnectedness between humankind and its natural environment. The francophone African authors of my selected texts – Lamko, Sow Fall, and Mabanckou attempt to focalize and thus valorize in their narratives the essential interdependence of the various factors within the ecosystem—human, animal, and plant.

La phalène des collines, *Douceurs du bercail* and *Mémoires de porc-épic* advocate for the sacredness and sanctity of all life forms in the biosphere: as tiny and delicate as the insect moth, as small and vulnerable as the rodent porcupine, as large, sturdy and traditionally valuable as the baobab tree, and as ingenious and intellectually resourceful as humankind. The conscious reflection on the psychological state of major characters as well as the imperatives of the African experience with natural earth, also insert the narratives within the discourse of the polemics of African identity in a globalized world. They highlight that by maintaining harmonious relationships with the natural world, one's psychic balance and spiritual wellness can be reclaimed, renewed and recovered. This would, in turn, strongly affirm the cultural identity of African humankind.

In all, the three novels deconstruct the Cartesian conception of human distinctiveness and keenly advocate for ecological justice for all of creation. They constitute a clarion call for the discontinuation of cruelty to animals, violence to humans, and degradation to the natural environment, making their prose fiction a green campaign communicative form that aptly registers the novels in the domains of ecomedia and zoomedia.

REFERENCES

Atilade, Kayode. 2022. "La tradition orale africaine comme outil de plaidoyer : l'écocritique dans Ijala d'Ogundare Foyanmu." *Mouvances Francophones*. https://doi.org/10.5206/mf.v7i1.14589.

Bassintsa-Bouesso, Aetius. 2017. «Alain Mabanckou et l'écriture de la migrance: enjeux éthiques et sociopoétiques». *Francisola* 5 (2): 158. https://ejournal.upi.edu/index.php/Francisola/article/view/9407. Accessed December 12, 2023.

Coupe, Lawrence. 2013. "Green Theory." In *The Routledge Companion to Critical and Cultural Theory*, 2nd ed. https://lawrencecoupe.co.uk/green-theory. Accessed January 16, 2024.

Derman, William. 2003. "Cultures of Development and Indigenous Knowledge: The Erosion of Traditional Boundaries." *Africa Today* 50 (2, Fall/Winter): 67–85.

Doudoroff, Michael J. 1989. "José Emilio Pacheco: An Overview of the Poetry, 1963–86." *Hispania* 72 (2): 264–76.

Eya'a Obame, Daisy Fabiola. 2021. *Pour une réflexion écocritique postcoloniale: lecture de Petroleum de Bessora, Les neuf consciences du Malfini de Patrick Chamoiseau, The Conservationist de Nadine Gordimer et la trilogie postcoloniale de Kate Grenville (The Secret*

River, The Lieutenant, Sarah Thornhill). Doctoral diss., Université de Bretagne Occidentale – Brest. NNT: 2021BRES0107. https://tel.archives-ouvertes.fr/tel-03789590. Accessed June 24, 2024.

Fioritti, Nathan. 2020. "The Interconnectedness of Human, Animal and Environmental Health." *Pursuit.* https://pursuit.unimelb.edu.au/articles/the-interconnectedness-of-human-animal-and-environmental-health. Accessed January 1, 2024.

Germain, Nathan. 2019. "Une poétique des espaces : lecture écocritique des géographies et langages hybrides dans *Verre cassé*." *Alternative Francophone.* https://www.semanticscholar.org/reader/765b138f3789257bad07cfe8c0aa0c2f840e3347. Accessed June 24, 2024.

Glotfelty, Cheryll. 1996. "Introduction: Literary Studies in an Age of Environmental Crisis." In *The Ecocriticism Reader: Landmarks in Literary Ecology,* edited by Cheryll Glotfelty and Harold Fromm, xv–xxxvii. Athens and London: University of Georgia Press.

Huggan, Graham, and Helen Tiffin. 2010. *Postcolonial Ecocriticism: Literature, Animals, Environment.* London and New York: Routledge.

Lamko, Koulsy. 2002. *La phalène des collines.* Paris: Le Serpent à plumes.

Love, Glen. 1996. "Revaluing Nature: Toward Ecological Criticism." In *The Ecocriticism Reader: Landmarks in Literary Ecology,* edited by Cheryll Glotfelty and Harold Fromm, 225–40. Athens: University of Georgia Press.

Mabanckou, Alain. 2006. *Mémoires de porc-épic.* Paris: Éditions du Seuil.

Magdelaine-Andrianjafitrimo, Valérie. 2018. "Terre rouge, eaux vertes: Blessures et énergie de la nature dans trois textes de Michèle Rakotoson." *Nouvelles Études Francophones* 32: 26–42. https://doi.org/10.1353/NEF.2017.0037. Accessed June 24, 2024.

Mason, Bethany. 2019. "An Ecocritical Approach to Identity Representation in Patrick Chamoiseau's *Chronique des sept misères.*" *Alternative Francophone* 2 (4): 25–41. https://doi.org/10.29173/af29377. Accessed June 24, 2024.

Regan, Tom. 1985. "The Case of Animals' Rights." In *In Defence of Animals,* edited by Peter Singer, 13–26. Oxford: Basil Blackwell.

Rueckert, William. 1996. "Literature and Ecology: An Experiment in Ecocriticism." In *The Ecocriticism Reader: Landmarks in Literary*

Ecology, edited by Cheryll Glotfelty and Harold Fromm, 104–23. Athens: University of Georgia Press.

Shales, Melissa. 2021. "The Baobab: Fun Facts About Africa's Tree of Life." *ThoughtCo.* https://www.thoughtco.com/fun-facts-about-the-baobab-tree-1454374. Accessed January 13, 2024.

Simon, Anne. 2015. "Animality and Contemporary French Literary Studies: Overview and Perspectives." Translated by Céline Maillard and Stephanie Posthumus. In *French Thinking about Animals,* edited by Louisa Mackenzie and Stephanie Posthumus, 75–88. East Lansing: Michigan State University Press. http://www.jstor.org/stable/10.14321/j.ctt13x0p3s.10.

Singer, Peter. 1975. *Animal Liberation: Towards an End to Man's Inhumanity to Animals.* Wellingborough, Northamptonshire: Thorsons Publishers.

Soper, Kate. 2005. "The Beast in Literature: Some Initial Thoughts." *Literary Beasts: The Representation of Animals in Contemporary Literature. Comparative Critical Studies* 2 (3): 303–9.

Sow Fall, Aminata. 1998. *Douceurs du bercail.* Abidjan: NEI.

Toivanen, Anna-Leena. 2011. "Retour au local: *Celles qui attendent* et l'engagement diasporique de Fatou Diome." *Relief* 24 (3): 48. https://www.revue-relief.org/articles/10.18352/relief.658. Accessed June 24, 2024.

Trout, Colette. 2020. "Les animaux et nous chez Marie Darrieussecq: une coexistence indispensable." *Précisions sur les sciences dans l'œuvre de Marie Darrieussecq.* https://doi.org/10.7202/1067880AR. Accessed June 28, 2024.

Vignola, Gabriel. 2022. "Écocritique, écosémiotique et représentation du monde en littérature." *Cygne noir.* https://doi.org/10.7202/1089937ar. Accessed June 24, 2024.

Vital, Anthony. 2008. "Toward an African Ecocriticism: Postcolonialism, Ecology and 'Life & Times of Michael K.'" *Research in African Literatures* 39 (1, Spring): 87–106.

Woodward, Wendy. 2008. *The Animal Gaze: Animal Subjectivities in Southern African Narratives.* Johannesburg: Wits University Press.

CHAPTER FIVE

Rhinos, Rangers, and (Eco) Returns in Contemporary South African Literature

Beverley Jane Cornelius & Jean Rossmann

INTRODUCTION

Three recent offerings in South African literature foreground the historical exploitation of and damage to the region's environment. *Decima*, by Eben Venter (2023), *Eye Brother Horn*, by Bridget Pitt (2023), and *Black Lion: Alive in the Wilderness*, by Sicelo Mbatha (2021) indicate an ecological turn in South African literature, offering a postcolonial ecocritical explanation for the current crises without catastrophizing the future.[1] They each also suggest—as a remedy—that spiritual awareness and connection to nature can foster environmental justice, through multispecies entanglements.

Eben Venter's novel, *Decima*, a hybrid blend of fact and fiction, highlights the current plight of the rhino, a creature that has been hunted to the point of near extinction. Bridget Pitt's historical novel, *Eye Brother Horn*, fictionalizes the colonialism and capitalism that decimated the landscapes of KwaZulu-Natal (Zululand), while Sicelo Mbatha's memoir, *Black Lion: Alive in the Wilderness*, advocates for an intuitive and mystical relationship with the fauna and flora of the Zululand biome. Venter, Pitt, and Mbatha urge a return to nature-wisdom and to an equitable

---

1   While this chapter offers a broad overview of shared ecocritical concerns across *Eye Brother Horn*, *Black Lion: Alive in the Wilderness* and *Decima*, two more sustained analyses subsequently emerged from this work: "Rekindling Eco-Ubuntu in Sicelo Mbatha's *Black Lion: Alive in the Wilderness*" (Cornelius and Rossmann 2024) and "Demythologising the Rhino: From Dürer to Venter, From Beast to Being" (Rossmann and Cornelius 2025).

community with nature. Through their 'activated storytelling' (Haraway 2016, 132), they reimagine multispecies possibilities.

In what follows, we focus on these three examples of South African literary ecology and undertake an ecocritical reading of the texts to ascertain how current environmental crises are represented in South African literature. We ask: What do these texts ascribe to the cause of these crises, what is their prognosis, and how can storytelling serve environmental activism and justice?

The landscape and the environment are always (and have always been) prominently featured in South African literature but have typically served as a backdrop to the human story. In recent years, a marked shift has occurred that sees the environment and ecological concerns overtly positioned, with a sense of urgency that foregrounds mass extinction and climate change. Flora and fauna are in the forefront of the three texts that form the focus of our study, limning and re-imagining the South African past, present, and future.

Foregrounding the entanglement of nature and culture/s, these tales reflect ecocriticism's "basic premise that literature both reflects and helps to shape human responses to the natural environment" (Hutchings 2007, 172). Literature can act as an agent for change, as Donna Haraway advocates in her notion of 'activated storytelling.' Brooke Stanley and Walter Dana Phillips note that South African ecocritical work is "especially generative [because it navigates] the imbrication of environmental and social problems [...], given conservation's troubling links to colonialism, apartheid, and more contemporary inequalities" (2017, n.p.). Postcolonial and ecocritical concerns are intertwined, and their vexed effects loom large in *Decima*, *Eye Brother Horn*, and *Black Lion*. As an antidote to capitalist-colonialist commodification of nature, these texts present nature as animate and spiritual, invoking a romantic sensibility, which aligns with indigenous knowledge systems.

Kevin Hutchings observes that Romantic literature provides fertile ground for ecocriticism because it "value[s] the non-human world most highly, celebrating nature as a beneficent antidote to the crass world of getting and spending, and lamenting its perceived destruction at the hands of technological industrialism and capitalist society" (2007, 172-202). The celebration and lamentation mentioned by Hutchings (2007) highlights the distinction that Peter Barry (2017) has identified: between a tone, in early examples of ecocriticism, that is either 'celebratory' or 'minatory', meaning that it seeks "to warn us of environmental threats emanating from governmental, industrial, commercial, and neo-colonial forces" (2017, 251).

The threat of technological industrialism and capitalist society that the Romantics recognized 200 years ago is now a crisis the world over and has reached apocalyptic proportions. Haraway's caution in 2013 is ever more pressing today (2023 [2013]) – "we live and die in a time of permanent war, multi-species surplus killings, and genocides. Coupled to that, but distinct from it, is the urgency of climate change. We inhabit a planet that is undergoing systemic transformations [...]. Rich worlds crucial to human and nonhuman flourishing can and do disappear. Things can be very gradual and then boom—systems changes mutate life and death radically and suddenly. Understanding that in the tissues of our flesh seems to be really urgent" (Haraway and Kenney 2023).

This sense of urgency is shared by Thom van Dooren, Eben Kirksey, and Ursula Münster, who point out that we are in a "period shaped by escalating and mutually reinforcing processes of biosocial destruction—from mass extinction to climate change, from globalization to terrorism" (2016, 3). In response, ecocritics have adopted numerous names for the current condition, such as "Anthropocene, Capitalocene, Plantationocene, Chthulucene, White-supremacy-cene" (3). This variety in nomenclature is indicative of the multifaceted nature of the field of ecocriticism, as well as of the breadth of the community.

This diversity, of course, explains debates about the naming of the field.[2] To clarify for the sake of this chapter, we see 'ecocriticism' as an umbrella term that brings together or connects multiple strands and various areas of study. Like Cheryll Glotfelty, we feel that 'eco-' (as in ecocriticism, ecoliterature, ecological) "implies interdependent communities, integrated systems, and strong connections among constituent parts" (1996, xx). Glotfelty and Harold Fromm stated nearly 30 years ago that they saw "ecocritical scholarship becoming ever more interdisciplinary,

---

2 "Other terms currently in circulation include *ecopoetics, environmental literary criticism*, and *green cultural studies*" (Glotfelty 1996, xx).

multicultural, and international" (xxv). Acknowledging that it had been "predominantly a white movement," they foresaw its transition to "a multi-ethnic movement when stronger connections [were] made between the environment and issues of social justice" (xxv). They were mindful that before a "community of [ecocritical] scholars" was formed, "each critic was inventing an environmental approach to literature in isolation" (xvii) and that there were voices "howling in the wilderness" (xvii). This naïve use of the word 'wilderness' in fact speaks to the occlusion of Africa and the Global South, which brings us to the importance of this work as a voice from the putative 'wilderness': Africa. Although the formal roots of ecocriticism as a literary theory can be traced to the USA and the UK, this does not mean that ecocrit and ecolit were not developing in other parts of the world. Now, in the 21st century, voices from the Global South are coming to the fore, writing back and "engaging with long histories of relational, agentic thinking from indigenous peoples" (Van Dooren, Kirksey and Münster 2016, 2).

This point (about where and by whom ecocrit/ecolit is being produced) has been taken up by William Slaymaker (2001), especially with regard to ecocriticism in Africa; to which Rogers Asempasash et al. (2022), as well as Stanley and Phillips (2017), have responded in their respective discussions about ecocriticism in/from Africa. At the onset of the new millennium, Slaymaker, differentiating between 'nature writing' and 'ecocriticism and/or ecoliterature', commented that the "African echo of global green approaches to literature and literary criticism [had] been faint" and that there was "no rush by African literary and cultural critics to adopt ecocriticism or the literature of the environment as they are promulgated from many of the world's metropolitan centers" (2001, 132).

In Stanley and Phillips's (2017) view, Slaymaker's argument depends upon an outmoded conception of nature as synonymous with wilderness. Moreover, as Asempasash et al (2022) point out, though "the ecology or environment has scarcely been central in [literary] discussions", this does not necessarily suggest that "African writers are insensitive to the plight of the physical environment, as Slaymaker (2001) alleges" (2022, 2). They argue that "if African writers and literary criticism have largely been anthropocentric, as Slaymaker claims, it is because African writers and critics have focused attention on interrogating postcolonial issues that caused the environmental crises rather than tackling the environmental issues head-on or in isolation". However, they are also surprised at this lack of critical attention "for, the environment that bore witness to the trade in human[s] and other postcolonial crises has suffered greatly from the human drama of wars, capture, slave escape, or flight" (Asempasash 2022, 2).

But Slaymaker, having decried the "low visibility of ecolit and ecocrit in recent Black African writing," also predicted that it is temporary and that "the green revolution will spread to and through communities of readers and writers of African literature, 'ecoing' the booming interest elsewhere" (Slaymaker 2001, 116). Stanley and Phillips counter, though, that ecocriticism's "foundational concepts [should be interrogated] by embracing a multidirectional ecocriticism, rather than asking black Africa to 'respond' to yet another white and/or Northern imposition" (2017, 7).

Emanating from the Global South (as well as from the Global North), a new branch of ecocriticism's tree is multispecies studies, summarized in Anna Tsing's pithy assertion that "human nature is an interspecies relationship" (2012, 141). Multispecies scholars challenge human exceptionalism, recognizing nature as an active, intelligent force and that all planetary life is interconnected and interdependent. Van Dooren, Kirksey and Münster explain: "while the 'the animal' and 'the environment' have in recent decades been the subject of new forms of scholarly inquiry [...] a multispecies approach focuses on the multitudes of lively agents that bring one another into being through entangled relations that include, but always also exceed, dynamics of predator and prey, parasite and host, researcher and researched, symbiotic partner, or indifferent neighbor" (2016, 3).

Multispecies scholars are thus concerned with giving voice to nature's "lively agents" and emphasizing interspecies relationships. Understanding these relationships requires cultivating "'arts of attentiveness' [which are] modes of both paying attention to others and crafting meaningful response" (1).

The literary texts discussed here feature human and animal characters who are "lively agents" and experts at the art of attentiveness. We begin with a text that opens in the South African present but also stretches back into the distant past: *Decima*. This text foregrounds, with a sense of urgency and foreboding, the lifeworld and subjectivity of the titular rhino. It is a story that reverses anthropocentric hierarchies that are the legacy of Western enlightenment discourse, promoting a philosophy of deep ecology. The novel interrogates the figure of the historical 'great white hunter' as well as the contemporary poaching crisis that is spurred by poverty and the Traditional Chinese Medicine Market (TCM). The second multispecies text we discuss returns to the beginnings of colonialism. *Eye Brother Horn*, set in 1800s Zululand, foregrounds a correspondence and tension between Wordsworthian ecospirituality and African animism. Finally, we turn to the present moment with the memoir *Black Lion: Alive in the Wilderness*, which stresses that a relationship to land based only on economic returns leads to social, spiritual, and ecological poverty. Rather, Mbatha urges us to weave ourselves into the tapestry of wilderness as an approach to the precarious future.

DECIMA: SHARED LIVES AND CONSEQUENTIAL RELATIONSHIPS

Decima is the tenth and most recent novel by South African author, Eben Venter, in which he takes up the *cause célèbre* of saving the rhinoceros from the brink of extinction. Venter's novel exposes the socio-economic complexities of the South African rhino poaching racket and imbues an individual rhino with subjectivity, selfhood, and agency. He names this rhino Decima, which is "Latin for one tenth, but also a largesse bestowed" (Venter 2023, 28). Her wealth cannot be measured instrumentally, in the form of rhino horn; Venter instead emphasizes her intrinsic value as a sentient being.

It is the rangers (and counter-intuitively, a poacher) who employ the 'art of attentiveness' to view creatures as more than "mere symbols, resources, or background for the lives of humans" (Van Dooren, Kirksey and Münster 2016, 6). Their attentiveness awakens a realization of "shared lives [and] consequential relationships" (6) that exist between human, animal, and all life. Attentiveness is co-extensive with "passionate immersion [which means] becoming curious and so entangled, 'learning to be affected' and so perhaps to understand and care a little differently" because of the shared and consequential nature of all planetary life (6). *Decima* is exemplary of what multispecies scholars refer to as "'thick' accounts of the distinctive experiential worlds, modes of being, and biocultural attachments of other species" (6).

Though explicitly labelled a novel on its cover, *Decima* is a hybrid text, an 'autofiction' that melds the facts and fictions of the author, Eben Venter, and his mother, Maureen Venter, with an unnamed narrator-protagonist and a fictional mother.[3] The protagonist is a writer who has returned from Australia to his birth country, South Africa, to research the scourge of rhino poaching in southern Africa. Through his investigations, the novel presents a multi-faceted perspective of conservation and poaching in the present day and delves into the far-reaching history of trophy hunting and the exoticization of animals that problematize anthropocentric and colonial binaries to defy any simple solution. Eben has also returned to visit his aging mother, who lives in a retirement village in the Eastern Cape, having moved from the family farm. During their time together in the narrative present, a visit interrupted by his research expeditions to various locations, they reminisce about their earlier rural life.

A philosophy of deep ecology permeates the narrative, "imagin[ing] a broader sociality that includes diverse communities of life on earth that are composed not only through biotic factors but also […] ethical relation, the valuing of other beings as more than just resources" (Næss 2005 [1973], 33). This ethics is signaled, in the novel, by the truism and moral litmus test of Venter's mother in the opening epigraph: "[i]f someone doesn't like animals there is something wrong with them" (2023, n.p.). Eben will later reflect, prompted by his mother's enquiry about his "new book", that "this time my writing is not for the sake of writing only, but for the sake of a particular animal, an attempt, if nothing else, to bring to the fore Decima's sentience, to try to understand it in the way the first-century poet Catullus expresses its meaning: *fieri sentio et excrucior*. I feel it and I am tormented" (137-38). Eben reappropriates the Roman poet's famous epigram on love to describe the intensity of his passionate immersion in the life of a rhino. To feel this deeply is torture, as the Latin excrucior alludes to being torn apart on a rack. *Decima* is, as Michael Titlestad

---

3   Though the narrator-protagonist is never named in the narrative, for clarity and ease of discussion, we will, from this point on, refer to the author as Venter and to the narrator-protagonist as Eben.

observes, a "novel about love, in a profound and manifold sense" (2023, n.p.). The narrator broadens his own empathy (and the reader's), placing the tale of the rhino matriarch, Decima, alongside reminiscences of his mother. Often, the two mothers' narrative strands follow consecutively, implying an affinity and kinship between human and animal. Avoiding an inaccurate self-sameness, he declares he "will not equate [his] mother's loneliness to that of a solitary rhinoceros in the bush [but that] there is a continuity between the feelings of two such creatures" (our emphasis, Venter 2023, 28). Beyond the quest for solitude, they share a maternal instinct to protect their young and their love of the fauna and flora of the Eastern Cape, and a desire to conserve it.

When Eben uses the word 'continuity', he challenges anthropocentric hierarchies, rooted, he notes, in biblical dogma. Recalling his father's evening devotions, which often turned to Genesis 1:28 ("have dominion [...] over every living thing that moveth on earth"), Eben foregrounds that the "kak began" with the mistranslation of dominion (Venter 2023, 51). The original Hebrew, *radah*, implied rather a more egalitarian "agreement" between human, animal, and the earth, "of respectful guardianship" (51). Rejecting religious dogma, Eben turns to the Romantic philosophy of sympathetic imagination as an ethical alternative to human/animal relations (76). Acknowledgements at the end of the novel cite Walter Jackson Bate's seminal essay on the topic, which describes the power of the imagination, "by an effort of sympathetic intuition [...] to penetrate the barrier which space puts between it and its object, and, by actually entering into the object, so to speak, secure a momentary but complete identification with it" (Bate 1945, 144). Drawing on the combined powers of sympathy and imagination enables a mystical, shamanic oneness with the earth and its creatures.

Eben contrasts two phenomenological approaches to understanding and perceiving an animal: sympathetic imagination versus stalking. The hunter stalks the animal and at the crucial moment, if there is time for hunter and hunted to see eye-to-eye, that moment is often lost because of insufficient time or light. But the ranger/conservationist "visits and revisits the [animal] in the bush" (Venter 2023, 76). Observing and learning from rangers, Eben notes that "over time, imagining the life and history of each animal becomes possible, the space between human and animal is erased, and for a moment at least the human identifies with the animal" (76). Although the two approaches (sympathetic intuition and stalking) seem to correspond directly with conservationist and hunter/poacher respectively, in fact, the delineation is not fixed. There is the possibility and hope that the stalker could desist; there is also Venter's depiction of the poacher's dire financial circumstances, the result of systemic inequality. The greed and machismo of the 'great white hunter' of the colonial period are juxtaposed with the bare and precarious existence of the contemporary poacher.

In the novel's climax, when the poacher, Athule, has Decima in sight, exposed under the full moon, there is an opportunity to shift his outlook. His attentiveness to her and the richness of the bushveld awaken in him a moment of sympathetic intuition:

> He is within seconds of shooting, yet he still gives himself the time of this moment. Night scents of bush and grasses and thorn tree he picks out, one different to the other. Like an animal he flares his nostrils and grants himself the bliss of it. The land and the bush are his too, as they are to this umkhombe in front of him, and the air, yes, even the air can be shared by both of them this night, even if it is just for now. This is the place he's had to come to, to be like this animal in front of him. They have become each other's equals, both lit by the moon. For it is the moon that makes the animal so sharply visible to him, not as a target to be killed, rather as a creature living here, eating and shitting and standing and sleeping and, when it wakes up, knowing. Now, full moon means alertness. And courage (170-171).

For a moment, the rhino is not a target, simply a fellow creature sharing land and air as an equal. Athule returns to a halcyon time when "the land and the bush are his too" (170), before the exclusionary politics of colonialism and apartheid. This is a moment of complete identification and kinship between human and animal: shared creatureliness and bare existence— "eating and shitting and standing and sleeping" (170)—but also shared knowing and sentience. It is the knowing that alerts the reader to the hard reality that this is a zero-sum game, and Athule must have the courage to choose his life. Decima's inevitable death and Athule's uncertain fate are all the more tragic because of this glimmer of Arcadian bliss. *Decima* encapsulates the present moment's sense of urgency and near-catastrophe, concluding almost hopelessly, but it offers a way forward through the compassion and passion of characters such as Ziyanda, the ranger/conservationist, and the protagonist, who foreground an iconic animal as a sentient being, eliciting empathy and conscientizing the reader.

EYE BROTHER HORN: RETURNING TO ECOSPIRITUALITY AND AFRICAN ANIMISM

Like *Decima*, the novel, *Eye Brother Horn*, features a rhino. The cover is a close-up shot of a rhino's head with the two horns clearly visible, while one small, gentle eye looks directly at you. In the novel's opening sentence, "the rhino bursts from the reeds" (1), leaving you in no doubt that this animal has potent energy as "[t]wo tons of bone and muscle hurtle towards the women gathering grass for weaving" (1). In just two sentences, we are presented with flora, fauna, and humans in a close encounter.

The novel thus begins with this thrilling encounter between human and nature as the rhino storms at a group of women, one of whom has a baby strapped to her back. She trips and falls, leaving herself and the baby helpless with the rhino looming over them. But having lunged at them three times, the rhino retreats, leaving the baby, Daniel, unharmed yet forever affected, with a "look of strangeness in his eye, as if he'd been lost in distant worlds" (1). Here, rhino and child meet eye-to-eye, where a multispecies kinship is sparked, giving meaning to the title, *Eye Brother Horn*.

Pitt has commented that her "activism has always been strengthened by fiction written with a critical social lens [because] storytelling is inherently transformative" (Selig 2022), an approach evident in the scene that follows this event, which foregrounds the tension between the differing cultural and spiritual relationships that the various characters have with this environment. At the (fictional) Umzinyathi Christian mission station in Natal[4] in the 1800s, there are disparate forces at play: an intersection of (interhuman) culture, religion, and language. Daniel's survival of the rhino encounter is described as "a miracle" by the Reverend, while other theories include "witchcraft, ancestral intervention, and good luck" (2).

Within the greater context of British colonialism, *Eye Brother Horn* is a subversive re-worlding of Zululand in an activated storytelling mode (Haraway 2016, 132); a tale that is political and that challenges 'official history' by not only retelling the history of the region from a postcolonial perspective but by, also, including the impact of colonialism on the wild plant and animal species. In the following paragraphs we comment briefly on two aspects of this tale: the depiction of the plantation, which is a literary commentary on the transformations of the land, and on Daniel's shamanic animal empathy—sympathetic intuition in the extreme—which functions as a damning indictment of the devastation of animal species for the sake of the hunter's trophy (and ego).

Eye Brother Horn is an imaginative return to the 19th-century kingdom of Zululand,[5] and responds to a yearning for this landscape as the natural environment it was before it was devastated by colonial enterprises (plantations, development, hunting). But this nostalgic yearning is not a "restoratively nostalgic" return, to use a phrase coined by Svetlana Boym (2001), meaning that it is not simply a sentimental visit to the past. The novel is, rather, a "reflectively nostalgic" (Boym 2001, xviii) engagement that reflects on the pain and trauma of the past; that considers what has been lost, and what 'might have been'. It responds to the problems of the postcolony by reanimating the past, so that the present—as Plantationocene (Haraway 2016, 206)—can be confronted and challenged, and the future reimagined. An alternative name for the geological era named the Anthropocene, the term Plantationocene is apt because "it is not just an environmental term, it is a social term, it is an ecological term, it is an economic term, it is a racial term, and it is a human vs non-human term [because it points] to plantations and the plantation system as an incubator of these kind of devastating ways of transforming the planet's

---

4   Natal is today known as KwaZulu-Natal (KZN), a province of the Republic of South Africa.
5   Zululand today occupies the northeastern region of the province of KwaZulu-Natal.

economy and ecology through racial capitalism, through exploitation, not only of plant life but also of human life" (Safier 2023).

When the character, Daniel, has matured to adolescence and is obliged to hunt and farm with his sugar baron-uncle, he witnesses these assaults on the landscape first-hand. He sees not only how much of the land is under crops of "coffee, cotton, and sugar cane" (Pitt 2023, 194) but that "you can almost hear the march of the sugarcane as it consumes ever-widening tracts of grassland and forest to grow more sugar" (194). Small traditional villages—umuzi—with "rising mounds of beehive huts surrounded by small fields of corn and vegetables" are affected by the "pressing of the English farmers around them" and there is worry that, "soon there will be no more place to graze our cattle" (195). But his uncle attempts to 'educate' him: "If you can look at a piece of land and see ahead, to the wealth that can be turned from it, if you can put in the hard work to see that wealth created, you'll go far in life. This is what distinguishes the British from the African native. The natives are content to grow enough merely to feed themselves. A true Englishman wants more" (197). This speech emphasizes the change and 'progress' imposed by the colonizing force, the type of progress that Huggan and Tiffin have called a "myth of development [that takes] false support from ideas promiscuously linked to the Enlightenment ideology of progress" (2010, 28).

Further afield than the sugar estate, Daniel is also obliged to accompany his benefactor-uncle on hunting expeditions in yet-uncultivated landscapes. This is excruciatingly painful for him because he has developed and acutely felt empathy with animals, an empathy that exceeds the sympathetic imagination that Bates and Venter describe. For example, when a wounding, non-lethal shot leaves a young rhino "dying a slow and agonizing death [...] he can feel every spasm" (311). His own body reacts: "he is curled up, clutching the tree branch, his body wracked with pain. A high-pitched wailing is tearing through his head and vibrating in his chest" (311). Where the poacher in *Decima* experiences a momentary one-ness with a rhino, Daniel in *Eye Brother Horn*, via his sympathetic intuition is "able to penetrate the barrier" between himself and the rhino; "and, by actually entering into the object [the rhino's consciousness], so to speak, secure a momentary but complete identification with it" (Bate 1945, 144). Daniel shares a mystical, shamanic affinity with the dying rhino.

BLACK LION: WEAVING INTO THE TAPESTRY OF WILDERNESS

Mbatha discusses his mystical connection with the natural world, including animals, plants, and insects of the Zululand biome, in his memoir *Black Lion: Alive in the Wilderness* (126). In this book, he explains that (eco)returns are to be had from a return to nature, from eco-ubuntu[6], and from a deep ecology. The memoir begins with Mbatha's childhood experiences of nature shaped by his socio-economic circumstances. Though raised in a poor rural village close to the iMfolozi Park in KwaZulu-Natal, he experienced not only the ubuntu of his community but also a wider eco-ubuntu that has sustained him throughout his life. As with the two fictional narratives we have discussed, this non-fiction ecological offering, too, exemplifies Glotfelty's fundamental premise, that "human culture is connected to the physical world, affecting it and affected by it" (xix). Mbatha explains that the community "endured the emotional and physical wounds of apartheid because of [their] rich cultural traditions, [their] social cohesion and the abundance that comes with living in harmony with nature" (169). Physical and emotional health were bolstered by "traditional healers and shamanistic izangoma [who] helped to keep the community free of illness. There was a wealth of knowledge about the healing herbs and plants that grew in the area" (170). In addition, rites of passage helped young people to "ground themselves, giving them a strong sense of identity and purpose" (170).

One of the wounds of colonialism and later apartheid is the exclusion of local people from the game reserves they live adjacent to, from the pristine wilderness that was originally theirs (as Pitt's novel describes). Mbatha, though, visited the Hluhluwe-iMfolozi Park regularly as a child because his father worked there as a horse groomer. "Most people in our district have never had the opportunity to enter its gates. But I was lucky

---

6 'Ubuntu' has "elusive and contest[ed]" definitions; but "is broadly encapsulated in the often-repeated maxim of the Nguni peoples of South Africa, '*umuntu ngumuntu ngabantu*' – that is, a person is a person through other persons" (Praeg and Magadla 2014, 29). A generalised definition is that Ubuntu or African humanness/ humanism is a philosophical world view that emanates values and principles about human beings, their modes of interaction and their relationship to one another. It includes the natural and spiritual world" (29).

to be able to visit my dad in the park – and later to work there myself," he says. Immersion in the wilderness led him to an epiphanic moment: the "essence of life is to walk in nature" and he "*had* to share it" (34). This spurred his "life's purpose" (34) and his resolve to become a ranger.

Now a spiritual wilderness guide who facilitates week-long expeditions into the African bush and an author, he shares his nature wisdom. What Bate, a westerner, names sympathetic imagination, Mbatha knows from the stories his elders told; an intuition that is part of ancient African Knowledge Systems (AKS). *Black Lion* forms part of a global turn to indigenous knowledge systems. Thus, Mbatha is an ecological activist who inculcates "arts of attentiveness" (Van Dooren, Kirksey, and Münster 2016, 1) on his trails, re-awakening an intuitive connection to nature. Notably, "as a Black trail guide and author, he brings an important perspective to African conservation that is missing from most accounts of this nature" (Stoddard 2023). Indeed, the memoir forms part of the new wave of African eco-activists marked by Wangari Maathai's memoir, *Unbowed* (2006). We must again stress that there is nothing new about African ecology, as Mbatha's book makes clear. Rather, African ecologists are simply no longer "howling in the wilderness" (as Glotfelty phrased it) but are, instead, voicing powerful and important knowledge from, and of, the continent. As Mbatha's memoir reminds us, African culture has always been rooted in deep ecology. Van Dooren, Kirksey and Münster note that "while the knowledges and practices of the sciences have played a key role in multispecies studies, the field has also sought out a range of other approaches, aiming to decolonize and more broadly challenge dominant assumptions about knowledge, expertise, and who is authorized to speak for Nature" (2016, 8).[7] Mbatha highlights that Zulu philosophy is influenced by cultural exchange with the San people, the autochthonous people of southern Africa. He notes: "long before my Nguni forebears arrived, the San people lived here. [...] I could drink the well-spring of my origins, and feel the generosity and kindness of my forebears, the wisdom of those who had lived and died steeped in

---

7   Another example of the global turn to indigenous knowledge is by the author Leah Penniman. Her collection of essays, *Black Earth Wisdom: Soulful Conversations with Black Environmentalists* (2023), explores Black people's spiritual and scientific connection to the land in the USA.

the practice of ubuntu" (33).

This notion of interconnection, of sharing spaces, and of kinship, is a recurring theme in *Black Lion*, but extends beyond inter-human relationships to include, also, all plant and animal life. This ecological ethics precedes Western notions of deep ecology; it is an eco-ubuntu. Mbatha answers to Archbishop Desmond Tutu's call to "widen the circle of our ubuntu as we become aware of the totality of what we are. Our bodies extend into the soil, into the air, into the rivers and oceans. Our families include our dogs, cats, horses, and cattle. Our species is a cell in a larger organism, a planetary body that functions to maintain life on earth" (Tutu 2007, n.p.).

Mbatha's eco-ubuntu developed from listening to the elders' stories in his childhood and, again, from his initiation to manhood when his grandfather taught him to emulate nature. Mkhulu warns him: human minds and bodies can "work together as a powerful force that can destroy the world, but that powerful force can be the medicine that heals the world. Together, our minds and bodies have the power to protect the village, the elders, disabled people, our country, and the world. To be insizwa is to allow your soul and heart to be imbued with wisdom of life and give birth to the true warriors of harmony and peace" (37).

Subsequently, Mbatha offers his memoir as "an invitation to step into the wilderness with [him], to heed the warning of the wind and wake up to the vibrancy of the earth, to open yourself to the transformation we need to heal our world" (27). Thus, *Black Lion* is both celebratory and minatory in tone; it cautions that the earth is vulnerable yet impels the reader to imagine a community with nature and its creatures. Having strengthened his resolve "to be a warrior for nature, a game ranger who could bring the wilderness to others" (41-42), he sets himself up as a role model for society at large. His quest is for others to discover the wilderness. But he also points out that "[f]rom the beginning, the story of the establishment of parks in Africa has been a story of exclusion" (95). He asks, "how can you protect something you have never laid your eyes on?" (94), and laments that, as a result, there is little wonder that people turn to poaching (a conundrum akin to that posed by Venter in *Decima*). Mbatha recounts an occasion, early in his career as a ranger, when two young poachers were caught. As they were taken away, he thought "of all the young men, like [himself], who had stood beyond the fence, looking with longing at the wilderness within" (96). He is determined to "find a way to open the path to the wilderness for [his] people" (96), to satisfy that longing for the wilderness.

CONCLUSION

As a sampling of contemporary South African literature, *Decima*, *Eye Brother Horn*, and *Black Lion: Alive in the Wilderness* indicate an ecological turn, providing philosophical reflections on African animist ontology and a new ethics of caring for the environment. In these examples of historical fiction, autofiction, and memoir, current crises and the historical events that have led us to this point of Anthropocene or Plantationocene are highlighted with a sense of hopefulness for the future that does not sentimentalize problems or trivialize the multiple cultural and socio-political challenges that must be addressed. Without shying away from the near hopelessness of some aspects of the crises, by using a storytelling mode to convey an ecological praxis, the prognosis offered is not entirely bleak. Instead, by returning to environmental sites, remembering them in their earlier, purer forms, and reconnecting to them through (eco)storytelling, an empathetic and spiritual connection to plants, animals, and landscapes forges an affective reconnection that we see as an (eco)return. Venter, Pitt, and Mbatha each also suggest—as a remedy—that spiritual awareness and connection to nature can foster environmental justice through multispecies entanglements.

REFERENCES

Barry, Peter. 2017 [1995]. *Beginning Theory: An Introduction to Literary and Cultural Theory.* 4th ed. Manchester: Manchester University Press.
Bate, Walter Jackson. 1945. "The Sympathetic Imagination in Eighteenth-Century English Criticism." *ELH* 12 (2): 144–64.
Boym, Svetlana. 2001. *The Future of Nostalgia.* New York: Basic Books.
Cornelius, Beverley Jane, and Jean Rossmann. 2024. "Rekindling Eco-Ubuntu in *Black Lion: Alive in the Wilderness.*" *Scrutiny 2* 28 (2): 142–57. https://doi.org/10.1080/18125441.2024.2389437.
Glotfelty, Cheryll. 1996. "Introduction: Literary Studies in the Age of Environmental Crisis." In *The Ecocriticism Reader: Landmarks in*

Literary Ecology, edited by Cheryll Glotfelty and Harold Fromm, x–xxxvii. Athens: University of Georgia Press.

Haraway, Donna, and Martha Kenney. 2023 [2013]. "Anthropocene, Capitalocene, Chthulucene: Donna Haraway in Conversation with Martha Kenney, in Santa Cruz, California in 2013." Edited and republished in *M+ Magazine,* September 7, 2023. Accessed January 5, 2024. https://www.mplus.org.hk/en/magazine/donna-haraway-critique-anthropocene-capitalocene/.

Huggan, Graham, and Helen Tiffin. 2010. *Postcolonial Ecocriticism: Literature, Animals, Environment.* New York: Routledge.

Hutchings, Kevin. 2007. "Ecocriticism in British Romantic Studies." *Literature Compass* 4 (1): 172–202.

Maathai, Wangari. 2006. *Unbowed.* New York: Alfred A. Knopf.

Mbatha, Sicelo, with Bridget Pitt. 2021. *Black Lion: Alive in the Wilderness.* Jeppestown: Jonathan Ball Publishers.

Næss, Arne. 2005 [1986]. "The Deep Ecology Movement: Some Philosophical Aspects." In *Selected Works of Arne Næss X,* edited by Harold Glasser and Alan Drengson, 33–55. Dordrecht: Springer.

Pitt, Bridget. 2023. *Eye Brother Horn.* El Paso, TX: Catalyst Press.

Praeg, Leonhard, and Siphokazi Magadla, eds. 2014. *Ubuntu: Curating the Archive.* Pietermaritzburg: University of KwaZulu-Natal Press.

Rossmann, Jean, and Beverley Jane Cornelius. 2025. "Demythologising the Rhino: From Dürer to Venter, From Beast to Being." *British and American Studies (B.A.S.) Journal* 31: 245–53.

Safier, Neil, host. 2023. "Plantationocene." *New Books in Environmental Studies,* episode 132 (podcast), November 17, 2023. Accessed January 7, 2024. https://podcasts.apple.com/za/podcast/new-books-in-environmental-studies/id425223410?i=1000635155023.

Selig, SarahBelle. 2022. "Author Q&A: Bridget Pitt." *Catalyst Press,* January 31, 2023 [Blog]. Accessed May 27, 2023. https://www.catalystpress.org/author/sarahbell/.

Stoddard, Ed. 2023. "*Black Lion* Is an Inspirational Walk on the Wild Side." *Daily Maverick,* January 23, 2023. Accessed November 11, 2023. https://www.dailymaverick.co.za/article/2022-01-23-black-lion-is-an-inspirational-walk-on-the-wild-side/.

Tsing, Anna. 2012. "Unruly Edges: Mushrooms as Companion Species: For Donna Haraway." *Environmental Humanities* 1 (1): 141–54. https://doi.org/10.1215/22011919-3610012.

Tutu, Desmond (Archbishop Emeritus). 2007. "Eco-Ubuntu." *Enviropaedia: Rethinking Reality.* Accessed September 26, 2023. http://www.enviropaedia.com/topic/default.php?topic_id=336.

Van Dooren, Thom, Eben Kirksey, and Ursula Münster. 2016. "Multispecies Studies: Cultivating Arts of Attentiveness." *Environmental Humanities* 8 (1): 1–23. https://doi.org/10.1215/22011919-3527695.

Venter, Eben. 2023. *Decima.* Cape Town: Penguin Random House.

CHAPTER SIX

Eco-activism, Eco-disasters, and Vulnerability in Niyi Osundare's "Our Earth Will Not Die" and Kinno Yukie's "God"

Sunday Olaoluwagbamila Dawodu & Gracious Ojiebun

INTRODUCTION

Environmental disasters are a critical threat to human well-being and the planet's health. They disrupt social and economic systems, displace communities, and in severe cases, contribute to the collapse of civilizations (Pelling 2011, 7). As these environmental challenges escalate, eco-activism has arisen as a potent force for societal change (McCarthy 2002, 15). This chapter examines the varied expressions of eco-activism, particularly in Nigeria and Japan, where literature and intellectual discourse have driven creative resistance against environmental threats.

Nigeria and Japan provide compelling case studies on the relationship between environmental disasters and eco-activism. In Nigeria, multinational oil companies have contributed extensively to environmental degradation, particularly in the Niger Delta (Ake 2004, 42). This has prompted writers like Niyi Osundare to employ satire and critique to shed light on human-induced environmental injustices in the region (Osundare 1986 [2011]). Conversely, Japan has faced the catastrophic effects of natural disasters, such as the 2011 Tōhoku earthquake and tsunami, which led to a surge in eco-activism. This movement is exemplified in the work of Japanese poet Kinno Yukie, who captures the profound impact of environmental disasters on both human and non-human life, highlighting the vulnerability of communities in the face of nature's power (Carruthers 2013, 182).

Osundare's commitment to eco-activism finds a parallel in the perspective of Samson Omofonmwan and Lucky Odia, who argue that human activities, including mineral extraction, are primarily responsible for environmental catastrophes in post-colonial nations. They note that this is driven by the misguided belief that the adverse effects of environmental degradation will be delayed, leading to complacency that wealth can remedy ecological damage through clean-ups and medical care for pollution-related diseases (Omofonmwan and Odia 2009, 25–30). They further argue that this belief has exacerbated ecological crises in postcolonial countries like Nigeria, where the assumption that degradation can be reversed with financial resources has hindered proactive environmental policies (Omofonmwan and Odia 2009).

Similarly, Cultural theorists such as Clifford Geertz (1973) and Stuart Hall (1990; 1996) underscore the inextricable tie between individual and community, illustrating that culture binds both and profoundly shapes personal and collective identities. Extending this view, Homi K. Bhabha (1994) highlights how cultural negotiation frames identity in dynamic and evolving ways. In times of ecological calamity, poets and writers, as noted by Lawrence Buell (1995) and Rob Nixon (2011), can harness their craft to reflect and strengthen the shared experiences and sentiments of their societies, thereby fostering unity and resilience. Yukie's work is particularly illustrative, as she explores the devastating effects of nature-induced environmental disasters on her community, capturing the feeling of helplessness that can accompany such tragedies. Her poetry reflects the depth of environmental challenges faced by her community, illustrating the scale of these disasters and the capacity of nature to render humans vulnerable.

Through their works, such as Osundare's "Our Earth Will Not Die" (1986) and Yukie's *God* (2017), the two poets use poetry as a medium to advocate for eco-consciousness and social stability. They incorporate eco-conscious themes, blending thematic concerns with literary techniques, to address environmental issues in a way that resonates across cultures and regions. This cross-cultural reading of their works creates a foundation for readers, critics, and writers to engage with their environment, encouraging individuals to recognize themselves as ecological subjects within a larger global context. Through their poetry, Osundare and Yukie exemplify the power of literary art to deepen individual and collective responses to ecocriticism, fostering awareness and urgency toward environmental preservation and responsibility.

The chapter, therefore, reveals how literature and eco-activism can serve as powerful tools in addressing environmental challenges. By examining the works of these poets, it becomes evident that eco-activism is not only a reaction to environmental disasters but also a proactive effort to cultivate eco-consciousness and sustainable thinking within and beyond the borders of Nigeria and Japan.

REVIEW OF RELATED LITERATURE

The field of ecocriticism, initially articulated by William Rueckert (1978), analyses literature through an ecological perspective, examining how literary works depict environmental themes, human-nature interactions, and their repercussions (Rueckert 1978). This approach goes beyond merely studying nature as a backdrop in literature, instead focusing on how representations of the environment affect human attitudes, actions, and awareness (Garrard 2004, 17). Ecocritics thus investigate the effectiveness of literature in addressing pressing environmental issues, encouraging readers to rethink their relationship with nature (Glotfelty 1996, xviii).

The Association for the Study of Literature and Environment (ASLE) has played a crucial role in advancing ecocritical scholarship by promoting research that investigates the relationship between literature, culture, and the natural world. As Oppermann (2006) observes, ASLE brings together scholars, teachers, and writers committed to exploring the ecological significance of literary texts. She argues that through engagement with literary representations of nature, ecocriticism inspires readers to value the importance of a sustainable environment and to acknowledge the harmful consequences of ecological degradation.

Lawrence Buell, a prominent voice in ecocriticism, underscores the interdisciplinary nature of this approach, suggesting that ecocriticism not only analyses environmental issues within literature but also seeks to inspire discourse on resolving these crises (Buell 1995, quoted in Dobie 2011, 239). Buell's work highlights the multifaceted dangers of ecological collapse—be it through pollution, deforestation, global warming, or industrial spills—that threaten the sustainability of human civilization.

These concerns are echoed by recent environmental crises, reinforcing the urgency of ecocriticism in understanding and addressing ecological problems.

Further strengthening Buell's interdisciplinary approach, Estok (2013) argues that ecocriticism transcends simply studying natural elements within literature. Instead, he describes it as an analytical theory committed to effecting change by scrutinizing how environmental elements, depicted in literature or other documents, fulfil various functions—be they thematic, artistic, or ideological (Estok 2013, 16). This aligns with ecocriticism's functional approach to cultural ecology, which links ecosystems and literary works, suggesting that literature can contribute to ecological regeneration within cultural frameworks.

In post-colonial contexts, including African nations, ecocriticism often addresses the enduring ecological impacts of colonial and neo-colonial exploitation. Initially viewed with skepticism by African writers as Eurocentric, the concept of ecocriticism has gained support from scholars like Elizabeth DeLoughrey (2015), Ogaga Okuyade (2013), and Rob Nixon (2011), who advocate for a postcolonial form of ecocriticism that addresses unique environmental concerns in these regions. African authors, such as Byron Caminero-Santangelo, have highlighted the ecological challenges faced by Africans, reflecting the pressing need for empathy towards the environment in African literature. Ogaga Okuyade (2013), for instance, explores the deep connection between African literature and the environment, while Augustine Nchoujie (2009) argues that ecocriticism, when framed as a global celebration of human-nature harmony, can be effectively applied worldwide.

Nchoujie's view provides insight into the connection between African or postcolonial eco-writers and the ecological issues they address. Sule Egya (2020) expands this perspective by analyzing Nigerian literature from an ecocritical standpoint, showcasing both well-known and lesser-known texts that engage with environmental themes. Egya's work demonstrates the richness of Nigerian eco-literature, which addresses the severe ecological degradation afflicting regions such as the Niger Delta.

Post-colonial ecocriticism diverges from traditional environmental movements, challenging notions that portray environmental literature as pastoral escapism. Instead, eco-conscious writings from post-colonial authors contend that ecocriticism must prioritize ecological crises caused by human actions. Moreover, post-colonial ecocriticism interrogates the role of religion, particularly Christianity's anthropocentric interpretations, in shaping exploitative attitudes towards nature. However, scholars like Huggan, Graham, and Helen Tiffin (2010) argue that the drive for excessive consumption—rooted in capitalist values—rather than religious misinterpretation, plays a primary role in ecological degradation in post-colonial settings. This critique of capitalism emphasizes that the pursuit of profit undermines efforts to preserve the environment, often leading to exploitation that disrupts the natural order and endangers future human well-being.

ECO-ACTIVISM IN NIYI OSUNDARE'S "OUR EARTH WILL NOT DIE"

Nigerian poet Niyi Osundare's eco-activist sentiments are vividly expressed in his poem "Our Earth Will Not Die," from his anthology *The Eye of the Earth* (1986). The collection, divided into sections titled "back to earth," "eyeful glances rainsongs," and "homecall," exemplifies Osundare's commitment to environmental advocacy. "Our Earth Will Not Die," part of the "homecall" section, addresses the critical degradation of Nigeria's environment, particularly as a result of industrial pollution. In this poem, Osundare echoes Frederick Buell's (2001) stance that imaginative engagement with the environment can be instrumental in addressing ecological issues, as opposed to relying solely on scientific or technological solutions, which often contribute to environmental harm.

Osundare's poem provides a powerful depiction of Nigeria's environmental struggles, portraying industrial waste, toxic fumes, and polluted waterways as sources of ecological harm. He describes the toxic effects of industrial pollutants on the ecosystem, where contaminated waste seeps into streams, and polluted rain threatens forests. The poet's portrayal of environmental deterioration highlights the consequences of unchecked industrial growth, such as the use of charcoal, fossil fuels, and gas flaring, which lead to harmful emissions and resource depletion.

In "Our Earth Will Not Die," Osundare mourns the devastation of Nigeria's natural landscapes, depicting a poisoned stream "staggering" under the weight of industrial contamination as it flows towards the sea.

This image symbolizes the pervasive impact of human actions on the environment, with oil spills, chemical waste, and pollution poisoning marine ecosystems. He describes humanity's destructive practices, including gas flaring, oil extraction, and chemical fishing, as acts of aggression against nature, invoking vivid imagery to depict the environmental toll of these activities.

The poem's language evokes both sorrow and urgency, as Osundare draws attention to the far-reaching consequences of pollution, acid rain, and climate change. He writes:

> And the rain
> the rain falls, acid, on balding forests
> their branches amputated by the septic daggers
> of tainted clouds
> (Osundare 1986, 51).

Here, Osundare portrays the damaging effects of industrial waste and atmospheric pollution, as "acid rain" erodes forested areas and disrupts ecosystems. The poet's language conveys a deep sense of loss and a call to action, warning that if humanity continues to ignore the environment's plight, the consequences will be catastrophic.

In 2010, the Nigerian Environmental Protection Agency issued a warning about the dangers of acid rain and the impact of rising sea levels due to global warming, particularly in coastal areas like Lagos, Calabar, and the Niger Delta. The agency warned that a one-meter rise in sea level could submerge 18,000 square kilometers of land, displacing millions (EPA Nigeria 2010). Osundare's poem anticipates these warnings, urging readers to consider the consequences of environmental neglect. His work underscores that ecological catastrophe is not a distant hypothetical but a present reality.

Through his poetic vision, Osundare demonstrates the power of literature to raise awareness about environmental degradation and encourage readers to consider their role in preserving the natural world. His eco-activism in *The Eye of the Earth* serves as a reminder that literature can inspire a more conscious relationship with the environment, using the imagination to illuminate the urgency of environmental preservation.

Osundare's poetry invites readers to see the natural world not as an expendable resource but as a shared heritage that must be protected for future generations.

VULNERABILITY IN KINNO YUKIE'S "GOD"

Kinno Yukie's poetry captures the deep vulnerability of her community, brought to its knees by a natural eco-disaster: the overwhelming tsunami that struck Japan on 11 March 2011. Her poem emphasizes the need to center the vulnerable in discussions on ecological collapse, particularly those events precipitated by natural forces. In Yukie's poetic frame, vulnerability extends to her community and the broader Japanese population devastated by this triune disaster. This definition of vulnerability is broad, encompassing children, women (especially pregnant women), the elderly, men, animals, birds, and the physical environment—all entities unable to extricate themselves from the immediate impacts of eco-disasters or recover without external assistance.

Susan Buckingham and Rakibe Kulcur argue that discussions on environmental disasters must foreground the vulnerable because they experience heightened risks of harm in ecological catastrophes (2009, 665). Yukie's poem, written in the wake of the tsunami, laments what she describes as the broken "harmonious relationship between humans and nature" (Wolfreys 2002, 165). Her poem underscores the fractured unity between humanity and nature—a rupture that, for her community, resulted in a dreadful ecological disaster. Yukie's choice to infuse her poem with the nuances of her indigenous language reflects her desire to "give voice to the battered and dispirited people throughout the region" (Takako, Arai, and Jeffrey Angles 2017, 2). This approach amplifies the collective experience of her community, enabling her to articulate her community's suffering through a culturally resonant lens.

In "God," Yukie captures the ravaging effect of nature on both the environment and human society. Written in the aftermath of Japan's March 11 disasters, which claimed the lives of around 20,000 people, the poem expresses her gratitude to God for her survival, even as it conveys her emotional and physical scars. The poem resonates with themes of pity, sorrow, sacrifice, introspection, and an examination of humanity's capacity for self-help amid catastrophes. The destruction inflicted on her community is palpable in her words, and her reflection on her survival is marked by an awareness of both gratitude and grief.

The tsunami wreaked havoc on Ōfunato, devastating the oyster farm and local market that sustained a thriving agrarian and commercial community. Yukie's poem embodies the intense pain, depression, and disorientation that permeated her community in the wake of this disaster. Her anguish and the collective feeling of helplessness among survivors are poignantly conveyed in her introspective question:

> But what am I supposed to do now?
> I'm like a tiny ant on the sandy beach…
> (Yukie 2017, 7).

Through this comparison to a "tiny ant on the sandy beach" (Yukie 2017, 7, l. 4), she captures her sense of insignificance against the vast and incomprehensible force of nature. The simile underscores her vulnerability; the ant, a small and nearly invisible creature on an immense shore, represents the frailty of human existence in the face of natural calamity. This line communicates not just her feeling of vulnerability but also a larger philosophical reflection on humanity's place within the natural world.

The poem further conveys the depth of Yukie's loss and her struggle to comprehend the extent of the tragedy. She speaks openly of the pain that has shattered her life, describing the toll of the tsunami:

> Four of my relatives are dead.
> What am I supposed to do?
> (Yukie 2017, 7).

Yukie's expression of her loss reveals her disorientation and sorrow, poignantly illustrating her struggle to find meaning amid devastation. The poet persona, reflecting Yukie's own experience, presses her anguish onto her readers by acknowledging the loss of "four of her relatives" (Yukie 2017, 7, l. 7). Her question—what she is to do now—reflects her confusion and desperation in the face of such unimaginable loss. As her poem shifts into a questioning tone, Yukie implicitly addresses God, probing the reasons behind her survival and others' deaths. This questioning can be understood as a plea for understanding the larger purpose, or lack thereof, behind her survival when so much around her has been destroyed.

Yukie's work can also be seen as a raw, candid expression of grief. The plaintive call to "God" conveys a profound sadness, marked by the inadequacy of words to capture her depth of emotion. Her cry evokes the intensity of her sorrow and loneliness, portraying a figure confronted by overwhelming grief and solitude. As she walks along the devastated shoreline, the shattered lives of her community weigh heavily upon her. She grapples with the painful sight of destruction, wondering about the larger significance of this suffering:

> God
> What are you telling me to do?
> (Yukie 2017, line 7).

Her tone is a blend of frustration, sadness, and helplessness as she calls out to God. Yukie's question to God expresses her desire to understand any purpose behind such widespread suffering. In the absence of a clear answer, her words convey a tone of despair and frustration, questioning why such ruin occurred. Her plea for divine guidance underscores her quest for meaning in the face of loss, as she attempts to reconcile her survival with the devastation around her.

Through her poem, Yukie highlights humanity's fragility in the face of nature's overpowering forces. Having witnessed the destructive power of the tsunami, she draws attention to the insignificance of human agency against natural calamities. This disaster reorients her understanding of her place within nature, underscoring the unpredictable power of the kami, or spirits, which inhabit the Shinto worldview. Within Shinto beliefs, these spirits permeate all elements of nature, acting as custodians of the natural world. Humans, within this framework, are at the mercy of these spirits and are shielded from harm only as long as nature allows. Unlike the anthropocentric views common in Western thought, the Shinto universe does not place humans at its center. According to Porcu (2017), this worldview underscores that human, while existing in favor of the kami, is not their primary concern. In the Shinto understanding, gods, creation, and even natural disasters are not designed to serve or focus on human welfare. These catastrophes occur because they are intrinsic to the rhythms of nature, leaving people vulnerable to the kami's will.

Yukie's poem thus conveys the vulnerability of humans within a natural order that is neither benevolent nor designed for their benefit. Her perspective highlights the contrast between humans and non-humans, as she comes to recognize the transient nature of human life in the face of immense natural forces. This understanding is distinctively Shinto, where nature exists independently, with its own purposes, and is not bound to human survival or welfare. Through her verse, Yukie invites readers to confront the implications of this belief, urging a reassessment of humanity's role within the larger cosmos and prompting reflection on our vulnerabilities in an indifferent natural world.

Words reveal her feelings of disorientation as she seeks to make sense of the calamity. Her unfiltered question to God reflects her desperation to comprehend whether any purpose underlies her survival amid so much destruction. As someone who has experienced the terrifying, untamable power of nature, Yukie further underscores the insignificance of humanity when confronted by the overwhelming forces of the natural world. This disaster leads her to reflect on the kami, the spirits believed in Shinto to inhabit all aspects of nature. She understands that these kami, integral to Japanese cultural and spiritual belief, wield powers far beyond human control. Unlike Western beliefs, where humanity often appears central to creation, Shinto emphasizes that while humans exist by the kami's favor, they are not its focus. This view, as Porcu (2017) highlights, portrays humans as marginal in the Shinto cosmology, which prioritizes nature and the spirits within it. Humans remain at the mercy of these natural forces, protected as long as the kami see fit but otherwise powerless to resist them.

In this respect, Yukie's poem offers a lens through which to view the transient and fragile position of humanity in relation to the natural world. Disasters, as in her community's experience, are not solely products of human error but intrinsic elements of nature's broader, uncontrollable processes. This spiritual perspective underscores the vulnerability of humanity as a part of, yet not above, the natural order.

CONCLUSION

In *Environmentalism and Literature* (1998), Lawrence Buell highlights the power of contemporary environmental discourse as reflected in poetry. This essay considers how Nigerian poet Niyi Osundare and Japanese poet Kiyoko Mori, also known by her pen name Yukie, use their work to explore the complex nature of environmental crises. These poets address urgent ecological issues, such as human-induced environmental degradation—pollution, and resource depletion—as well as the harsh impacts of natural disasters. Their works strongly support Buell's views, offering insightful reflections on the intricate connection between humanity and nature.

In Osundare's poem "Our Earth," a potent combination of irony, sarcasm, and vivid imagery serves as a powerful critique of human-caused environmental destruction. He points a finger at multinational corporations and corrupt governments for their greed-driven exploitation of resources, which leads to significant pollution and environmental damage. Osundare's poetic style demonstrates his strong ecocritical stance and commitment to eco-activism. By personifying the environment and giving it agency, he challenges readers to view the natural world not as an object to be used but as a living entity capable of suffering. This approach encourages a sense of empathy towards the environment, inspiring a greater sense of responsibility for its care.

In contrast, Yukie's work takes on a more direct, visceral engagement with nature-induced disasters, particularly likely inspired by the 2011 Tōhoku earthquake and tsunami. Her poem moves beyond metaphor, delivering a raw response to a real, devastating event. Yukie's work portrays a complete societal breakdown and exposes the vulnerability of humans when faced with such overwhelming natural power. Her poem's emotional depth lies in its portrayal of fundamental human emotions—fear, despair, anguish, pain, hopelessness, and helplessness. These themes resonate strongly, prompting readers to confront the harsh realities of environmental upheaval and its impact on human lives.

Together, Osundare and Yukie reveal the profound effects of environmental crises on humanity, each approaching the subject with distinct perspectives. Osundare's work calls attention to human accountability for ecological damage, while Yukie underscores humanity's vulnerability to nature's forces. Collectively, their poems exemplify the complexity of environmental discourse in contemporary ecopoetry, urging readers to recognize both our responsibility to protect the environment and our fragility within its vast, unpredictable scope. These works invite reflection on the dual role humanity plays as both a custodian of and a participant in the natural world, thus aligning with Buell's insights on the power of environmental discourse in literature.

REFERENCES

Awhefeada, Sunny. 2013. "Degraded Environment and Destabilized Women in Kaine Agary's *Yellow-Yellow*." In *Eco-Critical Literature: Regreening African Landscapes*, 95–108.

Bhabha, Homi K. 1994. *The Location of Culture*. London: Routledge.

Buckingham, Susan, and Rakibe Kulcur. 2009. "Gendered Geographies of Environmental Injustice." *Antipode* 41 (4): 659–683.

Buell, Frederick. 2001. "Globalization without Environmental Crisis: The Divorce of Two Discourses in US Culture." *Symplokē* 9 (1/2): 45–73.

Buell, Lawrence. 1995. *The Environmental Imagination: Thoreau, Nature Writing, and the Formation of American Culture*. Cambridge, MA: Harvard University Press.

———. 1998. "Toxic Discourse." *Critical Inquiry* 24 (3): 639–665.

———. 1999. "In Pursuit of Ethics." *PMLA* 114 (1): 7–19.

Caminero-Santangelo, Byron, and Garth Myers. 2011. *Environment at the Margins: Literary and Environmental Studies in Africa*. Athens, OH: Ohio University Press.

Caminero-Santangelo, Byron. 2007. "Different Shades of Green: Ecocriticism and African Literature." In *African Literature: An Anthology of Criticism and Theory*, edited by Tejumola Olaniyan and Ato Quayson, 698–705. Malden, MA: Blackwell Publishing.

Courtney, T. 2016. "Non-Anthropocentric Narrative Strategies in Recent Experimental US Fiction." *Literature Compass* 13 (9): 515–529. https://doi.org/10.1111/lic3.12337.

Dasylva, A. O. 2009. "African Writers on Environmental Degradation and the National Psyche." Paper presented at the Africa Conference on Science, Technology and the Environment, University of Texas, Austin.

Dawodu, Sunday. 2010. "Ecocritical Reading of Selected Poems of Niyi Osundare and Tanure Ojaide." Unpublished thesis, University of Ibadan.

DeLoughrey, Elizabeth. 2014. "Postcolonialism." In *The Oxford Handbook of Ecocriticism*, edited by Greg Garrard, 321–340. Oxford: Oxford University Press.

———. 2015. *A Postcolonial Environmental Humanities*. New York: Routledge.

DeLoughrey, Elizabeth, and George Handley. 2011. "Introduction: Towards an Aesthetics of the Earth." In *Postcolonial Ecologies: Literatures of the Environment*, 3–39. Oxford: Oxford University Press.

Dobie, Ann B. 2011. *Theory into Practice: An Introduction to Literary Criticism*. Boston: Wadsworth Publishing.

———. 2012. *Theory into Practice: An Introduction to Literary Criticism*. 3rd ed. Australia: Wadsworth Cengage Learning.

Egbuson, Vincent. 2008. *Love My Planet*. Ibadan: Kraft Books.

Egya, Sule Emmanuel. 2020. *Nature, Environment and Activism in Nigerian Literature*. Ibadan: Kraft Books.

Estok, Simon C. 2013. "Partial Views: An Introduction to East Asian Ecocriticism." In *East Asian Ecocriticism: A Critical Reader*, edited by Simon C. Estok and Won-Chung Kim, 1–13. London: Palgrave Macmillan.

Garrard, Greg. 2004. *Ecocriticism*. New York: Routledge.

Geertz, Clifford. 1973. *The Interpretation of Cultures*. New York: Basic Books.

Glotfelty, Cheryll, and Harold Fromm, eds. 1996. *The Ecocriticism Reader: Landmarks in Literary Ecology*. London: Routledge.

Hall, Stuart. 1990. "Cultural Identity and Diaspora." In *Identity: Community, Culture, Difference*, edited by Jonathan Rutherford, 222–237. London: Lawrence & Wishart.

———, 1996. "Introduction: Who Needs 'Identity'?" In *Questions of Cultural Identity*, edited by Stuart Hall and Paul du Gay, 1–17. London: SAGE.

Huggan, Graham, and Helen Tiffin. 2010. *Postcolonial Ecocriticism: Literature, Animals, Environment*. London: Routledge.

Iheka, Cajetan. 2019. *Naturalizing Africa: Ecological Violence, Agency, and*

Postcolonial Resistance in African Literature. Cambridge: Cambridge University Press.

Meeker, Joseph W. 1972. *The Comedy of Survival: Studies in Literary Ecology*. New York: Scribner's.

Nchoujie, A. 2009. "Things Fall Apart Fifty Years After: An Ecocritical Reading." In *Themes Fall Apart but the Centre Holds*, edited by Joseph Ushie and Denja Abdullahi, 106–118. Lagos: Association of Nigerian Authors.

Nixon, Rob. 2011. "Preface." In *Slow Violence and the Environmentalism of the Poor*. Cambridge, MA: Harvard University Press. http://www.jstor.org/stable/j.ctt2jbsgw.

Nixon, Rob. 2011. *Slow Violence and the Environmentalism of the Poor*. Cambridge, MA: Harvard University Press.

Ojaide, Tanure. 1986. *Labyrinths of the Delta*. New York: Greenfield Review Press.

———. 1989. *The Endless Song*. Lagos/Oxford: Malthouse.

———. 1998. *Delta Blues and Home Songs*. Ibadan: Kraft Books.

Okuyade, Ogaga. 2013. *Ecocritical Literature: Regreening African Landscape*. Lagos: African Heritage Press.

Omofonmwan, S. I., and L. O. Odia. 2009. "Oil Exploitation and Conflict in the Niger-Delta Region of Nigeria." *Journal of Human Ecology* 26 (1): 25–30. https://doi.org/10.1080/09709274.2009.11906161.

Oppermann, Serpil. 2006. "Theorising Ecocriticism: Toward a Postmodern Ecocritical Practice." *Interdisciplinary Studies in Literature and Environment* 13 (2): 103–128. https://doi.org/10.1093/isle/13.2.103.

Osundare, Niyi. 1986. "Our Earth Will Not Die." In *The Eye of the Earth*. Ibadan: Heinemann Educational Books.

Porcu, Elisabetta. 2017. "Contemporary Japanese Buddhist Traditions." In *The Oxford Handbook of Contemporary Buddhism*, 122. Oxford: Oxford University Press.

Rueckert, William. 1996. "Literature and Ecology: An Experiment in Ecocriticism." In *The Ecocriticism Reader: Landmarks in Literary Ecology*, edited by Cheryll Glotfelty and Harold Fromm, 105–123. Athens, GA: University of Georgia Press.

Wolfreys, Julian. 2002. *Victorian Haunting: Spectrality, Gothic, the Uncanny and Literature*. Basingstoke: Palgrave Macmillan.

Yukie, K. 2017. *God: Disaster Poems from Ōfunato*. Translated by Takako A. and J. Angles. Tokyo: Josai University Educational Corporation University Press.

CHAPTER SEVEN

Place and Socio-natural Environment in the Poetry of Akachi Adimora-Ezeigbo & Warsan Shire

Deborah Chinonyerem Uzoma

INTRODUCTION

Like other literary theories, ecocriticism has evolved significantly over time due to changing needs and developments. The practices of eco-literature and ecocriticism have emerged from a rich tradition of global writers expressing themes related to nature and the environment. This indicates a blending of traditional nature writing with contemporary ecological concerns. According to Slaymaker (2001, 129-44), creative literary works and analytical essays are expected to engage with environmental and ecological issues, drawing insights from disciplines such as Marxism, anthropology, geography, post-structuralism, philosophy, post-colonialism, and feminism, among others. Slaymaker's view suggests that the intersection of creative works and analytical essays fosters a deeper understanding of the complex relationships between humans and the natural world. These intersections incorporate insights from various disciplines, including resource exploitation, cultural perceptions of the environment, indigenous displacements, eco-feminism, environmental ethics, challenging dominant narratives, and the impacts of human activities on the ecosystem.

Based on the foregoing, this study examines how place and socio-natural environment are represented in the poetry of Akachi Adimora-Ezeigbo and Warsan Shire.

The interpretation of the poems would be done through the lens of Lawrence Buell's concept of place. Lawrence Buell is an American literary critic best known for his contributions to ecocriticism, which examines the relationship between literature and the environment. In his influential book *The Future of Environmental Criticism*, (Buell 2005, 75), explores the concept of place as it relates to literature and the environment. Buell suggests that the concept of place gestures in at least three distinct directions simultaneously. These directions, according to Buell, are "individual affect or bond." This multidimensional understanding of place makes it a rich and intricate arena for environmental criticism.

Buell's[1] first direction, "toward environmental materiality," encompasses the physical and tangible aspects of the natural world. Places are inextricably linked to specific landscapes, ecosystems, and geographical features that shape their unique characteristics and significance. Secondly, Buell's notion of place gestures "toward social perception or construction." This refers to the understanding that places are defined through human interactions, cultural practices, and collective representations. The way people perceive and engage with a place is crucial in shaping its meaning and significance. The third direction, "toward individual affect or bond," evokes the personal feelings, attachments, memories, and sense of belonging that individuals develop with particular places. This subjective dimension of place highlights the emotional and experiential aspects that individuals associate with their environments. By exploring these three intertwined directions of the concept of place, Buell offers a nuanced understanding of how place functions in literature and environmental criticism.

The researcher's interest in Adimora-Ezeigbo's *Heart Songs* and Shire's *Our Men Do Not Belong to Us* arises from their detailed home country experiences and the societal stereotypes associated with them. Their poetry collections raise concerns about the socio-natural effects on vulnerable individuals of their inhabitance, especially women. For instance, Warsan Shire is a British writer and poet. She was born to Somali parents in Kenya. Shire has been writing poetry and her work is also influenced by her experiences as a Somalian immigrant in the United Kingdom. Shire's poetry captures the complexities and emotions associated with displacement, identity, migration, and the challenges refugees and marginalized communities face. Adimora-Ezeigbo, born and raised in Eastern

---

1   Lawrence Buell, *The Future of Environmental Criticism*, (Buell 2005, 55)

Nigeria, has been in academia. Foremost, she is known as a novelist rather than a poet. Adimora-Ezeigbo's works explore cultural identity, gender, family dynamics, societal issues, and the impact of colonialism and post-colonialism in Nigerian society.

Adimora-Ezeigbo's *Heart Songs* serves as a fervent critique and a contribution from a female perspective, aiming to transform her country into a more suitable society and productive environment (Chukwuloka and Asika 2011, 357). Here, the duo argue that Adimora-Ezeigbo's poetry elicits a profound response, evoking emotions that resonate deeply, offering a glimpse into the deteriorated state of their nation and society.

Similarly, studying Shire's *Our Men Do Not Belong to Us* explores issues that stem from the backdrop of civil war, delving into themes of physical, social, and psychological disarray. Adimora-Ezeigbo and Shire present some striking similarities in their exploration of place, gender, and the environmental question. They do this in ways that draw attention to the universal nature of the environmental sentiments that course through 21st-century arts and humanities scholarship, besides what is revealed in the material and social environmental studies.

In exploring the poets' representation of the socio-environment and place, two poems each from the poetry collection have been selected to explore the relationship between human interactions and the socio-natural environment from the lens of Buell's three directions of place. It is worth mentioning that by "socio" and "natural," the researcher refers to the society and the natural environment, which are mutually influential and intertwined, shaping and being shaped by each other. It acknowledges that human activities, cultural practices, and social structures are influenced by and have consequences for the natural environment, including ecosystems, resources, climate, and biodiversity.

ENVIRONMENTAL MATERIALITY AND SOCIAL PERCEPTION IN AKACHI ADIMORA-EZEIGBO'S *HEART SONGS*

The dynamics of place-attachment are intricately linked to social and economic structures when Buell suggests that place "under modernization, however, place-attachment spreads out to look more like an archipelago than concentric circles. The workplace is increasingly outside the home, in extreme cases a country or even a hemisphere away, requiring breadwinners to live apart from their families for long periods" (Buell 2005, 82). Buell's assertion about the dynamics of place suggests the complex and evolving nature of place-attachment in modern society, where factors such as work, distance, and separation can shape individuals' connections to particular locations and challenge the traditional concentric circles model of place-attachment. Places are dynamic and subject to change over time, which affects the environmental materiality and social perception of the socio-natural world.

In the poem "Tornado Jam London", Adimora-Ezeigbo depicts the impact of a natural disaster on a specific location, "London" (46). The poem recalls an eyewitness account in London. It recalls the speaker's experience of a sudden storm or tornado. A "tornado" represents a destructive wind or storm that changes the physical transformation of a place or an environment. Structurally, the poem is written in pidgin, which gives rise to humor in the poem. In other words, the influence of Pidgin English enables the use of humor in exploring the social realities of human and natural behavior as depicted in the poem.

In English translation, we have the poem opens:

> My brother, I have seen something
> That made me so much afraid in this world
> But nothing shocked more like the Tornado
> That tore London like old rag.
> (Adimora-Ezeigbo 2009, 46).

Adding to our discussion, the imagery of chaos and destruction conveys the overwhelming force of the natural disaster. The poem captures how a natural disaster can transform a place and cause pain to its inhabitants. It reveals the disruption of things in the environment and the changes human and non-human beings encounter due to climate change. The breaking of "wall," the "uprooting of the tree," and the destruction of "cars" (46), etc., reflect the changes of natural disaster in a place. It leaves the speaker to question, "What kind of thing is this?"/ Wind that shifts cars // Across the Streets/ Fling brick and bin into the air" (46- 7). While seeking refuge, the speaker observes the immediate response of health workers in London to rescue her citizens. This led the speaker to compare such incidents to those in his home country, as there is a lack of similar resources and responses readily available in his country.

It also suggests the connection between individuals and their environment in the face of natural environmental issues. The speaker further reveals that his own country has an artificial tornado created by politicians and thugs. The speaker discloses that the political violence and destruction perpetrated by "thugs," with "guns," "rocks," and "clubs," contribute to the man-made disaster which is referred to as an "artificial tornado". This situation leaves the speaker to reassess the underlying disparity between the support and recovery efforts in London and the lack thereof in his country.

The mention of specific places like "Awka" and "Odi" (47) suggests the political turmoil of the artificial "tornado" and its impact on the speaker's country home. This shows where certain regions and communities are better equipped and supported in times of crisis, while others face ongoing challenges without adequate assistance. The speaker expresses hope that the affected areas in London will be repaired with an adequate response; he avers that such immediate health intervention does not exist in his own country. He tells us that what happens in his own country is caused by political unrest. The poem concludes with sorrow for both the country and the speaker's encounter. It also highlights that disasters can be natural as well as caused by humans, which brings a transformation to the physical and social environment of a place.

In another poem titled, "Chicken Gizzard," Adimora-Ezeigbo addresses the theme of social stereotypes against women, the injustice and oppressive cultural practices against women in the Igbo cultural milieu. It exposes the underlying power and patriarchal control that perpetuate such injustices. Thus, the poem opens by highlighting the cultural significance and guarded ritual surrounding the consumption of Chicken Gizzards:

> Gizzard culture
> Guarded ritual
> of ancient culture
> Bizarre cult

> 'O Woman
> This meat is taboo to you -
> His vulgar spite-coated voice
> Assaults her long-suffering ears
> Chastised by a din of dos and don'ts-
> Dressed in any form (58).

The above excerpt from the poem suggests that the metaphor "gizzard" symbolizes exclusion and taboo for women, who are explicitly forbidden from partaking in it. The voice represents the oppressive nature of tradition and the assault it inflicts upon women's involvement with non-human species. The "gizzard" from its description in the poem symbolizes an ancient and bizarre culture that prohibits women from eating it, thus emphasizing its time immemorial with the history of a place. It also signifies the connection between cultural practices and the specific places where they originate and their persistence over time. The voice describes the initial reaction of a woman, portrayed as "grim-faced" and "aghast," at the oppressive culture she is in.

As a social perception, the poem expresses the persona, the woman's growing defiance and mourning anger against the oppressive practices. No matter how the anguish seems, she cannot eat the gizzard. In order to obey the law of the land, the woman seizes the gizzard and forcefully removes it from the slaughtered chicken, symbolizing her rejection of the cruel customs imposed upon her. The woman's mind runs through centuries of oppression and unnumbered seasons of this suppression, which serves as a form of societal injustice to women.

The poem concludes that a society's cultural context, traditions, and rituals play a crucial role in shaping the perception and treatment of the gizzard, thereby influencing human experiences and power dynamics. It further evaluates the concept of place as a source of bond and history that endures the influence of historical practices on present-day customs. There is a need "to re-write and represent women as individuals with conscience, able to question the system that marginalizes and disempowers women."[2] By this statement, Onwueme advocates a more nuanced

---

2 Tess Onwueme, "Personal interview," Eau Claire (2003, 8).

representation of women as "individuals with conscience," thoughtful of themselves, "able to question" and challenge institutions, societal norms, and structures that marginalize and disempower them. In essence, it creates room for autonomy and social changes with regard to the concept of place.

SOCIAL PERCEPTION AND SPEAKING VOICE ATTACHMENT TO PLACE IN WARSAN SHIRE'S *OUR MEN DO NOT BELONG TO US*

Buell refers to social perception or construction as the understanding that places are defined through human interactions, cultural practices, and collective representations. In addition, individual affect or bond evokes feelings, attachments, memories, and a sense of belonging that individuals develop with particular places.

In the poem "Haram", the speaker's older sister breaks the societal stereotypes associated with women in her religious practice. As depicted in the poem, the speaker's older sister takes the neighbor's husband, and there is a change in the sister's body. These actions are influenced by the social stereotypes that shape the speaker's older sister into such an act. The excerpt reads:

> My older sister soaps between her legs, her hair
> a prayer of curls. When she was my age, she stole
> the neighbor's husband, burned his name into her skin.
> For weeks she smelled of cheap perfume and dying flesh
> (Shire 2014, 18).

From the above excerpt, there is the intertwining of environment and social construction, and the speaking voice affect within the concept of "place." The interrelationship between humans and the perceived values or laws of the places they inhabit is exemplified by the speaker's older sister, who engages in a lifestyle that is considered taboo in the family and community. The imagery of the speaker's sister "soaping between her legs" and the mentioning of her "tender breast being bruised from sucking" allude to the sexual objectification.

People tend to react to the environment in which they are confined.

Furthermore, there is evidence of a ban from the mother to the speaker's sister from mentioning God's name - "Anything that leaves her mouth sounds like sex / our mother has banned her from saying God's name" (16). The ban from the mother conforms to obeying certain social norms. The speaker's older sister is not permitted to mention the word "sex" or call on the name of "God". Adding to our discussion, the sister's statement "Boys are haram; don't ever forget that"(18), reflects the gender roles and expectations that are embedded in their culture. It also explains how the sister's behavior challenges these norms and how this is perceived as a transgression of the established order. It is on this premise that Lewis (1969, 45) argues that social norms are "customary rules of behavior that coordinate our interactions with others. Once a particular way of doing things becomes established as a rule, it continues in force, because they prefer to conform to the rule given the expectation that others are going to conform." This also implies the effects of patriarchal norms on religious practices attached to a place. The poem calls for re-assessing some established order that contributes to social injustice in women's lives and the environment in which they live.

The poem "Conversation about Home (At the Deportation Center)" portrays the experiences of forced migrants and the societal injustice accompanying it. The speaker speaks of the trauma and harsh experiences of refugees, immigrants, and others who are forcibly displaced from their homes. The poem reveals the importance of recognizing the human meaning and significance of place, and forced migration on one's relationship with their homeland. It begins with the following often quoted sentences:

> Well, I think home spat me out, the blackouts and curfews like
> tongue against Loose-tooth. God, do you know how difficult it is,
> to talk about the day your own city dragged you by the hair,
> past the old prison past the school gates, past the burning torsos
> erected on poles like flags? [...]
> No one leaves home unless home
> is the mouth of a shark (20).

The above passage portrays the speaker's harrowing experience of being uprooted from their home due to violence and oppression. It conveys the pain, fear, and displacement many individuals face when forced to flee their homeland, emphasizing the desperate and life-threatening circumstances that drive people to leave everything behind.

Just as the title depicts, it opens with a conversation leading to memories of injustices such as "the blackouts and curfews," the missing, the memory of ash on people's faces, and the comparison of leaving to a "wild animal, Shark." In the same vein, the poem traces the story of its speaker from an unspecified East African country (most probably Somalia, given Shire's background and the allusions to the horrors of civil war, but it may also allude to Libya, Sudan, Congo, or Eritrea). It exemplifies the sense of loss and disconnection that the speaker feels from their homeland. The line, "I've been carrying the old anthem in /my mouth for so long that there's no space for another song/ another tongue/or another language" (20) depicts a homeland identity that the speaker carries with loss and memory.

As pertained to the environment and perception of things, the reference to "the Libyan deserted red with immigrant bodies/ the Gulf of Aden bloated" (20), depict the dangers that the refugees face when crossing borders. The vivid imagery of "countries like uncles who touch you when you're young and asleep" (20), portrays the abuse and exploitation the refugees experience during their journey. The line "I am the sin of memory and the absence of memory" (21), captures the trauma that the speaker carries with them, as well as the loss of their homeland and the experiences they had there.

The poem mentions the ocean as a contested space. The depiction of the ocean in the poems reflects its dual nature – a contested space where power dynamics are at play, and a space of transformative potential that offers possibilities for change and liberation. This aligns with Buell's assertion on space and place regarding the environment. Buell suggests that space and place are important for analyzing how humans interact with their environments and how they shape the meaning of the spaces they inhabit. Space is "associatively thick, rich in associations, memories, and cultural meanings; while place refers to the social and cultural meanings attached to those particular locations. In the poem, the ocean becomes a symbol that captures the complexities of human experiences of displacement and the interplay between control and freedom. The loss from the persona also speaks to Buell's concept of place as a site of experience and bond-to-place attachment.

PROJECTION FOR THE FUTURE

Nature and the environment, from Buell's concept of "Place," which the analysis of the poems are largely anchored on, seek to inspire reflection, awareness, and action from everyone to actively engage in the preservation of environmental materiality and social change amidst globalization.

The concern for environmentalism in Adimora-Ezeigbo and Shire's poetry reflects and shapes the reader's attitude positively towards environmental literature or eco-critical studies. Therefore, there is a need for continuous environmental writing from African female poets. From the two poetry collections examined, the two poets have consciously used their poems to decry all forms of dehumanizing practices as a weapon for the reformation of the socio-natural environment. Hence, Achebe in "The Black Writer's Burden" encourages writers to express their thoughts and feelings, even against themselves, without the anxiety that what they say will be taken as evidence against their race. (1996, 138-139). Achebe's view also creates an opportunity for dialogue, understanding, and ultimately, the possibility of combating racial injustice inherent in society. As African writers, they are encouraged to express themselves freely, without the fear of their words being used against their racial group.

My reading of Adimora-Ezeigbo and Shire's poetry reveals that "place" depends largely on lived experiences, place attachment, and social constructs inhabited by human and non-human beings.

CONCLUSION

This research adds to the corpus of eco-criticism and environmental literature from a new perspective on the reintroduction of the exploration of place. By using the poetry written by two African women, Adimora-Ezeigbo *Heart Songs* and Shire's *Our Men Do Not Belong to Us,* it presents the interactions and changes human and non-human beings have within a place that is tied to environmental materiality, social perception or construction, and individual bond or affect in a given place.

Based on these, I make a case that poets from African cultures have unique and recognizable values that arise from a combination of their literary traditions and a strong sense of purpose, which should be explored. This chapter aims to explore the African literary ecosystem through the two African female poets, Adimora-Ezeigbo and Shire. The insights from their collection reveal the aftermath of war, migration, forced societal stereotypes, labor, or violence within a place. In essence, there is a need for more African writers, especially women, to fully embrace nature writing. There is a need for African writers to actively look into changes in the environment, land issues, landscape themes, and cultural border claims from colonialism into post-colonialism, and the exploitation of indigenous resources for immediate intervention and preservation of the ecosystem.

REFERENCES

Achebe, Chinua. 1966. "The Black Writer's Burden." *Présence Africaine* 31 (59): 135–140.

Adimora-Ezeigbo, Akachi. 2009. *Heart Songs*. Ibadan: Kraft Books Limited.

Buell, Lawrence. 2001. *Writing for an Endangered World: Literature, Culture, and Environment in the United States and Beyond*. Cambridge, MA: Harvard University Press.

———. 2005. *The Future of Environmental Criticism: Environmental Crisis and Literary Imagination*. Oxford: Blackwell Publishing Limited.

Carter, David. 2006. *Literary Theory*. United Kingdom: Pocket Essentials.

Chukwuloka, Chukwuloo C., and Ikechukwu E. Asika. 2011. "Words as Bullets: Poetry as a Veritable Tool for Social Criticism and Reformation: A Study of Akachi Adimora-Ezeigbo's *Heart Songs* and *Waiting for Dawn*." *African Research Review* 3: 354–68.

Ede, James Ogbonna. 2018. "A Country in Chaos: A Reading of Warsan Shire's *Our Men Do Not Belong to Us*." *Academia*, February 4, 2018. http://www.academia.edu/38028824/.

Ekwueme-Ugwu, Chinonye C. 2015. "Energy Environmental Crisis in Nigerian Novels and the Renewable Alternative." *Bassey Andah Journal* 7 (8): 130–38.

Glotfelty, Cheryll. 1996. "Literary Studies in an Age of Environmental Crisis." In *The Ecocriticism Reader: Landmarks in Literary Ecology*, edited by Cheryll Glotfelty and Harold Fromm, xv–xxxvii. Athens: University of Georgia Press.

Iheka, Cajetan N. 2015. "African Literature and the Environment: A Study in Postcolonial Ecocriticism." PhD diss., Michigan State University, USA.

Lewis, David. 1969. *Convention: A Philosophical Study*. Cambridge, MA: Harvard University Press.

Ohaeto, Ezenwa. 1994. "Pidgin Literature, Criticism and Communication." *African Literature Today* 19: 49–51.

Onwueme, Tess. 2003. Personal interview. Eau Claire, WI.

Shire, Warsan. 2014. *Our Men Do Not Belong to Us*. New York: Slapering Hol Press.

Slaymaker, William. 2001. "Ecoing the Other(s): The Call of Global Green and Black African Responses." *PMLA* 116 (1): 129–144. https://doi.org/10.1632/S0030812900105085.

CHAPTER EIGHT

Environmental Degradation
Interrogating Triggers and Paradigms in Select African Imaginaries

Victory O. Okpala, Ezinwanyi Edikanabasi Adam, &
Arinze T. Okpala

INTRODUCTION

Our world is currently confronting an unprecedented environmental catastrophe. This problem poses a substantial threat to the fundamental structure of our existence, as it disrupts the intricate balance of our planet's ecosystems and endangers the prospects of all living organisms. The unwavering drive for industrialization, the rapid increase in the human population, and the irresponsible exploitation of natural resources have cumulatively brought our environment to the verge of collapse. Environmental degradation refers to the deterioration of the natural environment resulting from human activities. These repercussions extend beyond national borders, affecting every part of our interconnected world. Environmental degradation is caused by various factors, including urban economic development, floods, typhoons, droughts, politics, and socio-economic factors. From a literary viewpoint:

> ecological degradation is a global phenomenon that centres on the depletion of natural resources through various inordinate attitudes of humans which usually triggers ecological activism towards instilling necessary core values and consciousness among people for the restoration of the environment from the shackles of human devastation (Olughu 2019, 40).

Creative writers showcase their dedication to protecting the environment and opposing harmful activities that harm the ecosystem's well-being. The emergence of eco-critical literary criticism lends credence to this commitment. Ecocriticism is the "study of the relationship between literature and the physical environment" (Glotfelty and Fromm 1996, xviii).

According to Kumar, it is the "analysis of literature and environment from an interdisciplinary perspective where all sciences join their hands together to investigate the environment and to reach potential resolutions for the improvement of the present-day environmental condition (2017, 263). Environmental literary analysis delves into the complex relationship between humans and the environment in greater depth. Glotfelty, a prominent advocate of ecocriticism, asserts that ecocriticism scrutinizes the portrayal of nature in literature, the misrepresentation of the concept of the wild, and the receptiveness of science to literary exploration. Thus, Neema (2015, 370) suggests that ecocriticism is conceived as an interdisciplinary method that examines how nature is portrayed in literary works, aiming to address environmental problems and suggest solutions. Ecocriticism, as defined by Glotfelty (1996, cited in Okoye-Ugwu 2013, 157), shares similarities with Marxist and feminist criticisms in that it adopts an activist viewpoint. Moreover, it expands the human understanding of the global community to include nonhuman living forms and the physical environment. As a theoretical framework, Okoye-Ugwu (2013, 158) asserts that ecocriticism investigates the connections between the human and nonhuman elements may be extended to include the other goal of ecocriticism, which is to advocate for the elimination of detrimental activities that endanger the health and integrity of the natural environment.

POLLUTION AND PIPELINE ISSUES IN WATSON'S TINY SUNBIRDS FAR AWAY

Watson's *Tiny Sunbirds Far Away* advocates both environmental justice and well-being. The author analyzes the various environmental problems that have plagued the Nigerian ecosystem.

The novel explores several instances of environmental deterioration, focusing particularly on different types of pollution. It also examines the factors that contribute to these issues within the context of the story. The author scrutinizes the metropolis of Lagos and reveals the prevailing environmental degradation within it. Allen Avenue in Ikeja exemplifies an area plagued by air pollution, which reduces and alters the quality of air people breathe. The extent of environmental pollution is captured thus: "on Allen Avenue, every house or apartment had a generator. The hum they made was constant, day and night" (Watson 2011, 2). This excerpt illustrates the presence of noise pollution resulting from the continuous operation of generators, as well as air pollution caused by the release of harmful fumes into the atmosphere. These factors have negative impacts on the purity and well-being of both the environment and human beings.

The town's urban planning exacerbates environmental degradation. Despite being a residential area, Allen Avenue is located near a market that emits various odors. Additionally, the presence of open gutters in the region further contributes to the dissemination of unpleasant scents. In addition, the protagonist experiences a mixture of strong and appealing odors from "open gutters, the fresh fish, raw meat, akara, puff puff, and suya" (Watson 2011, 2), which simultaneously evoke feelings of nausea and hunger. The environment is experiencing a decline in air quality, which is detrimental to human health. The novel criticizes inadequate urban planning that contributes to environmental damage. Consequently, it urges town planners to adopt necessary measures for efficient town planning.

Similarly, Blessing provides a detailed account of air pollution in locations such as Makoko, situated beneath the primary bridge in Lagos. She says of it: "smell of fish and human waste and rubbish is so strong that if it fills your nostrils it takes all day to remove" (Watson 2011, 17). This depicts an environment that has been poorly managed and poses a risk to human health. More so, Warri experiences a high level of air pollution. Upon arriving in Warri, Mama and her children are greeted by the sight of pipeline fires. Mama's driver, Zafi, explains that the fumes emitted from the burning oil are the cause of this pollution. This statement similarly illustrates that air pollution is a type of environmental deterioration.

Deductively, this literary imaginary provides precise knowledge and awareness of the current environmental issues in Nigerian cities, necessitating immediate attention and resolution. At first, Mama's family's move to Warri as a result of her divorce is met with apprehension. Ezekiel inquires of Warri and discovers that it is plagued by "oil bunkering, hostage taking, illness and poverty" (Watson 2011, 11). He expresses trepidation and doubt about their relocation to Warri, due to the widespread environmental damage in the Niger Delta region of Nigeria. He tells Mama: "and if we don't get shot the bacteria and parasites will surely kill us" (Watson 2011, 11).

In addition, improper garbage disposal is a significant environmental concern prevalent in Alhaji and Grandma's house, leading to environmental and water pollution. Interestingly, Grandma's family retains refuse for one year, namely during the rainy season, after which it is disposed of into the river and then washed away. This practice causes a decline in value and damages aquatic life due to the discharge of hazardous substances into the river by the waste. Over time, water becomes polluted, posing a threat to both human and aquatic creatures such as oysters, fish, and crabs. Likewise, the waste disposal procedure practiced in Alhaji's household results in air pollution.

Clearly, the individuals residing in this location are breathing in contaminated air that originates from waste dumped over the past year and is decomposing, thereby releasing harmful compounds into the atmosphere. The narrator explains: "I followed Grandma and Celestine to the area at the side of the outhouse where the rubbish was held until the rains come to wash it down the river. They rustled when we arrived. Grandma had told me they saved it all every year, God washed it away. I wondered where the rubbish ended up, and who lived at the end of the river" (Watson 2011, 85). This approach is detrimental and causes instability in the mind of young Blessing. It is disheartening that Grandma is complicit in the deterioration of the ecosystem and believes that God is responsible for the waste disposal. Olughu (2019, 44) confirms that the local population is an accomplice in the degradation of the environment, as demonstrated by their disposal of waste in the river.

Consequently, Blessing is perplexed about where the waste ends up, as certain materials are indecomposable. Undoubtedly, Blessing resided in Lagos, attended a reputable educational institution, and was well enlightened about proper waste management and maintaining a healthy environment. These practices align with the core principles of ecocriticism philosophy, which seeks to preserve and improve the natural environment by offering solutions to environmental problems. In summary, Blessing's response to this inappropriate waste disposal practice displays her opposition to environmental injustice.

Pipeline mishaps in Nigeria, according to Johnson et al. (2022, 637), are a significant cause of environmental degradation, resulting in detrimental impacts on both people and the environment. Specifically, a pipeline explosion occurs when individuals known as oil bunkers deliberately open pipes, leading to an explosion. This phenomenon occurs when "a premixed gas cloud is formed by mixing combustible gas with air, which is fully mixed with air on the ground" (Yan et al. 2023, 1). This has been a recurring event in the South-South part of Nigeria. Blessing affirms that: "it had happened before. We were getting so used to explosion noise waking us from sleep that it should not have made me feel so sick. I looked at the smoke rising in the darkness like a cloud" (Watson 2011, 347).

Paradoxically, this occurrence results in Ezekiel becoming a victim, since he is severely burned to the point where his appearance is practically unrecognizable. Blessing describes the event: "I could not see Ezekiel as he was held in the air, but I could smell his burning. Burnt skin, like suya that had been barbecued for too long and was beginning to turn black" (Watson 2011, 348). He becomes a member of the Sibeye boys, a group involved in pipeline vandalism, and as a consequence, he experiences a fire mishap involving a pipeline. Grandma informs Celestine that: "it was Ezekiel said Grandma eventually joining that gang of Sibeye boys. Over twenty boys in hospital now. Breaking a pipeline. An explosion like that imagine" (Watson 2011, 354). Unfortunately, pipeline explosions lead to environmental contamination due to the release of hazardous, polluted gases.

Notably, the pipeline vandalism carried out by the Sibeye boys can be seen as a form of protest against the European oil firms' neglect of the Niger Delta, which is considered to be inhumane. Ezekiel directs his hatred towards Dan Mama's fiancé because of their job at the Western oil firm. He believes that Dan is responsible for the problems in the Niger Delta. Consequently, he vociferates at him: "you people come here Ezekiel slammed his fist down onto the tabletop making us jump 'And take our women' he looked at Mama 'and our money. And our jobs. He looked at Alhaji. Nobody moved. 'You pay people to kill us and you rape our land then our women" (Watson 2011, 258)!

From the foregoing, Ezekiel's actions reveal his rage and defiance at the neglect and marginalization of his community. He denies Dan the opportunity to marry his mother; instead, he questions Dan's presence in their family. He inquired: "what are you doing here? … said Ezekiel as he walked towards Dan causing Dan to step back towards the house. I said what are you doing here?" … "Dan tried to hug Ezekiel. Ezekiel pushed Dan so far backward that he nearly fell into the doorway" (Watson 2011, 263). He categorically asserts that the actions of the oil giants are aggressive and tantamount to sexual assault. Overall, Ezekiel serves as an advocate against the unequal treatment of his community, which leads to environmental degradation and impacts the people living in the Niger Delta region.

Similarly, ecological activism in the Niger Delta is stirred by "environmental injustices meted by the oil companies" (Olughu 2019, 42). Subsequently, Watson demonstrates her support for ecocriticism in response to anti-environmental behaviors, inspired by Ezekiel's actions and stance. Besides, Ezekiel informs Blessing about the insufficient focus on FFIN, who are requesting reparation from the oil firms for extracting oil from their territory. He tells Blessing that "more direct action is required" (Watson 2011, 289). As a result, multiple factions in the Niger Delta region participate in the abduction of Caucasian oil industry employees, whom they label as 'white Gold'. In addition, Ezekiel's animosity towards Dan motivates him to orchestrate the abduction of Dan by the Sibeye group. He intimidates Mama and Dan, uttering the words: "a white man?" A fucking oil worker! He's going to get what he deserves. He flicked his head at Mama, then back at Dan. I'll show you, white Gold. Me and the Sibeye Boys" (Watson 2011, 331)!

Without a doubt, the inhabitants of the Niger Delta are portrayed as impoverished, lacking access to clean and drinkable water. One of the women protesters shouts: "we want to drink water that has no oil in it" (Watson 2011, 382). Ironically, the Western oil firm is located in this setting, while the indigenous people reside in shacks instead of proper homes and suffer from hunger. The narrator articulates their dissatisfaction with the disregard for the Niger Delta region, which is depicted as follows:

> Women waved at us on the way, from their roadside huts, where they could see. The Western Oil Company buildings are in the distance. It was still inside my head. I wanted ask the women about how it felt, to watch the glass building from where they lived in shacks and were hungry. I was so angry. It felt good to be angry. I let it grow inside me. The anger burned my throat. I was angry with the western oil company, who gave the government the money with full knowledge that on the other side of the gate, children were hungry, and had no school, no electricity, no future (Watson 2011, 378).

As a result, the women come together to protest against the environmental injustice inflicted upon the Niger Delta, which has endangered their environment and, consequently, their health. Shehu and Ojeyokan (2022, 243) aver that "Watson in the spirit of activism equally presents women and their role in the vanguard of fighting against the atrocities of the Western Oil Company and military government in the Niger Delta region" (243). Their demonstration reveals the struggle against the exploitation of the Western oil industry, which has led to environmental deterioration. One of the women says: "we no want dangerous gas burnt in all this pipeline fire give us cancer, coughing, asthma, like our lungs are less important than any other place. We want our fruits to grow, our animals to be able to eat grass, our animals to be able to eat grass and not drop dead. We want to drink water that has no oil in it" (Watson 2011, 382).

Logically, the existence and exploration of oil in the Niger Delta expose the ecosystem to damage and resource depletion. It is sufficient to state that capitalist aspirations and motives are responsible for another aspect of environmental destruction. The government, functioning as a capitalist entity, abuses the general population, prioritizing economic gain over their well-being. They obtain financial compensation from oil firms in exchange for conducting oil exploration, despite the various negative impacts, such as environmental damage and depletion of natural resources, which adversely affect the population. The female demonstrators express their disappointment and assert: "we are sick of the failed promises. Sick of sickness, sick of our environment filled with pollution, and our rivers filled with oil spills. Sick of no electricity. Sick of our government putting billions of pounds in their own pockets. We are sick of the oil companies giving these men money, knowing it will not go to the people" (Watson 2011, 383).

Furthermore, the demonstration provides a glimpse into the environmental degradation caused by the presence of oil firms in the Niger Delta, to the extent that all forms of life in the area are affected. Grandma tells the journalist, "let our fish live in the river and our trees grow" (Watson 2011, 384). Environmental degradation leads to the extinction of aquatic organisms and hinders the germination and growth of trees due to oil spills and other actions that undermine agricultural sustainability.

The protest aims to combat environmental deterioration and serves as a platform to condemn unethical behavior. Furthermore, it serves as a means to articulate and educate not only the oil corporations but also to universally denounce the abnormality, thereby fostering unity in the face of the threat. Essentially, it is a proactive initiative aimed at addressing the mistreatment of the Niger Delta. Grandma urges the world to observe them as they have exposed themselves completely throughout the demonstration. This is recorded in this manner: "the press arrived shortly afterwards to find hundreds of naked women. One press van nearly crashed into the security office. The cameras started flashing; it became impossible to see… The cameras flashed at Grandma. 'Look at us!' She shouted. 'Your sisters and daughters and mothers! Look at our disgrace. You feel shame. Now you all feel shame!"(Watson 2011, 381).

DESTRUCTION OF WILDLIFE, DEFORESTATION, AND GOLD MINING IN TADJO'S IN THE COMPANY OF MEN

The novel, *In the Company of Men*, chronicles the process of environmental degradation through the destruction of wildlife, deforestation, and mining. In Tadjo's work (2021), the account of two brothers who aggressively assault a colony of dormant bats, causing their demise, and subsequently indulge in the delectable meal is depicted. However, the delicious supper ultimately proves to be their demise. The pair engages in the assault and annihilation of animals, which constitutes a manifestation of environmental degradation. Their act of killing the two bats symbolizes the decline of wildlife, a component of the environment. Regrettably, the animals serve as disease carriers for a highly contagious and untreatable illness, resulting in their demise along with that of their mother. The Bat Conservation Trust (2023) holds the view that the transmission of a virus or other disease vector from wild animals to humans typically occurs due to environmental changes. This increased proximity can lead to instances of viruses spilling over into human populations, either directly or through an intermediate host. Significantly, humans choose animals as a source of food out of necessity during periods of starvation and famine.

Moreover, the author gives voice to trees and expresses sorrow for the harm inflicted upon plant life as a result of human actions. The annihilation of "our hopes" (Tadjo 2021, 9) is articulated in this manner. Again, the investigation delves into the environmental deterioration caused by deforestation, which is described as follows: "our trunks crash to the ground with a sound like thunder. Our naked roots mourn the end of our dreams.' You cannot destroy the forest without blood" (Tadjo 2021, 10). Moreover, the story highlights the beneficial nature of trees, thereby condemning the heartless cutting down and destruction of them. Deforestation can be seen as a violent act, as it often results in the killing of animals who try to escape from their habitats when humans invade. The author expresses support for the battle against deforestation, which poses a grave threat to vegetation and wildlife.

The relentless character of human desires is revealed as they delve deeply into the depths of the earth. They submerge into the oceans. They will continue until there is complete depletion. The detrimental and inconsiderate use of natural resources by humans is condemned, while the benefits of trees to humanity, animals, and the cosmos are depicted and praised. The safeguarding of natural resources from harmful exploitation is advantageous for both humanity and the global community. The author personifies many species of trees, giving them a voice to condemn the cruel actions of humans towards natural resources, ecosystems, wildlife, and natural habitats. The impact of human activities on the environment is clearly demonstrated through deforestation, which depletes the land's nutrients and hinders its intended productivity.

Consequently, these harmful removals of natural resources lead to food shortages and famine. The primary motivation behind these actions is materialism. One of the trees expresses its sorrow, stating: "they see in us nothing but marketable goods" (Tadjo 2021, 11). Nevertheless, the baobab tree effectively mitigates certain natural calamities, such as landslides and mudflows, due to its unique characteristics. Therefore, it admonishes humans for their lack of foresight and comprehension, as the harm inflicted upon trees ultimately harms humans as well. The baobab tree speaks:

> If only man were clear sighted! If only man he could foresee his own decline, the depletion, the degradation. Maybe he would finally understand that he depends on us, and that in this century beset by so many disasters, hundreds of forest dwelling communities have disappeared along with their languages, their knowledge and their beautiful traditions. If only man could realize how misguided he is, he would surely end the violence and lay down his axes and machetes. He would silence his chainsaws, stop his bulldozers and lock away his heavy trucks, those gigantic iron monsters that haul timber and death. None of that brings him anything good or makes him happy (Tadjo 2021, 12).

Without exception, when humans engage in deforestation, it leads to the complete disappearance of human communities along with their customs and languages. Human-induced deforestation is "breaking the chains of existence" (Tadjo 2021, 13). This situation involves animals being denied food, which leads to migration.

The work provides additional insight into another type of environmental deterioration, known as bush burning, which notably leads to the demise of animals and the extinction of numerous species. The motivation for the pursuit of financial gain by those who engage in this behavior is highlighted by the author, who notes that some individuals prioritize their financial gain to the extent that "only some of them run industrial-scale palm oil, rubber, cocoa, and eucalyptus plantations for financial gain" (Tadjo 2021, 14). Yet, there are alternate methods of generating income that do not involve the exploitation of natural resources.

The relentless assault on the natural world by people is seen as a departure from past norms. This is recorded in this manner:

> things were not always like this. There was a time when men used to talk to us, the trees. We shared the same gods, the same spirits. If one of us had to be cut down, our pardon would be begged first… Those were the old days, in times past, when the ancestors who founded the village would plant me right in the centre of their lives. As the centuries passed, I grew into a symbol of the close link between Nature and Humanity. I was the tree of wisdom, the one to which people would turn when they wished to find an answer to the troubles of human existence" (Tadjo 2021, 15).

Without a doubt, the act of felling trees and engaging in activities that exhaust natural resources did not occur initially. Instead, it arose due to shifts in economic conditions, globalization, and urbanization. The author depicts the symbiotic connection between humans and trees. The baobab tree, renowned for its exceptional robustness, serves as a representative for other trees, highlighting their essential contributions. It precisely represents the prominent position it holds. It tells the story in this way: "if a conflict was brewing, any attempts to settle it took place in my presence, including the chiefs' consultations among themselves. My cool shade was the only place where lengthy deliberations could be brought to a successful conclusion… Life decisions were taken in the cocoon of my embrace, where all topics were discussed: marriages, births, funerals, good harvests and bad droughts, the laudable or reprehensible conduct of a young man or a young girl, divine protection, protection against sorcery, and alliances with neighboring villages. Everything revolved around my good will" (Tadjo 2021, 17-18).

Another form of environmental degradation is gold mining. The merciless method employed in this process leads to the contamination of rivers with mercury, which "killed the fish, the plankton and dark–green algae. So the water became acid. Toxic. Life became poisonous." (Tadjo 2021, 19) As a result, the pursuit of wealth leads humans to forsake their sustainable means of living in favor of alternative activities that have detrimental effects on the environment and nature. The consequence of these behaviors is the anthropogenic devastation of the animals' natural environment. The event is captured thus: "The villagers turned into driver ants, formidable predators determined to annihilate everything in their path. The past had to be wiped out as well as from one day to the next, they abandoned their fields, their legends, their customs, their beliefs, the trees that crashed to the ground took climbing animals and crawling animals with them" (Tadjo 2021, 20-21).

Lastly, the author highlights that the Ebola virus outbreak that devastated Africa in 2014 was a result of human interference in the form of degradation and depletion of the earth's resources. This resulted in humans becoming infected with the virus and ultimately caused the deaths of numerous individuals. Fortunately, the villagers rely on plants, particularly neem leaves, although they struggle to get them due to the deforestation of their trees. From a deductive standpoint, it is evident that natural resources, like trees, provide significant benefits to humanity. Consequently, the act of cutting down these trees would lead to immediate or eventual problems that would hurt humans.

CONCLUSION

Tadjo and Watson demonstrated unwavering solidarity in their support for the battle against environmental degradation in Africa. The examination of environmental protection and justice, which serve as the fundamental principles of eco-criticism, is thorough enough. This discussion portrays uneducated yet patriotic young men with a strong desire to restore integrity to their exploited surroundings, even if it means resorting to drastic measures. The youths' misguided attempts to address environmental degradation tragically led to the loss of life.

The investigation of environmental degradation in Africa reveals that it serves as a means of survival for the impoverished and economically disadvantaged populations and communities. This inquiry aims to address and combat environmental injustice. The opposition to oil exploration symbolizes the struggle against environmental exploitation.

Environmental degradation arises from both visible and underlying factors. Both deliberate and unintentional actions cause environmental deterioration. On one hand, there are the oil firms, and on the other hand, there are the indigenous inhabitants of the Niger Delta who are struggling to make a living. Poverty-induced hunger is a significant catalyst for human violations of environmental regulations. The chapter concludes that natural calamities do not solely cause environmental deterioration in Africa in the twenty-first century, but are also influenced by socio-economic and political factors. It is safe to say that this is a global issue, which severe economic circumstances have exacerbated.

REFERENCES

Bats Conservation Trust. 2023. "Bats and Health." Accessed [month day, year]. https://www.bats.org.uk.

Glotfelty, Cheryll. 1996. "Introduction." In *The Ecocriticism Reader: Landmarks in Literary Ecology*, edited by Cheryll Glotfelty and Harold Fromm, xv–xxxvii. Athens and London: University of Georgia Press.

Johnson, I. Francis, Richard Laing, Bassam Bjeirmi, and Marianthi Leon. 2022. "Examining the Causes and Impacts of Pipeline Disasters in Nigeria." *AIMS Environmental Science* 9 (5): 636–57. https://doi.org/10.3934/environsci.2022035.

Kumar, Saurabh. 2017. "Historical Perspective on Emergence of Eco-Critical Theory: A Review." *International Journal on Arts, Management and Humanities* 6 (2): 262–71.

Neema, Bagula. 2015. "Ecocritical Approach to Literary Text Interpretation." *International Journal of Innovative and Scientific Research* 18 (2): 369–78.

Okoye-Ugwu, Stella. 2013. "Going Green: An Ecocritical Reading of Chinua Achebe's *Things Fall Apart*." *Okike: An African Journal of New Writing* Chinua Achebe Memorial Edition 50: 154–65.

Olughu, Michael Ikenna. 2019. "Unmasking Policies in the Niger Delta Narrative: Eco-degradation and Activism in Tanure Ojaide's *The Activist* and Christie Watson's *Tiny Sunbirds Far Away*." *Journal of Literature, Languages and Linguistics* 52: 40–49. https://doi.org/10.7176/JLL/52-06.

Shehu, Garba Sunusi, and Ojeyokan John Egwabor. 2022. "Environmental Degradation: Women and Youth Protest in Niger Delta: Analysis of Christie Watson's *Tiny Sunbirds Far Away*." *International Journal of Sustainable Development Research* 8 (3): 239–46. https://doi.

org/10.11648/j.ijsdr.20220803.20.

Sule, Emmanuel Egya. 2018. "Sexualized Body, Exploited Environment: A Feminist Ecocritical Reading of Kaine Agary's *Yellow Yellow* and Christy Watson's *Tiny Sunbirds Far Away*." *Journal of the African Literature Association* 12 (2): 1–13. https://doi.org/10.1080/21674736.2018.1454846.

Tadjo, Véronique. 2021. *In the Company of Men*. Lagos: Narrative Landscape Press.

Watson, Christie. 2011. *Tiny Sunbirds Far Away*. London: Quercus.

Yan, Liu, Lin Chen, Xuting Wang, Yaqi Zhao, Zhen Zhao, Chen Zhang, and Jinghan Xu. 2023. "Study on Overpressure Explosion of Oil and Gas Pipelines and Risk Prevention and Control." *Journal of Physics: Conference Series* 2520: 012028. https://doi.org/10.1088/1742-6596/2520/1/012028.

PART TWO

ECOCRITICAL ISSUES FROM NIGERIAN ART, LITERATURE, THEATRE AND ORATURE

CHAPTER NINE

Outrage and Marginal Communities
Postcolonial and Ecocritical Meditations on Jerry Buhari's Landscapes of the Soul (1993-2022)

Dominic James Aboi

INTRODUCTION

"How can you measure progress if you didn't know what it cost and who has paid for it?"
–Arundhati Roy (*The Algebra of Infinite Justice*, 2002, 60).

There has always been a struggle between the binaries of man and nature, tradition and modernity, among other factors that either promise economic prosperity or offer solutions to environmental challenges. From the Industrial Revolution of the nineteenth century to the present, the binary oppositions have never aligned; instead, they have been pushed further apart, with the widening gap between the proletariat and bourgeoisie, to borrow an orthodox Marxist term, and between the Global North and the South. Said (1979, 11) observes that "the world is made up of two unequal halves, Orient and Occident," whose system of relationship is referred to as Orientalism. Orientalism, therefore, is how corporate institutions deal with the Orient. It is an established Western style of dominating, restructuring, and having authority over the Orient.

This division transcends individual levels to engage national and continental boundaries, distinguishing classes, races, and socioeconomic stratifications in a manner that confirms the uneven relationship between the colonized and colonizer, which has been neutralized to appear normal or natural. Such postulations solicit a postcolonial ecocriticism that includes "examining the implications of fundamental narratives, problematizing assumptions of a universal subject and of an essentialized nature, and examining how forms of dominance are naturalized" (Deloughrey 2014, 321). It is along this train of thought that the German sociologist Wolfgang Sachs asserts that the international development debate tends to mimic "the rise and fall of political sensibilities within the [affluent] Northern countries," referring to the West, therefore suggesting that the "unfettered enthusiasm for economic growth in 1945 reflected the West's desire to restart the economic machine after a devastating war" (Huggan and Tiffin 2010, 27-28). These dialectics of uneven representation, along with other ethical and aesthetic considerations, played out in the distribution and exploration of natural resources, which invigorated Buhari's engagements in *Landscapes of the Soul* (2022) and provided him with the artistic "vocabulary of protest" (Guha and Martinez-Alier 2006, 13).

The gap in elaborating the unequal relationship between rich and poor countries, despite the lauded doctrines of sovereignty and racial equality, confirms rich nations as the determinants of what development is and when to switch on or switch off the engines of imperialist advantages. The aforementioned calls forth Roy's rhetoric in the epigram above. It contests what development means to the Global South, specifically whether it entails the destruction or sacrifice of their natural resources in order to benefit from modern projects and global economies. Huggan and Tiffin (2010) also pose a series of similar questions: What is development? How should it be defined and measured, and whose interest does it serve? What is development's historical relationship to colonialism and imperialism? Whither development in an increasingly globalized postcolonial world? Is development sustainable, and what is its connection to the environment? This uneven relationship divides the world into developed regions and less developed ones, between the North and South, as referred to in *The Brandt Report* (1980). According to Slovic, Rangarajan, and Sarveswaran (2015, 2), this report is best known for identifying economic disparities across the planet. They further contend that:

The so-called Brandt Line advocated the economic development of Third World societies to the south of the thirtieth parallel, which separates North and Central America, passes above Africa and India, but does not include Australia and New Zealand which are considered de facto members of the North. Both "rich" and "poor" nations today fall on either side of the Brandt Line (2).

For Australia and New Zealand, which both share a long history of capitalist exploitation of the Aborigines and the Maori, respectively, to be exempted from this categorization in spite of being within Willy Brandt's demarcation calls into question the authenticity of the claim and the imperialist effort to draw a distinctive line between rich and poor nations. Like the concepts of race and gender, which are social constructs, the notion of the Global North and South is also a socioeconomic and political construct designed to exploit the wealth of nations considered weak or lacking military or economic support to protect their sovereignty. This stimulates a postcolonial ecocritical investigation that interrogates "imperialist modes of social and environmental dominance" (Huggan and Tiffin 2010, 2), especially when Euro-American scholars overlook once colonized landscapes in situating the place of nature in the history of Western thought.

There is an urgent need to highlight how colonization, with its destructive impact on the material resources and human capital of former colonies, which also serve as sources of their wealth, ushered in the modernity that the Global North boasts of today. Unfortunately, the Global South is at the receiving end, and should write back to the Empire because "plunder exhausts the noncommodified relationships that allow capital accumulation to proceed," since "capitalism is always in search of new commodity frontiers for extraction and appropriation" (Deckard 2015, 39). However, what postcolonial ecocriticism and its critics are saying is that the problems of the environment with regards to the Global South, like the "legacy of colonialism is as much a problem for the West as it is for the scarred lands in the world beyond" (Young 2004, 165). This also lends weight to why Buhari's *Landscapes of the Soul* matters.

Buhari's *The Landscapes of the Soul* (spanning three decades) is a personal meditation with global intimations that captures marginal communities and their rage. Akinwande (2022) avers that the catalogue is Buhari's "personal recreation of his own world, and an intimate portrait of the peace on the inside, one that is devoid of chaos on the outside," and further states that, it is an "inward journey, working in watercolor, each box represents cities and moments from his travels" (22-23). Again, in an interview with Sabo Kpade (2022), Buhari admits his travels fertilized the creation of the landscapes and submits that "the idea was to create as many worlds as possible in such a small space. So, you could travel to so many cities and explore many jungles, without moving from your comfort zones" (56). It is no surprise that Obodo and Anikpe (2014) assert that Buhari's work is a "narrative that talks of a physical reality in which nature's resources are exploited and mismanaged" (10). It demonstrates Buhari's unreserved sensitivity towards environmental degradation that is encroaching on the Nigerian state, and how he artistically launches ecocritical investigations into natural landscapes once celebrated but have given way to capitalism. Buhari interrogates the despoliation of national/ natural resources by powers, mostly from the Global North, to facilitate their smoking industries and imperialist ambitions, which continue to widen the gap in relationships between the rich and the poor. Buell (1995), for instance, observes that since 1970, there has been an unprecedented discussion on a national and global scale, about "the need to set limits to technoeconomic growth" (3) and submits that if such a thing as global culture comes into being, environmentalism will surely be one of the catalysts. This concern, until recently, has always been about the Global North alone.

With the rapid change unfolding around the globe, Iheka (2018) posits that "Postcolonialism needs to be attuned to the ecological implications of colonial and neocolonial oppression and ensure that its responses are not complicit in the problems it seeks to address" (85). On this pedestal, it is essential to deploy postcolonial ecocriticism in the evaluation of Buhari's paintings, which can be situated alongside environmentalists such as Arundhati Roy, Tanure Ojaide, Wangari Maathai, Indra Sinha, and Gabriel Okara, who all lament the loss of virgin forests to capitalist exploitation. One of the foremost voices in this struggle is Ken Saro-Wiwa, who was unfortunately martyred by a military junta alongside eight (8) of his Ogoni elders in 1995. The claim made by Saro-Wiwa needs to be quoted at length to elucidate the impact of colonial imperialism and exploitative capitalism on the environment:

> Oil exploration has turned Ogoni into a waste land: lands, streams, and creeks are totally and continually polluted; the atmosphere has been poisoned, charged as it is with hydrocarbon vapours, methane, carbon monoxide, carbon dioxide and soot emitted by gas which has been flared twenty-four hours a day for thirty-three years in very close proximity to human habitation… the rain forest has fallen to the axe of the multinational oil companies, all wildlife is dead, marine life is gone, the farmlands have been rendered infertile by acid rain and the once beautiful Ogoni countryside is no longer a source of fresh air and green vegetation. All one sees and feels around is death (Saro-Wiwa 1995, 95-96).

Though Saro-Wiwa infuses his personal grief into the despoliation of Ogoni land, his claims are both national and global regarding community rights to natural resources, basic human rights, their violations, and environmental degradation. Saro-Wiwa's cries echo a society on the brink of annihilation because its material, human, and cosmological makeup has been shattered. The Abacha regime, in connivance with Shell Oil, "martyred" the environmental activists to avoid cleaning up the environment, as well as "reducing Shell's profits and power" (Pressley-Sanon 2018, 163). In reverse, Buhari (2022) in "Soft Landscape with Two Soft Elements" (38) offers, in acrylic and watercolor, a countryside that is one with nature and at peace with itself. He depicts a virgin landscape that is a haven for the animals within, offering shelter and clean air to the respective communities.

The thriving atmosphere on "Soft Landscape with Two Elements," portrays a tropical mangrove rainforest and features a scurrying squirrel within the brush over a wash of sunlight illuminating the thickest areas of the forest. The clarity of air, registered by the mustard yellow rhythms dancing on the flush vegetation is a testament to landscapes not abused by capitalist intrusion and ecological destitution that Nixon (2011) calls "slow violence" which is a "violence that occurs gradually and out of sight, a violence of delayed destruction that is dispersed across time and space" (2).

Figure 9.1.
"Soft Landscape with Two Soft Elements," Acrylic on paper, Jerry Buhari, 15x22 inches, 2007.

It is to this type of toxic build-up and what Johan Galtung calls "indirect or structural violence" (Nixon 2011, 10), that features unequal morbidity that results from commodified health care, to racism among others, that postcolonial ecocriticism advocates.

Jerry Buhari is one of Nigeria's foremost artists. Born on July 11, 1959, at Akwaya, Kachia Local Government Area of Kaduna State, Buhari is a Professor in the Department of Fine Arts at Ahmadu Bello University (ABU), Zaria, where he has been teaching since 1982. Alongside administrative and academic commitments, Buhari's intellectual reach extends globally, encompassing institutions such as Princeton University (USA), where he served as a Visiting Professor in 2013, and Kansas Wesleyan University (KWU) in 2007. He was also a Visiting Lecturer/Artist at the Savannah College of Art and Design (USA) in 2007; a Visiting Lecturer at the University of Nigeria, Nsukka (UNN) in 2008, and at the University of Jos (Nigeria) in 2019. As a Pan-Africanist, ecologist, activist, artistic mediator of art and society, as well as a cultural ideologue with conference attendance in Germany, Ghana, USA, Japan, Senegal, the UK – over 50 within Nigeria, and a bustling oeuvre of over 100 publications, Buhari bestrides the theoretical and practical worlds of visual arts as a colossus with quintessential messages for the present and the future.

POSTCOLONIAL ECOCRITICISM AND ECOCRITICAL DISILLUSIONMENT

On a global scale, outraged communities often result from resource wars, uncompensated exploitation, and disregard for human capital and the environmental consequences of natural resource extraction. Iheka (2018) designates three manifestations colonialists have used to "naturalize" the African continent, and locates the second dimension in the project of colonial modernity, saying: "In their bid to justify their colonial processes, including the despoliation of the African environment, the colonizers sought to civilize the Africans and their environment" (10). In other words, they sought to "naturalize" Africans and their environment into a global modernity that is similar to the acquisition of citizenship through naturalization. This naturalization takes the form of capitalist expansion of Western markets that serve imperialist interests. In this sense, a haunting atmosphere is birthed to the detriment of the indigenous landowners or inhabitants. An atmosphere that Nixon (2011; see also Guha and Martinez-Alier 2006, 3-16) calls the environmentalism of the poor. Nixon (2011, 17) speculates that it is triggered when an official language is forcibly imposed on a vernacular one, and further clarifies:

> A vernacular landscape, although neither monolithic nor undisputed, is integral to the socioenvironmental dynamics of the community rather than being wholly eternalized – treated as out there, as a separate nonrenewable resource. By contrast, an official landscape – whether governmental, NGO, corporate, or some combination of those – is typically oblivious to such earlier maps; instead, it writes the land in a bureaucratic, externalizing, and extraction-driven manner that is often pitilessly instrumental.

This imposition of foreign values that are capitalist-driven does not serve the political economy of the colonized, as it violently snatches away their local industries and means of livelihood. In most cases, it collapses the socioeconomic bridge between subsistence production and commercial sustenance. Without considering the sociocultural and ecological implications of this capitalist mapping, the colonial imperialists impose conditions that make indigenous populations become conduits in their own exploitation. State-sanctioned "slow violence" of this type on spaces with natural resources often harbors imperialist undertones, usually denied by the ruling class. Similar trends whether in the construction of hydroelectric dams, mining tunnels, shipping lanes, logging, creation of coffee, tea, rubber plantations from tropical mangrove forests, to despoliation of pastoral settlements into wastelands for oil exploration, or violation of sovereignty for fisheries on the coastlines of countries in the Global North, have been experienced in Gabon, India, Congo, Sri Lanka, Nigeria, Central African Republic, and Somalia among others (Deckard 2010, 34; Nixon 2011, 43; Saro-Wiwa 1995, 96). These create outrage in the exploited societies.

Ecological crises are sometimes caused by elites within a given community or foreign powers that have an interest in the country's material resources. Along this line of logic, Ursula (2010) argues that "postcolonial ecocriticism attempts to make new contributions to the analysis of how imperialism, colonialism, neocolonialism, and postcolonialism not only create basic conditions of inequality between colonizer and colonized," but also "give rise to complex material and symbolic transition between the different tribes, classes, nations, and interest groups that situate themselves differently in these basic conditions, and that define and determine each other unevenly" (255). The expression of these outraged communities is embedded in the brushstrokes of Buhari's *Landscapes of the Soul*. This effort to demand environmental justice is captured by Deckard (2010, 32):

> Within the developing field of postcolonial ecocriticism, critics are increasingly exploring the efficacy of postcolonial literatures and literary criticism [and art] to formulate resistive discourses to the economic dispossession, social justice, and environmental degradation resulting from the continuing forms of colonialism and processes of global development across the world.

The aforementioned are rooted in most colonized spaces. Thus, Ursula (2010, 251-253) contends that postcolonial ecocriticism emphasizes that environmental problems cannot be solved without addressing issues of wealth and poverty, overconsumption, underdevelopment, and resource scarcity. Postcolonial critics have highlighted diverse ways in which historical struggles over colonial and neocolonial power structures as well as contemporary conflicts over economic globalization have involved and continue to revolve around fundamental environmental questions like land ownership, energy needs, uses of natural resources, agricultural systems, pollution, and exposure to risk which has local and global patterns of consumption.

BUHARI'S ECO-POETICS, AND THE AESTHETICS OF GLOBAL GREEN MORALITY

The Global North advocates for green energy and a clean environment, because "greenness is the ultimate luxury of the consumer society," which shows that the growing interest in nature was not so much a rejection of the modern world, but a proper fulfilment of it

(Guha and Martinez-Alier 2006, xiv). The desire for capitalist ventures makes it appear as though the postmaterialist framework does not allow for the expression of environmental concern in the less developed world (suggesting African villagers and Asian peasants), where "nature is not a friend but a hostile force to be propitiated" (2006, xiv). This is probably why Lawrence Summers, then president of the World Bank, with a voice loaded with global managerial reasoning, suggests "a scheme to export rich nation garbage, toxic waste, and heavily polluting industries to Africa" (Nixon 2011, 2), which is not only a form of toxic imperialism, but environmental racism.

In the eyes of the Global North, the less developed are less concerned about organic gardening, but in fertilizers, pesticides, and fungicides, the very things that give renewed strength to the opponents of modern technology. In a similar vein, Eric Hobsbawm argues that "the main support for ecological policies comes from the rich countries and from the comfortable middle classes" because the poor, "multiplying and under-employed, wanted more 'development', not less" (Guha and Martinez-Alier 2006, xiv-xv). This establishes an imbalance between the Self and the Other, the Orient and the Occident. This informs Buhari's ecocritical sensibility and aesthetic notions of a global green morality. In trying to contain the bastardization of regional landscapes, socioeconomic violence unfolding in the skyrocketing prices of staple foods and overbearing control of international bodies meddling in the social and political economy of Nigeria during the military era, Buhari (2022, 56) launches a postcolonial shield that triggers his survival instinct because it is ecocritical as well when he posits:

> Restricted by the scarcity of fuel and a crippling decline in purchasing power, the early nineties were a prison of sort – a social prison, political prison, economic prison, emotional prison, and so on. I found that the safest way to be safe, to be mobile, and travel is to travel into the self. So, the grid composition provided me with that landscape and that organized, orderly environment.

In this light, Buhari's unique paintings talk back to Empire in a visual voice which, decades ago, as a subaltern subject, lacked representation (Spivak 1999, 273; Ashcroft, Griffiths and Tiffin, 2003, 28), but finds aesthetic expression with perspectives that even the most well-intentioned outsider cannot approximate. Thus, one of the outstanding achievements of Buhari's collection, particularly in "The Landscapes of the Soul," is the designation of different states and stages of environmental metamorphosis that contrast with the earlier peaceful atmosphere. It demands not a technical solution, rather ecological problems that requires "making choices and decisions – about what to produce, what to consume, on what energy to rely – which ultimately concern the very way of life of a people; as such, they are not technical, but are eminently political in the most radical sense of involving fundamental social choices" (Zizek 2009, 25). It suggests that an existentialist path, one that is both political and socially conscious, must be taken towards the restoration of landscapes undergoing destruction to their original state.

"Anthills of Nsukka" is a 2008-2009 painting executed in 96 dream-like grids, concerned with an Eastern Nigerian landscape. The title coincidentally intimates the historic birth of a literary Renaissance that unfolded at the University of Nigeria (UNN), as captured by Maik Nwosu (2005) in "Children of the Anthill: Nsukka and the Shaping of Nigeria's 1960s Literary Generation." The word "Anthill," aside from being the name of an art collective at Nsukka that draws a rich roll call of Nigeria's writers like Chinua Achebe, who has a novel titled *Anthills of the Savannah* (1987), Odia Ofeimun, Tunde Fatunde, Niyi Osundare, Obiora Udechukwu, Ezenwa Ohaeto, Ifi Amadiume, Ossie Enekwe, Chimalum, among others, holds ecological and metaphysical significance. Here is what Nwosu (2005, 38) says about its most dominant feature:

> Shaped in part as hills that seemed to have been anthills once upon a time or as a network of anthills aspiring to become bigger hills, depending on one's angle of perception, Nsukka exuded a cultural aura rooted in a spiritual aesthetic relatable to its rituals and festivals.

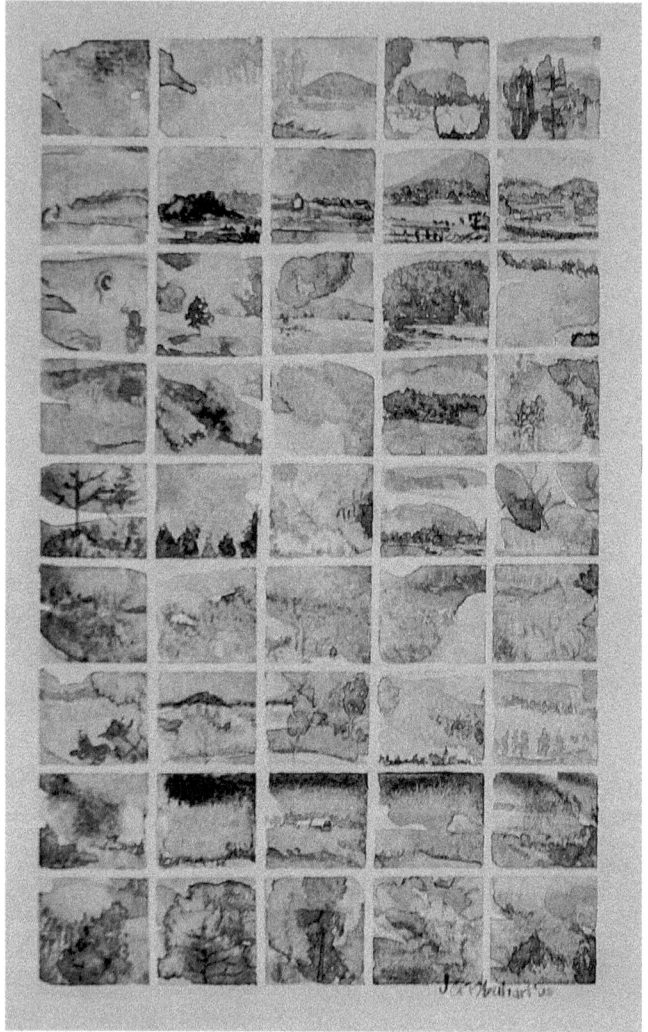

Figure 9.2.
"The Landscapes of the Soul," Watercolor on paper, 6.4x9 inches, Jerry Buhari, 2005.

Buhari's ecocritical consciousness captures the natural environment in its unaltered state, with the mindful understanding that ants can only build to such a magnitude in an ecosystem that suits them. Buhari contributes to a pastoral nostalgia for the wild. His "Anthills of Nsukka," epitomizes landscapes that extol beautiful notions of a wilderness, "signifying nature in a state uncontaminated by civilization," and "is the most potent construction of nature available to New World environmentalism. (Garrard 2004, 59). It exudes the type of atmosphere Garrard posits is "mobilized to protect particular habitats and species, and is seen as a place for the reinvigoration of those tired of the moral and material pollution of the city" (59). Buhari's painting (Figure. 9.4) below is symbolic of a rural countryside with mudbrick and thatched huts, capturing natural habitats that straddle the borders of Nigeria and are the heart of a university town referred to as its intellectual anthill (Nwosu 2005, 38).

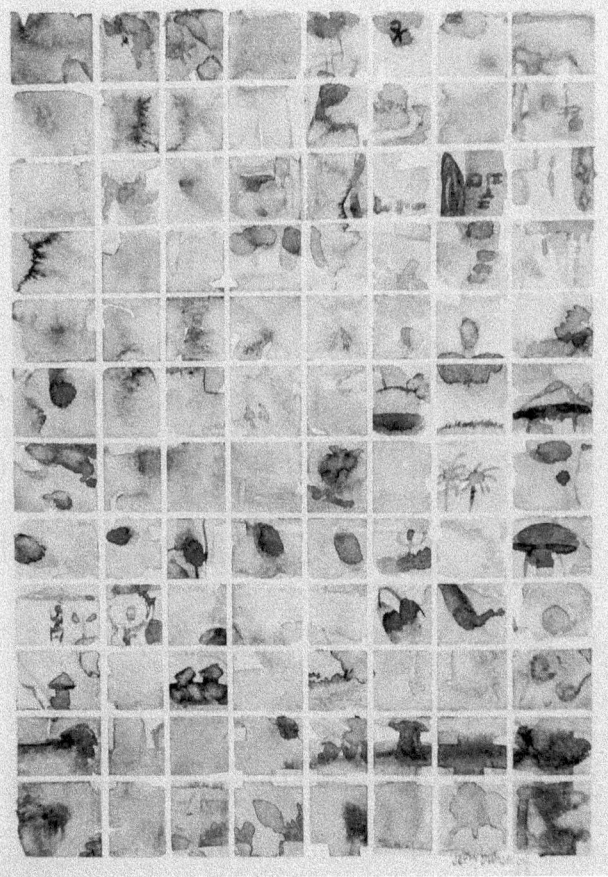

Figure 9.3.
"Anthills of Nsukka," Watercolor on paper, 9x13 inches, Jerry Buhari, 2008-2009.

ECOLOGICAL LAMENTATIONS AND THE DIALOGUES OF TOMORROW

Ronald Inglehart, in Guha and Martinez-Alier (2006), contends that "rapid economic growth since World War II had, through the creation of a mass consumer society, led to the satisfaction of material needs and expectation for the vast majority of the population" (xiv). At the same time, Nixon (2011, 106) warns that the greater a nation's reliance on a single product for its economic survival, the higher its chances of being riddled by corruption and unsettling its income distribution, which unfortunately is the Nigerian situation. Buhari captures an environmental crisis and its implications on the Niger Delta region in "Warm Spillage." The painting is in conversation with the Nigerian landscape, where oil is drilled for export and revenue generation. Buhari calls attention to rural areas, farms, or creeks where the people depend on their livelihoods by presenting the bottom soil with its little patch peeping from above, as illustrated in figure 9.4.

The bottom shows the earth bleeding from different runnels of earth that cascade in liquids of diverse colors, like tributaries. The red hue spilling from the earth could be inferred as the blood of the innocent victims who have lost their homes or lives for the soil. It pictorializes their blood mixing with the oil, amidst other minerals, including sap from the wounded roots of trees cut down during excavations to reach the "black gold". The painting epitomizes the environmental crisis of the Niger Delta and narrativizes ecological degradations happening below sea level. The cut-out round pipes, which could be the product of oil bunkering or vandalism, amidst holes that may later permit gas flares, offer a graphic but grim picture of a brewing disaster. There is a double narrative here: the loss of Mother Earth at the bottom and the loss of livelihood for the inhabitants at the top, signaling the Mexican proverb that where there is land, there is bloodshed. Buhari's "Warm Spillage," lends its colors to the voice of Ojaide (1994) – a native of the Niger Delta, who in "No Longer Our Own Country," laments the senseless destruction of "our original neighbors, the trees and animals" (16) thus:

Figure 9.4.
"Warm Spillage," Mixed media on paper, 11x18 inches, Jerry Buhari, 2016.

> Our sacred trees have been cut down
> To make armchairs for the rich and titled;
> Our totem eagle, that bird of great heights,
> Has been shot at by thoughtless guardians…
> …

> Where are the tall trees
> that shielded us from the sun's spears,
> where are they now that hot winds
> blow parching sands
> and bury us in dunes?

Ojaide, like the Kithiko-Hachiko *satyagraha* in India, which was an affirmation of peasant claims over disputed property, is not merely asserting ownership of the land, but rhetorically asking: What are trees for? (Guha and Martinez-Alier 2006, 13). He addresses the loss of the natural environment around the 1970s and 1980s, thereby showing that the loss never stops, as Buhari's painting of 2016 testifies. The oil boom, unfortunately, became a curse for the inhabitants. It resonates with Rachel Carson's warning that "if left unchecked, capitalism's appetite for the unregulated, specialist consumer product will leave behind a trail of non-specialist fatalities" (Nixon 2011, x). Buhari's *Landscapes of the Soul* reminds us that Global warming did not happen overnight, but was given impetus by neoliberal intensification of resource excavation and capitalist industrialization, which fuels the material hunger of expanding markets. Roos and Hunt (2010, 3) refer to it as "globalism," which is perceived as latter-day colonialism strategically based on economic and cultural imperialism. Buhari's paintings are knitted in a manner that thematizes environmental degradation with regard to the for-profit industrialists and political leaders who are power-thirsty and wish to have the last sentence. "Dark Melting Planet" in figure 9.5 exemplifies the outcome of such greed.

Morton (2016) in his concern about the planet argues that "Just as World War II was the viral code that broke the program of a certain imperialism, one wonders whether global warming will be the viral code that breaks the machinations of a certain neoliberal capitalism and whether this will shut down agrilogistics [an agricultural program so successful that it now dominates agricultural techniques planetwide] itself" (46). Morton further interrogates the "development" for the price paid in part because "agrilogistics is the smoking gun behind chimneys responsible for the Sixth Mass Extinction – global warming, and underlies all 'civilized' forms thus far, from slave-owning societies to Soviets" (43, 46).

Figure 9.5.
"Dark Melting Planet," Mixed media on paper, 14x14.6 inches, Jerry Buhari, 2016.

Morton argues that the very concept of the "world" as the temporality region suffused with human destiny emerges from agrilogistics functioning (46). As Buhari's *Landscapes of the Soul* demonstrates, the region of ecological catastrophe does not limit its planetary harm, and calls for a need to care about even nonhumans in a more dignified way because "ecological awareness means thinking and acting ethically and politically on a lot of scales, not just one," as everything is connected in this "fragile web of life" (Morton 2018, 23) and we have the whole world in our hands.

Buhari's "Soft Masquerades Pretending to be Iroko," metaphorically interrogates the motif of political leaders with regard to their environment, and how they pretend to be messiahs of their society. In this case, saviors of the environment. Particular attention should be given to the fact that in Yoruba cosmology, "the iroko tree takes a special designation as the abode of the spirits, which protects it from indiscriminate exploitation" (Iheka 2018, 7), and is perceived as bearing rooted connections to the people's destiny. Buhari responds to the scary political situation in Nigeria, as can be seen in Figures 9.7 and 9.8, that the painting is populated with human forms, representing leaders who are ready to sacrifice the future of the country for their electoral seats (Akinwande 2022, 24).

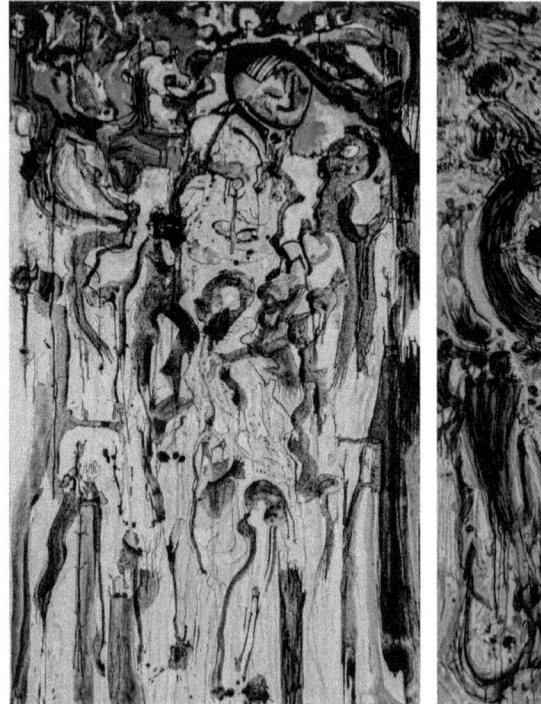 

Figures 9.6. & 9.7.
Figure 9.6. (L) "Soft Masquerades Pretending to be Iroko Trees," Acrylic on Canvas, 36.2x60.2 inches, Jerry Buhari, 2022, and Figure 9.7. (R) "Landscapes of Angels and Devourers," Acrylic on canvas, 35.8x58.3 inches, Jerry Buhari, 2020-2022.

The figures, like leaders in the Global South, are environmentally sensitive, but give way to foreign investors willing to stash their coiffures at the detriment of the poor. This has a postcolonial ecocritical twist because of the imperialist implication of signing off a people's natural resources to industrialists in the Global North who claim to bring development to communities, but have proven to act contrary to their promises. There is a synergy between the paintings; one permits the other to happen, and as replicated in other climes where communities are at the receiving end of ecological degradation, Guha and Martinez-Alier (2006) posit:

> To put it in more explicitly ecological terms, these conflicts pit 'ecosystem people' – that is, those communities which depend very heavily on the natural resources of their own locality – against 'omnivores', individuals and groups with the social power to capture, transform and use natural resources from a much wider catchment area; sometimes, indeed, the whole world. The first category of ecosystem people includes, the bulk of [India's] rural population: small peasants, landless labourers, tribals, pastoralists, and artisans. The category of omnivores comprises industrialists, professionals, politicians, and government officials – all of whom are based in the towns and cities as well as a small but significant fraction of the rural elite, the prosperous farmers in tracts of heavily irrigated, chemically fertilized Green Revolution agriculture (12).

The omnivores in this case—devourers in Buhari's painting —capture resources to feed their industrial machines at the expense of local production, development, and growth, thereby collapsing the subsistence of the ecosystem. This sets in motion the concept of the "environmentalism of the poor" which Guha and Martinez-Alier (2006) aver could be understood as "the resistance offered by ecosystem people to the process of resource capture by omnivores: as embodied in movements against large dams by tribal communities to be displaced by them, or struggles by peasants against the diversion of forest and grazing land to industry" (12). In this light, Buhari's aforementioned paintings draw attention to ecological degradation through impressionist and abstract portrayals of societal realities, challenging subordinating narratives. It captures Global Warming. Morton (2018, 5) refers to it as the sixth extinction in human history, and further states that it should not be called Global Warming, but rather mass extinction, which could be the age we are living in.

CONCLUSION

The care of the planet and its concomitant concerns are not the exclusive domain of the rich or the Global North, but have become a universal responsibility that can be initiated through a global green morality. Buhari's *Landscapes of the Soul* (2022) presents an expansive examination of the beauty of our cultural, physical, and sociological landscapes, as well as the impact of environmental degradation on not only the Global South but also the North. Postcolonial Ecocriticism as explored in this chapter, calls attention to social and environmental justice as a Siamese subject that must be confronted if progress is to be made, first, in confronting the environmentalism of the poor usually found or created in the Global South or outraged communities; and to being more sensitive towards the Anthropocene effect on the changing planet. Though Buhari's environmentalist paintings caution against capitalist greed and a consumerist culture that has neglected the moral arc of conscience, he remains optimistic about the need and search for credible solutions to the environmental crises and resource wars still bedeviling the Global North and South, as well as the planet.

REFERENCE

Akinwande, Ayo. 2022. "Proverbs of Ashes, Defenses of Clay." In *Landscapes of the Soul*, 21–25. Lagos: Ko Publication.

Ashcroft, Bill, Gareth Griffiths, and Helen Tiffin. 2006. *The Post-Colonial Studies Reader*. 2nd ed. London: Routledge.

Buell, Lawrence. 1995. *The Environmental Imagination: Thoreau, Nature Writing, and the Formation of American Culture*. Cambridge, MA: Belknap Press of Harvard University Press.

Buhari, Jerry. 2022. *Landscapes of the Soul*. Lagos: Ko Publication.

Deckard, Sharae. 2010. "Jungle Tide, Devouring Reef: (Post)colonial Anxiety and Ecocritique in Sri Lankan Literature." In *Postcolonial Green: Environmental Politics and World Narratives*, edited by Bonnie Roos and Alex Hunt, 32–48. Charlottesville: University of Virginia Press.

———. 2015. "'The Land Was Wounded': Ecologies, Commodity Frontiers, and Sri Lankan Literature." In *Ecocriticism of the Global South*, edited by Scott Slovic, Swarnalatha Rangarajan, and Vidya Sarveswaran, 35–53. Lanham, MD: Lexington Books.

DeLoughrey, Elizabeth. 2014. "Postcolonialism." In *The Oxford Handbook of Ecocriticism*, edited by Greg Garrard, 320–40. Oxford: Oxford University Press.

Garrard, Greg. 2004. *Ecocriticism*. London: Routledge.

Guha, Ramachandra, and Juan Martínez-Alier. 1997. *Varieties of Environmentalism: Essays North and South*. London: Earthscan.

Heise, Ursula K. 2010. "Postcolonial Environmentalism and the Question of Literature." In *Postcolonial Green: Environmental Politics and World Narratives*, edited by Bonnie Roos and Alex Hunt, 251–79. Charlottesville: University of Virginia Press.

Huggan, Graham, and Helen Tiffin. 2010. *Postcolonial Ecocriticism: Literature, Animals, Environment*. London: Routledge.

Iheka, Cajetan. 2018. *Naturalizing Africa: Ecological Violence, Agency, and Postcolonial Resistance in African Literature*. Cambridge: Cambridge University Press.

Iheka, Cajetan, and Jack Taylor, eds. 2018. "Introduction: The Migration Turn in African Cultural Productions." In *African Migration Narratives: Politics, Race, and Space*, 1–15. Rochester, NY: University of Rochester Press.

Kpade, Sabo. 2022. "Faith in Painting: Jerry Buhari in Conversation with Sabo Kpade." In *Landscapes of the Soul*, 52–77. Lagos: Ko Publication.

Morton, Timothy. 2016. *Dark Ecology: For a Logic of Future Coexistence*. New York: Columbia University Press.

———. 2018. *Being Ecological*. Cambridge, MA: MIT Press.

Nixon, Rob. 2011. *Slow Violence and the Environmentalism of the Poor*. Cambridge, MA: Harvard University Press.

Nwosu, Maik. 2005. "Children of the Anthill: Nsukka and the Shaping of Nigeria's 1960s Literary Generation." *English in Africa* 32 (1): 37–50.

Obodo, Eva, and Ekene Anikpe. 2014. "Engaging the Mundane: The Art of Jerry Buhari, Kuti Usman, Uche Onyishi and George Osodi on the Environmental Question." *Art and Design Studies* 24: 8–15.

Ojaide, Tanure. 1994. "I Want to Be an Oracle: My Poetry and My

Generation." *World Literature Today* 68 (2): 16–19.

Pressley-Sanon, Toni. 2018. "Noo Saro-Wiwa's Migration of the Heart." In *African Migration Narratives: Politics, Race, and Space*, edited by Cajetan Iheka and Jack Taylor, 160–72. Rochester, NY: University of Rochester Press.

Roos, Bonnie, and Alex Hunt. 2010. "Narratives of Survival, Sustainability, and Justice." In *Postcolonial Green: Environmental Politics and World Narratives*, edited by Bonnie Roos and Alex Hunt, 1–13. Charlottesville: University of Virginia Press.

Roy, Arundhati. 2002. *The Algebra of Infinite Justice*. New Delhi: Penguin Books India.

Sachs, Wolfgang. 1992. *The Development Dictionary: A Guide to Knowledge as Power.* London: Zed Books.

Said, Edward W. 1979. *Orientalism.* New York: Vintage Books.

Saro-Wiwa, Ken. 1995. *A Month and a Day: A Detention Diary.* London: Penguin Books.

Slovic, Scott, Swarnalatha Rangarajan, and Vidya Sarveswaran, eds. 2015. *Ecocriticism of the Global South.* Lanham, MD: Lexington Books.

Spivak, Gayatri Chakravorty. 1999. *A Critique of Postcolonial Reason: Toward a History of the Vanishing Present.* Cambridge, MA: Harvard University Press.

Young, Robert. 2004. *White Mythologies: Writing History and the West.* 2nd ed. London: Routledge.

Žižek, Slavoj. 2009. *First as Tragedy, Then as Farce.* London: Verso.

CHAPTER TEN

Art and Society
An Ecocritical Reading of Aliyu Kamal's Fire in My Backyard and EE Sule's Makwala

Abubakar Shehu Usman

INTRODUCTION

Literature, as a discourse about social life, constantly interrogates humanity and its environment. This implies that the environment has always been a part of literature, giving rise to several approaches in literary representation and interpretation. Within the context of Art and Society, creative texts raise awareness about how humans constitute a danger to their natural environment through their quest for survival and desire to maximize profits. It aims to proffer solutions to human and ecological problems through stories that will change human perceptions and relationships with nature, especially those practices that have adverse effects on the environment and, by extension, humanity.

Therefore, the exploitation of nature by humans is bound to bring negative repercussions that can affect both human beings and other non-human organisms. The abuse of resources as represented in the selected texts calls for scrutiny of environmental destruction and the question of injustice, and this can be achieved through ecocriticism. As such, the study undertakes an ecocritical reading of the selected texts to validate the assumptions and objectives of the paper.

POSTCOLONIAL ECOCRITICISM: BACKGROUND AND CONCEPT

This paper employs Postcolonial Ecocriticism as its framework, as ecocriticism and postcolonial theory share similarities that can facilitate a valuable exposition of the works under review. Ecocriticism has its source from two Greek words, Eco (oikos) and Critic (kritis), meaning "house judge." Ecocriticism is a movement known by various names, including Green Cultural Studies, Eco-poetry, Environmental Literary Criticism, Green Poetry, Eco-literature, and Eco/environmental Studies. Historically, Ecocriticism began with the pioneering works of British critic Raymond Williams, who wrote a seminal critique of pastoral literature titled *The Country and the City* in 1973, and the American Joseph Meeker, who wrote *The Comedy of Survival: Literary Ecology and Play Ethics* published in 1974. Ecocriticism, as a movement, owes much to Rachel Carson's *Silent Spring: An Environmental Expose*. These works propose that the environmental crisis is caused primarily by a cultural tradition in the West of separating culture from nature and the elevation of the latter to moral superiority. "Ecocriticism" was coined by William Rueckert, who introduced the term in a 1978 essay titled, *Literature and Ecology: An Experiment in Ecocriticism* and focuses on "the application of ecology and ecological concepts to the study of literature" (Glotfelty and Fromm 1996, 107). In the mid-1980s, the need to establish Ecocriticism as an approach within criticism was addressed through the publication of two seminal works on ecocriticism: Cheryl Glotfelty and Harold Fromm's *The Ecocriticism Reader* (1996) and Lawrence Buell's *The Environmental Imagination* and *Literature and the Environment: An Experiment in Ecocriticism*.

As defined by Lawrence Buell, Ecocriticism is the "study of the relationship between literature and the environment conducted in a spirit of commitment to environmentalist praxis." Buell rejects harmful theoretical notions representing nature as an ideological screen. For Buell, literary texts should contribute to man's interaction with the natural world. Ecocritics encourage others to think seriously about the relationship between humans and nature, about the ethical and aesthetic dilemmas posed by the environmental crisis, and about how language and literature transmit values with profound ecological implications. Cheryl Glotfelty, as one of the major proponents, explains Ecocriticism as the study of the relationship between literature and the physical environment. Just as feminist criticism examines language and literature from a gender-conscious perspective and Marxist criticism brings an awareness of modes of production and economic class to its reading of texts, Ecocriticism takes an earth-centered approach to literary studies (Glotfelty 1996, xviii).

Since the emergence of Ecocriticism, there have been different shades of it, although all emphasize the welfare of the ecosystem, employing eco-philosophy, environmental ethics, evolutionary biology, eco-psychology, ecology, and other related disciplines. The enormity of the environmental crises the world is witnessing today demands urgent attention to environmental issues and calls for immediate action to salvage the situation. Henry Thoreau, as quoted in Bertens (Thoreau 1854, quoted in Bertens, 199), opines that, "By avarice and selfishness and a groveling habit, from which none of us is free, of regarding the soil as property, or the means of acquiring property chiefly the landscape is deformed, husbandry is degraded with us, and the farmer leads the meanest of lives". The gravity of these problems becomes a primary call to action for all to come on board and provide solutions to a colossal problem facing humanity.

However, Scott Slovic (2000, 160-162) offers a broad description of "Ecocriticism as the study of explicitly environmental texts from any scholarly approach or, conversely, the scrutiny of ecological implications and human-nature relationships in any text, even texts that seem, at first glance, oblivious of the nonhuman world". Similarly, Simon Estok (2001, 220) in his contribution explicates that Ecocriticism is more than "simply the study of nature or natural things in literature. Rather, it is a theory that is committed to affecting change by analysing the function- thematic, artistic, social, historical, ideological, theoretical or otherwise of the natural environment or aspects of it represented in documents – literary or others that contribute to material practices in material worlds". This definition echoes the functional approach of Ecocriticism, which analyses the analogies between ecosystems and imaginative texts and posits that such texts potentially have a regenerative function in the cultural system (Estok 2001, 223).

For some African critics, such as Slaymaker (2002, 684), "Ecocriticism… appears as another hegemonic discourse from the Metropolitan West…." He further adds that "the suspicion that environmentalism in all its various shades of green is a 'white' thing borne out by the explosive growth of research and participation by white scholars in and outside

Africa has contributed to the low visibility of ecocriticism in recent African writing." This is temporal as Black African-Nigerian poets such as Niyi Osundare, Tanure Ojaide and Nnimmo Bassey have joined their counterparts in this globalized interest that "environmental literature and ecological criticism are resonating dynamic signals which generate concern for the health of the earth and its resources" (Slaymaker 2002, 691). Moreover, Ecocriticism has much to offer and Karla and Kathleen (31) posit that "the applications and theory that Ecocriticism develops… broadens understandings of how modern cultural assumptions about the environment have developed." Lawrence Buell (2005, 33) postulates the following four principles in appraising any literary composition eco-critically:

> The environment is present not merely as a framing device but as a presence that begins to suggest that human history is implicated in natural history.
>
> The human interest is not understood to be the only legitimate interest.
> Human accountability to the environment is part of the text's ethical orientation.
> Some sense of the environment as a process rather than as a constant is at least implicit in the text.

The application of ecological efforts to postcolonial criticism is relatively new. Its introduction has led to debate on issues of "settler culture" and the use of territorial metaphor to reflect on the changing patterns of land use and spatial perception. The intersection between postcolonial ecological concerns and ecocriticism is, however, gaining momentum in recent times.

Postcolonial Ecocriticism, according to Mukherjee (2011, 177), is the "complex interplay of environmental categories such as water, land, energy, and habitat, migration with political or cultural categories such as state, society, conflict, literature and visual arts." He asserts in the same vein that "any field purporting to attach interpretative importance to the environment must be able to trace the social, historical and material coordinates of categories such as forest, rivers, bio-regions and species" (Mukherjee 2011, 145). Since postcolonial studies is a rejection of the viewpoints fostered on colonized communities through education and religion, one that includes a reaction and portrayal of nature and the environment, Postcolonial Ecocriticism thus becomes a veritable marriage where discourses challenging colonial imagination can be explored. According to Dominic Heads, in both Ecocriticism and Postcolonial theories, there is "an informed recentring common to the different branches of post modernism such as post-colonialism and ecologism". Mukherjee (2011, 178) gives the historical account of the Postcolonial and Eco-Studies and submits that both fields developed and entrenched "roughly in the same historical moment".

For Graham Huggan and Helen Tiffin (2010, 6), "Postcolonial ecocriticism and Ecocriticism are hedged about with seemingly insurmountable problems. The two fields are notoriously difficult to define, not least by their practitioners. Beginning with Post-colonialism, this theory examines and responds to the cultural and ideological legacy of colonialism. The theory offers intensive studies of people and the culture affected by colonialism; certainly, literature plays a crucial role in imparting knowledge to people about colonial and non-colonial descent. This theory celebrates the historicity of events, sculpture, documents, music, art, and people. Moreover, post-colonialism attacks the centuries of slavery and economic and physical exploitation of native people and their lands and resources. It dismantles the social hierarchical structure, which is based on Western thought and epistemology, and empowers the colonized and marginalized to speak for themselves. Postcolonial Ecocriticism is therefore a variety of Ecocriticism that addresses "concerns with conquest, colonization, racism, sexism, along with its investments in theories of indigeneity and diaspora and the relations between native and invader, societies and cultures." Huggan and Tiffin (2010, 6) explicate ecocritical modes of Feminist Ecocriticism, Romantic Ecocriticism, and Postcolonial Ecocriticism as the "need to be understood as particular ways of reading" (Huggan and Tiffin 2010, 13). Irrespective of the different discourses about Ecocriticism and Postcolonial Ecocriticism, this study posits that "Postcolonial Ecocriticism cannot be appraised without delving into environmental issues just as Ecocriticism or Eco/environmental Studies cannot be addressed without delving into postcolonial issues alongside imperialism" (Clarke 2011, 7). Suffice it to mention that many great scholars such as William Rueckert, Cheryl Glotfelty, Harold Fromm, and Greg Gerrard, among others, have attempted and presented acceptable definitions.

Huggan and Tiffin (2010, 79) opine that "postcolonial ecocriticism preserves the aesthetics function of the literary text while drawing attention to its social and political usefulness, its capacity to set out symbolic guidelines for the material transformation of the world". The advocacy strength or the protest powers of postcolonial ecocriticism has made some critics refer to it as Eco-Socialist. Reacting to the eco-socialist label, Anthony Vital, in his essay "Toward an African Ecocriticism", suggests that "reconciling postcolonial criticism and eco/environmental criticism might need taking the complex interplay of social history with the natural world and how language both shapes and reveals such interactions" (Vital 2008, 90).

Bonnie Roos and Alex Hunt emphasize the importance of paying attention to a variety of issues or problems related to postcolonial environments:

> As we see it, postcolonial green scholarship must define itself not as a narrow theoretical discourse, but as a relatively inclusive methodological framework that is responsive to ongoing political and ecological problems and to diverse kinds of texts… Our goal is not to suggest a universalizing approach through some magical half-way, in between 'common ground,' but rather to grapple with the issues that each of the various writers presented here offers us (Ross and Hunt 2010, 9).

Postcolonial Ecocriticism rejects the idea of development that propels the growth of global corporate interests and proposes an alternative development that takes cognizance of the people's culture, history, and future. It frowns upon development that destroys the people's habitat and preoccupation, reducing humans to expendable materials. This is the attraction and the nature of postcolonial ecocriticism. It is a theory that is responsive to the socio-political and psychological needs of people who have been battered by political bastardization, economic slavery, colonialism, intellectual subjugation, and crass servitude.

The basic assumptions and generalizations of Postcolonial Ecocriticism constitute the tenets that define the theory. These assumptions of postcolonial Ecocriticism theory center on the relationship between Literature and the postcolonial environment. Postcolonial Ecocriticism projects a review of all colonial manifestations, whether material, historical, or ideological, which may also include environmental issues. It, however, promotes cultural and primordial attachment to place. According to Huggan and Tiffin (2010), "Postcolonial Ecocriticism concerns itself with conquest, colonization, racism, sexism along with its investments in theories of indigeneity and diaspora and the relations between native and invader, societies and cultures" (6).

Moreover, Postcolonial Ecocriticism examines environmental issues from a socio-political angle, particularly in relation to the exploitation of resources for political or economic gain. Postcolonial Ecocriticism preserves the aesthetic function of the literary text while drawing attention to its social and political usefulness, its capacity to establish symbolic guidelines for the material transformation of the world. It is a theory that is responsive to the socio-political and psychological needs of people who have been battered by political bastardization, economic slavery, colonialism, intellectual subjugation, and crass servitude. Additionally, Postcolonial ecocriticism helps generate an alternative perspective on the issue of nature and the environment, shifting away from the previously dominant exploitative view imposed on colonized minds.

Therefore, an ecocritic is a person who judges the merits and faults of writings that depict the effect of culture upon nature with the view of celebrating nature, bearing its despoilers and reversing their harm through political actions (Rueckert 1996, 107). To this end, ecocritical examinations of environmental exploitation, destruction of human and non-human habitats and how these motifs are expressed or disguised in a text may also be readily applied to the existing body of post-colonial theory.

POSTCOLONIAL MANIFESTATION AND ENVIRONMENTAL ADVOCACY IN ALIYU KAMAL'S FIRE IN MY BACKYARD AND E.E. SULE'S MAKWALA

Capitalism is a concept and way of life with various dimensions; while some believe it broadens economic opportunities, others recognize it as an exploitative system that leads to the erosion of traditional ways of life. Capitalism has the potential for both positive and negative effects on development, just like any other economic system, mainly depending on how its essential elements are applied; unfortunately, in many societies, governments violate these principles, making it impossible to defend the proposition of the existence of pure capitalism (Ali 2016, 103).

For Urry (2011, 50), "capitalism has gone too far, devouring the very preconditions of economic and social life, problematising its own long term viability... and demonstrating extraordinary level of dysfunction and disequilibrium." Therefore, Nigeria's ecological problems are the outcome of structures of hegemony and elitism geared to exploit the common people and the natural world. Sule's novel condemns the industrialists and their cohorts who scheme to plunder Nigeria's natural resources for profit. On the contrary, the novelist suggests a sustainable relationship with the ecosystem in opposition to the inclination for modern technological progress. As such, Sule depicts the relationships between the factory owners, who are mostly invaders, and the people of Makwala. Most of the youth in Makwala are factory workers and they are not paid well, but rather are maltreated by police men in the factory. Michael said:

> Oga sorry o. Hm, dis policemen be wan kill you o. But Oga you no see say wetin Ogaja Boy talk na true? Dis factory owner dem be real wicked o. Na so de MD dey use police deal with people anyhow (2018, 175).

In the streets of Makwala, life is not easy, and everyone is struggling for survival. Government is not helping them, fighting and stabbing are very normal in Makwala. Both males and females go to work; some open shops for business, while others have drinking joints. ".... each house frontage boasting a bar where in the afternoon men, bare chested, their arms growing muscular from factory work, sat and played draughts." Sule's

(2018, 239) postcolonial ecocritics are responsive to the social-political and psychological needs of people who have been battered by capitalism, political bastardization, and economic slavery. Sule depicts how the people of Makwala are being battered by their political leaders and elites. Thus:

> They want to maim all of us. They want to use our blood to make their money. Then they will take the money away to their country and leave us all broken in our own country. See all the factory owners in this layout are Indians, Pakistanis and Lebanese. What they do to maximize profits is to bring machines that will take our blood, after all there are modern machines that don't hurt people, but they will not buy them (2018, 166-167).

Regarding these expressions, the novelist advocates a pragmatic approach to saving the earth. He believes that industrial civilization is fundamentally unsustainable; thus, it must be dismantled to secure a livable future for all species. Sixtus Ibekwe (2019, 7) posits that "Rapid industrialization that took place mainly in the cities of Nigeria brought along with it a special kind of social movement that involved large amount of people moving away from the rural areas to the urban areas in search of jobs and other opportunities." As a consequence, money became the only valuable thing, and the government started rapid privatization of the economy; as a result, the economy became capitalist-based. From an ecocritical perspective, *Makwala* confirms that Nigerian rulers, in alliance with multinational companies, subvert the Nigerian ecological order by overexploiting natural resources for power, wealth, and profit. Therefore, Sule offers ideas on how to take necessary actions to salvage the Nigerian space. Consequently, human accountability to the environment, environmental awareness, and the notion of environmental praxis are observable in Sule's *Makwala*.

The title of the novel, *Fire in My Backyard*, connotatively suggests a catastrophic disaster that is close to our environment. Kamal tries to draw the attention of the members of his society to take some precautionary measures to avert it before it gets out of control. In other words, he aims to raise awareness about the dangers of rampant tree cutting, wood burning, and other forms of environmental degradation. In *Fire in My Backyard*, Kamal discusses the inappropriate use of the natural environment by the people of Northern Nigeria. He describes the inconsiderate relationships between people in rural areas and those in the city with their environment. Such inconsiderate relationships include excessive tree logging and wood consumption, inadequate drainage in the city, and the excessive use of diesel engines and machines. All these are what Kamal discusses, and he considers these activities as the agents of desertification and pollution. For instance, He describes how trees are being rampantly cut as follows:

The first identifiable incident occurs when Umar-Farouq visits his aunt's house and finds that the beautiful tree that used to shade them has been cut down. "There only tree in the house had been cut. Their compound looked stark, bare, barren" (Kamal 2004, 25). And he continues to talk about the regular wood logging. "Logging continued even while the desert sands were creeping slowly towards the denuded fields" (Kamal 2004, 26), and it is also seen that in the urban areas, the source of fuel is wood. For example, when Umar-Farouq visits his aunt, Dija, he finds that they use wood to cook. The author also describes the dry season as the time when tree destruction reaches its peak, during which even living trees are put to death by the use of poisonous chemicals. Kamal also continues to show how wood logging persists in the Kano metropolis, as people are busy expanding their farms and converting forests into bare land.

Additionally, the scarcity of green grass during dry seasons prompts herders to pluck and cut branches of trees to provide nutritious food for their animals.

> Unfortunately the tree leafed only in dry weather and so attracts the sticks of herdsmen who plucked the nutritious leaves as a supplement to the lost of carotene in dull, a brown grass (Kamal 2004, 128).

Furthermore, the issue of environmental degradation continues, as explained by Kamal when Umar-Farouq arrives in Kano. The destructive acts in Kano include the noise of diesel engines, which makes the atmosphere less conducive, the smoke that covers the sky, and inadequate drainage systems. Kamal describes:

> There was no underground drainage in this metropolis-soiled water collected where it would after, from clogged, open gutter or backyard drains pipe...used carrier bags innumerably black, added to the muck; others were blown about and getting entangled with threadbare roadside emissions, davish coos and the deafening reverberation of the local diesel grinding machines (Kamal 2014, 25).

Kamal also describes how Kano is gradually destroyed by the people in chapter thirteen of the novel.

> ...the deposition of rubbish, uncovered and ill-assorted all over the place ...The pavement with the smelly drains, usually left partially-open, offers the exorbitant rental fees to display their wares...the flyblown gutter pills, with the miasma of car and bike exhaust fumes drifting, like the smoke of incense sticks, all over the hubbub the surge of humanity... (Kamal 2004, 206-207).

Again, Kamal describes the nature of people's activities in Kano: "The common urban noise...There was no underground drainage in this new metropolis..." (Kamal 2004, 24).

Expressively and implicitly, Kamal portrays and foresees some negative consequences of people's inappropriate relationship with their natural environment. One of the significant looming dangers Kamal foresees is desert encroachment. He demonstrates that desertification is inevitable if excessive logging persists. Kamal sounds like an environmentalist who wants to prevent the Kano region from desert encroachments. He clearly shows that through the thoughts of his central character, Umar-Farouq. For example, "logging continued even while the desert sands were creeping slowly towards the denuded fields" (Kamal 2004, 126). Again, in another part of the novel, he shows the negative consequences of logging.

> This discovery proved Umar-Farouq right confirmed his

> hypothesis...deprived Kano of its environmental heritage, further slowing down the trend towards modernization and paving the way for speedy ... borgie of the Sahara desert (Kamal 2004, 125).

Additionally, Kamal views pollution as one of the major environmental problems. The pollution can be either air or noise pollution. This danger is anticipated to occur if sound drainage systems are not built within the city and if local diesel engines and machines are used excessively. It is also unavoidable if refuse is dumped anywhere. Kamal here, seems to explain that excessive use of local diesel engines and machines will make the atmosphere noisy and smoky, thereby polluting the air and affecting our hearing. A lack of good drainage produces soiled, dirty, and odorous water, which may help spread diseases.

Therefore, Kamal clearly portrays the destructive activities of people in Kano against their environment, including deforestation, inadequate drainage in urban areas, and other environmental degradation. He also advocates for people to be environmentally conscious by portraying the disasters that will endanger the well-being of the people and their environment. And these looming dangers he foresees in his work, *Fire in My Backyard*, will bring people to their conscious and careful handling of their dear natural environment.

CONCLUSION

Unlike the other eco-critical writers, Aliyu Kamal and Emmanuel Egya Sule's voice of fighting against environmental degradation resonates with all individuals, regardless of class or geographical area, as well as Non-governmental Organizations, the government, and even international communities. They demonstrate that every individual has a role to play in mitigating environmental disorder. To this end, the chapter shows the socio-environmental relevance of *Fire in My Backyard and Makwala* in that it does not merely address diverse areas of environmental problems, but also pinpoint the adverse causes, effects, as well as man's role, either individually or collectively, directly or indirectly, locally or internationally to the aggravation of environmental crises.

REFERENCES

Abubakar, Tanimu A. N., Ezekiel S. Akuso, and Edward O. Abah. 2014. "An Exploration of the Hermeneutical Phases of Ecocriticism." *Global Journal of Arts, Humanities and Social Sciences* 2 (7): 1–6.

Ali, Abbas J. 2016. *Capitalism: An Islamic Perspective*. London: Routledge.

Becket, Fiona, and Terry Gifford. 2007. *Culture, Creativity and Environment: New Environmentalist Criticism*. Amsterdam and New York: Rodopi B.V.

Buell, Lawrence. 1995. *The Environmental Imagination: Thoreau, Nature Writing in the Formation of American Culture*. Cambridge, MA: Belknap Press.

Estok, Simon C. 2001. "A Report Card on Ecocriticism." *AUMLA: Journal of the Australasian Universities Language and Literature Association* 96 (November): 200–223.

Glotfelty, Cheryll, and Harold Fromm, eds. 1996. *The Ecocriticism Reader: Landmarks in Literary Ecology*. Athens: University of Georgia Press.

Gogoi, Gitanjali. 2014. "An Eco-Critical Approach to Achebe's *Things Fall Apart* and *Arrow of God*." *IOSR Journal of Humanities and Social Science* 19: 1–20.

Huggan, Graham, and Helen Tiffin. 2010. *Postcolonial Ecocriticism: Literature, Animals, Environment*. London: Routledge.

Ibekwe, Sixtus. 2019. *Urbanization and Industrial Development in Nigeria*. Lagos: University of Lagos Press.

Kamal, Aliyu. 2010. *Fire in My Backyard*. Kaduna State: Ahmadu Bello University Press Limited.

Mukherjee, Pablo. 2011. "Surfing the Second Wave: Amitav Ghosh's *The Hungry Tide*." In *Literature and Globalization: A Reader*, edited by Liam Connell and Nicky Marsh, London: Routledge.

Plumwood, Val. 2002. *Environmental Culture: The Ecological Crisis of Reason*. London: Routledge.

Roos, Bonnie, and Alex Hunt, eds. 2010. *Postcolonial Green: Environmental Politics and World Narratives*. Charlottesville: University of Virginia Press.

Rueckert, William. 1996. "Literature and Ecology: An Experiment in Ecocriticism." In *The Ecocriticism Reader: Landmarks in Literary Ecology*, edited by Cheryll Glotfelty and Harold Fromm, [page numbers if available]. Athens: University of Georgia Press.

Slaymaker, William. 2002. "Ecoing the Other(s): The Call of Global Green and Black African Responses." In *African Literature: An Anthology of Criticism and Theory*, edited by Tejumola Olaniyan and Ato Quayson. London: Blackwell.

Sule, Emmanuel E. 2018. *Makwala*. Lagos: Parresia Publishers.

Sule, Emmanuel E. 2020. *Nature, Environment, and Activism in Nigerian Literature*. New York: Routledge.

Urry, John. 2011. *Climate Change and Society*. Cambridge: Polity Press.

Vital, Anthony. 2008. "Toward an African Ecocriticism." *Research in African Literatures* 39 (1): 87–96.

CHAPTER ELEVEN

Towards Harmonious African Ecosystems
Estrangement and Resilience in Ibirawi Ikiriko and Nnimmo Bassey's Poetry Collections

Abundance Amamchukwu

INTRODUCTION

As long as humans inhabit the earth, ecocriticism will remain a vital avenue for exploring literature's response to environmental issues. Beyond being a fusion of disciplines like ecology, biology, and literature, ecocriticism offers a critique of humanity's interactions with the environment. The Niger Delta, one of Africa's most resource-rich regions, has experienced severe socio-economic and ecological degradation due to extensive oil extraction (Bassey 2002; Ikiriko 2000). This backdrop sets the stage for the exploration of the themes of ecological estrangement and resilience in Ibirawi Ikiriko's *Oily Tears of the Delta* and Nnimmo Bassey's *We Thought It Was Oil but It Was Blood*. Ibirawi Ikiriko and Nnimmo Bassey are both Niger Delta poets, and the titles of their poetry collections under study present a snapshot of what to expect in their poetry. *Oily Tears of the Delta* employs personification to portray the human character of the Delta region, depicting it as being in tears due to the exploitative oil practices (Ikiriko 2000). Similarly, Bassey's "*We Thought It Was Oil But It Was Blood*" takes an ironic stance, depicting the fact that the oil, which is often thought to be a symbol of wealth, is instead a metaphor for blood, death, and decay in the region (Bassey 2002). To this end, Chidi Maduka (2013) is of the view that in the face of this unquantifiable damage to the region, it has produced an enduring body of literature. Just as the trauma of the civil war generated Civil War Literature and the denial of rights to women produced Women's Literature, poets, novelists, playwrights, and literary critics decry the enormity of environmental abuse witnessed in the region, hence the emergence of Niger Delta literature.

Ecocriticism, "the study of the relationship between literature and the physical environment" (Glotfelty 1994), is an essential tool for investigating the themes of ecological estrangement and resilience in the works of Ikiriko and Bassey. It also advocates for environmental justice, calling for reparation of both physical and spiritual environments (Garrard 2002). Ecological estrangement refers to the separation of humans from nature, which results in a destructive relationship. Environmental philosopher Val Plumwood introduced this concept in 1991, arguing that humans' separation from nature leads to its exploitation (Plumwood 1991). Plumwood critiques the Western view of nature as distinct from humans, which fosters an exploitative mindset, while many other cultures emphasize continuity between humans and the natural world.

Central to the theme of estrangement is Robert Nixon's idea of slow violence, outlined in *Slow Violence and the Environmentalism of the Poor* (Nixon 2013). Nixon argues that environmentalism of the poor arises when people are dispossessed of their lands and left to suffer the slow, incremental effects of environmental destruction, such as oil spills and deforestation. Slow violence, which unfolds gradually and invisibly, disproportionately affects impoverished communities. This dispossession leads to estrangement from one's land and community, as represented in both poetry collections under study.

Ken Saro-Wiwa's writings and activism are foundational to understanding the intersection of literature, environmentalism, and social justice in the Niger Delta. His *A Month and a Day: A Detention Diary* (1995) highlights the environmental degradation and human rights abuses caused by oil extraction in Ogoni land. His legacy of resistance to environmental and social injustice laid the groundwork for Ikiriko and Bassey, whose poetry blends ecological concerns with social justice. Helon Habila's *Oil on Water* (2010) is also essential for understanding the consequences of oil exploitation in the Niger Delta. The novel portrays environmental destruction through the experiences of journalists documenting the region's crisis. It explores ecological estrangement on both a psychological and social level, mirroring the themes in Ikiriko and Bassey's poetry.

Both *Oily Tears of the Delta* and *We Thought It Was Oil but It Was Blood* extend the discourse on slow violence and ecological estrangement by focusing on the emotional and spiritual toll of environmental degradation. Bassey's poetry, like Saro-Wiwa's activism, serves as eco-resistance, demanding environmental restoration and social justice.

Niger Delta literature, like that of Tanure Ojaide's *Delta Blues & Home Songs* (1998) and Niyi Osundare's *The Eye of the Earth* (1986), continues to critique the environmental devastation caused by oil exploration. These works emphasize the interconnectedness of human and non-human life and advocate for environmental justice. Literature plays a crucial role in documenting and resisting the environmental degradation of the Niger Delta. Ikiriko and Bassey's poetry not only mourns the destruction but also highlights the resilience of the people who continue to fight for their land and future. This paper examines the complex relationship between humans and their environment, with a focus on ecological alienation and its social and ecological repercussions, as depicted in the poetry collections.

ECOLOGICAL ESTRANGEMENT IN OILY TEARS OF THE DELTA & WE THOUGHT IT WAS OIL BUT IT WAS BLOOD

Estrangement always creates a feeling of disconnection or separation between one thing and another. Ikiriko's *Baseless Compass* presents a stark portrayal of the loss of connection between humanity and nature, highlighting the ecological crisis that people face as a result of the activities of oil exploiters in the fictional setting of his poems. The opening lines of *Baseless Compass* suggest this sense of disconnect:

> We are adrift
> On a spaceship
> With all our rights
> And benefits suspended

The lines "We are adrift / On a spaceship," rather than grounded on solid earth, highlight that the poet-persona and his compatriots have lost their connection to the natural world and are now living in a state of detachment from the environment that sustains them. The use of the word "adrift" also implies a sense of aimlessness and uncertainty, as if humanity has lost its sense of purpose in the absence of a connection to nature (Ikiriko 2000). "With all our rights / And benefits suspended," the persona further drives home the point that even in this state of hopelessness, uncertainty, and disconnect from their environment, their rights have also been taken away from them.

The second stanza of the poem continues to develop the theme of ecological estrangement, with the imagery of "Hope leaks out from our insides / Leaving us empty as a basket of water" (Ikiriko 2000). Here, the poet-persona suggests that human beings have lost their sense of optimism and vitality in the absence of a meaningful relationship with the natural world. The use of the word "basket" also implies that when the connection to nature is lost, the poet-persona and others in his community find themselves empty and depleted like a basket that cannot hold water. The poem then shifts its focus to the concept of "a ship of state" with a "Baseless compass / Bereft of our cardinal point." This image suggests that the society in which the speaker finds himself has lost its sense of direction and purpose, navigating blindly without a clear understanding of its place in the world. The poem's final stanza brings the theme of ecological estrangement to a personal level:

> So, we, the Aborigines of the base,
> Stay, shattered like
> A calabash of crabs
> Crashed on concrete

The "Aborigines of the base" are deeply affected by the loss of connection to nature; they are broken into pieces like "A calabash of crabs / Crashed on concrete" (Ikiriko 2000). The imagery employed in the poem serves to reinforce the sense of despair and futility that can arise from ecological estrangement, ultimately underscoring the urgent need for a reconnection with the environment.

Bassey uses *Gas Flares* to highlight the environmental destruction, displacement, and physical harm caused by these flares, which serve as symbols of exploitation and disregard for the well-being of the local population. The opening line suggests a violent assault on the planet: The earth gassed / Dynamites rocked the storehouse / Of life. The word "gassed" in the first line of the poem has a double meaning, suggesting not only pollution but also a sense of suffocation and asphyxiation. "Dynamites rocking the storehouse of life" describes the impact of human activity on the environment, signifying that the earth is a precious resource that has been depleted (Bassey 2002). The repeated refrain of "The earth gassed" underscores the idea that the planet is under assault and that its natural systems are disrupted in ways that are harmful to other living beings. The speaker uses metaphors in these lines—"A fart delayed / Belching dragons attack / Leaping tongues lick / Roofs, farms"—to describe the destructive impact of these assaults, suggesting a sense of violence and danger (Bassey 2002). In the face of the belching dragons that attack and have destroyed their roofs and farms, and the gassing of the earth which releases harmful toxins signifying air pollution, the people are in a fix. The natural order has been disrupted, they are separated from the earth they once knew, dynamites have rocked their storehouses, and they are left in a dilemma:

> Now the sky is ablaze
> Where will the people go?
> Flee the flames
> Dive into the creek
> Fly!
> The last tortoise is gone
> Escape the raging flames (Bassey 2002, 10).

The speaker submits that the people have been separated from the sky by "Belching dragons…" and "Leaping tongues" (Bassey 2002). However, amid the dilemma to escape, the urgency of action commands them to "Flee the flames / Dive into the creek" and "fly" as a solution to "Escape the raging flames" that threaten to terminate their existence (Bassey 2002). Yet, that solution does not suffice. They are still faced with an utter sense of hopelessness and helplessness: "Now the sea is ablaze." The sea could not save them, and the panic and desperation resurface; the speaker repeats the question, "Where will the people go?" to highlight the displacement caused by the destruction of the natural environment. In the face of "A million explosions" and "A shower of soot," the speaker's clever play on the words, "Oil's not well / That starts a well," provides commentary on the disastrous effect of the exploitation of natural resources, which has caused the people to be alienated from the sky and sea (Bassey 2002).

Similarly, this separation of people from their natural habitat is evident in the poetic setting of *Facial Marks* in Bassey's collection. *Facial Marks* is a commentary on the alienation of indigenous peoples from their land and cultural heritage due to environmental degradation and resource extraction. Bassey uses the poem to highlight the importance of the land and its connection to the people who live on it:

> Facial marks help folks
> Pick out members of the clan
> Environmental scars traced
> By seismic lines and illegal loggers
> Transnational eco-devourers
> Alienate us from our land
> We are strangers to our own soil (Bassey 2013, 10).

The poem opens with imagery of facial marks, which are traditional in some Nigerian cultures and serve as a means of identifying community members. However, the marks are contrasted with "Environmental scars traced / By seismic lines and illegal loggers," which result in the alienation of the people from their land (Bassey 2002). The speaker uses the phrase "Transnational eco-devourers" to portray the predatory role of multinational corporations in exploiting their natural resources and causing environmental destruction. As a result, "We are strangers to our own soil" (Bassey 2002). The use of this phrase highlights the psychological impact of ecological estrangement on individuals and communities in the poetic setting. The degradation of the environment has caused people to lose their connection to their land, culture, and identity, leading to feelings of dislocation and alienation.

Social-ecological Resilience

The concept of social-ecological resilience, as Folke et al. (2010) submit, highlights the importance of understanding the complex interactions between social and ecological systems and the need for interdisciplinary approaches to managing these systems. Ikiriko and Bassey's poems under study not only cry foul at the unjust exploitation of their natural resources by these multinationals, but they also convey an urgent call for action to arise, fight, and reclaim their land. This tone of resilience is prevalent in the title poem in Bassey's collection, *We Thought It Was Oil but It Was Blood*. The poem begins with a joyful scene of people dancing in the streets, believing that they are free:

> The other day
> We danced in the street
> Joy in our hearts
> We thought we were free
> Three young folks fell to our right
> Countless more fell to our left
> Looking up,
> Far from the crowd
> We beheld
> Red-hot guns (Bassey 2013, 12).

However, this joy is quickly overshadowed by the violence that unfolds amidst the celebration. A sense of despair and loss characterizes the image of fallen young people on either side of the crowd. The speaker then looks up and sees red-hot guns, which they initially mistake for oil. The juxtaposition of joy and violence highlights the complexity of life in the poetic setting, where the violence of the oil industry and the government constantly threatens moments of happiness and freedom. The repeated refrain, "We thought it was oil, but it was blood," highlights the notion that the region's oil wealth is founded on the blood of its people (Bassey 2013).

Despite the death, alienation, and despair the people face, there is an urgent call to action towards the end of the collection, which reads:

> They may kill all
> But the blood will speak
> They may again all

But the soil will RISE
We may die
And yet stay alive
Placed on the slab
Slaughtered by the day
We are living
Long sacrificed (Bassey 2013, 32).

The final lines highlight the strength and resilience of the people of the Niger Delta, who have endured immense hardship but continue to fight for justice.

Canadian scholar C.S. Holling introduced the four phases of the adaptive cycle, which characterize the dynamic changes in ecosystems. Holling's adaptive cycle metaphor provides a qualitative description of the development of a dynamically evolving complex system. In discussing the resilience of socio-ecological systems, a resilient system is one that successfully navigates all phases of the adaptive cycle. The four phases of Holling's adaptive cycle include exploitation, conservation, release, and reorganization (Holling 1986).

In Holling's adaptive cycle, the concept of ecological estrangement is observable during the phase of exploitation. During this phase, human beings often exploit the environment for resources without considering the long-term consequences. This exploitation leads to the degradation of flora and fauna, resulting in detachment from the previously harmonious and balanced environment. As a result, human beings become estranged from the wholesome environment they once knew and relied upon (Folke et al. 2010). However, in the subsequent phase of reorganization, the theme of resilience becomes prominent. Despite the damage it has suffered, the environment possesses inherent resilience and the capacity to adapt and transform. This phase is characterized by collective efforts to restore and revitalize the environment, with human beings playing a crucial role as facilitators in the process of reorganization (Folke et al. 2010).

The theme of resilience is highlighted through the lens of Holling's phases of the adaptation cycle in the poem "IV" from Ikiriko's collection *Oily Tears of the Delta*:

Then possess,
O over-possess forever
The midwives
Of these cares
And let this houselessness,
This homelessness,
This total dispossession
They visited on others
Be their lot
Let it be
The lot of their children's children (Ikiriko 2000, 14).

The first phase, "exploitation," is represented by the "midwives of these cares," who over-possess and exploit their power to cause displacement and dispossession. The use of the word "over-possess" implies overexploitation, where resources are used beyond their sustainable limits. The second phase, "conservation," is represented by imagery of houselessness, homelessness, and total dispossession. The third phase, "release," is highlighted by the desire for these exploitative powers to be visited upon the children of those responsible for the exploitation. Finally, the fourth phase, "reorganization," is implied in the call to "shoo these cares," suggesting a renewal process through collective efforts (Ikiriko 2000).

Folke et al. (2010) argue that the purpose of adaptive management and governance is to enhance the adaptive capacity of social-ecological systems, thereby avoiding undesirable thresholds, absorbing shocks, mitigating disruptions, and managing transitions. In this context, Bassey's *We Have One Earth* highlights the collective responsibility required to build resilience in social-ecological systems (Bassey 2013).

The repeated questions in Bassey's poem set a reflective tone, while the image of water slipping away underscores the need for decisive action:

Now we seek to re-discover
Ourselves—dreamers, chanters, cries
Sealed beneath departed mayonnaise long snatched
We must be ready to face
Taking a stand to keep apace

Outside the rat race
We have one earth; we are all in one place! (Bassey 2013, 45).

The speaker urges a fundamental shift in behavior and values, emphasizing that "Men must give nature a break" and calling for the restoration of balance between humans and nature (Bassey, 2013). By emphasizing collaboration, sustainability, and long-term commitment, the poem reaffirms the importance of building resilience in socio-ecological systems (Folke et al. 2010).

CONCLUSION

Ikiriko and Bassey's poems serve as a critique of the devastating ecological disruptions caused by oil exploitation, leading to the alienation of local communities from their natural environment. To achieve a more sustainable and resilient future, prioritizing environmental protection, community engagement, and the adoption of renewable energy is vital. Strengthening regulations, engaging with local communities, investing in restoration, and promoting renewable energy can pave the way for an equitable and prosperous future. Literature, exemplified by the works of Ikiriko and Bassey, plays a pivotal role in catalyzing social-ecological transformation, raising awareness, and fostering solidarity. Embracing resilience thinking, sustainable development, and the power of literature, collaborative efforts are necessary to achieve a sustainable and harmonious future for African ecological systems.

REFERENCES

Bassey, Nnimmo. 2002. *We Thought It Was Oil but It Was Blood*. Ibadan: Kraft Books.

Folke, Carl, Stephen R. Carpenter, Brian Walker, Marten Scheffer, Thomas Elmqvist, Lance Gunderson, and C. S. Holling. 2016. "Social-Ecological Resilience and Biosphere-Based Sustainability Science." *Ecology and Society: A Journal of Integrative Science for Resilience and Sustainability* 21 (3). https://doi.org/10.5751/ES-08748-210341.

Garrard, Greg. 2002. *Ecocriticism*. London and New York: Routledge.

Glotfelty, Cheryl. 1994. "What Is Ecocriticism?" Position paper presented at the meeting of the Western Literature Association, Salt Lake City,

Utah.

Habila, Helon. 2010. *Oil on Water*. London: Penguin Books.

Holling, Crawford. 1986. "The Resilience of Terrestrial Ecosystems: Local Surprise and Global Change." In *Sustainable Development of the Biosphere*, edited by W. C. Clark and R. E. Munn, 292–317. Cambridge: Cambridge University Press.

Ikiriko, Ibirawi. 2000. *Oily Tears of the Delta*. Ibadan: Kraft Books.

Maduka, Chidi. 2013. "The Niger Delta as the Predator's Paradise in Tanure Ojaide's *Tales of the Harmattan*." In *Critical Issues in African Literature: Twenty-First Century and Beyond*, 339–58. Port Harcourt: University of Port Harcourt Press.

Nixon, Rob. 2013. *Slow Violence and the Environmentalism of the Poor*. Cambridge, MA: Harvard University Press.

Plumwood, Val. 1991. "Nature, Self, and Gender: Feminism, Environmental Philosophy, and the Critique of Rationalism." *Hypatia* 6 (1): 3–27. https://doi.org/10.4324/9781315239897-13.

Saro-Wiwa, Ken. 1995. *A Month and a Day: A Detention Diary*. Ibadan: Spectrum Books.

CHAPTER TWELVE

Theatrical Design, Environment, and Children's Theatre Practice in the ABU Studio Theatre

Franklin Pyokpung Zaure

INTRODUCTION

Scenography is a crucial component of theatre and the performing arts. This is because it plays a decisive role in shaping the performance and audience experience. It involves the major visual elements, such as set/scenery, lighting, costume, makeup, sound, and others, which collectively create the ambiance for a performance. As the concept of scenography for stage performance evolves, transforming the spatial relationship between the audience and performers, scenography has also moved beyond traditional paradigms, branching into and incorporating other areas of concern that have a broader impact on humanity. Moreover, for over twenty years, ecocriticism has gained popularity in African literary studies. Although it is frequently used in literature and humanities to examine environmental issues, discussions on eco-scenography in Nigerian theatre and performing arts are relatively few, particularly regarding the built environment that aids in situating and housing performances. Therefore, the performing arts are well-positioned to play a leading role in investigating and showcasing options for sustainable practice as the world enters a new era of environmental consciousness. Notably, scenographers worldwide are beginning to refocus their attention by becoming more environmentally conscious, moving beyond mere creativity and aesthetics. Being "ecological" entails paying attention to how scenographic work impacts and connects to the larger environment, as well as its broader implications. To construct recyclable, biodegradable, restorative, and/or regenerative performance environments, ecological principles must be incorporated. Therefore, this research appraises the 2023 Children's theatre experience at the Ahmadu Bello University Studio Theatre, which features eco-scenography. Ecological design theory undergirds this study.

THEATRE

The term "theatre" involves a broad range of meanings, from a classroom or hospital operating room to a football stadium. However, in the context of the performing arts, a theatre refers to a specialized building designed for hosting performances, such as songs, dances, festivals, and productions. Theatre in the performance arts is an activity or performance in which participants use their bodies—voices, eyes, legs, hands—to communicate or tell stories, for the entertainment and/or education of others. Theatre has been an integral part of human society, with every community developing its unique form of theatre over time and reflecting its distinct way of life (Illah 2004).[1] This is evident in various forms of expression, such as songs, dances, masquerades, storytelling, and dramas, which serve as a reflection of our culture, religion, and outlook. Furthermore, theatre activities are enhanced by theatrical designs, also known as scenography, which include set/scenery, lighting, costumes, makeup, and sound. These elements work in harmony to elevate theatre performances on both stage and film.

THEATRICAL/STAGE DESIGN

The significance of theatrical and stage design in theatre practice is paramount. This is because it forms the very foundation of theatre. It involves the major visual elements of theatre, such as set and scenery, lighting, costume, makeup, and sound, among others. This ensemble is also referred to as scenography and is designed to delight audiences through audiovisual aesthetics, comprising non-verbal communications and imagery that often accompany actions, movement, and renditions on stage. As Enendu (1993, 54)[2] aptly notes, "The practice of scenography is,

---

[1] The design components of theatre which enhances the performance, have also been a part of the human society.
[2] Scenography gives the performance 'form' through visual representations of objects like furniture, actors' costumes, make-up, lighting design, and other forms that bring the performance to life

therefore, an integral part of every theatrical production, as it gives the performance form and situates the production within a culturally acceptable domain, being 'a dwelling place' of the performance." Theatrical/stage design aids in establishing the locale, time, and context of a performance, effectively housing the performance. Moreover, as an integral part of the theatre, scenography assumes a semiotic and symbolic role by contributing to meaning-making through projections of ideas and messages in the form of images, impressions, and colors that support the intent and concepts of a performance or activity. Scholars such as Asomba (2001), Hameed (2011), and Gillette (2013, 165) have emphasized the importance of scenography in various contexts, highlighting its ability to establish the mood and atmosphere of a performance or activity, thereby reinforcing the theme(s). Particularly, McKinney and Butterworth (2009, 7) observe that "Theatrical design defines an active role for the audience because it is completed by the spectator." This emphasizes the function of design in aiding the audience's assimilation of messages contained in the actions and performance, as they become immersed in the entire performance.

THE INTERRELATIONSHIP BETWEEN ECO-SCENOGRAPHY AND ECOCRITICISM

Eco-scenography and ecocriticism share a common concern for the relationship between human culture and the natural environment, in different contexts and media. This connection is rooted in their shared goal of promoting environmental awareness and sustainability. Moreover, ecocriticism is an academic field that studies the representation of nature and the environment in literature and cultural texts. It explores how literature and culture reflect and influence attitudes toward the natural world. It aims to raise awareness of environmental issues, critique anthropocentric perspectives, and promote sustainable practices. Buell (1995) defines ecocriticism as a study of the relationship between literature and the environment conducted in a spirit of commitment to environmentalist praxis. Vaghani (2023, 8)[3] further emphasizes that:

---

3   Ecocriticism is an intentionally broad approach that is by its very nature interdisciplinary. It draws its sustenance from the existing literary theories.

ecocriticism advocates sustainable development for a better future of mankind in general. All organisms have the right to survive in their way. The plants, the animals, the women, the men, the marginal, the tribal - all have their role to play in keeping up the earth's basic life support system. Limited use of resources will ensure the safe and secure future of the generations to come.

In contrast, eco-scenography refers to sustainable and environmentally conscious practices in theatrical design and production. It emphasizes the use of materials that reduce environmental impact, promote ecological awareness, and incorporate natural elements into design. Eco-scenography also aims to minimize the ecological footprint of theatrical productions and engage audiences with themes of sustainability and environmental consciousness. According to Beer (2015, 3):[4]

> Eco-scenography is the integration of ecological principles into all stages of scenographic thinking and production. Ecological thinking acknowledges that materiality and environments are mutually dependent in making beings, things, and places, it recognizes humans as part of nature's system, rather than a separate entity to use nature at its disposal. As a result, the effectiveness of eco-scenographic work is determined not only by its aesthetic results but also by how it interacts with and affects social and environmental systems outside of the theatre.

Scholars like Rachel Hann (1965) (*The Ecological Theatre*) and Una Chaudhuri (2016) (*The Stage Lives of Animals*) have explored the intersection of theatre and ecological themes, demonstrating how eco-scenography can engage audiences with environmental issues. Eco-scenographers often draw inspiration from ecocritical analyses, incorporating recycled materials, renewable resources, and energy-efficient technologies into stage design.

---

4   Man should learn to collaborate with nature for a more sustainable future.

Both eco-scenography and ecocriticism focus on the environment, emphasizing the importance of the natural environment and the impact of human activities on ecological systems. Eco-scenography is a practical application of ecocriticism's theoretical concerns from a theatrical design perspective. While ecocriticism provides a critical framework for understanding environmental themes in literature and culture, eco-scenography translates these ideas into tangible practices within the performing arts. The philosophies and insights of ecocriticism can inspire eco-scenography by providing a deeper understanding of how cultural narratives shape environmental attitudes. Equally, eco-scenography can offer ecocriticism examples of how environmental consciousness can be incorporated into artistic practice, demonstrating art's potential contribution to environmental sustainability.

ECO-THEATRICAL PRAXIS

The integration of ecological ethics and sustainable design techniques is transforming stage design and scenography practice in both conventional and avant-garde theatre. This is due to the progressive development of eco-theatrical praxis. As the world enters a new era of environmental consciousness, the performing arts are well-positioned to take a leading role in presenting possibilities for environmentally sustainable practices. Every theatre activity presents an opportunity to be more environmentally conscious, which involves thinking ahead, considering the big picture, and resisting the status quo in favor of innovation. This process requires as much creativity as it does organization (Miller 2012, 199[5]).

To be environmentally conscious is to simply consider the sustainability of the environment and ecological factors when doing theatre-related tasks. In this instance, the theatre professional considers sustainability at every step of the planning process (analysis, conceptualization, design, development, and implementation), allowing for the early exploration of thematic, aesthetic, and ecological elements. The pursuit of environmentally sensitive design in the performing arts has given rise to "eco-scenography."

---

5   In addition to part-gardening, part-theatre approach to eco-scenography, there are approaches of repurposing, recycling, and reusing objects.

Since ecological consciousness is taken into consideration during performance and design preparations, stage design plays a significant role in the practice of eco-scenography by altering social and environmental systems outside the theatre. To be "ecological" means to consider the broader ramifications of scenographic work, and how it affects and connects to the surrounding environment (outside the theatre). Ecological concepts must be taken into consideration when building recyclable, biodegradable, restorative, and/or regenerative performance environments. This is essentially the nature of eco-scenography practice.

When approaching eco-scenography, material choices must be carefully considered. In this light, Beer[6] (2016, 161) posits that:

> Today, the production of theatre design demands that we think carefully about waste management, energy efficiency, and about the long-term impacts of our work. Often, these considerations will be seen as constraints. Yet ecological considerations also present opportunities for rejuvenation and innovation; opportunities to consider how ideas of ecology, nature, and culture can lead to new forms of creative expression in spatial design. Considering the interconnections between humans and non-humans can have profound effects on the way scenographers approach their practice, their choices of material, and their creative processes.

Beer's focus on the long-term effects of our labor as theatre professionals has given rise to the global practice of eco-scenography, which considers the impact of climate change. Although many theatre professionals have worried that the practice would be restrictive, it appears to have the capacity to inspire innovation and change. Additionally, it is an eco-friendly and eco-efficient activity. The eco-efficient practice has been defined as having a carrying capacity approach to minimizing waste, pollution, and natural resource depletion while still satisfying human needs (DeSimone and Popoff 1997).

---

6   Dr. Tanja Beer is the founder of eco-scenography. She is a Senior Lecturer in Design at Griffith University, Australia.

It is often possible to incorporate eco-efficient or eco-friendly measures (such as material reuse and waste minimization) without compromising design principles, building methods, or aesthetics. Eco-efficient practices promote the use of locally obtained, recovered, and reused resources to reduce excess waste and energy use. The performing arts, with all their potential, have been slow to adopt the tenets of ecological practice. Many people believe that theatre and sustainability are incompatible, and current conceptions of sustainability are viewed as restrictive and stifling. Consequently, Morris (2007) points out the linear, inefficient techniques frequently used in theatre design. He contends that stage designers must embrace the potential of sustainable practice and inspire the theatre business to abandon its wasteful practices.

The environmental effects of theatre design are still not well understood, and methods for updating present design practices to adhere to ecological principles have not been thoroughly investigated, especially in Nigeria (Africa). As Arons (2007, 93) asserts, humanity's relationship to the environment is an issue of urgent concern and one that can and should be addressed by anyone engaged in critical and intellectual pursuits, including theatre artists and scholars. Accordingly, Woynarski (2015, 1) proposes that researchers and practitioners of performance should address ecology as it can bring something unique to their engagement with it, in addition to engaging with it as all other fields should.

While there are works in the field of ecocriticism that enable researchers to describe the relationship between nature, humans, science, and the arts through literary works (poems, novels, drama, and others), not much has been done recently around eco-scenography in children's theatre practice, which is a crucial aspect of theatre performance in Nigeria. Eco-theatre addresses local and global concerns about climate change through film production, radio drama, dance, television drama, and stage performance. When an eco-scenographer uses readily available natural and repurposed materials, a distinct natural style gradually emerges. The impact of the goods we use and create is what matters, not how quickly and flawlessly the work is completed (Kastell and Myers 2019, 5[7]). Using readily available natural materials reduces costs, helps the

---

7   Eco-friendly and biodegradable materials are underexplored in theatre design

audience experience a more natural feeling through the aesthetics that accompany their appearance, and, above all, these natural materials are environmentally friendly because they decompose more readily than plastics and other harmful materials that harm the ecosystem.

Another method of implementing sustainable theatre through design is to salvage reusable or degradable items. Kastell and Myers (2019, 5) further explain:

> The wooden stumps were salvaged from street bins following Christmas waste droppings. Real plants were chosen over fake foliage as a deep respect for the natural world who then became fully fledged members of the cast. Also, the carpet was retrieved from a theatre company when their show run ended; it was stitched together to create a patchwork of grass… It is wise to focus on the values already existing in objects and what they can bring to the scenographic industry, rather than just thinking about reducing waste. Knowing that most of the materials I used would later go back to Nature through composting helps me feel at peace with creating work that will not harm the world.

Eco-scenography takes various forms. For instance, one form combines gardening and performance (theatre), focusing on promoting green life, food production, and afforestation. Additionally, a widespread practice across disciplines involves recycling harmful waste to reduce ecosystem damage. Furthermore, eco-scenography also encompasses the exploration of eco-friendly materials. This research examines two key aspects: the integration of gardening and theatre, and the use of locally sourced eco-friendly materials and reclaimed objects, to promote environmental sustainability in theatrical design practice.

The goal of eco-scenography, which is composed of the words "Ecology" (Eco) and "Scenography," extends beyond the scope of the term scenography itself to promote environmental sustainability. "Scenography," as defined above, enhances performances and provides the audience

---

practice, which is why it is important to investigate their use.

with a beautiful visual experience. By considering "ecological concerns" and "environmental sustainability" in the practice of scenography in the theatre space and beyond, "Eco" refers to this kind of scenographic practice as going above and beyond the traditional practice of designing to enhance performance(s).

However, given that wood is the primary material utilized for set designs nationwide, Nigerian theatre appears to be supporting tree chopping in opposition to climate sustainability. Numerous stages that have been taking place across the nation have demonstrated this. According to Agoba (2008, 200-201), in his thesis (Modular Concepts in National Theatre Scenic Design), "the joinery methods used were dependent largely upon... the predominant use of lumber and plywood... in constructing entire forms on stage." To bolster his claim, he says, "The utilization of a sizable collection of 'stone-hill' platforms holding levels but still made of wood significantly lessens the overpowering presence and repetition this background item creates. The full platform units are situated halfway between the wall unit's left and right sides. Most of the production's sets were made of wood" (Agoba 2010, 170-173). Agoba's statement here highlights the dominance of wood in stage construction for Nigerian theatre productions, justifying the need for ecological ethics and designs in the industry. Given the implications of scenography on climate change, eco-scenography is crucial for addressing the urgent challenges of climate sustainability through theatre practice, particularly from the perspective of scenography and stage design. Therefore, this research aims to evaluate the 2023 Children's Theatre activities at Ahmadu Bello University's Studio Theatre for their adoption of sustainable theatre practices. aims to evaluate the 2023 Children's Theatre activities at Ahmadu Bello University's Studio Theatre for their adoption of sustainable theatre practices. Since the story and the actor have always taken center stage, the visuals also play a significant role due to their aesthetic and symbolic effects on the audience (Nasir 2012, 667[8]; Ofora and Nwafor 2018).

This study aims to demonstrate how green scenography, or "green

---

8   Though scholars have argued otherwise that designs have also taken center stage, the argument design not taking center stage is in the context of theatre practice and environmental sustainability

life," and environmental sustainability can be promoted with scenography in performances. To achieve this, this study will investigate the use of substitute materials, such as recovered or reclaimed artifacts, recycled or reused materials, and locally sourced materials, to produce accessories and scenery while minimizing environmental impact. Ecological design theory underpins this study, providing the necessary framework and guide for addressing the research needs.

SOURCING MATERIALS

Eco-scenography offers a cost-effective approach for theatre practitioners by encouraging the use of objects and materials found in the environment. This includes repurposing objects that are left littering the environment or have been dumped. The primary focus of this research is to explore eco-friendly and biodegradable materials, such as paper, cartons, cardboard, cotton and fabric materials, wool, and pruned tree branches, for use in children's theatre activities and tree planting (part gardening) initiatives. Additionally, the pruning activity by the ABU University Health Services' Afforestation unit provided an opportunity to source materials. The unit's pruning of branches within and around the university yielded materials used to create various shapes and sizes, which enhanced the beauty of the drama village environment, from the entrance gate to the theatre. The designs created from found objects and reused materials produced a natural environment that excited the children. Moreover, the tree-planting activity is crucial to green theatre practices, promoting environmental sustainability and a greener lifestyle in Zaria communities. The materials explored in this research include found woods, pruned branches, leaves from the Ahmadu Bello University farms and environment, paper materials, fabrics, reused stage properties, and live plants.

The two images overleaf show distinct features of the Studio Theatre (Drama Village) environment. On the left is a display of multi-colored cardboard paper used for decoration. On the right is the Zaure, which serves as both the entrance to the Drama Village and the ticket room. The Zaure is adorned with decorative elements, including wool, rope, pruned tree branches found within the environment, and balloons.

Figure 12.1. & Figure 12.2.
Images of the Studio Theatre (A.B.U. Studio Theatre) (Drama Village)

Figure 12.3. & Figure 12.4.
Inside the Studio Theatre (A.B.U. Studio Theatre)

Inside the Studio Theatre, the image on the left showcases a creative design using found objects (pruned trees) to create a passage or entrance to a sacred ground, where the children's audience is seated before the stage. The image also features multi-colored cardboard papers used for decoration. On the right is another passage that utilizes paper decoration to enhance the existing wall design, aligning with green practices. The painting on the right, depicting a flower vase, is done in various shades of green, complementing the overall aesthetic. The image also shows part of the decoration featured in the image on the left.

Figure 12.5.
Inside the Studio Theatre

Figure 12.5 above features designs made of wool, cardboard, colors, paintings on paper, pruned branches, and other decorative elements.

Figure 12.6. & Figure 12.7.
Picture of plants shared with the children

The images above show the plants shared to the children, so they can take them to their communities to be planted and maintained.

Figure 12.8.
Image of children given plants to plant in their communities

CHILDREN'S THEATRE

Children's theatre is an entertaining and educational performance activity that combines drama, music, dance puppetry, and other forms, often featuring both children and adults performing for children's audiences. Similarly, Goldberg (1974, 5) defines children's theatre as a "formal[9] theatrical experience in which a play is presented for an audience of children." He adds that the goal of children's theatre is "to provide the best possible theatrical experiences for the audience." Eluyefa (2017, 82) also defines children's theatre as "a piece of performance that involves children as actors/or as the audience." He continues that children's theatre is "specifically created and performed for children's audience either by children's actors or professional adults or a combination of both." Furthermore, Omoera (2011, 210) asserts that children's theatre is "an educational instructional approach which focuses on development through drama,

---

9   Children's theatre must not necessarily be formal, there are traditional/local forms of children's theatre that are practiced

providing a relaxed kind of theatre that is geared towards developing the participants."

Children's theatre-making, like other theatrical activities, comprises several elements, including stage and theatrical design. This aspect is key in preparing for children's theatre, as children are attracted to artistic design. The creative use of colors, shapes, and other visual elements featured in children's theatre excites and immerses them in the activities.

ABU STUDIO THEATRE

In addition to being entertaining, African theatre can also be deeply committed to aesthetics, politics, social justice, and spirituality, often combining all these qualities at once. African theatre engages and feeds off a highly responsive, interested, and vocal audience. It offers a holistic experience that encompasses the mind, body, and soul. Modern African theatre combines ideas of drama derived from Western colonization experiences with indigenous performance traditions, including dance, music, storytelling, and mime. Since the University's Drama program was established in 1975, Ahmadu Bello University in Zaria, Nigeria, has witnessed growth in its theatre practice.

The technique that inspired the Drama program was already becoming increasingly common in Southern Africa, particularly in Botswana and Zambia, where theatre had quickly become a tool for addressing social issues. This grassroots foundation was "with an orientation of social commitment," that is, the theatre was focused on social issues pertinent to its environment. This type of theatre origin led to its being labeled as an "indigenous theatre practice" (Abah 2003).

Consequently, in 1975, the Ahmadu Bello University Studio Theatre was constructed. Its distinctive architecture features areas designed to reflect northern Nigeria, including circular huts, thatched roofs, and an outdoor performance arena. The theatrical productions at Drama Village showcase a range of themes, directing styles, and audiences from various ethnic backgrounds and genders. With its creative layout and incorporation of native shapes and materials, the Ahmadu Bello University Studio Theatre (Drama Village) is a versatile art space that hosts theatrical productions and workshops. Steven Ehrlich is credited with creating a theatre design reminiscent of the traditional cloistered architecture of the old Hausa cities of northern Nigeria, which featured mud-walled compound buildings (https://eyrc.com/work/ahmadu-bello-university-theatre, 2019). The theatre consists of four round thatched huts connected by compound walls arranged in a circle for the main performance area. This design allows for a variety of layouts, including theatre-in-the-round and the conventional proscenium stage. The huts are adaptable and can be used as separate studio workshops, auxiliary performance venues, and seating areas for the audience.

When the ABU Studio Theatre was first constructed, environmentally friendly natural materials were used. One of Stephen Ehrlich's early students, Segun Oyekunle, mentioned in an interview that Ehrlich aimed to combine elements of native architecture with modern architecture to serve its intended purpose today. Oyekunle noted:

> Even though there is no specific theatre, such as the Globe Theatre in London, built for drama in our African communities, we have always had the village square as emblematic of drama and dance performances and festivals in our communities. Every village has always had its all-purpose village square for gatherings, dances, and festivals. However, the square is not square but round, hence theatre in the round. Ehrlich's concept for Studio Theatre, therefore, is to transpose the open-air village round into a partially closed theatre in the round (Oyekunle 2019, quoted in Liman & Franklin-Pyokpung 2020, 93[10]).

According to Oyekunle, the ABU Studio Theatre aimed to construct a space where native artists could perform and where the concept of colonial engagement with Africa could be reinterpreted. Oyekunle further explained:

> Since he believes, as we do, that the proscenium stage, with

---

10 Oyekunle, Segun. 2019. In a discussion with the author in Abuja, Nigeria on the history of the ABU Studio Theatre. He was also one of the first sets of students under the department of English & Drama

its curtain opening and closing, is not African but an export model from Western culture, the multiple round stages of four in the Studio Theatre make it possible to change scenes without closing and opening curtains. Act and scene changes occur automatically, representing the entries and exits at different points of the Village Round. It also allows for the utilization of Peter Brook's minimal staging techniques in plays written specifically for the theatre, such as my play-text, *Katakata for Sofahead* (Oyekunle 2019, quoted in Liman & Franklin-Pyokpung 2020, 94).

The four circular stages in the ABU Studio Theatre are set up for action as the drama progresses from scene to scene, as demonstrated by numerous stage productions held there. The audience for these performances is seated in the well. However, in some performances, such as *Katakata*, the audience is seated on three tiers, while the action takes place in the circular well.

Though it has a northern architectural design, the architecture provides flexible space to mimic any indigenous society. The play and the director's subjective perception of it determine precisely how the theatre and its round stages are used. For instance, Oyekunle observes that the *Man Pickin* production—a Michael Etherton transposition of Bertolt Brecht's *The Good Woman of Setzuan*—used the main performance space, while the walkway—the aisle between the well—was utilized as the street that the gods and other characters traveled while the audience was seated inside the well. Despite its broad orientation, it is argued that the unique architectural design of the Drama Village has a cultural impact on its diverse stage performances, considering the various modifications the Drama Village has undergone. Sadiq Balewa supports this assertion when he states that:

> The building originally used local resources and materials, and the architecture was traditional, reflecting the environment instead of constructing a huge multimillion-naira concrete western structure. It was meant to reflect the people of the culture—North, Nigeria, Africa. The idea was to break

away from traditional Western concepts of theatres and drama to create something different; that's why the creation of an adaptable space. Most productions were done in the round, but they comprised different kinds of stages (Balewa 2019[11], quoted in Liman & Franklin-Pyokpung 2020, 96). As the stage is divided into various sections, rising higher from the well to the center, then to the highest section of the stage—the architectural plan is indeed well-laid out and flexible, allowing actors plenty of space and partitioning for movement from one area to another. This design facilitates visibility from every angle.

The designer created what Bappah (2019) describes as "traditionalizing the acting space"—a notion that gives the actor or dancer a sense of awareness and connection within the performative culture, helping them understand and connect to the performative truths in the world of the play. He elaborates:

> Two concepts were merged. The first is the Zaure concept, where Soro is the entrance to Zaure; you don't go beyond that in traditional culture. The second is the performance area, the Dandali concept, which is the well, where people from different places meet at the center. These two concepts were combined to create architecture. Steven Ehrlich, the architect, worked with Tsarkin Maginan Tsarkin Zazzau, a building specialist, who was contracted to build the structure. They used local building materials and though cement later played a more prominent role in the structure, it did not affect the architecture (Bappah 2019,[12] quoted in Liman & Franklin-Pyokpung 2020, 96).

---

11   Balewa, Sadiq (2019) was a Lecturer in the Department of Theatre and Performing Arts Amadu Bello University, Nigeria and one of the early students of the then Department of English and Drama.
12   The late Bappah, Salihu (2019). Senior Staff, Department of Theatre and Performing Arts, Ahmadu Bello University, Zaria.

Several philosophical motifs of acting and performance are conveyed in Bappah's description of the ABU Studio Theatre. As he notes, Zaure is the doorway leading into any traditional building. Every Zaure entrance, or Soro, must be passed through to enter the main house. Bappah further explains: "The initial concept was both the traditional performing space and the Zaure. You enter the Zaure, move into the forecourt of the actual house, and sit down to watch performances. The architecture was deliberately designed in the round, with the structure facing each other" (Bappah 2019, quoted in Liman & Franklin-Pyokpung 2020, 97).

The Well, a traditional performance space that symbolizes relationships within the Hausa community, is a gathering place where neighbors congregate to talk and socialize. From a philosophical standpoint, the Well serves as a platform for relationships and communication among community members.

CONCLUSION

Eco-scenography and ecocriticism are interconnected through their shared emphasis on the relationship between human culture and the natural environment. Eco-scenography employs sustainable and environmentally conscious practices in theatrical design and production, aiming to minimize ecological impact and foster ecological awareness. Ecocriticism, on the other hand, analyses how nature and the environment are represented in literature and cultural texts, seeking to raise environmental awareness and critique anthropocentric views. The connection lies in eco-scenography's practical application of ecocriticism's theoretical concerns, demonstrating how environmental consciousness can be integrated into artistic practices. This was illustrated through the Children's Theatre experience at Ahmadu Bello University, where the performance featured designs guided by ecological thinking and gardening (planting) to project environmentally sustainable practices for children.

REFERENCES

Abah, Oga Steve. 2003. "Methodological Conversations in Researching Citizenship: Drama and Participatory Learning and Action in Encountering Citizens." In *Geographies of Citizenship in Nigeria*, edited by Oga Steve Abah. Zaria: Tamaza Publication.

Agoba, Ernest Obukohwo. 2008. "Towards Modular Concepts in Scenic Design Heuristics: Influences from Production Sceneries in The Cinema Hall 2 of the National Theatre of Nigeria (1995–2001)." Master's thesis, University of Jos.

Agoba, Ernest Obukohwo. 2010. "The Set Design Process in The Nigerian Theatre: A Designer's Rendition of Ahmed Yerima's *Trials of Oba Ovonramwen.*" *Nigerian Theatre Journal*, edited by Iorapuu T. 10 (1): 167–78.

Arons, Wendy. 2007. "Introduction to Special Section on Performance and Ecology." *Theatre Topics* 17 (2): 93–94.

Asomba, Domba. 2001. *Scene Design: Art and Craft*. Ibadan: Caltop Publications (Nigeria) Limited.

Balewa, Sadiq. Interview by Franklin P. Zaure. Kaduna, December 5, 2019.

Bappah, Salihu. Interview by Franklin P. Zaure. Zaria, December 10, 2019.

Beer, Tanja. 2015. "The Living Stage: A Case Study in Eco-scenography." *Etudes* 1 (1): 1–16.

Beer, Tanja. 2016. "Ecomaterialism in Scenography." *Theatre and Performance Design* 2 (1–2): 161–72. https://doi.org/10.1080/23322551.2016.1179437.

Buell, Lawrence. 1995. *The Environmental Imagination: Thoreau, Nature Writing, and the Formation of American Culture*. Cambridge: Harvard University Press.

DeSimone, Livio D., and Frank Popoff. 1997. *Eco-efficiency: The Business Link to Sustainable Development*. Cambridge: MIT Press.

Eluyefa, Dennis. 2017. "Children's Theatre: A Brief Pedagogical Approach." *Arts Praxis* 4 (1): 79–83. https://bgro.repository.guildhe.ac.uk/id/eprint/166/1/Eluyefa_Childrens%20theatre_2017.pdf.

Enendu, Molinta L. O. 1993. "Modern Technology and Theatre Production in Nigeria." *Theatre Studies Review* 1: 243–65.

Goldberg, Moses. 1974. *Children's Theatre: A Philosophy and a Method*. Englewood Cliffs, NJ: Prentice-Hall.

Hameed, Lawal O. 2011. *Fundamentals of Theatre Arts*. Ibadan: Glory Land Pubs. Company.

Illah, Egwugwu J. S., ed. 2004. *Child Rights Theatre for Development Training Manual*. Department of Theatre Arts, University of Ibadan, and UNICEF.

Kastell, Mona, and Hannah Myers. 2019. "Ecoscenography in Action: Bridging Stage Design with Nature Connection to Shape Sustainable Communities and Wellbeing." *Scene* 7 (1-2): 29-44. https://doi.org/10.1386/scene_00004_1.

Liman, Rasheedah-Aliyu, and Franklin-Pyokpung Zaure. 2020. *Architecture, Stage Design and Performance: The Case of Ahmadu Bello University Studio Theatre*. Scene Dock 4 (6): 91-109.

McKinney, Joslin, and Philip Butterworth. 2009. *The Cambridge Introduction to Scenography*. Cambridge: Cambridge University Press.

Miller, Justin A. 2012. "The Labor of Greening *Love's Labour's Lost.*" In *Readings in Performance and Ecology*, edited by Wendy Arons and Theresa J. May, 191-201. New York: Palgrave Macmillan.

Morris, Damond Guy. 2007. "Towards a Recycled Theatre: Industrial Ecology Theatrical Applications for the Next Industrial Revolution." Master's thesis, Western Washington University. http://faculty.skagit.edu/news3.asp?pagenumber=2711&dept=156&yrq=B892.

Nasir, Taofiq Oaide. 2012. "The Interface between Theatre Technology and Stage Performance: Interview with Duro Oni." In *Fireworks for a Lighting Aesthetician*, edited by S. E. Ododo, 665-77. Lagos: CBAAC.

Ofora, Emeka, and Friday Nwafor. 2018. "Amorphous Lighting Design: Issues in Dan Kpodoh's Stage Production of Julie Okoh's *Victims of Violence.*" *International Journal of Current Research in the Humanities*: 243-65.

Omoera, Osakue S. 2011. "Repositioning Early Childhood Education in Nigeria: The Children's Theatre Approach." *Academic Research International* 1 (2): 206-14.

Vaghani, Daya. 2023. *Ecocriticism: A Study of Environmental Issues in Literature*. ResearchGate. https://www.researchgate.net/publication/376829159_Ecocriticism_A_Study_of_Environmental_Issues_in_Literature. https://doi.org/10.13140/RG.2.2.12963.02085.

Woynarski, Lisa. 2015. "A Brief Introduction to the Field of Performance and Ecology." Royal Central School of Speech & Drama, University of London. https://www.academia.edu/11045059/A_Brief_Introduction_to_Performance_and_Ecology.

CHAPTER THIRTEEN

Greg Mbaijiorgu's Wake Up Everyone and the Scourge of Climate Change on Food Security

Hameed Olutoba Lawal & Tijime Justin Awuawuer

INTRODUCTION

Climate change is one of the major challenges to food security in Africa and globally. In recent times, it has added considerable stress to our societies and the environment. Fangs of climate change range from shifting weather patterns that threaten food production to rising water levels that increase the risk of flooding and erosion. The impact of these shifting weather patterns is global in scope, unprecedented in scale, and inimical to food security. Many research findings indicate that the climatic vagaries caused by climate change have adverse effects on agricultural productivity in Nigeria, resulting in reduced productive outputs. This situation has led to a shortfall and disruptions in food supplies, resulting in increased food prices. Food insecurity intensified across Nigeria due to climatic factors that have limited agricultural productivity.

Climate change-induced alterations such as droughts, heavy precipitation, flooding of farmlands, rising temperatures, increasing aridity and soil acidity, changes in relative humidity, and increased evaporation, among others, have adverse effects on agricultural productivity and food systems in Nigeria (Ani, Anyika, and Mutambara 2022, 151). Nigeria is physically and climatically diverse, and the vulnerability of each geographical zone to sudden and perennial climatic changes is determined by its topography and climatic conditions. These environmental challenges confronting the country include deforestation, desertification, soil degradation, erosion, flooding, and pollution. While the northern states of Nigeria are prone to desert encroachment and drought, flooding, pollution, and erosion are rampant in the southern states. The menace of climate change and environmental degradation can be attributed to both natural causes and human activities. The consequences of the destruction of farmlands and rivers are typified by food scarcity and high food prices. For farmers, a poor harvest and resulting loss of revenue can be devastating and frustrating. Famine, on the other hand, can unleash unimaginable hunger on the populace.

Government intervention over the years has been through scientific forecasts of possible floods and droughts that could change the climatic conditions in states prone to such natural disasters. However, this does not take into account the security threat posed by farmers' and herders' clashes, which have led to the destruction of farmlands and the relocation of farmers for their safety in recent times. While the meteorological forecast of weather is hardly taken with the seriousness it deserves by the farmers, government, and agricultural agencies, palliatives to cushion the effects of environmental degradation are like a drop of water in the ocean.

Inadequacies in forecasts and palliatives necessitate more preventive and proactive measures by farmers, agricultural agencies, and the government. Orientation programs on electronic media should incorporate dramatization of the causes of climate change, its threat to food security, and proactive and preventive measures to be taken to mitigate its devastating effects on the environment and society. To create more awareness, the participatory nature of drama and the universality of its language on stage and screen should be explored in enlightenment campaigns, as it is in furtherance of orientation and outreach to rural farmers, making eco-theatre inevitable. Eco-theatre expatriates is the dramatist's creative interpretation of the essence of nature, where the causes and effects of climate change are seen as the core thematic motif. In tandem with these definitions, scholars such as Bate (1991 and 2000), Scigay (1999), Murphy (2000), and Aghalino (2005 and 2010) explicate the relevance of culture workers, environmentalists, dramatists, novelists, and poets in sensitizing on climate change and its effects (Adeoye 2013, 575).

THEORETICAL FRAMEWORK

Over the last few decades, the environment has posed a significant threat to human society. The extensive misuse of natural resources has left us on the brink of collapse. The rainforests are being cut down, fossil fuel supplies are rapidly decreasing, the seasonal cycle is out of order, ecological disasters are frequent around the globe, and our environment is on the brink (Mishra 2016, 168). Under these circumstances, a new theory of reading nature writing emerged during the last decade of the previous century, known as Ecocriticism. It is a worldwide movement that emerged as a reaction to humanity's anthropocentric attitude of dominating nature. This paper examines the ecocritical perspectives presented in Greg Mbaijiorgu's *Wake Up Everyone*, focusing particularly on its treatment of climate change and food security.

Ecocriticism, as conceptualized by William Rueckert in 1978, critically examines the relationship between literature and the environment, challenging anthropocentric views that position humanity as dominant over nature. This approach interrogates the intricate interdependence of human and ecological systems, focusing on how literature reflects environmental degradation and its consequences. Mbaijiorgu's play serves as fertile ground for an ecocritical analysis, as it portrays the catastrophic impact of climate change on food security—a pressing issue in developing nations. The destruction of natural ecosystems, symbolized by deforestation, disrupted seasons, and dwindling natural resources, becomes a central theme in the play, aligning with ecocritical discourse on environmental justice. Thus, Frederick opines that "the modern ecological consciousness has a feeling that the balance between human and the natural world must be maintained. A perfect ecology is one in which plants, animals, birds, and human beings live in such harmony that none dominates or destroys the other" (Frederick 2012, 147).

The unequal distribution of climate-induced hardships, particularly affecting marginalized communities, ties into the core tenets of ecocriticism, which seeks to expose the socio-economic dimensions of environmental crises. Developing nations, such as those in sub-Saharan Africa, bear the brunt of food insecurity as a direct result of environmental degradation. Ecocriticism thus provides a framework for examining these socioeconomic dimensions, particularly how the most vulnerable communities are disproportionately affected by the ecological crisis.

Nature in *Wake Up Everyone* can be seen as an active character rather than a mere backdrop. Through its depiction of ecological disasters and their direct effect on human livelihoods, Mbaijiorgu's work positions the environment as a dynamic force, reacting to human exploitation. This representation emphasizes the agency of nature, resonating with Lawrence Buell's assertion that ecocriticism must explore the human-non-human relationship while maintaining an ethical commitment to environmental praxis. To this end, Frederick asserts that "the most common measure to tackle environmental crisis is sustainable development." (Frederick 2012, 128). In this light, the play is not merely a narrative about climate change; it is a clarion call, using literary devices to warn of the impending ecological disaster. The play thus becomes a medium through which the principles of ecocriticism can be explored, illustrating the urgent need for environmental stewardship and equitable responses to climate-induced food insecurity.

THE CONCEPT OF CLIMATE CHANGE AND FOOD SECURITY

Climate change and food security are issues that affect the lives of the human species. There cannot be a good harvest without a favorable climate. Thus, safeguarding food security in the face of climate change also implies avoiding disruptions or declines in global and local food supplies that could result from changes in temperature and precipitation regimes, as well as new patterns of pests and diseases (Killmann 2008, xi). This could be imminent due to their high exposure to natural hazards, their direct dependence on climate-sensitive resources such as plants, trees, animals, water, and land, and their limited capacity to adapt to and mitigate the impacts of climate change. Sanober Naheed (2023, 1) holds that:

> climate change is increasing the frequency of climate-related disasters, creating greater risks of hunger and the breakdown of food systems. The sustainability of our planet is currently a major concern for the global community and has been a central theme for several major global initiatives in recent years. Climate change has prevalent, multi-faceted, and temporal impacts on food security. Higher temperatures, water scarcity, extreme events like droughts and floods and greater CO_2 concentrations in the atmosphere have already begun to

impact staple crops around the world. The warming climate is already taking a toll on human health, causing widespread hunger and illness that will grow exponentially worse, and will pose a major threat to human well-being.

Climate change thus threatens to reverse the progress made in the fight against hunger and malnutrition. As highlighted by the latest assessment report of the Intergovernmental Panel on Climate Change (IPCC), climate change increases and intensifies risks to food security for the most vulnerable countries and populations. Four out of the eight key risks induced by climate change identified by IPCC AR5 have direct consequences for food security: Loss of rural livelihoods and income; Loss of marine and coastal ecosystems, and livelihoods; Loss of terrestrial and inland water ecosystems, and livelihoods; and Food insecurity and breakdown of food systems (Killmann 2008, ix). This means that some of these risk-inducing factors are both natural and human-made. For instance,

> the rapid population growth in Nigeria and unmatched agricultural productive output point to an aggravated food security crisis. This condition is attributed to the stresses that are connected with climate change. Climate change undermines the ability of developing countries to meet targeted agricultural output. The persistence of this shortfall indicates intense food security crisis. Climate change also affects aquatic ecosystem. Sea warming, changes in sea salinity and increasing sea acidity are some of the physical changes that climate change brings. Several incidents of mass aquatic deaths in the Niger Delta are indications of the horrendous consequences of climate change. Such losses threaten the livelihood of riverine communities that heavily dependent on food and trade (Ani, Anyika and Mutambara 2022, 154).

Based on the above, it is therefore evident that the Niger Delta region in Nigeria faces more ecological challenges than any other region in Nigeria. This is simply because some of the climatic or ecological challenges are man-made and natural. In some regions, climatic crises are caused by bushfires. Some regions are affected by desert encroachments, particularly the Northwest and Northeast. It thus becomes imperative that all these pose threats to food production and human life, as Nigeria is not shielded from the rest of the world in terms of the effects of climate change. This eco-catastrophe is felt in every part of the globe, and it is increasingly evident on African shores. Changes in rainfall patterns across Nigeria have significantly impacted the food supply, and the recent rise in the cost of foodstuffs is a testament to the growing effects of climate change. Hence, in Nigeria, the response to these ecological challenges over the years has been to silence the voices that dare to speak out, either through military might or monetary inducements in the name of compensation (Ebere 2016, 86). Whereas the outcomes of climate change have been felt across Nigeria's vegetative regions. It is against this backdrop that this paper attempts an eco-reading of Greg Mbaijiorgu's *Wake Up Everyone* as a dramatic response to climate change and food security.

ECO-THEATRE AND CLIMATE CHANGE IN NIGERIA

Before the environmental degradation in the Niger Delta region of Nigeria, caused by years of oil exploration and the attendant agitations and militancy, much attention was not given to dramatizing environmental issues in Nigeria. The allusion to the environment by some Nigerian dramatists before the degeneration of protests and agitations in oil-producing communities in Nigeria into criminality was more of a metaphor to satirize the unfolding events in our social reality. While some of these plays exhibit eco-theatrical features in terms of setting and characterization, the environmental degradation caused by both natural and human factors is not clearly presented. This conforms with the definition of eco-theatre, a form whose motif and aesthetics are dedicated to exploring environmental degradation and conscious efforts at solutions to problems of climate change (Adeoye 2013, 581). In this regard, many Nigerian playwrights have explored the environmental issues in Nigeria through their various works. For instance, Bode Sowande's *Mammy Water's Wedding* exemplified this kind of metaphorical enactment of environmental degradation. In the play, the need for a harmonious living of earth and water is personified in the love affairs of Akinla and Tarrella. A young man (Akinla) based in Lagos drowns in a rainstorm despite being a good swimmer. He does not die but finds himself in a world below the sea, among mermaids, called mammy water. Akinla is charmed by Tarella's beauty in the world below the sea. Tarrella decides to help Akinla return to Lagos, but the barrier to their love is the environment. To transform into a human, Tarella is born to a wealthy Lagos businessman named Adagun-Odo, who goes by the name Okuntoro. Adagun-odo trade is waste dumping into the sea, which later sets him on a collision course with the destined love between Okuntoro and Akinla.

The natural harmonious relationship between earth and water, which is essential to food production and healthy living, is destroyed by Adagun-odo's act of dumping waste into the sea to pollute it. The dramatization of Adagun-odo atoning for his sins of environmental degradation is enhanced by thematic songs, just as the symbiotic relationship between the earth and sea is personified in the marriage of Akinla and Tarella. The sensitization on the sanctity of the environment is captured in these two stanzas of the songs:

> First stanza
> People of the world, don't
> Wreck the world.
> People of the world, don't
> Pollute the sea
> People of the world
> Let us reflect
> People of the world, don't
> Wreck the earth
> People of the world, don't
> Spoil the earth
> People of the world don't
> Wipe out the world.
>
> Second stanza:
> Toxic waste in water is horrible
> Water pollution is bad
> Pollution in the forest is bad

> Filth at home is bad
> Air pollution is horrible
> Polluting the sky is bad (Sowande 2014, 58-59).

The lesson in this play, Sowande (2014, iv) avers, "is that pollution is a serious problem which has serious consequences for the quality of life on earth." Consummation of the love affair of Akinla and Tarella (Okuntoro) is thus a token of faith that a healing bond can occur between the earth and the sea.

Furthermore, tears, sorrow, and blood that trailed the militancy of youth of the Niger Delta region of Nigeria, as characterized by kidnapping, hostage taking, killings, and bunkering, inspired an artistic approach to the struggle for emancipation. This manifested in plays and poems that capture the travails of oil-producing communities to raise awareness among national and international communities. While the cineastes dramatized the agitations, militancy, degraded environment, blood bath, death, and trauma, the playwright emphasizes psychological and emotional trauma and the senselessness of killing the innocent ones caught in the web of violence. These scenarios are aptly re-enacted in Yerima's *Hard Ground* (2005) and *Little Drops* (2009). *Hard Ground* depicts the psychological and emotional trauma that a family has to contend with when the fate of its son is in the hands of the dreaded militant leader, Don. Yerima's craftsmanship, as noted by Azeez Akinwumi Sesan (2021, 187), is evident in how he fuses family tension with national tension.

Deceit, treachery, and secrecy, which had been frustrating efforts aimed at reconciliation, rehabilitation, and resolution in the Niger Delta crisis, played out in the home of Baba and Nimi, the protagonist." *Little Drops* unfolds the travails of women in the confrontation between the Niger Delta militant youth and the armed forces. In recalling their ordeal, they lament how the militancy in the region has caused family dislocations and unending trauma as a result of the loss of loved ones, including husbands, brothers, children, and pupils. The play concludes with an appeal for the laying down of arms for dialogue (Sesan 2021, 89). One can summarize these crises as a response by the Niger Delta militants to the ecological disorders found within the region, resulting from air and water pollution, which is the concern of this paper.

THE PLAY, WAKE UP EVERYONE

Set in an agrarian community in Ndole land, Southeastern Nigeria, the play *Wake Up Everyone* dramatizes Professor Aladinma's crusade against the devastating effects of environmental degradation caused by climate change and human activities. The approaches of the retired professor of Agricultural Extension and drama enthusiasts to sensitization and mobilization against climate change and threats to food security are through official channels, extension services to farmers, and dramatization.

The official eye approach is dramatized in his visits to the local government chairman to advocate for proactive and preventive measures to mitigate impending floods and the consequences on food production. However, the chairman, who rose to power through the activism of protest and agitation over the degraded environment and the attendant loss of his father, turned a deaf ear to the advocacy and advice of Professor Aladinma. The extension services method entails an educational campaign on the types of seeds to plant, when to plant, and how to plant them during challenging times of climate change. This was stepped up with dramatic enactments of the causes of climate change, its devastating effects on food production, and the traumatic experience of the dislocation of families and the death of loved ones. The eventual occurrence of the flood, as forecasted by Professor Aladinma, and its trail of destruction of farmlands and properties instigated mass action among the peasants of Ndole land against the recalcitrant chairman.

SENSITIZATION AND MOBILIZATION AGAINST THE THREAT OF CLIMATE CHANGE TO FOOD SECURITY: WAKE UP EVERYONE

Segmented into three Acts with eight scenes, the play utilizes characterization, dialogue, and pantomime, fused with songs and dances, to convey the playwright's sensitization and mobilization regarding the threat of climate change to food production. This approach sensitizes the government at the grassroots, enlightens peasant farmers, and enacts the consequences of ignorance and a nonchalant attitude. The play opens with Professor Aladinma's visit to the local government, presenting a brilliant proposal to address the menace of climate change and its attendant environmental degradation, as typified by flooding, pollution, and erosion. Not even the suggestion of counterpart funding from the state, the local government, and the oil companies could convince the local government chairman, who is not on the same page with the professor. The chairman's reluctance stems from selfish motives. The oil companies are captured in this response to the Chairman in the play:

> CHAIRMAN: (He points his glasses at Prof in strange defensive mode) Listen, this Local Government headquarters was recently refurbished by Zodiaqc Oil, the three eighteen seater buses and two Toyota Hilux trucks out there were donated by Continental Petroleum, my sport utility vehicle and two hundred and fifty KVA soundproof generating set that is powering this Local Government Secretariat came three weeks ago as birthday gift from the MD of Diamond Oil, and don't forget that all these oil companies came together to raise a campaign fund with which I ran the election for this position. I have not even started thinking of how to pay back the money and you are asking me to go back to them, cap in hand like Oliver Twist, asking for more? With due respect for your concern for this community Prof. I don't think this local government is ready to get involved in such projects. After, all, it is based on more speculation (Mbaijiorgu 2021, 24).

The above statement confirms that the personal interests of political elites in the oil-producing states of Nigeria have been a significant hindrance to palliative and rehabilitative packages by the government at all levels. Furthermore, the oil companies have aimed to empower impoverished peasants and rehabilitate polluted rivers and barren soil.

In Act One, Scene Two, the impact of Professor Aladinma's extension services to farmers, in terms of orientation on species of seed yam to mitigate the devastating effects of sudden climate change, unfolds as the Cooperative Society of Local Farmers rejoices over bountiful harvests. It was while the farmers were still basking in the euphoria of heeding the advice of an agricultural expert that Dimkpa lamented his poor harvest for being lackadaisical.

> Dimka: Oh! I, Dimkpa, Okaji of Ndoli! The great yam farmer whose efforts had never been flouted nor ridiculed in the past, not by the weather, not by man or woman I, the pride of yam harvest, whose hands mother earth has always blessed with a bountiful harvest, now does not have even a yam tuber to boast of, this season (Mbaijiorgu 2021, 34).

Dimkpa's nonchalant attitude reflects the primordial belief that attributes climate change and poor harvests to the wrath of the gods. Dimkpa's ignorance and disdain for a scientific method of processing and transforming animal wastes and decomposed organic substances into natural fertilizer are exposed in this mockery of the process.

> DIMKPA: My wife attended that one she said he taught our farmers how best to process cow dung, dog shit, fowl shit, goat shit, and shit of Agama lizard into fertilizer. (They laugh). What arrant nonsense! Why must I meddle with all the different excrements on earth before putting my seed yam into the soil (they laugh) (Mbaijiorgu 2021, 36)?

In Act Two, Scene One, the dramatic aspects of sensitization and mobilization against the devastating effects of climate change on the environment and food production are enacted in a rehearsal session of Professor Aladinmu's drama troupe in his rehearsal studio. This is heralded with songs and exercises that progress into a reflection on the causes of climate change, its global dimension, oil exploration, and the side effects of spillage and pollution. The militant reaction against environmental degradation is also captured in the ruminative dialogue of Obioma and Nweke. The sensitization in the lamentation of causes and effects of climate change on the environment and food production is spiced up with a rendition of the theme song that goes thus:

> Wake up! Wake up everyone (×2)
> To build our world a new no burning down our bushes no polluting our rivers
> Mo more deforestation

> To guarantee our future
> No greenhouse gas emission
> No heating up our planet
> Wake up!
> Let's stop oil pollution.
> No more flaring of gases
> No cutting down our forests
> Wake up!
> Let's stop oil pollution
> No more flaring of gases
> No cutting down our forests
> Wake up ... (Mbaijiorgu 2021, 65).

Professor Aladinma's passion for deploying music, dance, and drama as strategies for social mobilization and mass enlightenment is thus an eye opener on the relevance of eco-theatre in the orientation of mostly illiterate rural farmers on what constitutes climate change, its effects on food production, and the proactive and preventive measures to avert poor harvest. The edge this dramatic mode has over the mass media of radio, television, and social media is its participatory nature, in terms of the involvement of its audience in the presentation and the use of its artistic idiom, including songs and dances.

Overcoming the technical language barrier of the sciences through the medium of drama could change the mindset of the conservative and recalcitrant individuals in the Nigerian agrarian communities, who often attribute the devastating effects of climate change to supernatural sources. This deep-seated belief in superstition came to the fore in the lamentation of Muzi Chinedum (fisherman) and Anayo (farmer) over poor catches and harvest in Act Three, Scene Two:

> ANAYO: Forget Prof Aladinna and all his shit about climate. There is nothing like climate, it is just that the gods are angry with us. You made sacrifices to the gods before the last harvest season, didn't you?
> MAZI CHINEDUM: I did. You see, I expressed fear in the past, but why should the gods be angry with us? Where have

we gone wrong?
ANAYO: Someone may have done something that provoked the wrath of the gods. Do you remember last year when the priest of Ndoli River refused to make the annual sacrifice to the deity of the river, remember, the river changed its course and headed to the priest's compound well until he rushed and quickly made the necessary sacrifices and the river returned to its normal course.
MAZI CHINEDUM: (waves his hand). That is superstition the river changed its course by accident.
ANAYO: You called that superstition? Is that superstition to you? If it happened by accident, why did the river return to its normal course immediately the necessary sacrifices were made (Mbaijiorgu 2021, 78-79)?

The deduction from this dialogue on superstition is that, while we are not averse to the traditional ways of preventive rituals against the devasting effects of climate change our illiterate farmers should also embrace the scientific methods being spearheaded by the likes of Prof. Aladinma for the dual approach to mitigating environmental degradation and poor harvests that may result from sudden climate change.

The reality of Prof. Aladinma's scientific forecast of an impending flood stares the people of Ndoli in the face when the flood finally comes, leaving in its wake destruction of farmlands, loss of lives, and property. Now convinced of the wake-up call from Prof. Aladinma, which was initially received with reservations, the farmers are mobilizing themselves to vent their anger at the local government chairman over his nonchalant attitude towards proactive and preventive measures to fortify the riverbanks against flooding for food security.

CONCLUSION

A critical reading of the play, *Wake Up Everyone*, revealed an exploration of the causes of climate change, both globally and nationally, as well as its devastating effects on the environment, both globally and locally. Its devastating effects on the environment and society, and threat to food production are enacted in three acts of eight scenes. Sensitization and orientation through drama are employed at three levels: raising awareness among the rulers at the grassroots, educating peasant farmers on a new farming method to mitigate the adverse effects of climate change, and shifting their focus from appeasing gods to mitigating the threat of climate change to food security. Taken together, this study suggests that governments at all levels should pay more attention to proactive and preventive measures to mitigate the effects of climate change on food production. This entails, among others, channeling more funds to environmental protection than to palliative measures of compensation after the disaster.

Agricultural extension workers in local government should go beyond supplying fertilizer and seedlings to orient farmers on climate change and scientific methods of mitigating its effects. This approach will enable farmers to key into global best practices for tackling climate change and make them adopt the crusade in such a manner that it becomes a way of life among them.

The ritual approach of appeasing the gods to prevent flooding and drought and ensure a bountiful harvest should be combined with the scientific approach of consulting a meteorologist's advice and adopting improved seedling and planting methods to avoid being caught unaware.

REFERENCES

Adeoye, Abdulrasheed Abiodun. 2013. "Eco-theatre and Climate Change in Nigeria." In *Arts, Culture and Communication in Postcolony: A Festschrift for Lawrence Olanrele Bamidele*, edited by Ameh D. Akoh and Stephen E. Nnegbe. United Kingdom: Alpha Crownes Publishers.

Ani, Kelechi Johnmary, Vincent Okwudiba Anyika, and Emmanuel Mutambara. 2022. "The Impact of Climate Change on Food and Human Security in Nigeria." *International Journal of Climate Change Strategies and Management* 14 (2): 148–167.

Frederick, Suresh. 2012. *Contemporary Contemplation on Ecoliterature*. New Delhi: Authors Press.

Killmann, Wulf. 2008. *Climate Change and Food Security: A Framework Document*. Rome: Food and Agriculture Organization of the United Nations.

Mbaijiorgu, Greg. 2021. *Wake up Everyone*. Ibadan: Kraft Books Limited.

Mishra, Sandip Kumar. 2016. "Ecocriticism: A Study of Environmental Issues in Literature." *BRICS Journal of Educational Research* 6 (4): 168–170.

Naheed, Sanober. 2023. "An Overview of the Influence of Climate Change on Food Security and Human Health." *Archive of Food Nutritional Science* 7: 001–011.

Sesan, Azeez Akinwumi. 2021. "A Study of History Polemics of Oil and the Quest for Justice in Yerima's *Hard Ground*, *Little Drops* and *Ipomu*." In *One Muse, Many Masks: Reflections on Ahmed Yerima's Recent Drama*, edited by Gbemisola Adeoti, 183–203. Ibadan: Kraft Books Limited.

Sowande, Bode. 2014. *Mammy Water's Wedding*. Ibadan: Book Builders.

Uzoji, Emmanuel Ebere. 2016. "Playing Earth: Eco-Pedagogy in Nigerian Drama." PhD diss., University of Jos.

WFP, FAO, IFRC, OXFAM, WVI, CARE, CARITAS, WHO, and Save the Children. 2009. *Climate Change, Food Insecurity and Hunger: Key Messages for UNFCCC Negotiators*. Technical Paper of the IASC Task Force on Climate Change. Accessed March 12, 2023. https://www.unscn.org/en/resource-center/archive/climate-change-and-nutrition-archive?idnews=1484.

Yerima, Ahmed. 2005. *Hard Ground*. Ibadan: Kraft Books Limited.

Yerima, Ahmed. 2009. *Little Drops*. Ibadan: Kraft Books Limited.

CHAPTER FOURTEEN

The Nigerian Creative Writer and Ecocritical Challenges in the 21st Century
An Appraisal of Adamu Kyuka "Usman's Death of Eternity"

Suleiman A. Jaji

INTRODUCTION

For our purposes, creative writers are defined as those individuals who use their imagination to create, compose, and or put together works of art that, given the craft and aesthetic status, are qualified to be considered as literature. This could be in any language, although our focus here is on the use of the English language as a medium of expression. In this regard, creative writing is the process of producing works of literature that may be considered as such in the English language. The originating forms and the final point of reference of these works are their existence as literature. Their appeal to our sensibilities as readers, critics, or even publishers could emanate from their being either prose, poetry, drama, or other genres of literature, such as life writing, etc., with theme, setting, and content that directly or indirectly is preoccupied with the socio-cultural, political and aesthetic interests of our humanity.

The creative writer in Nigeria faces numerous challenges in the twenty-first century. Some of these challenges date back to pre-colonial times. This chapter, however, examines only three of the problems that are considered more important in the context of the 21st century. These challenges are: a) the attitude and societal consideration of the writer, and b) the conception, often a misconception, that the business of creative writing in Nigeria, in general, and in northern Nigeria in particular, is still in its infancy. c) The third is the challenge of addressing the issue of thematic concern, particularly the need for Northern Nigerian creative writers to shift their focus from emphasizing culture and cultural nationalism to more pressing topical issues of the day. These include existential modernist or postmodernist corollaries, such as migration, ecology, and nature, and their impact on human society, rather than perpetually dwelling on the good old culture and its preservation or reintegration in an age of rapidly increasing change and transformation that radically affects the conceptions of everyday acceptances and assumptions.

THE WRITER AND THE CHALLENGES OF THE 21ST CENTURY

One of the challenges facing writers in Nigeria is that creative writing in the country, particularly in northern Nigeria, is often perceived as being in its infancy. This is acceptable only to the extent that African literature, as a whole, is relatively new compared to its Euro-American counterpart. This 'convenient' generalization has been repudiated by scholars such as Nnolim in Asoo (2006) and others. Nevertheless, coming back nearer home, Abubakar (2009, 15), has also drawn our attention to the facile view that "the development of creative writing that designates the postcolonial condition has not reached iconic levels in all parts of Nigeria it is assumed (by many a critic) to be in a state of perpetual childhood in the north" (of Nigeria). This contention by the scholar is roundly discountenanced, given the practical application of artistic practice by one of the consistently patriotic creative writers from the northern region of Nigeria.

Secondly, quite recently, the view has been expressed by critics and writers of the need for African literature to keep up with the global trends of charting new ways and discovering or exploring new themes, settings, and characterization away from its predominant preoccupation with restricting its thematic and literary concerns with African continent only and "African culture and return to the source" mentality It is implied by this statement that there is a need for African creative writers to "invade" other continents and cultures such as Europe and America in their art instead of restricting their artistic forays to Africa only. There is what Emenyonu (2009, 262) refers to as the "retour aux sources fixation, which informed the Negritude aesthetics, and the African writers should expand their thematic scope by venturing into other continents to acquire a global outlook in their imaginative praxis.

The other challenge closely related to this is the need for African or Nigerian writers to experiment with the modernist and postmodernist literary canvas to explore more relevant and topical themes of pressing concerns to humanity, rather than perpetually dwelling on outdated, traditional culture. Although the emergence of the literature of Nigerians in the Diaspora may seem to have fallen into this line of artistic concern, two northern Nigerian novels namely, Kamal Aliyu's *Fire in My Backyard* and Adamu Kyuka Usman's *Death of Eternity* have struck a chord in the attempt to answer to this significant call to respond to the challenge of the changing dimensions of Nigerian and African literature. Our concern in this chapter is, however, limited to Kyuka's *Death of Eternity*.

THE CREATIVE WRITER AND DISCRIMINATION IN NIGERIA

It is observed that there is a general discriminatory treatment of creative writers and literary creativity in Nigeria, which may be a hangover from colonial days and is detrimental to creativity and the socio-economic and political well-being of both the writer and society. This discrimination is evident not only in the socio-economic status of writers in Nigeria but also in the criteria for their career progression in Nigerian Universities, where considerations of high regard for creative writers are expected but not considered, which, however, turns out to be contrary to social justice and common sense. For this reason, our creative writing programs and the creative writers in our institutions are unlikely to make a significant impact in our march to produce world-class literature. For example, in most Nigerian universities, creative writers are not given a fair deal. Ike (1983, 144) has since cried out on this score when he said that:

> Creative writing programs are not likely to succeed if they are taught by literary critics who have never published any creative writing themselves. They will not retain any practicing creative writers unless the Universities review their criteria for promotion. Undoubtedly through a lack of appreciation of the creative process, Universities attach a higher value for the scholar who publishes a review of a novel in a so-called learned journal than the author of the novel itself. Hence for

> a creative writer who wants to advance within the university system must allow his creative talent to atrophy while he engages in a sterile exercise of reviewing the works of other creative writers... it is indefensible that while a lecturer in Chemistry may qualify for promotion by writing a textbook (in Chemistry) for university students, a lecturer in creative writing who publishes a novel receives no similar recognition for his creative work.

For this reason, many creative writers from Nigeria find it challenging to remain in the country and therefore migrate to areas where opportunities are more abundant. Examples are legion: Achebe, Habila, Ojaide, Adichie, Omotoso, Usman, and others.

Thus, despite the recurrent call for a change in basic assumptions in the practice and criticism of African literature, writers have remained despondent to the challenge on the continent. Of the few Nigerian writers in recent times who have responded to this challenge, Adamu Kyuka Usman is presumably one of those who have tried to write outside the usual African or Nigerian literature's obsession with the theme of culture and African identity, as seen in his novels, especially *Death of Eternity*. At this point, the novel, *Death of Eternity*, is examined as a modest attempt to demonstrate the breakaway from what Emenyonu (2005) describes as the "retour aux sources" mentality that has been haunting African writers in general and Nigerian writers in particular. The novel, as well as its ambitious thematic focus, is a clear index of not only the fact of maturity in literary craftsmanship but also a worthy attempt at internationalizing Nigerian novel tradition by the deliberate act of experimenting successfully, with literary exploration of the theory and practice of environmentalism or what can be conceived as Postcolonial Eco-Critical concerns.

POSTCOLONIAL CRITICISM, HUMANITY AND THE ENVIRONMENT IN LITERATURE

According to Kerridge and Sammels (1998), Ecocriticism was coined in the 1970s to denote the science or art that investigates the interrelations of all forms of plant and animal life that are ordinarily considered part of the natural world with their physical environment. It critically examines the relationships between literature and the biological, physical, and social sciences, as well as the physical environment. This is done with a keen awareness of the devastation caused to the environment by human activity.

The history of the representation of the natural environment in literature is as old as writing itself. According to Gottlieb (2003), this is also reflected in the accounts of the Garden of Eden in the Bible and other religions and the Pastoral (poetry) forms of literary representations by ancient Greeks and Roman poets such as Virgil who idealized the depiction of rural life as the survival of simplicity, peace, and harmonious co-existence that later generations of humanity have regretfully lost due to the involvement with the complexity and consumerism of urban industrial society.

These literary forms, which culminated in the 18th century's nostalgic view of a return to nature to rescue the "lost simplicity" that 18th-century Naturalism and Romantic poetry loudly echo and are nostalgic about, are typical examples. The development transformed into what we now refer to as nature writing, which consists of intimate, realistic, and detailed descriptions in prose, portraying the natural environment that novelists such as Emile Zola typify in his novel *Germinal*. This led to the evolution of what is known as "naturalism" in writing, which is a kind of extreme (scientific) realism of sorts.

Moreover, in the 20th century, the threats posed to the environment by rapid and large-scale urbanization, industrialization, and the increasing alarm occasioned by the rapid and extensive human despoliation of the natural environment led to the establishment of environmental protection movements by individuals and associations. One such example is the famous Wangari Maathai's Green Belt Movement in Kenya, and in the U.S., the environmental movement known as the Association for the Study of Literature and Environment (ASLE). It aims to preserve the remnants of the American wilderness, a theme that the media has explored through programs such as "Wild America", a television program anchored on the premise of "enjoy[ing] our wild America." In the Kenyan case, one such example is Wangari Maathai's Green Belt Movement of Kenya, through which she launched a robust advocacy effort to conserve the African fauna and flora.

Other sources of warnings about the dangers of our "civilized" lifestyles are also found in works by scientists and conservationists, including Aldo Leopold's *A Sand County Almanac* (1949) and Rachel Carson's *Silent Spring* (1962). These books, among many others, document the degradation of the environment and the devastation caused by chemical pesticides to wildlife in land, sea, and freshwater ecosystems. It is, however, common knowledge that the realization that the earth is in an environmental crisis is no more news. This crisis is manifested in the industrial and chemical pollution of the biosphere, which threatens the purity of water and air, which are essential to human life. Similarly, the depletion of forests and other natural resources increases the inevitability of the relentless extinction of plant and animal species, with the concomitant expansion of deserts and climate change, which have now become a global concern. These are real causes for grave concern.

Going cheek-by-jowl with these is the explosion of human population in an ever-decreasing agricultural space and with the potential for a virtual war, particularly in third world countries, where like in Nigeria and some West African countries, "the farmers/herders" clash has become a household word resulting in massive loss of human and animal life and destruction property. Given all these potential/kinetic disasters, efforts have been made over time to stem the tide of environmental destruction in various ways by individuals and organizations but more relevant to this chapter are the efforts of the Association for the Study of Literature and the Environment (A S L E) with its journal – *Interdisciplinary Studies in Literature and the Environment - ISLE*. (Huggan and Tiffin 2010, 21)

Although Huggan and Tiffin's (2010) report indicates the diversity and differences in the objectives of the Association's members, they note that they share some common grounds, namely that a) the postmodern civilization is anthropocentric, i.e., man-centered as opposed to and superior to nature. This argument, according to critics, is correct, implying that nature is for man to plunder and exploit regardless. This potentially destructive tendency is hinged on many reasons, including religion and transcendental conceptions that are rooted in ideas about God and nature that are sometimes couched in ornate binaries. Similarly, members of the Association agreed on the need to discard this binary: man/ woman,

man/culture, black/white, culture/civilization, rationality/emotion, etc.

It is argued and correctly so, that this discourse (of binary) elevates man as a rational subject while the woman is projected as the object and the weaker sex. Its dualism posits that man is a rational subject and woman an object and Other. The opposition then continues between rationality and emotion, culture and nature, etc. Nature is often assumed to be a gendered female, so women are perceived as territories for adventure, a wilderness to be tamed, owned, and controlled. Ecofeminists and literary critics in general, however, dispute all these claims and put man and woman on an equitable pedestal from a discursive point of view.

As pointed out by Brydon (1993, 50), Judith Williamson suggests that the insinuations positing the other, "woman is the 'desert island', an ideal location to be more easily colonized than an entire continent and picturing the colony as female, makes it so much more conquerable and receptive." This is what she calls an example of the "conflation of body politic, the female body, national place, and dominance."

In contrast to the discriminatory ideology that the binary "discourse" entails, members of *I SL E* perceive the binary situation as mutually constitutive and therefore interrelated: "We and our country create one another, depend upon one another, are part of one another ... our culture and our place are images of each other and inseparable from each other" (Berry in Huggan and Tiffin 2010, 210).

CRITIQUE OF ECOCRITICISM

Kerridge and Sammels (1998, 5) interrogate the essence of eco-criticism by questioning its objectives. Is it advocacy, a call to action, or is it "an imprisoned manifestation of late capitalism" masquerading as theory? Is Ecocriticism from an ecological perspective part of the problem and not the solution? From all indications, as Kerrides and Sammels (1998) suggest, a marriage of ecological thinking and literary studies promises to give a "theory" that extends its concerns on textuality as a complement to the call by Ecology for action on the environment. Thus, the insights provided by theory can be put to useful purpose to reinforce our ecological understanding of the relations between man, the environment, and literary representation. From this perspective, postcolonial Ecocriticism can be perceived as a theory and discourse that pays close attention to the question of how nature is constructed and/or represented in literary works. It therefore examines the representation of landscape and nature in its pristine state. It becomes an eco-centered rather than an anthropomorphic or man-centered theory. Therefore, ecocriticism from this perspective seeks to evaluate texts and ideas in terms of their adherence and faithfulness in response to environmental crises.

Buell in Abrams (2009) informs us of the major features of Ecocriticism, which is that the non-human (i.e., natural environment) is presented in writing and literature not just as a framing device or an invariable "setting" but also as an integral presence, which implies that human history is implicated in natural history. Similarly, for an ecocritic, the human interest is not the only legitimate interest in literature and literary investigation. Therefore, the argument goes, accounting for the role of man and human interest in the environment is part of the texts, and by implication, the author's ethical concerns. Moreover, the text or author should project "some sense of the environment" as a process, rather than a constant or a given or implicit in the text. In other words, the environment is not static. Finally, it is incumbent on the eco-critic to ensure that if the text does not live up to these ecocritical standards, it is the function of the critic to point out in which way and why the text or author fails to do so.

DEATH OF ETERNITY AND ENVIRONMENTALISM

Death of Eternity is an ambitious literary venture in which the writer attempts to engage in a variety of topical thematic areas that artistically portray elements that are outside the "normal", mundane concerns with what has come to be known as the dispensable aspects of culture: a concern with tradition and how the central character or authorial point of view valorizes the culture of the people and how s/he integrates into the dominant culture of the locale. This is a major feature of Kyuka Usman's *Death of Eternity*.

The novelist delves deeper into the modern and postmodern domains of futuristic and ecological phenomena confronting humanity and his society. Futuristic in the sense that the underlying, implicit thematic concern is more about the fate of man in general than about the immediate concern with culture and tradition only; contemporary, topical, and artistic as it is. Moreover, the adoption of a European character to tackle an African and universal theme sets the novel apart, regardless of its apparent similarity to African novels like *The Radiance of the King*.

THE NOVEL DEATH OF ETERNITY

The beginning of the novel reveals the protagonist, Tibor, at home in his country in Europe. He is plagued by many problems, such as a fastidious girlfriend, a wayward brother, and the need to find his mother's corpse. These problems, however, pale into insignificance when compared to his self-imposed mission of liberating Africa from the environmental disaster posed by the debilitating, postmodern, late capitalist consumerism. The urge to accomplish this mission leads him to Africa, among the locals of the Nunsa community, where he is revered as a hero of sorts. He leads the people of the local community against the global industrial complex through which the bastion of capitalist industrialist exploitation is threatening to exterminate the flora and fauna in the process of destroying the life and society of Nunsa, or by implication, the people living around the Kaduna Oil Refinery in northern Nigeria.

Here, oil spillage from the Kaduna Refinery has inhibited agricultural production, and the consequences of this on their existence are violence, hunger, disease, and terrorism. Youth unemployment and idleness further compound the tragic drama being unleashed on the Nunsa community as "the strange white man", Tibor, faces assassination as he assumes the role of a folk hero in the community where toxic material from the refinery is flushed into the River Kaduna. After exhausting all legal and civic means of redress, the people resort to violence and terrorism. This state of affairs creates a scenario of a "Bermuda Triangle" in which oil pollution, tree-cutting or logging, and HIV / AIDS combine to produce a catastrophic possibility of the total annihilation of life, property, and the entire flora and fauna of the community.

There is a sense in which in *Death of Eternity*, man, the environment, and the flora and fauna are interconnected and form an organic whole: the survival of one is crucial to the survival of the others. This relationship is implied in Tibor's makeup and personal disposition. He is obsessed with nature in its raw state, with the zeal of a romantic philosopher. For this reason, he communicates with the open sky in a form of nature worship, "enjoying the thrills of taking coffee in the sky" (Usman 2007, 8), and while in a state of delirium, he implores it to "come and take me, father winter I am all yours" (Usman 2007, 9). Other living creatures, including flora and fauna, are also shown to be intimately connected to the rest of the environment and the fate of humanity and society as a whole. Tibor's love and admiration for the fly and cockroach are only dwarfed by his missionary zeal and his affection for the Puli, which he symbolically nurtures; this is a pointer to his passion for preserving wildlife and conserving nature. Regarding wild animals, he prevents the British hunter from killing an old deer, despite the hunter's license. Tibor can, in this sense, be compared to the author of the novel in the latter's artistic attempts to provide a solution to social problems through artistic praxis.

Although Tibor, unlike the writer of the novel, is a typical romantic conservationist who finds friendship and personal fulfillment with Sergeant, his dog, he differs significantly from the writer of the novel, whose concern is with society in general. Instead, Tibor, typical of a European romantic tourist, is more enamored of the flora and fauna than with fellow human beings. His affection for trees is so overflowing, as it were, revealing his genuine enthusiasm as that of a modern tourist who cares more for the exotic scenery and natural vegetation than for people. His attitude towards the "dead mahogany" tree speaks volumes of his concern for nature when he:

> Stretched himself full-length on the tree and hugged it in a way he had never hugged a human being. After lying on the tree for what to an onlooker might appear to be an inordinately long time but to him was a fleeting moment, he got up and went back to the land cruiser (Usman 2007, 165).

Nature is portrayed as the canvas on which man's actions and inactions are played out, being a more potent force and phenomenon than man in all conditions of existence. But the enormity of the threat to human and social existence by the adverse effects of the activities of man is vividly illustrated by the indiscriminate industrial waste disposal into rivers, seas, and oceans as well as mining activities, industrial logging, and the ills of scientific inventions and technological manipulations of and use of chemicals, artificial fertilizers, pesticides that are often injurious to humanity and the environment.

The "Bermuda Triangle" is the metaphor for the aftermath of the possible evil results of human actions in the bid to achieve development, which ironically also threatens humans and the environment, is the evil "Trinity" of the forces of global terrorism, environmental pollution, degradation, and diseases such as HIV/AIDS:

> The trinity of environmental pollution, HIV/AIDS, and terrorism will destroy the world before the biblical trinity of God the Father, God the Son and God the Holy Spirit can save it...the new Bermuda Triangle has placed the death of eternity before us all. (Usman 2007, 77).

THE DIALECTICS OF MAN, NATURE, AND THE ENVIRONMENT IN DEATH OF ETERNITY

Through the use of symbolism, imagery, and allusions to scripture, the novelist navigates the terrain of environmentalism by depicting a powerful, imaginative picture of the possible disaster that has befallen humanity in Nunsa, and by extension, Nigeria and the world in general, in a dialectically involved relationship. The novelist's artistic depiction of the intimate, organic, and dialectical relations between human characters, nature (including fauna and flora), and the social environment is a palpable manifestation of his commitment to environmental philosophy and the theory of literary representation.

For instance, Francis' exploitation of nature for selfish, material reasons is an outright attitude of damning the consequences of deforestation. He ignores the warning from Tibor and the community in the mindless pursuit of his logging enterprise. Nature, however, through nemesis, takes back its pound of flesh when Francis dies because "those who live by the felling of trees will eventually be killed by the trees they have been killing" (p. 168). Similarly, the Pollution Control Manager, whose greed and corruption led him to corner millions of naira meant for waste management, but which he corruptly enriches himself monthly, is by implication the cancer that is responsible for polluting River Kodewa or River Kaduna.

The river stands as a source of life and sustenance for many families, animals, and plants, but the industrial waste being flushed into it due to the manager's corruption becomes a source of death for humans, animals, and plants. The deformation and dying plantain stock powerfully symbioses the dialectical relationships between human activity and its effect on nature and the environment:

> Man is the cancer of the earth. Excessive desire generates excessive greed. The beast of the jungle is better than man. The lion kills only when it is hungry and kills only to meet its hunger. For days when the lion is not hungry, it sleeps side by side with the zebra and plays with it. But man, full or starving devours the world. (Usman 2007, 93).

The dialectical relationship of man, nature, and the environment is further emphasized by the writer's artistic portrayal of Mmanya's experience on the riverbank when:

> For the third time, (Mmanya) peered at the reflection in the not–too–blue water but did not have a good view of his face as he had in the same place some nine years ago. Even though other parts of his body, like his teeth had been aging, his eyes curiously, had refused to join...so if he could not get a good glimpse of himself in the water, it could not be due to his poor sight, but due to something in the water...something dark and grey seem to have flowed into the river, *it was as though the river, like him was developing grey hair and might soon die.* (Usman 2007, 36, emphasis added).

This passage is a fitting demonstration of one of the key tenets of postcolonial ecocriticism, which suggests that human history is inextricably linked to natural history. It vividly links Mmanya's health with that of the river and therefore with nature as a living, breathing phenomenon. Thus, the juxtaposition of aging grey hairs on Mmanya's head and the "dark, grey" particles that flow into the river is a metaphor for the river's aging, and, hence, like Mmanya and the surrounding vegetation, it is on the path of death. However, like the cancerous disease that man is, he shares a strong connection with the death of eternity. In other words, if nature catches a cold, a man sneezes: "There is a close link between the unnatural (i.e., polluted environments) environment and evil" (Usman 2007, 96). Thus, the writer has artistically succeeded in depicting the conviction that accounting for the role of man and human interest in the environment is part of the text, and by implication, the author's ethical concerns. Moreover, the text or author projects "some sense of the environment" as an integral process of the environment, rather than a constant or a given or implicit (setting) in the text only, as is the case with conventional settings in conventional novelistic writing.

It is in the context of the dialectics of nature, man, and the environment that Tibor resorts to violence and terrorism as an antidote to environmental destruction, pollution, and degradation, which ultimately leads to the failure of his mission. This is because his resort to violence undermines the ecological missionary undertaking, and thus, like Francis, Tibor becomes a victim of his own self-indulgence. Like the other characters in the novel, he also becomes an enemy of nature. There is, therefore, a connection between Zolta's killing of Puli and Tibor's killing of the pet dog, Sergeant. The implication of all this is that Humanity is destined for doomsday or the end of existence because it has violated the covenant of the symbiotic relationships that are the essence of life on the planet.

If Tibor were able to achieve his aim in life and succeed in his mission at Nunsa, he would have succeeded in attaining, through enlightenment and action, the loud bang that his father wanted him to achieve in life, but Tibor lacks the talent and humanity to do so:

> Let me tell you something my son, talent is the call, the flash and rambling of destiny. As lightning becomes thunder, so talent becomes destiny…what I want from you is a long lightning followed by a loud bang of thunder…any human being that wants to register his presence in the world …can only do so through a loud bang (Usman 2007, 16).

Tibor's recurring questions and tendency to interrogate the essence of his quest are reflections to "ever create the big bang my (his) father wanted me to create" (Usman 2007, 292) and thunder and lightning are the metaphors of nature used to illustrate the dialectical relations of the essence of symbiosis or the interdependence of all living things on nature and the environment. Just as Tibor struggles with the evil "Bermuda Triangle" of HIV/AIDS, deforestation, and oil pollution in the Nunsa community, so is the writer in Africa grappling with the forces of discrimination, poverty, and deliberate marginalization from both society and the socio-political establishments.

Similarly, Mmanya's life is shown to be intimately tied to the prevalence of natural elements and other characteristics of the animal kingdom. For instance, Mmanya possesses a "running walk of a dog" (Usman 2007, 38) and he perceives death as the "snake of Egbudu but there is no stick to crush it" (Usman 2007, 39). On his part, Tibor describes Odoko as a snake, and the latter proves fatal later on when he becomes responsible for the outbreak of HIV/AIDS in the community. Symbolically, therefore, the novel *Death of Eternity* could be read as the reflection of the trials and tribulations of not only the enthusiastic foreign conservationist but also that of the writer in Africa who strives to minister to social benefits but who is nonetheless unappreciated by society.

Even in the use of language such as the proverbs deployed by the writer, the allusion to the primacy of nature is unmistakable. For example, "we are ants in an anthill that is crumbling; we are fishes in a small brook whose water is fast drying up", all these are deliberate artistic devices used by the writer to drive home the power of the thematic effort that drives his imaginative endeavors. And they all point to the fact that all are involved in one another and share the same fate when it comes to the business of life and existence on Earth.

The description of the virgin landscape and vegetation, as well as the appreciation and display of the authenticity of the life of the flora and fauna, are unique literary enactments of the biblical story of the fall of man from the Garden, careering towards doomsday, which is occasioned by the destructive nature of human activity. Another instance of the predominance of nature in the course of humanity's survival is depicted in the image of the river in *Death of Eternity*. This is symbolically enacted to portray it as the essence of life. It represents the life-giving elixir that the writer employs to depict the intimacy of life and the survival of all living creatures. The river is shown to be aging by the way it is drying up, and therefore gradually dying in the process, during which pollution from industrial toxic waste from the oil refinery destroys the environment. Moreover, in a startling but apt symbolism, Tibor compares himself to a "beehive, bees without children, or hope of any, labor [ing] for children of others for weeks without food and water until they wear themselves out. I am such a bee" (Usman 2007, 70). The lack of children is an indirect reference to the effects of the AIDS scourge, which may prevent the current generation from reproducing heirs that will inherit them into the next generation. This symbolism aptly captures also, the fate of the creative writer in Africa whose progress and development are hampered by not only the lack of material and social appreciation but also by the lack of succeeding generations of writers that will continue with the writing given the brain drain and lack of encouragement to the existing generation of writers to toe the creative line in our universities.

All said and done, the idea that literature in Northern Nigeria is still in its infancy is a very questionable premise given the literary maturity and recent artistic efforts from writers in Northern Nigeria, such as Adamu Kyuka Usman's novelistic forays in *Death of Eternity* and many of his novels, such as *Last Saints* and *Hope in Anarchy*. Within the scope of his entire works, Kyuka Usman warns through his depiction of violence, which implicitly reveals the outcome of social injustice. His futuristic depiction of violence has indeed foreshadowed the current spate of violence not only in Africa but specifically in contemporary Nigeria. We can therefore say that the author has succeeded in many ways in shifting the traditional paradigm of the obsession with culture and tradition to a contemporary concern with modern and postmodern issues of immediate and dire consequences for humanity.

CONCLUSION

This chapter explored the significant challenges that creative writers face from both practical and theoretical perspectives, while also scrutinizing the argument that literary creativity in Nigeria, particularly in the northern region, remains underdeveloped. However, writers such as Adamu Kyuka Usman are rising to the challenge of meeting up with postmodern literary trends and motifs. In the final analysis, this chapter holds the view that the assumption that literary artistic practice in Nigeria is in its infancy is out of tune with contemporary realities in Africa, Nigeria, and, in particular, northern Nigeria. This position is demonstrated through the application of postcolonial ecocriticism as a major canvas to explore environmentalism in the novel *Death of Eternity*. It is argued that the novel, far from being "childish" is a mature, bold, and postmodern attempt by the writer to not only create "a loud bang" on the African literary scene but also an instance of a foray into the futuristic domain that has taken him away from the "return to the source" mentality of most African novels. The adoption of a non-African central character and some aspects of the setting attest to the writer's brave acceptance and picking up the gauntlet in response to Emeyonu's relevant but long-neglected challenge to African writers to effect a paradigm shift and new directions in creativity. Although the novel may not be numerically representative of the overall literary output of the region, it significantly attests to the exception to the generalization of novelistic infancy. Similarly, the novel symbolizes, to some extent, the myriad problems faced by the African creative writer in contemporary African society. This novel promises to elevate the status of African literature to a global reckoning, much like the emerging and burgeoning literature of Africans in the Diaspora. The vitality and energy with which the narrative enacts the chilling sense of future shock and impending doom with which Kyuka's novel resonates, is a testimony to the writer's de facto announcement of his arrival to the elite precinct of African literature with a loud bang in contradistinction to Tibor's efforts in *Death of Eternity*.

REFERENCES

Abdu, Sale K. 2006. "Environmentalism and Self-Exploration in Aliyu Kamal's *Fire in My Backyard*." In *Toward Sustaining Creative Writing in Northern Nigeria: Proceedings of the First Summit of Northern Nigerian Writers*, edited by Abdullahi Samaila, Ismaila Garba, and Kamar Hamaza, 67–72. Ibadan: Kraft Books.

Abrams, M.H. 2009. *A Glossary of Literary Terms*. Boston: Wadsworth Cengage Learning.

Alkali, Zaynab. 2007. "Sustaining Creative Writing in Northern Nigeria." In *Toward Sustaining Creative Writing in Northern Nigeria: Proceedings of the First Summit of Northern Nigerian Writers*, edited by Abdullahi Samaila, Ismaila Garba, and Kamar Hamza, 47–60. Ibadan: Kraft Books Limited.

Bertens, Hans. 2001. *Literary Theory: The Basics*. London: Routledge.

Brydon, Diana. 1993. "The White Inuit Speaks: Contamination as Literary Strategy." *Australian-Canadian Studies* 11 (2): 37–52.

Buell, Lawrence. 1995. *The Environmental Imagination: Theory, Nature Writing, and the Formation of American Culture*. Princeton: Princeton University Press.

Carson, Rachel. 1994. *Silent Spring*. New York: Houghton Mifflin Company.

DeLoughrey, Elizabeth, and George Handley, eds. 2011. *Post-Colonial Ecologies*. Oxford: Oxford University Press.

Emenyonu, Ernest. 2005. "New Directions in African Literature." In *African Literature Today* 25. Ibadan: African World Press and H.E.B. Nigeria.

Gottlieb, Roger, ed. 2003. *This Sacred Earth: Religion, Nature, and the Environment*. New York: Routledge.

Huggan, Graham, and Helen Tiffin. 2010. *Postcolonial Ecocriticism: Literature, Animals, Environment*. London: Routledge.

Ike, Chukwuemeka V. 1983. "Problems of the Book Industry in Nigeria." In *Culture and the Book Industry in Nigeria: Proceedings of NAFEST '83 Seminar*, edited by Sule Bello and Augie Abdullah R., Maiduguri, Borno State. Lagos: National Council for Arts and Culture.

Leopold, Aldo. 1949. *A Sand County Almanac and Sketches Here and There*. London: Oxford University Press.

Mathaai, Wangari. 2007. *The Green Belt Movement: Sharing the Approaches and the Experience*. New York: Lantern Books.

Morretti, Franco. 2008. "The Novel: History and Theory." *New Left Review* 52 (July/August).

Richard, Kerridge, and Neil Sammels, eds. 1998. *Writing the Environment: Eco-Criticism and Literature*. London: Zed Books.

Usman, Adamu K. 2007. *Death of Eternity*. London: Athena Press.

CHAPTER FIFTEEN

Folktale as a Pedagogical Agent for Social Justice
An Ecocritical Perspective

Tayo Olubunmi Agboola

INTRODUCTION

The interaction of orality and environmentalism is essential to modern literary scholarship. To convey social realities, the African literary artist consistently recreates sociocultural and economic experiences, including issues related to orality and environmental discourse, as reflected in the oral narratives of specific environments in both oral and written media (Agboola 2022, 1). "Art is and has always been in the service of man," writes Chinua Achebe (1975, 175). Similarly, Wole Soyinka asserts that "the artist has always functioned in African society as a recorder of his society's mores and experiences and as a voice of vision in his own time (Soyinka 1997, 36)." The artist creates the text from the environment, conveying the sensibilities of the people to whom it is attributed (Agboola 2022, 2). The representation of ecological experiences and justice in literature attests to literature's utilitarian value. Social justice and environmental discourses are essential aspects of human experiences that literary artists frequently depict in oral and written forms. This discourse examines the significance of folktales in shaping laws governing ecological, intra- and interpersonal relationships, communal cohesion, ethical regimes, and justice systems among the Yoruba.

To different degrees, oral art forms in Africa have conveyed African sensibilities and consciousness, including experiences that border on managing the natural environment. From a classical viewpoint, in traditional African societies, myths and other forms of oral narratives, such as folktales and legends, were used to define, describe, and give meaning to all aspects of life—natural, civil, sacred, and social. This classification is evident in the Yoruba folktales, which guide the society in sustaining and ensuring its continuity. Oral narratives, such as folktales, can awaken people's interest in social justice issues and allow them to participate in society. The community observes and adheres to how punishment is used to mend society and create order through the stories.

The Yoruba have a well-developed system of conflict resolution mechanisms and principles that govern the administration of justice. Furthermore, religion and rituals are employed for social control and the imposition of sanctions. Peacemaking between conflicting parties is central to the Yoruba adjudication process, which aims to maintain social equilibrium. In the Yoruba belief system, punishment, which is also an aspect of justice, is referred to as ìjìyà and can include flogging, whipping, beating, tying, chaining, imprisonment, execution, ejection or banishment, razing an offender's house to the ground, and so on (Ajisafe 1946, 36). It is facilitated by socially defined sins (èsè) that violate culturally defined norms and laws, destroying social harmony among natural beings and between the natural and spiritual realms of existence. In short, sin is an offense committed against man within a culture. It destroys another's life force, especially that of the community. For example, such wrongs violate the invisible realm and disrupt the cohesion of an ordered world, resulting in injustice. The implication is that one must maintain harmonious relationships among community members and take the necessary steps to bridge every breach of harmony and strengthen the community bond, primarily through justice and sharing. It shows that the Yoruba firmly hold the principle of justice, as its absence may disrupt communal living. It means that everybody is treated fairly under the law and the norms of the land. No individual can be unjustly treated for a crime they know nothing about as its consequence, and if attempted, it may be grievous for the entire community (Taiwo 1998, 210). Complementary balance is thus the goal of justice for the Yoruba. As the Yoruba believe that all lives are interconnected and exist in a conjoining web, justice that brings balance among all humans and non-humans is essential.

Extant African studies have examined the representation of justice and ecological issues in oral narratives. Still, they have not sufficiently explored how the Yoruba justice system in folktales contributes to the preservation and maintenance of the environment. Additionally, while nature has been used as a backdrop in several critical works, few studies have critically employed ecocriticism theory in their discussions. Sunday Owoade (2020) examines the employment of folklore in literary arts as a viable way of preserving and documenting the culture, while Oluwole Coker and Adeshina (2008) investigate how the knowledge of law among the Yoruba is entrenched in having a deep understanding of the folklore as consisting in the elements of culture, tradition, language, and religion. Adeeko Adeleke (2017) and Ayo Kehinde (2010) have investigated the importance of festivals and folktales to Yoruba society. Kehinde has specifically examined how folktales are essential to the Yoruba environment. He examined the didactic nature of folktales and their impact on people, without considering the environment and its preservation. Additionally, Enongene (2018) examines the relevance of folktales in promoting social values in Africa, illustrating how these narratives offer insight into a community's social norms, values, thoughts, concepts, and ideas, drawing implications for positive change. It is based on the assumption that African folktales, particularly those from Cameroon, promote social and ethical values, foster human understanding, facilitate the elimination of anti-social behavior, and contribute to the construction of social identity.

Furthermore, Sanusi (2015) elaborates on the role of women, particularly mothers, as critical agents in educating children about the dangers of climate change. While the research emphasizes folktales as an effective tool for imparting knowledge about climate change to children, it overlooks the complementary role of men, specifically fathers, within Yoruba culture. Similarly, Berat, Dilara, and Sibel (2014) examined 15 children's pictorial texts from Aboriginal and American Indian cultures to understand how these cultures address nature and environmental issues. While this research is essential for children's knowledge development, it is limited by its focus on specific cultural contexts, thereby not fully encompassing cultural diversity. Finally, Raymond Ogunade (2005) examines the approach to environmental issues in Yoruba religion and its implications for leadership and society in Nigeria.

Despite the rich research in Yoruba people's folklore and oral literature, a void remains in orality and environmental studies, particularly in the discourse of law and order as it pertains to the natural environment.

Using the literary analytical research method, the study examines the representation of justice and environmental experiences in selected Yoruba folktales. The data were obtained from Olagoke Ojo's *Ijapa Tiroko Oko Yannibo* (1973) and Harold Courlander's *Tales of Gods and Heroes* (1973). Drawing insights from a theoretical perspective informed by studies in ecocriticism, this study analyzed the selected tales (*Moremi and the Egunguns, Elephant and Tortoise,* and *Tortoise and Olokun*) in the light of their engagement with environmental degradation that occurs synchronously with the breakdown of law and order, and how this is corrected.

ECOCRITICISM: A THEORETICAL FRAMEWORK

William Rueckert (1978) coined the term ecocriticism in his critical essay "Literature and Ecology: An Experiment in Ecocriticism." The term 'eco' is derived from the Greek root word 'oi kos,' which means 'household or earth,' and 'logy' is derived from the Greek root word' logos,' which means logical discourse. They refer to criticism of the house and the environment as depicted in literature. Ecocriticism, according to Rueckert, incorporates ecology or ecological principles into the study of literature. According to Lawrence Buell, ecocriticism is "a study of the relationship between literature and the environment conducted in a spirit of commitment to environmentalist's praxis." (1995, 430).

Furthermore, ecocriticism is more than just a study of nature; it has distinguished itself from traditional nature writing, first by taking an ethical stand and committing to the natural world, and then by linking the human and non-human worlds. According to Buell (1995, 138), there are two waves of ecocriticism. "The first wave of ecocritics concentrated on nature writing, nature poetry, and wilderness fiction." They used to support the organism philosophy. Here, environment refers to the natural environment (Buell 1995, 21). The wave aimed to protect the "biotic community" (Coupe 2000, 4). This wave's ecocritics discussed "the effects of culture on nature, intending to celebrate nature, berate its despoilers, and reversing their harm through political action." (Howarth 1996, 69). As a result, ecocriticism initially focused on environmental protection. The second wave of ecocritics is more concerned with environmental justice and a 'social ecocriticism' that values urban landscapes as much as natural landscapes (Buell 1995, 22). This school of thought is known as revisionist ecocriticism. It seeks to locate natural remnants in cities and exposes eco-injustice crimes against society's marginalized sections. The Ecocritic interprets texts on nature writing. They use them as a context for analyzing the principles and our society's customs concerning nature. The result is frequently a critique of how our culture devalues and degrades nature.

Despite its novelty, particularly in the African context, the concept of ecocriticism is not new to indigenous Africans and African literary writers. This notion is most likely based on the fact that, contrary to Eurocentric perceptions of Africans and their relationships and attitudes toward ecological units (cf. Martin, 2012), Africans have consistently demonstrated environmental consciousness. This assertion is supported by some available literature (cf. Traore, 2019; Mwangi, 2019; Huggan and Tiffin, 2015; Iheka 2015). Although this literature highlights some of the current environmental issues confronting the African state, it also suggests that Africans are becoming increasingly environmentally conscious. Iheka discusses environmental justice in Achebe's *Arrow of God*, pointing out that in Achebe's novel, the snake – the royal python – is a sacred deity that connects the people and their gods. Thus, the killing of the snake by Oduche, under the influence of his Christian belief, is tantamount to the disruption of the harmony of communal living. As such, there is a need for justice for the snake (2015, 86).

The deep-seated environmental logic in this conceptualization of the snake is that the survival community is culturally dependent on the survival and functionality of the snake. Such an analysis underscores pre-colonial society's symbiotic relationship between humans and non-humans. In addition, scholars have examined the representation of other environmental issues bedeviling the postcolonial African state. For instance, Traore engages in the adoption of recycling within an African context. Basing his argument on Camara Laye's *The African Child*, Traore proposes a practical solution to addressing the issue of waste management within an African context (2019, 260).

One distinguishing feature of African ecocriticism is the combination of justice and environmental exaltation while paying attention to indigenous knowledge and arts of the African community. When discussing the African and, by extension, the Yoruba environment, special attention must be paid to the people's spirituality and culture, as this is the foundation of pedagogy in all African communities. These lessons help reinforce the ecocritical perspective on justice and preservation as it applies to Africa's diverse cultures.

ENVIRONMENTAL DEGRADATION AND INJUSTICE IN THE SELECTED YORUBA FOLKTALES

Environmental degradation and injustice are evident in the following tales: *Moremi and the Egunguns, Tortoise and Olokun,* and *Elephant and Tortoise.* In the tales, we see the injustices between humans and non-humans. The environment described in these tales is one of depravity and toxicity. The narrative, *Moremi and the Egunguns,* is a legendary tale that centers on the character Moremi, an indigene of Ife, whose heroic exploits delivered her people and land from the marauding visitation of the Ile-Igbo community. Ife, a productive land, is hounded by the Ile-Igbo warriors due to the lack of fertile land in Ile-Igbo. Moremi's sacrifice and bravery helped rescue her people and land from being deserted. In the narrative, *Moremi and the Egunguns,* the effect of climate change is visible between the two cities (Ile-Igbo and Ife), separated by a thick forest. In Ile-Igbo, due to soil degradation caused by environmental changes, their land is no longer suitable for planting, and when they do plant, their crops yield poorly. The King of Ile-Igbo laments: The land of Ile-Igbo did not grow enough food, and often, some families had to eat wild roots because their crops were poor (Courlander 1973, 5).

From the King's lamentation, due to the poor crops in Ile-Igbo, the people are faced with food scarcity, which is evident in what they eat. Some of the features of climate change, such as erosion, compaction, nutrient imbalance, pollution, acidification, and increasing salinity, have been affecting soil across the globe, reducing its ability to support plant life and grow crops. This is where the Ile-Igbo community finds itself, lacking arable land, which forces families to forage for wild roots. Unfortunately, since women are homemakers in indigenous settings, the land degradation issue will hugely affect the productivity and sustenance of their various families. Additionally, a comparison is made between the communities of Ile-Igbo and Ife to illustrate the extent of soil degradation in one community and the presence of fertile soil in another. Ife represents a land filled with milk and honey, where the harvest of Mother Earth blesses the citizens. The hunter from Ile-Igbo gives a vivid description of this green land:

> Then they came to the edge of the forest and saw Ife standing there. They saw Ife's field on all sides. They saw the fertile gardens and the granaries filled with food. Its granaries are full of grains. Its market is full of people selling manioc, corn, and yams (Courlander 1973, 5).

From the above excerpt, two features are evident: firstly, the fruitfulness of the Ife land. The people cannot go hungry with the fertility and greenery of their land. The Ife community, due to their arable land, will be employers of labor and grow cash crops for the survival of their immediate families and society. Women and men in this community will obviously not endure the hardship of trekking long distances to find edible food that may adversely affect their health. Secondly, we can see an apparent economic boom in Ife. Agriculture has helped the economy of Ife and provided a means of survival due to its arable land. Growth in agriculture helps attain global food security, and reducing hunger hinges primarily on this role. Food insecurity prevails in the Ile-Igbo community, prompting the warriors to migrate spatially due to environmental changes. As evident in the narrative, the Ile-Igbo warriors pretend to masquerade to despoil the Ife community to get food for their families and community. Though migration is not permanent but seasonal or spatial, the Ile-Igbo community constantly lures the Ife people to become part of their lives:

> The looting of Ife became a way of life for the Ile-Igbo, whose people neglected their gardens even more than before. Now, there was plenty of food for everyone in Ile-Igbo, and there was no need to worry about the crops in the fields (Courlander 1973, 5).

Migration due to environmental changes leads the characters in the narratives to move and dominate other communities. They establish various "isms" by dominating and plundering, with the weak continually fearing the strong, as evident in *Moremi and the Egunguns*. Migration also results in overpopulation, causing food scarcity in the region to which it migrates, as the agricultural output cannot sustain the increased population. This situation is surmised in the text:

> Life in Ife became hard. Though the people there worked industriously, they no longer had enough to eat. They planted and gathered their crops, and then the mysterious Egunguns came out of the forest and took everything away (Courlander 1973, 6).

Migration, therefore, aids in the imbalance challenged by ecocritics. The imbalance gives room for a dual or hierarchical positioning in any society. Ecological scholars, therefore, call for environmental ethics or the green movement to preserve and conserve a changing environment. Additionally, from the excerpts, we observe the neglect of Mother Nature, which fosters a hierarchical attitude between humans and non-human beings. By neglecting Mother Nature, the Ile-Igbo warriors have introduced a volatile method of acquiring food that disregards the survival of their fellow humans, thereby breaking the circle of connectivity. To reconnect the broken cycle, Moremi reinvents herself by shedding her traditional passive role to become Ife's savior in the mentioned text. The narrative surmises her stance thus:

> In Ife, there was a woman named Moremi. She went to the Oba of Ife, saying, "These spirits from the forest, where do they come from? Where do they go? Why do dead spirits need to consume the food of the living? If things go on this way, Ife itself will die and become a dead spirit. We should find out about these Egunguns. Therefore, when they come again, I will remain in the city and learn why they continue to harass us (Courlander 1973, 7).

Moremi's penchant for saving Ife leads to her being captured by the disguised Egungun of Ile-Igbo, whose King finds her beautiful and marries her, thereby giving her access to the secret of the Egunguns. Using her sexuality, carved in her beauty and sex, she achieved her aim and returned to Ife, where she divulged the secret of the Egunguns and saved her people from the constant raiding of their land, produce, and harvest. In this context, the female body becomes a preserving and protective tool used to save her community and Mother Nature.

Subsequently, Man's neglect of nature is also evident in the legendary tale of Moremi and the Egunguns, leading to food scarcity in the Ile-Igbo community. In the tale, the people of Ile-Igbo neglected their land as a result of their decision to raid Ile-Ife. They were content with stealing instead of tending to Mother Nature. The continuous neglect of the earth results in them being impoverished: "The looting of Ife became a way of life for Ile-Igbo, whose people neglected their gardens even more than before" (Courlander 1973, 5).

Famine in this town is caused by man's decision not to see himself as part of nature. The community lacks environmental ethics that can help sustain the environment, which inevitably leads to famine and a lack of sustenance for its people. The extent of famine in this community is alarming, as the people feed on dung to survive, showing how debased humanity can become when faced with hunger. Arable land, combined with sustainable environmental ethics, can help control food scarcity. By relying on immoral acts of survival, humans have initiated a gap in the web of life, drastically affecting both humans and non-humans in society. The effects range from famine to loss of life and sickness.

Furthermore, in *Elephant and Tortoise's* folkloric narrative, we see the Elephant terrorizing the community and further destroying their farmlands. Symbolically, the Elephant represents the bourgeoisie and their oppressive nature towards the proletariat. Their impact on the have-nots is repressive and intimidating. The community dreads this giant creature and silently mourns the loss of their livelihood and mental health. Animals, especially cattle, goats, and other livestock, straying into farmlands and destroying farm produce, are a rampant problem in the Nigerian environment. With the herders' situation in Nigeria, the loss of millions of investments has gone down the drain due to the assault of these straying and controlled animals. Just as we have in the narrative, *Elephant and Tortoise*, the Nigerian communities continue to live in perpetual fear due to the occurrence of loss of lives when the herders are challenged. The narrative sums up this fearsome manifestation thus:

> Bi o ti dun fun awon ara ilu yii to, sibe won ni ota. Ota won naa buru to bee ti ki i se asodun ti a ba pe e ni. Ota orun ko gbebo. Eni ti o doju ota ti a wi yii ko awon ara ilu naa ni ogbeni Erin!

> Notwithstanding the way people of this town enjoy, they had an enemy. Their enemy is evil. He should be referred to as a 'sworn enemy'. The person who waged the enmity war against the town's people was Mr Elephant! The Elephant turned all their farms into his home. He ate and destroyed all their farm produce (Olagoke 1973, 115).

The Elephant is an enemy because it deliberately destroys the farmland of this community without regard for the survival of the people of this town. Once their farmlands are destroyed, food scarcity is invariably not far from this once-flourishing community. Animal invasion of farmlands is a prevalent occurrence in Nigeria, attributed to herders' nomadic mode of living. Besides causing the loss of the fauna and flora in the environment, this method also leads to tribal wars and financial instability among farmers within the migrating environment. The more fertile the land is, the more abuse the animals inflict on it. It is, therefore, ironic that the land that is supposed to nurture man is severely abused by animals, controlled by men, and left to die. There is, therefore, a need for them to fight and defend their farmland. To seek justice, they asked for the help of the Tortoise, who had conceived a way to trap the Elephant and stop his terror. The Tortoise directs the community thus:

> Kabiyesi, pase nisinsinyin ki awon gende ilu gbe koto nla kan ni aarin agbala yin, oba. Ki koto naa fe ni ogun ese bata, ki jijin re si je ogbon ese. Ki won fi ogbon ati laakaye te eni ati aso alarabara si ori re. ki gbogbo ilu si pejo sibe pelu ilu ati orin nigba ti mo ba mu Erin wo ilu wa lati fi je oba yeeriye, ati ayederu. Bi Erin ba si ti jokoo lori aga naa, bee ni yoo rii esin ara re. nigba naa, ki awon gende ma jafara lati ko ponpo

bo o mo inu koto naa.

His Majesty, direct able men to dig a big pit in your backyard now, let the hole be wide at twenty feet and deep at thirty feet. They should apply wisdom to spread mats and design clothes on them. The whole town should gather there with drums and songs when I take in Elephant to install him as a fake and false king. When Elephant sits on the throne, he would be put to shame. Then, the able men should quickly hit him with clubs inside the pit (Olagoke 1973, 117).

The Elephant is tricked into believing he will be a king, so he dances into the village and falls into his death pit, just as intended. The village obtains justice, and the Tortoise is richly rewarded for his courageous role in fighting their terrible foe. In addition, the *Elephant and Tortoise* folktale conveys how the strong in society feast on the weak. The Elephant in this tale threatens the community in which the Tortoise resides, and in a bid to save the community, the Tortoise goes on a journey. In the tale, the oppressive nature of the Elephant is on display. He destroys and feasts on the farmland of this community without recourse to the community's survival. Due to his size, it is difficult to challenge Mr Elephant, who will trample upon any animal that dares to challenge him:

Gbogbo oko ti won n da ni Erin fi se ibudo, ti o si n je awon nnkan ogin won ru. Ohun isoro gbaa ni oro yii je fun won, won ko si mo bi won o ti se segun re, nitori pe Erin koja eran ti a a fi takute mu, bee ni Ajanaku si kuro ni eran ti a a fi Aja pa.

The Elephant turned all their farms into his home. He ate and destroyed all their farm produce. This issue was a big problem for them, and they didn't know how to overcome it because the Elephant is more than an animal to be caught in a trap; also, the Elephant is more than an animal that one can hunt with dogs (Olagoke 1973, 115).

In his oppressive state, the Elephant was turning the community into a subservient one by killing their source of livelihood—farmland—thereby starting a gradual famine in the land. Due to his size, his selfishness, and control (power), he became a dictator who could not be admonished or dialoged with. As a dictator, a patriarchal male is prone to narcissistic tendencies, making him feel he must be in control—no wonder the patriarchal individual seeks ways to control other humans and non-humans to demonstrate his importance.

Also, the folkloric tale of *Tortoise and Olokun* conveys Tortoise's sojourn to the domain of Olokun in search of food for his community and the resultant effect of the journey. Like the Ile-Igbo community, which eats wild roots, the community in the tale *Tortoise and Olokun* is anguished at the loss of arable land that has affected their community. The land has refused to yield a good harvest, causing the animals and humans in the society to be malnourished and on the verge of death. In desperation, the King called a meeting and mourned thus:

> A gbin isu, ko ta, a gbin agbado, ko gbo, a gbin eree ati awuje, ko si okankan ti o so nitori naa ni mo se pe yin ki a jo jiroro lori oro naa, ki a si wa nnkan se si.

> We cultivated yam, but it didn't grow; we planted maize, it didn't mature; we planted cowpea and cocoyam, but none of them yielded; that is the reason why I called you so that we can deliberate on the issue and find a solution (Olagoke 1973, 91).

The above excerpt indicates a deficiency of land nutrients and acidification of the community's soil, which reduces fertility and hinders plant germination. Unfortunately, farmers in this community are not economically viable since their source of livelihood has become bleak and futile. Poverty becomes the result of climate change as the working class and non-working citizens battle the lack of food. Food, which is a basic necessity, is now a scarce commodity due to the environmental degradation evident in the community's deplorable and languishing state. The famine affected both the rich and the poor, with no disparity between community members. The narrator asserts thus:

Ni igba laelae, iyan mu pupo ni ilu kan bayii to bee ti o fi je pe o nto ojo keta ki oba paapaa to maa ri ounje eekan soso je, ki a ma sese so ti awon mekunnu laarin ilu.

Once upon a time, there was a famine in a town. The famine was severe to the extent that even the King ate once in three days, not to talk of commoners in the town (Olagoke 1973, 91).

The poor, women, and children are more affected by climate change because they are at the bottom of the food chain. These "others" in society are vulnerable to depraved behaviors detrimental to their society's growth.

CONCLUSION

Utilizing an ecocritical perspective, folktales emerge as potent pedagogical tools for advancing social justice. Rooted in cultural heritage, these narratives offer a distinctive framework for interrogating environmental ethics and societal norms. Educators can effectively leverage folktales to foster social equity and environmental awareness among students by integrating ecocritical viewpoints. This approach enriches the educational process and facilitates a deeper understanding of the interconnections between natural systems and human societies. As enduring sources of wisdom, folktales provide a creative means for cultivating empathy, critical thinking, and a sense of collective responsibility. In addressing the complexities of social justice and ecological sustainability, it is imperative to incorporate folktales into educational practices, thus nurturing informed and responsible global citizens rather than merely acknowledging traditional narratives.

REFERENCES

Achebe, Chinua. 1975. *Morning Yet on Creation Day: Essays and Studies in African Literature*. London: Heinemann.

Adeeeko, Adeleke. 2017. *Arts of Being Yoruba: Divination, Allegory, Tragedy, Proverb, Panegyric*. Bloomington: Indiana University Press.

Agboola, Olubunmi Tayo. 2022. "Gender, Environmentalism and Oral Arts: Ecofeminist Readings of Selected Yoruba Oral Narratives." PhD diss., Ajayi Crowther University.

Ahi, Berat, Dilara Yaya, and Sibel Oszoy. 2014. "The Concept of Environment in Folktales from Different Cultures: Analysis of Content and Visuals." *International Electronic Journal of Environmental Education* 4 (1): 1–17.

Ajisafe, Ajayi Kolawole. 1946. *The Laws and Customs of the Yoruba People.* New York: Routledge & Sons, Limited.

Buell, Lawrence. 1995. *The Environmental Imagination: Thoreau, Nature Writing, and the Formation of American Culture.* Cambridge: Harvard University Press.

Courlander, Harold. 1973. *Tales of Yoruba Gods and Heroes.* New York: Crown Publishing.

Coupe, Laurence. 2000. *The Green Studies Reader: From Romanticism to Ecocriticism.* New York: Routledge.

Enongene, Sone. 2018. "The Folktale and Social Values in Traditional Africa." *Eastern African Literary and Cultural Studies* 2 (6): 1–21.

Howarth, William. 1996. "Some Principles of Ecocriticism." In *The Ecocriticism Reader: Landmarks in Literary Ecology*, edited by Cheryll Glotfelty and Harold Fromm, 69–91. Athens: University of Georgia Press.

Huggan, Graham, and Helen Tiffin. 2010. *Postcolonial Ecocriticism: Literature, Animals, Environment.* New York: Routledge.

Iheka, Cajetan. 2015. "African Literature and the Environment: A Study in Postcolonial Ecocriticism." PhD diss., Michigan State University.

Kehinde, Ayo. 2010. "Story-Telling in the Service of Society: Exploring the Utilitarian Values of Nigerian Folktales." *Journal of Social and Cultural Studies* 21 (2): 29–45.

Martin, Glen. 2012. *Game Changer: Animal Rights and the Fate of Africa's Wildlife.* Berkeley: University of California Press.

Mwangi, Evan. 2019. *The Postcolonial Animal: African Literature and Posthuman Ethics.* East Lansing, MI: Michigan State University Press.

Ogunade, Raymond. 2005. "Environmental Issues in Yoruba Religion: Implications for Leadership and Society in Nigeria." *Science and Religion: Global Perspectives* 6 (1): 4–8.

Ojo, Olagoke. 1973. *Ijapa Tiroko Oko Yannibo.* Nigeria: Longman Schools Division (a Pearson Education Company).

Oluwole Coker, and Adesina Coker. 2008. "Folklore as Folklaw in Yoruba Indigenous Epistemology." *Journal of Afro-European Studies* 2 (1): 1–20.

Owoade, Sunday Caleb. 2020. "Folklore in Yoruba Novels: A Potential Tool for Culture Documentation and Preservation." *Ihafa: A Journal of African Studies* 11 (1): 154–186.

Rueckert, William. 1978. "Literature and Ecology: An Experiment in Ecocriticism." *Iowa Review* 9 (1): 71–86.

Sanusi, Chinade Ibrahim. 2015. "Women, Children and the Environment: The Use of Folktales in Managing Climate Change." *An International Journal of Language, Literature and Gender Studies (LALIGENS)* 4 (2): 164–169.

Soyinka, Wole. 1997. "The Writer in an African State." *Transition* 31: 350–56. https://doi.org/10.2307/2935430.

Taiwo, Olukayode. 1998. "Traditional versus Modern Judicial Practices: A Comparative Analysis of Dispute Resolution among the Yoruba of South-West Nigeria." *Africa Development: A Quarterly Journal of CODESRIA* 23 (2): 209–226.

Traoré, Moussa. 2019. "An Ecocritical Reading of Camara Laye's *The African Child*." In *African Culture and Performance Dynamics in the Dramaturgy of AbdulRasheed Abiodun Adeoye*, edited by Ojediran Oludolapo, Arinde Tsimeon Tayo, and Gborsong Arthur Philips, 253–268. Nigeria and Ghana: University of Ilorin and University of Cape Coast.

PART THREE

ECOCRITICISM AND ENVIRONMENTAL COMMUNICATION FROM CAMEROON AND NIGERIA

CHAPTER SIXTEEN

Language Framing of Climate Change and Ecocritical Consciousness in Nigerian Newspapers

Zulfaa Yushau-Waziri

INTRODUCTION

Climate change is a global issue affecting countries worldwide, including Nigeria. The country is particularly vulnerable to the impacts of climate change, due to its geographical location and reliance on agriculture. The devastating effects of climate change in Nigeria include increased temperatures, erratic rainfall patterns, desertification, and flooding. These changes have led to food and water insecurity, loss of biodiversity, and displacement of communities. Understanding the background of climate change in Nigeria is crucial for comprehending the language framing of this prevalent issue in Nigerian newspapers.

Climate Change is recognized as one of humanity's most formidable challenges, transcending geographic, cultural, and political boundaries and impacting societies worldwide. Its consequences are far-reaching, affecting ecosystems, economies, and the well-being of present and future generations. The United Nations Framework Convention on Climate Change (UNFCC) defines climate change as "a change that is attributed directly or indirectly to human activity that alters the composition of the global atmosphere and in addition to natural climate variability observed over comparable periods" (United Nations 1992). Amid this global crisis, the language used to communicate climate change becomes a critical aspect of shaping public understanding and fostering meaningful action. This study undertakes an ecocritical exploration and content analysis of the language framing of climate change within the context of Nigerian newspapers, aiming to reveal the subtle yet powerful ways in which linguistic choices contribute to the broader discourse on environmental issues.

Climate change discourse, as disseminated through the media, particularly in Nigeria, using the *Daily Trust Newspaper* and *Vanguard*, informs public opinion, influences policy decisions, and shapes societal responses. The language framing used by the media has the potential to evoke emotions, construct narratives, and shape perceptions that, in turn, impact the urgency attributed to environmental concerns (Ayittey 2010). Climate change is a phenomenon that requires public education on its nature and how to cope with the situation, and it is the media that have the clout to inform their audience on the subject. As such, understanding the nuances of how climate change is linguistically portrayed in Nigerian newspapers is paramount, considering the country's unique socio-cultural and environmental landscape. In the realm of ecocriticism, scholars argue that literature, culture, and language play pivotal roles in shaping human perceptions of the environment. Applying this lens to media discourse allows for a deeper exploration of the connections between language, culture, and environmental consciousness. Through an analysis of the language framing of climate change in Nigerian newspapers, this research aims to contribute to the broader field of ecocriticism and environmental communication.

The importance of language framing in media cannot be overstated, as it plays a significant role in shaping public opinion. This article identifies common language framing techniques used in Nigerian newspapers. The implications of language framing on public perception are significant for accurate and balanced reporting, which can help improve climate change discourse. Thus, newspapers play a crucial role in shaping public opinion on climate change. Through their language framing, they have the power to influence how the public perceives the issue. The role of newspapers in this regard is to educate the public through the language used in their coverage of climate change; this allows one to understand the extent to which newspapers contribute to shaping public opinion. The influence of language framing on climate change discourse is examined, highlighting its potential impact on shaping public perceptions and attitudes. Through this analysis, this study gains insights into the implications of language framing and makes recommendations for improving the discourse on climate change in Nigerian newspapers, emphasizing the importance of accurate and balanced reporting. Overall, this study offers an ecocritical perspective on the language framing of climate change in Nigerian newspapers and its implications for public understanding and action.

A HISTORICAL PERSPECTIVE OF CLIMATE CHANGE

The 18th and 19th centuries marked a significant turning point in human history, bringing unprecedented economic and technological advancements during the Industrial Revolution. However, it also initiated a trajectory of increased greenhouse gas emissions into the Earth's atmosphere (Weart 2003). The combustion of fossil fuels, a hallmark of industrialization, released substantial amounts of carbon dioxide, contributing to the gradual warming of the planet (James 1998). As scientific understanding evolved, early climatologists, such as Svante Arrhenius, began to explore the link between human activities and changes in the Earth's climate (Tolman 1899). Despite initial skepticism, subsequent research has corroborated the idea that human-induced factors play a crucial role in altering the planet's climate patterns (Jones 2010). The mid-20th century witnessed a growing awareness of environmental issues, leading to the establishment of international agreements and organizations dedicated to addressing climate change (Nations 1992). The Intergovernmental Panel on Climate Change (IPCC), established in 1988, has become a central hub for synthesizing scientific findings and disseminating information on the anthropogenic impact on the climate (Heerdegen 1991).

MEDIA FRAMING AND ENVIRONMENTAL ISSUES OF CLIMATE CHANGE

Entman explains that framing essentially involves the selection and salience of information (Entman 1993). That is, to frame is to select some aspects of a perceived reality and make them salient in a communicating text, in such a way as to promote a particular problem definition, causal interpretation, moral evaluation, and/or treatment recommendation for the item described.

Similarly, Nisbet and Dominique Brossard (2017) assert that media framing influences how the public perceives issues. In the context of climate change, media frames can accentuate specific aspects of the issue, thereby shaping public understanding and influencing policy discourse. Many scholars have defined media framing in different ways. For instance, Gamson and Modigliani, cited in Baysha and Hallahan (2004), define a media frame as "as a central organizing idea or storyline that provides meaning to an unfolding strip of events." Again, (Ngoa 2012) sees framing as "a means through which an issue is given a particular meaning" furthermore, she explains that: Framing, means the selection of some aspects of a perceived reality and making them more salient in a communication text, in such a way as to promote a particular problem definition, causal interpretation, moral evaluation and/or treatment recommendation for the item described. Gitlin (Reid 1981) pointed out that "the definitional power of frames relates to the general concerns over the power of the news media to shape and reinforce dominant ideology. Some aspects omitted in the frame do not come to the audience's attention". As a result, framing dictates where the audience directs its attention. A well-crafted framing capitalizes on preexisting attitudes, ideas, and views by emphasizing some aspects of a problem over others. Gitlin says news frames represent persistent patterns of selection, emphasis, and exclusion that furnish a coherent interpretation and evaluation of events.

Media framing of environmental issues has been a central focus in communication studies. The work of Boykoff and Boykoff (2007) on the "politicization of science" in media coverage of climate change highlights the power dynamics inherent in framing environmental narratives. Additionally, Painter and Ashe (2012) argue that media framing influences public perceptions of climate change impacts, mitigation, and adaptation. Scholars within ecocriticism have increasingly turned their attention to indigenous knowledge systems and environmental philosophies (Bracke 2016). In the context of Nigeria, with its rich cultural diversity and deep connection to the environment, indigenous ecocriticism offers a valuable perspective for understanding the media's language framing of climate change. The works by Ojaide (2015) and Okpewho (2014) on indigenous environmental literature provide a foundation for exploring how traditional ecological knowledge may influence language choices in media representations of climate change. The media, according to Tagbo (2010), can play a crucial role in disseminating valuable information to effectively guide public debate and understanding of weather and climate change. He stated that regular and accurate communication about climate change is the first step toward developing coping mechanisms in Africa.

Similarly, Climate change has emerged as a significant development issue, but it has been overshadowed by other pressing issues that receive greater public attention, according to Aniegbunam (2010), cited in Tagbo (2010). Aniegbunam also states that climate change issues should not be reported on the front page of newspapers unless there is a strong local, political, and economic dimension to them, which is rarely the case. Most African journalists struggle to report on climate change due to a lack of understanding of the issue. This assertion can also be attributed to Nigerian newspapers, as some journalists do not fully grasp the understanding and reporting of climate change issues. This lack of understanding of the issue stems from the fact that climate change is a complex scientific theory that cannot be accommodated in their daily routine due to the deadline culture.

ECOCRITICISM AND LANGUAGE

The term "ecology" was introduced by Ernst Haeckel in the 1860s to describe the relationships between organisms and their environment, with an emphasis on the mutual interdependence and interconnectedness of all living systems within an ecosystem. Ecocriticism, in its simplest sense, involves the study of the relationship between the physical environment and texts, focusing on how and to what effect nature is conceptualized and represented in various literary, cultural, critical, and disciplinary contexts (Gersdorf and Mayer, 2006). On the other hand, Ecolinguistics has been defined as "the ecological study of language and the linguistic study of ecology" (Busse, 2006). The linguistic study of ecology acknowledges that language use is always correlated to socio-cultural practices and ideologies in each historical context. Hence, it sheds light on the interaction between language, nature, and environment by elucidating the role of language in shaping the cultural aspects of the natural environment.

Ecocriticism, as an interdisciplinary field, has evolved as a valuable lens for examining the intersections of literature, culture, and the environment. Scholars within this field contend that language is not merely a tool for communication but a fundamental force in shaping human perceptions of nature. Drawing on the foundational works of Grusin and Buell (2002) and Garrard (2004), ecocriticism posits that literature and language contribute to the construction of environmental narratives, influencing societal attitudes toward ecological issues. Ecocriticism, as a theoretical framework, has significantly enriched our understanding of the intricate interplay between literature, language, and the environment. This approach scrutinizes how language shapes and reflects our perceptions of nature, offering a nuanced focus through which to analyze the ecological dimensions embedded in literary works.

Language, in the context of ecocriticism, serves as a mediator that constructs the narratives of our relationship with the natural world (Glotfelty 1996). It is through language that authors evoke the majesty of landscapes, capture the essence of ecosystems, and cultivate an ecological consciousness in their readers. The representations of nature in literature, meticulously analyzed by ecocritics, transcend mere descriptions; they become a means to explore cultural attitudes toward the environment (Grusin and Buell 2002).

Anthropocentrism, a central concern in ecocriticism, underscores the need to critically examine language for its inherent biases that prioritize human interests over the broader ecological web (Merchant 1980). When interrogating linguistic choices, ecocritics unravel the deeply ingrained anthropocentric perspectives that have contributed to environmental degradation. Nature writing, a genre scrutinized by ecocriticism, is the powerful manifestation of language's role in fostering environmental awareness (Slovic 2015). The genre's vivid descriptions and keen observations aim to cultivate a sense of place, inspiring readers to forge a deeper connection with the natural world. Furthermore, the semiotics of nature unravel in the hands of ecocritics, who examine the symbolic meanings embedded in language (Alaimo and Susan Hekman 2008). Metaphors and symbols related to the environment become potent tools through which authors communicate ecological truths, and ecocriticism provides the interpretive framework to decode these messages.

In the realm of environmental activism, ecocriticism emphasizes the potential of language to galvanize communities and effect change (Garrard 2004). Critical language awareness, as advocated by ecocritics, encourages a reflective engagement with language, fostering a deeper understanding of its implications for environmental thought and action. This suggests that ecocriticism and language engage in a dynamic dialogue, unraveling the rich tapestry of nature's narratives woven into literature and critically examining the use of language.

NEWSPAPER FRAMING OF CLIMATE ISSUES IN NIGERIA

A content analysis of headlines in Nigerian newspapers regarding the framing of climate change issues was conducted. Six online newspapers were collected, each featuring a spread of three headlines within 2023, resulting in a total of eighteen articles by different authors.

Article 1: Daily Trust Newspaper

i. **"FG Calls for Adoption of Climate Resilient Technique" by Umar Adamu, 26th December 2023.**

The article discusses the Federal Government of Nigeria's (FG) call for the adoption of climate-resilient techniques to mitigate the impacts of climate change. It emphasizes the importance of implementing sustainable practices in agriculture, infrastructure, and other sectors to withstand the changing climate. It highlights the government's role in advocating resilience-building measures, which may address the need for policy support and public awareness.

The language is directive, with the government urging action and urgency, reflecting the immediate need to address climate-related challenges. The tone may be supportive, encouraging the adoption of new techniques, and motivational, aiming to inspire stakeholders to act. The article mobilizes stakeholders across various sectors to adopt climate-resilient practices, emphasizing the government's commitment to mitigating the effects of climate change through proactive measures.

ii. **"Climate Change: Sand, Dust Storms Devastate Communities in Yobe" by Habibu Gimba, 13th December 2023**

The article focuses on the devastating effects of sand and dust storms on communities in Yobe, a state in northeastern Nigeria. Vulnerability and

Exposure: Highlights the vulnerability of these communities to extreme weather events exacerbated by climate change, resulting in significant disruptions to livelihoods and daily life. Humanitarian Concerns: Addresses the humanitarian issues arising from such environmental events, including displacement, health risks, and economic losses.

The language is descriptive, painting a vivid picture of the devastation caused by the storms, and sympathetic, showing concern for the affected communities. The tone may be alarmist, emphasizing the severity of the situation, and emotive, aiming to evoke a response from readers and possibly prompting them to call for assistance. The article raises awareness about the severe impacts of climate change on vulnerable communities in Nigeria, stressing the urgent need for both immediate relief and long-term resilience strategies.

iii. "Heat, Disease, Air Pollution: How Climate Change Impacts Health" by Daily Trust, 26th November 2023

This article examines the various ways in which climate change affects public health, including increased heat, the spread of diseases, and worsening air pollution. Comprehensive, it discusses the complex relationship between climate change and health, potentially covering topics such as heatwaves, vector-borne diseases (like malaria), respiratory issues, and mental health. It suggests measures to mitigate these health risks, including public health interventions, enhanced healthcare infrastructure, and community education.

The language is informative, providing data and scientific explanations of the health impacts, as well as some technical details. The tone may be concerned, reflecting the serious health risks posed by climate change, and cautionary, warning readers of potential future dangers. The article informs readers about the broad health implications of climate change, emphasizing the need for comprehensive public health strategies to mitigate these risks.

COMPARATIVE ANALYSIS

All the selected articles focus on climate change, but they address different aspects, including governmental action, environmental impacts, health risks, and mitigation efforts. The first article is directive and urgent, calling for the immediate adoption of climate-resilient techniques. The second article is descriptive and alarmist, focusing on the devastating impacts of sand and dust storms. The third article is informative and cautionary, discussing the health risks associated with climate change. The first article targets policymakers, urging them to implement resilient practices. The second article focuses on the affected communities and the broader public, aiming to raise awareness about environmental disasters. The third article addresses public health officials and the public, informing them of the health implications of climate change.

Each article calls for action in policy implementation, disaster relief, public health preparedness, and environmental restoration. They collectively stress the urgency of addressing climate change through various strategies and initiatives. These articles provide a multifaceted perspective on climate change in Nigeria, emphasizing the need for comprehensive approaches that encompass policy advocacy, disaster response, public health measures, and environmental conservation.

Article 2: Vanguard Newspaper

i. **Nigeria's climate change impact worsening, demand increased funding — CAPPA By Gabriel Ewepu, Abuja 24th October 2023**

The article discusses the increasing severity of climate change impacts in Nigeria, including extreme weather events, rising temperatures, and environmental degradation. It highlights the urgent need for increased funding to combat these worsening effects, focusing on the calls from the Corporate Accountability and Public Participation Africa (CAPPA) for more resources. The article also explores the concept of climate justice, highlighting the importance of equitable resource distribution and support for the most vulnerable communities.

The language is urgent, reflecting the worsening situation, and pleading, calling for immediate and increased financial support. The tone highlights inadequacies in current funding levels and advocates for greater financial commitment from both national and international sources. The article aims to draw attention to the escalating impacts of climate change in Nigeria, highlighting the urgent need for increased funding to support mitigation and adaptation efforts and advocating for immediate action.

ii. WMO, UN, NiMeT urge immediate action on climate change in Nigeria, globally By Ezra Ukanwa, Abuja, 28th November 2023

This article reports on the joint call from the World Meteorological Organization (WMO), the United Nations (UN), and the Nigerian Meteorological Agency (NiMeT) for urgent climate action in Nigeria and globally. It emphasizes the need for immediate action to address the accelerating pace of climate change and its wide-ranging impacts. The article also emphasizes the importance of collaborative efforts among national governments, international organizations, and other stakeholders in addressing climate challenges.

The language is directive, urging immediate action and conveying urgency, reflecting the critical nature of the climate crisis. The tone is collaborative, emphasizing the need for unified global efforts and unifying, bringing together various stakeholders to work towards common goals. The article stresses the importance of urgent and collaborative action to combat climate change, highlighting the roles of various international and national bodies in driving these efforts forward.

iii. Climate change funds inadequate to tackle impact – Stakeholders by Gabriel Ewepu, Abuja, November 25th, 2023.

This article addresses the concerns expressed by various stakeholders regarding the inadequacy of current climate change funding to effectively mitigate its impacts in Nigeria. Stakeholder Concerns: It highlights the views of experts, NGOs, and other stakeholders who argue that more resources are needed to address the growing challenges posed by climate change. The article advocates for better financial mobilization, both domestically and internationally, to ensure that adequate funds are available for climate resilience and adaptation projects.

The language reflects the serious challenges posed by inadequate funding and critical questioning of the sufficiency of current financial commitments. The tone may be advocacy-driven, pushing for more substantial financial contributions, and urgent, emphasizing the immediate need for additional funds. The article highlights the gap between the funds currently available and the actual needs required to effectively address climate change in Nigeria, calling for increased financial efforts to bridge this gap.

COMPARATIVE ANALYSIS

Common Themes: All articles address the issue of climate change in Nigeria, focusing on national commitments, the worsening impacts, the need for immediate action, and the challenges posed by inadequate funding.

Tone and Approach: The first article is urgent and pleading, calling for increased funding to address the worsening impacts of climate change. The second article is directive and collaborative, emphasizing the need for immediate and unified action against climate change. The third article is concerned and critical, highlighting the inadequacy of current funding and the need for more financial resources.

Each article calls for action in different areas—policy implementation, financial mobilization, collaborative efforts, and funding adequacy. Together, they present a comprehensive view of the challenges and necessary actions to address climate change in Nigeria.

Article 3: Punch Newspaper

i. **Expert trains 85 Kwara youth on climate change by Olumide Idowu, 14th May 2023**

This article covers a training initiative designed to educate and empower 85 youths in Kwara State on climate change issues. The focus is on equipping young people with knowledge and skills to tackle climate challenges, fostering a new generation of climate advocates. The training is presented as a way to influence broader community awareness and action on climate change.

The language emphasizes the importance of youth participation and education in addressing climate issues. The tone may be optimistic, encouraging youth to take an active role in climate action. The article highlights the role of youth in climate action, emphasizing the importance of education and capacity building in addressing environmental challenges in Nigeria.

ii. Climate change: UN agencies seek protection for children. Damilola Olufemi, 24th November 2023

This article discusses the increased vulnerability of children to climate change, with UN agencies advocating for stronger protective measures. The focus is on the role of international organizations in pushing for policies that safeguard children from the adverse effects of climate change. The article outlines the specific risks that climate change poses to children's health, safety, and well-being.

The language raises awareness about the urgent need to protect children from climate-related dangers. The tone reflects the gravity of the situation and emphasizes the need for immediate action. The article emphasizes the critical need for targeted efforts to protect children from the impacts of climate change, urging policymakers and stakeholders to take immediate action.

iii. Farmers lament the effect of climate change on output by Ademola Adegbite, 25th October 2023

This article outlines the adverse impacts of climate change on agricultural productivity, with farmers expressing concerns about reduced crop yields and unpredictable weather patterns. The discussion may include the broader economic implications, such as increased food insecurity and financial losses for farmers. The article might explore the challenges farmers face in adapting to changing environmental conditions, possibly calling for more support and resources.

The language is used to vividly describe the difficulties faced by farmers, with a sympathetic tone that highlights their struggles. The tone emphasizes the need for immediate interventions to support the agricultural sector. The article highlights the severe impact of climate change on agriculture, calling for increased support to help farmers adapt and sustain their livelihoods in the face of environmental changes.

COMPARATIVE ANALYSIS

The articles share a common focus on the impacts of climate change and the various responses required, ranging from youth education and protection of vulnerable populations to addressing agricultural challenges and enforcing compliance with climate policies.

Each article targets different stakeholders—youth, farmers, NGOs, and government authorities—highlighting the multifaceted nature of climate change response. Across the articles, a consistent sense of urgency and a call for advocacy are evident, whether it involves empowering youth, protecting children, supporting farmers, advocating for girls, or ensuring policy compliance. The tone and language used in the articles vary according to the target audience and the specific issue being addressed. However, all the articles aim to raise awareness and prompt action on climate-related challenges in Nigeria. The articles collectively provide a comprehensive view of the different dimensions of climate change in Nigeria, emphasizing the need for targeted actions and collaboration across various sectors to effectively address the ongoing and future challenges posed by climate change.

Article 4: Tribune Online Newspaper

i. **Nigeria is projected to lose $460bn to climate change by 2050 if… Climate change increasing hunger, poverty, others by Nurudeen Alimi, 28th November 2023**

The article projects a significant financial loss for Nigeria due to climate change, amounting to $460 billion by 2050. It also discusses the broader socioeconomic impacts of climate change, including increased hunger, poverty, and other related issues. The phrase "if…" suggests that these projections are contingent upon certain actions or inactions related to climate policies or mitigation efforts.

The language is cautionary, warning of the severe economic consequences that will result if climate change is not adequately addressed. The tone underlines the potential risks and the need for immediate action. The article emphasizes the urgent need for Nigeria to adopt effective climate mitigation strategies to prevent catastrophic economic losses. It serves as a wake-up call to policymakers and the public about the tangible financial and social costs of inaction on climate change.

ii. Why Nigeria will engage youths in the fight against climate change —Minister by Ifedayo Ogunyemi, November 19th, 2023

This article focuses on the government's plans to involve young people in the fight against climate change, recognizing their potential as agents of change. It discusses the role of the Ministry in fostering youth involvement through education, awareness, and possibly policymaking. It also highlights the importance of harnessing the creativity and energy of young people to develop innovative solutions to climate challenges.

The language is inspirational and aims to motivate young people to take an active role in climate action. The tone is strategic, outlining the government's vision and plans for engaging the youth demographic in climate efforts. The article emphasizes the critical role of youth in addressing climate change, advocating for their involvement as a key strategy in national climate action plans. It aims to mobilize and empower young Nigerians to contribute to the fight against environmental degradation.

iii. 110 million children in Nigeria at risk, more vulnerable to climate change — UNICEF As floods displace 650,000 Nigerian children in 7 years, by Ishola Michael, 20th November 2023

The article highlights the alarming number of children in Nigeria who are at risk due to climate change, with a focus on displacement caused by floods. It discusses UNICEF's role in raising awareness about the severe impacts of climate change on children, particularly in terms of displacement, health, and safety. It also emphasizes the growing humanitarian crisis linked to climate-induced disasters, affecting millions of children over the past years.

The language is empathetic, focusing on the plight of vulnerable children, and urgent, stressing the need for immediate intervention. The tone is descriptive, providing vivid accounts of the scale of the problem to elicit concern and prompt action. The article seeks to raise awareness about the specific risks climate change poses to children in Nigeria, calling for urgent humanitarian and policy responses. It highlights the need for targeted interventions to protect children from the escalating threats of climate change.

COMPARATIVE ANALYSIS

All articles discuss the impact of climate change in Nigeria, focusing on its economic, social, and demographic consequences, including risks to children and women, the role of youth, and the associated financial implications.

Tone and Approach: The first article adopts a cautionary tone, emphasizing the severe economic and humanitarian impacts of climate change. The second article adopts a motivational and strategic tone, emphasizing the proactive engagement of youth in climate action. The third article highlights the specific risks to vulnerable populations and the need for targeted interventions. The first article centers on government strategies involving youth. The second and third articles emphasize the vulnerabilities of specific groups (children and women) and the need for international and national support.

Despite their differing focal points, all articles emphasize the need for urgent and coordinated action to address the multifaceted impacts of climate change in Nigeria. They highlight the importance of both national and international efforts in mitigating these effects and protecting vulnerable populations.

Article 5: The Nation Online Newspaper

i. Climate Change: Tinubu solicits partnerships for Nigeria, Africa for new green economy, Abuja, December 12th, 2023

The article discusses President Tinubu's efforts to solicit partnerships for Nigeria and Africa to transition to a green economy. It focuses on the shift towards sustainable economic practices that minimize environmental impact and promote renewable energy. It also emphasizes the need for collective action within Africa, recognizing the continent's unique vulnerabilities to climate change and its potential for green growth.

The language is diplomatic, emphasizing collaboration and mutual benefits in tackling climate change. The tone seems visionary, highlighting long-term goals for a sustainable future and economic growth. The article aims to highlight Nigeria's proactive approach to seeking global partnerships that foster a green economy. It underscores the importance of international collaboration in achieving sustainable development and mitigating climate change in Africa.

ii. Nigeria lost 6 billion dollars to climate-related change-related issues in 2022 – Ex-lawmaker, Abuja, October 20th, 2023

This article focuses on the significant financial losses Nigeria incurred due to climate-related issues in 2022, amounting to $6 billion. The involvement of an ex-lawmaker suggests a political angle, possibly critiquing government policies or advocating for more robust climate action. It also discusses the broader implications of these losses, including the need for improved policies and investment in climate resilience.

The language centers on the severity of the economic impact and the need for urgent action. The tone may be analytical, using specific financial figures to underline the magnitude of the problem. The article serves as a warning about the severe economic costs of climate inaction, urging policymakers to prioritize climate change mitigation and adaptation efforts. It highlights the financial vulnerabilities that Nigeria faces due to environmental changes.

iii. UK okays £100m for vulnerable countries to tackle climate change by Lucas Ajanaku, December 5th, 2023

The article discusses the UK's approval of £100 million in aid to help vulnerable countries, including Nigeria, tackle climate change. It highlights the specific focus on aiding countries that are particularly vulnerable to the impacts of climate change, recognizing the need for global solidarity and cooperation. It also emphasizes the financial aspect of the support, reflecting the importance of funding in addressing climate-related challenges.

The language is supportive, reflecting a commitment to helping vulnerable nations cope with climate change. The tone emphasizes the global nature of the climate crisis and the need for collective action. The article emphasizes the significance of international financial support in combating climate change, particularly for vulnerable countries like Nigeria. It reflects the global responsibility to assist those most affected by climate impacts.

COMPARATIVE ANALYSIS

All articles discuss climate change, focusing on various aspects such as economic impact, partnerships, corporate responsibility, and international aid. The first article has a diplomatic and supportive tone, focusing on international partnerships and aid. The second article adopts a critical and alarming tone, highlighting the significant economic losses Nigeria faces due to climate change. The third article takes a collaborative and practical approach, emphasizing the role of corporate partnerships in promoting sustainable practices. The articles underscore the need for action, whether through international partnerships, corporate responsibility, or more robust national policies. They reflect the multifaceted nature of climate change challenges and the diverse responses required to mitigate its impact. The articles present a comprehensive picture of the ongoing efforts and challenges in addressing climate change in Nigeria, illustrating the importance of collaboration across different sectors and borders.

Article 5: The Sun Online Newspaper

i. **Climate Change: Disasters Don't Recognise National Boundaries** —Uba, Environmental Activist, 25th June 2023 by Josfyn Uba

The article emphasizes that climate change and its associated disasters are not confined by national borders, affecting multiple countries regardless of their actions. It highlights the need for global cooperation in addressing climate change, as its effects are universally shared. The perspective of an environmental activist adds urgency and a call to action, emphasizing the shared responsibility of all nations.

The language is urgent, emphasizing the immediacy of the issue and calling for collaborative efforts across nations. The tone may be realistic, acknowledging the harsh realities of climate change while warning against the consequences of inaction. The article underlines the interconnectedness of climate-related disasters and the importance of collective global action. It emphasizes that no country is immune to the effects of climate change, underscoring the importance of international cooperation.

ii. Climate Change with Vengeance, 28th September 2023

The title of the article suggests a focus on the increasingly severe and possibly unpredictable nature of climate change impacts. The article discusses extreme weather events, environmental degradation, and the rapid pace of climate change. The phrase "with vengeance" suggests an emotional and perhaps dramatic portrayal of climate change, likely intended to evoke a strong response.

The language is dramatic, using vivid imagery or emotional appeals to convey the severity of the issue. The tone is alarmist, aiming to persuade readers of the critical need for immediate action. The article serves as a stark reminder of the increasingly aggressive impacts of climate change, urging immediate and significant action to mitigate its effects. It may focus on conveying the urgency and scale of the problem to spur public and governmental response.

iii. Climate Change: Threat to World Peace, 27th October 2022

The article positions climate change as a significant threat to global peace and stability, linking environmental issues with geopolitical tensions. It also discusses how climate change exacerbates resource scarcity, leading to conflicts over water, food, and habitable land. It expands the conversation beyond environmental damage to include the political and social ramifications of climate change.

The language is analytical, connecting climate change to broader geopolitical issues and concerns, reflecting the profound implications for world peace. The tone forewarns and alerts readers to the potential for increased global conflict, and suggests ways to address these risks. The article highlights the broader implications of climate change, particularly its potential to disrupt global peace and security. It underscores the need for integrated approaches that address both environmental and political challenges.

COMPARATIVE ANALYSIS

All articles address climate change from various perspectives, including its global impact, severity, security threats, and national challenges. Tone and Approach: The first article adopts an urgent and collaborative tone, emphasizing the transnational nature of climate disasters. The second article adopts a dramatic and emotive tone, emphasizing the severe and escalating impacts of climate change. The third article uses an analytical and concerned tone, linking climate change to global peace and security. The first article highlights the significance of global stakeholders and the necessity for international collaboration. The second article is likely intended for the public, aiming to raise awareness through emotional appeal. The third article focuses on global leaders and policymakers, stressing the geopolitical implications of climate change

Each article calls for action, whether through international cooperation, an immediate public response, strategic security planning, or the development of national policy. They all emphasize the urgency and necessity of addressing climate change from different angles. The articles present diverse views on climate change, highlighting its far-reaching impacts and the varied responses required to address this global crisis effectively.

Article 6: The Guardian Online Newspaper

    i. **A Call for Environmental Justice: Amplifying Africa's Voice in the Global Climate Discourse by Dozy Mmobuosi, 15th December 2023**

The article emphasizes the need for environmental justice, particularly for Africa, which contributes minimally to climate change but suffers disproportionately from its effects. It emphasizes the importance of amplifying Africa's voice in global climate discussions, ensuring that the continent's unique challenges and needs are acknowledged and addressed.

It advocates for a more equitable approach to climate change policies and actions, where Africa's concerns are given due consideration.

The language is advocative, pushing for greater representation of Africa in global discussions and empowering, giving voice to those often marginalized in the climate debate. The tone is passionate, reflecting a strong commitment to justice, and assertive, demanding recognition and action from the global community. It stresses the importance of fairness and equity in addressing the global climate crisis.

ii. WHO alerts to rise in malaria burden due to extreme weather changes by Chukwuma Muanya, 2nd December 2023

The article examines the relationship between extreme weather changes resulting from climate change and the increasing burden of malaria, particularly in vulnerable regions. It highlights the World Health Organization's warning about the increased health risks due to changing climatic conditions, such as the expansion of malaria-prone areas. Additionally, it highlights the potential for climate change to exacerbate existing public health issues, thereby transforming them into larger crises.

The language is cautionary, alerting readers to the profound health implications of climate change, and informative, providing data and insights from health authorities. The tone is urgent, reflecting the immediate health threats posed by climate change and urging action to mitigate these risks. The article serves as a warning about the intersection of climate change and public health, emphasizing the need for proactive measures to address the increasing malaria burden. Overall, it highlights the broader impact of climate change on human health and underscores the need for integrated responses.

iii. Climate Change: Stakeholders task farmers to adopt digital technology By Owede Agbajileke, Abuja, 13th December 2023

The article discusses the call for farmers to adopt digital technologies as a means of mitigating and adapting to climate change. It focuses on the specific challenges faced by the agricultural sector due to climate change, such as unpredictable weather patterns, and explores how technology can help address these challenges. It also highlights the importance of innovation and modern farming techniques in increasing resilience and sustainability in agriculture.

The language is practical, offering actionable advice and solutions, and solution-oriented, with a focus on the benefits of technology adoption. The tone encourages and motivates farmers to embrace new methods and is optimistic, emphasizing the potential positive outcomes. The article advocates for the modernization of agriculture through digital technology as a critical response to the challenges posed by climate change. It emphasizes the need for farmers to innovate to maintain productivity and sustainability.

COMPARATIVE ANALYSIS

All the articles address climate change but focus on different aspects—environmental justice, health impacts, international aid, and technological adaptation.

Tone and Approach: The first article has an advocative and empowering tone, focusing on amplifying Africa's voice in the global climate discourse. The second article adopts a cautionary and urgent tone, highlighting the health risks associated with climate change. The third article takes a practical and solution-oriented approach, focusing on the role of technology in agriculture. The first article highlights the importance of global stakeholders and the need for equitable representation of Africa in climate discussions. The second article targets public health officials and policymakers, stressing the health implications of climate change. The third article focuses on the agricultural sector, encouraging farmers to adopt digital technology.

Each article calls for action in different areas—global equity, public health preparedness, and technological innovation. They all underscore the urgency of addressing climate change through various lenses. These articles offer a comprehensive overview of the diverse challenges and opportunities related to climate change, highlighting the need for multifaceted responses that consider environmental justice, health, and technological advancements.

ECOCRITICAL ANALYSIS OF LANGUAGE FRAMING AND ENVIRONMENTAL ISSUES

Ecocriticism, as an analytical framework, extends beyond traditional literary analysis to engage with the cultural, social, and linguistic dimensions of environmental discourse. In media analysis, ecocriticism provides a lens through which to explore the relationships between language, culture, and the environment. This section applies ecocritical perspectives to interpret the language framing of climate change in Nigerian newspapers, acknowledging the inherent connections between media representations and ecological consciousness. This involves examining the cultural dimensions embedded in the language framing of climate change. As cultural artifacts, Nigerian newspapers carry the imprint of societal values and beliefs. By scrutinizing the use of ecological imagery, cultural metaphors, and references to indigenous knowledge, this analysis aims to unravel the intersection of cultural narratives with environmental discourse. For instance, the portrayal of climate change impacts may draw on local ecological metaphors, connecting the global issue to local experiences and understandings.

Power dynamics are integral to ecocritical analysis, especially in media representations of environmental issues. Understanding who controls the narratives and how power structures influence the framing of climate change is crucial. The power dynamics are inherent in the selected newspapers, considering the influence of governmental, corporate, and cultural entities in shaping the discourse on climate change. By critically assessing the sources of information and the prominence given to different perspectives, this analysis seeks to identify potential biases and ideologies that may underpin the media's portrayal of climate change. Indigenous ecocriticism provides a valuable perspective for understanding the language framing of climate change in Nigerian newspapers. These offer alternative ways of engaging with ecological issues. The tension between global and local perspectives is a recurring theme in ecocritical analysis. Nigerian newspapers, as mediators between global environmental discourses and local realities, navigate this tension in their language framing of climate change.

Acknowledging the limitations of an ecocritical analysis within the context of media discourse is crucial. The inherent subjectivity of interpretation and the potential for multiple readings underscore the importance of reflexivity. This study acknowledges that ecocriticism entails a dialogue between the analyst and the text, recognizing that personal perspectives can influence interpretations. As such, the researcher's positionality acknowledges the complexity of interpreting language framing through an ecocritical lens. The ecocritical analysis complements the linguistic analysis, providing a deeper understanding of the cultural, social, and power dimensions that shape the language framing of climate change in Nigerian newspapers.

The analysis reveals a mosaic of linguistic strategies employed by the reporters in framing climate change. Metaphors such as "climate crisis" are prevalent, suggesting a heightened sense of urgency in the discourse. The tone varies, with some newspaper writers adopting an alarmist stance, emphasizing the severity of climate change impacts. In contrast, others maintain a more neutral tone, presenting information in a balanced manner. For instance, cultural references are also discernible, reflecting the news reporters' efforts to contextualize climate change within the Nigerian socio-cultural landscape. Additionally, a blend of scientific language and accessible communication is evident, suggesting a deliberate effort to bridge the gap between scientific knowledge and public understanding.

CONCLUSION

This chapter has explored the language framing of climate change in Nigerian newspapers, employing both linguistic analysis and ecocritical perspectives. The analysis revealed diverse linguistic strategies, including tone variations, metaphors, cultural references, and the integration of indigenous knowledge. The study highlights the cultural dimensions, power dynamics, and the interplay between global and local perspectives that shape the media representation of climate change in Nigeria. The findings of this study show that language framing influences public perception and contributes to constructing environmental narratives. Recognizing the cultural dimensions and power dynamics inherent in language choices is vital for fostering a nuanced and culturally sensitive discourse on climate change. This study contributes to the broader field of ecocriticism by applying its analytical tools to media analysis within a specific cultural context. By integrating linguistic analysis with ecocritical perspectives, this research demonstrates the potential of ecocriticism to reveal hidden layers of meaning in media representations of environmental issues. The study highlights the importance of ecocritical scholars engaging with diverse cultural and linguistic contexts to enrich the field's theoretical frameworks.

REFERENCES

Alaimo, Stacy, and Susan Hekman, eds. 2008. *Material Feminisms*. Bloomington: Indiana University Press.

Ayittey, Sherry. 2010. "Media Should Prioritise Education on Climate Change." *MyJoyOnline*, November 18.

Baysha, Olga, and Kirk Hallahan. 2004. "Media Framing of the Ukrainian Political Crisis, 2000–2001." *Journalism Studies* 5 (2). https://doi.org/10.1080/1461670042000211203.

Boykoff, Maxwell T., and Jules M. Boykoff. 2007. "Climate Change and Journalistic Norms: A Case-Study of U.S. Mass-Media Coverage." *Geoforum* 38 (6). https://doi.org/10.1016/j.geoforum.2007.01.008.

Bracke, Maud. 2016. *Indigenous Whaling in the North Atlantic: Perspectives on Its Cultural and Environmental Sustainability*. New York: Berghahn Books.

Busse, Thomas. 2006. "Ecocriticism and the Teaching of Literature." *Forum for World Literature Studies* 1 (1): 45–54

Entman, Robert M. 1993. "Framing: Towards a Clarification of a Fractured Paradigm." *Journal of Communication* 43: 51–58.

Garrard, Greg. 2004. *Ecocriticism*. London: Routledge.

Grusin, Richard, and Lawrence Buell. 2002. "Writing for an Endangered World: Literature, Culture, and Environment in the U.S. and Beyond." *The Journal of American History* 89 (2). https://doi.org/10.2307/3092237.

Heerdegen, Richard. 1991. "Book Reviews: Houghton, J.T., Jenkins, G.J., and Ephraums, J.J. 1990: Climate Change – the IPCC Scientific Assessment." *Progress in Physical Geography: Earth and Environment* 15 (3). https://doi.org/10.1177/030913339101500310.

James, Smith. 1998. *The Carbon Conundrum: Source, Sink, and Solution*. San Diego: Academic Press.

Jones, Sarah K. 2010. "Industrialization and the Rise of Greenhouse Gas Emissions: A Historical Perspective." *Environmental History* 15 (1): 105–30.

Merchant, Carolyn. 1980. *The Death of Nature: Women, Ecology, and the Scientific Revolution*. New York: Harper One.

Nations, United. 1992. "United Nations Framework Convention on Climate Change."

Nisbet, Matthew C., and Dominique Brossard. 2017. "Science Communication and the Media." In *The Oxford Handbook of the Science of Science Communication*, edited by Kathleen Hall Jamieson et al. Oxford: Oxford University Press.

Ojaide, Tanure. 2015. *Indigeneity, Globalization, and African Literature*. https://doi.org/10.1057/9781137560032.

Okpewho, Isidore. 2014. *Our Land Was a Forest: An Ainu Memoir*. Lexington: University Press of Kentucky.

Painter, James, and Teresa Ashe. 2012. "Crossing Divides: Representations of Climate Change in the Indian Press." *Global Environmental Change* 22 (1): 81–93.

Reid, Herbert G. 1981. "Todd Gitlin. *The Whole World Is Watching: Mass Media in the Making and Unmaking of the New Left*. Pp. xiv, 327. Berkeley: The University of California Press, 1980. $12.95." The ANNALS *of the American Academy of Political and Social Science* 456 (1). https://doi.org/10.1177/000271628145600152.

Slovic, Scott. 2015. *Ecocomposition: Theoretical and Pedagogical Approaches*. Albany: State University of New York Press.

Tagbo, E. 2010. *Media Coverage of Climate Change in Africa: A Study of Nigeria and South Africa*. Reuters Foundation.

Tolman, Cyrus F. 1899. "The Influence of the Carbonic Acid in the Air upon the Temperature of the Ground." *Philosophical Magazine and Journal of Science* 41. *La Revue Générale Des Sciences*. Svante Arrhenius. *The Journal of Geology* 7 (6). https://doi.org/10.1086/608462.

Weart, Spencer R. 2003. *The Discovery of Global Warming*. Cambridge, MA: Harvard University Press.

CHAPTER SEVENTEEN

Archeological Alternatives
Towards Africa's Eco-cultural Sustainability

Arthur Nebengou Njume Ndeley

INTRODUCTION

Eco-sustainability is a state in which demands placed on the environment can be met without reducing its capacity to allow people to live well, now and in the future. It can equally mean the capacity of the ecosystem to maintain its essential functioning processes and retain its biodiversity in full measure. This implies that non-renewable and other resources should not be depleted for short-term improvements (Hongie and Ngwa 2015, 354). Many things in today's world would cease to exist if eco-consciousness were not intensified. Many of the historic treasures and cultural values we hold dear are going extinct. The attack on our eco-cultural heritage is so severe and needs urgent critical attention. The response to this threat requires innovative strategies.

One way to preserve culture and nature is by educating posterity about past cultural beliefs, practices, and values that are embedded in our archaeology. This archaeological approach, coupled with the role of totemism and taboos in ecological sustainability, has received limited scholarly attention. This chapter seeks to demonstrate the extent to which African beliefs, rites, or practices could restore or preserve environmental elements as depicted in Chinua Achebe's *Arrow of God* and Camara Laye's *The African Child*. Against this backdrop, one questions how archaeological aesthetics, such as totemism and tabooism, are used to minimize threats and establish sustainable ecological heritage.

REVIEW OF RELATED LITERATURE

Some postcolonial critics have attempted to suggest critical solutions to ecological heritage. A few have dwelt on the role of totemism and tabooism, alongside other belief systems, in ecological conservation. K. Lucy Mandillah and Georges-Ivo Ekosse (2019) investigate how totems, as cultural belief systems, have been used in Africa to promote the conservation of natural resources. Qualitative methods (based on literature) were used to explore the values and perceptions that underlie the use of totems. They reiterate:

> Animal, plant and insect totems in Kenya and South Africa have symbolic meanings attached to them. The symbolic meanings are usually accompanied by taboos believed to have special spiritual and cultural associations. Due to these cultural associations and taboos, totems are protected against harm by the respective tribes, conserving species diversity and ecosystem diversity (218-19).

Among the Bakweri people of Fako in Cameroon, for example, the elephant is a totem. Their deity incarnates as an elephant and dwells on Mount Fako. Other sages in the village also have totems. This cultural belief has limited poaching in that locale, as the elephants are considered spirits. Given that the elephant is an endangered species in this zone, the belief has therefore contributed to its conservation. In this same vein, Mandillah and Ekosse submit that,

> Totems have helped to conserve not only the natural environment, but also traditional belief systems. Indigenous African belief systems in the form of totems have contributed immensely and effectively to the reduction in the incidence of wildlife and biodiversity loss. Some plant and tree species, animals and insects are conserved due to their significance to the community as totems. They are treated with reverence and protected for future use due to their sacred value and role in rituals. Totemic animals and plants are maintained mainly through two useful prohibitions: the first against

killing and eating the totemic animal and the second against the destruction of plants and their habitats. These traditional belief systems are capable of protecting species biodiversity in particular and the environment in general (214).

This chapter also explores the significance of indigenous or archaeological African belief systems in environmental management. This study therefore agrees with and adds to, such credible discourse by Mandillah and Ekosse on ecoculture, as exemplified above, and incorporates the role of archaeology in this process of revaluing African identity.

Like Nigeria and South Africa, the Kenyan landscape has received a plurality of critical attention in the domain of cultural ecology. Collecting primary data from the Wanga Luo Akamba and the Bukusu clans of Kenya, Sussy Gumo et. al. have attempted a fair analysis of African spirituality and ecology. Sussy Gumo et. al. (2012) state:

> Most African communities believed that the environment was the abode of the spirits, the living dead and ancestors. The natural environment has spirits which define the relationship between humans and nature, which is linked and is interdependent. Therefore, taboos, religious beliefs, sacred rites and totems provide a framework for defining Religions (542).

The myth of totemism is not just a literary concept but an ecocultural concept, given that totems are usually natural symbols that have spiritual relevance. Further critical views along this line of thought are factored into the analyses of this chapter.

ANIMALS AS TOTEMS AND WATER BODIES AS HABITATS

There is synergy between man, nature, and his culture. Plants, roots, leaves, bark of trees, water, oil, soil, animals, and other natural forms interact with humans and shape their culture through the practice of healing, food culture, and infrastructure. Natural features, such as lakes, rivers, mountains, forests, valleys, plants, trees, and animals, serve both physical and spiritual purposes according to African cosmology.

In Chinua Achebe's *Arrow of God*, Oduche, the son of Ezeulu, who joins the missionaries, locks up the royal or sacred python in his box specially designed by the "mission carpenter" (43). Idemili, the deity, owned this royal python. This act of Oduche's is a taboo –it desecrates the land, given that the sacred python is the totem of the people of Umuaro. It is not an ordinary python; it has been consecrated and given a more profound epistemological and cosmological status in the spirit realm. No one was allowed to harm this reptile in any way. We are told by the omniscient narrator that 'the outrage which Ezeulu's son committed against the sacred python was a very serious matter' (59). This explains why Ezidemili sends a young emissary to ask Ezeulu "how you intend to purify your house of the abomination that your son committed" (54). Appeasement must thus proceed totemic abuse.

We must not lose sight of the ecocultural impetus revealed to us through this taboo act. African culture emanates from the cultural environment, including plants, animals, water, hills, and so on. Ancient gods could dwell in water, animals or carved objects. African people are often eco-sensitive and eco-friendly.

Totems are engraved for many people to the point where they establish proverbs that are tied to some totems. An example of such a proverb is the Igbo saying that "when a man sees a snake all by himself he may wonder whether it is an ordinary snake or the untouchable python" (Achebe 1974, 142). Such a proverb can be classified as a "totemic proverb". The snake may therefore be considered as an ecocultural symbol.

In Camara Laye's *The African Child,* we also notice that snakes serve as totems in Guinean cultures. Laye's mother educates him when he sees a snake in his father's compound. She restricts him from killing the snake, saying, "My son, this one must not be killed: he is not as other snakes…. This snake is your father's guiding spirit…. Look…. the serpent is going to pay your father a visit" (15). Sometime later, Laye sees the snake and says, "I would watch him guide through the little hole in the wall. As if information of his presence, my father at that instant would turn his eyes to the hole and give a smile…. Never did I see the little snake attempt to do the slightest harm to my father" (21). We must thus understand that keeping totems plays a vital role in environmental preservation. Totemism has helped preserve certain endangered species. Restricting animals from being killed because of their metaphysical relevance to people has helped most of these animals to survive hunters' bullets in the physical realm. In West Africa, for example, the King and Queen Cobra are endangered species. They are found only in these tropical zones. Treating them as deities has deterred many villagers and hunters from killing this natural element.

Water bodies are an integral part of ecoculture. They serve as habitats for deities. Rivers, lakes, seas, or streams can serve humans in diverse capacities: they entertain as children swim, they are used for cooking, washing clothes, industrial work like molding sun-dried bricks, and for agricultural purposes such as irrigation. Beyond these useful functions for humans and even animals, most water bodies in traditional communities have cosmic functions. This underscores the importance of conserving and treating these bodies with honor, given their mythological significance.

In *Arrow of God,* for example, we learn that the stream, "Ota, had been abandoned since the oracle announced yesterday that the enormous boulder resting on two other rocks as its source was about to fall and would take a softer pillow for its head. Until the *alusi* who owned the stream and whose name it bore had been placated no one would go near it" (7).

This demonstrates that deities are believed to predict natural disasters, not just modern science. It also shows that nature not only shares values with humans but can also have a destructive side, many of which can be interpreted through an anthropological lens.

In Camara Laye's *The African Child*, water bodies have a similar dual function. Laye's mother has an ancestral bond with water. Her totem is the crocodile, a deity she "had naturally inherited from my grandfather his totem, which is the crocodile. This totem allowed all Damans to draw water from the Niger with impunity" (61).

Rivers thus serve as a habitat for aquatic totems like crocodiles, pythons, or even fish. People, therefore, are permitted to draw water from particular rivers depending on their totemic bond with these natural yet metaphysical bodies. Unlike the river that permits the Damans to draw water, the Niger is a little more accommodating, though seasonally. Laye says while everyone fled from the crocodiles at the river, his mother 'did not since the crocodile is her totem.' He adds that,

> But my mother continued to draw water from the river. I will watch her draw water from the part where there were crocodiles…. the crocodiles could do no harm to my mother; and this privilege is quite understandable: the totem is identified with its processor: this identification is absolute, and of such a nature that its processor has the power to take on the form of the totem itself (62).

The above excerpt indicates that the community was aware of people's spiritual prowess. African peoples must make the 'Other' aware that our culture is eco-friendly. 'Wild' animals are part of some of us, and we are part of some wild animals. We fight against environmental degradation because of our physical and spiritual connection to plants, animals, and natural features. The snake, for instance, is an animal that possesses both natural and symbolic value. The case is similar in Ola Rotimi's *Our Husband Has Gone Mad Again,* where Lejoka-Brown has a snake for his pet. The good luck python is called Freedom. He believes this snake will give him luck in his political endeavors. Ironically, his political career is aborted and a fruitless venture, not because the totem is dysfunctional per se, but due to his selfish attitude and corrupt ambition. This suggests that African spirituality is aligned with ethics.

The situation is not dissimilar in *Arrow of God,* where we have the "royal python." This snake is a protector of the land and is not supposed to be killed. Unfortunately, Oduche, Ezeulu's recently converted son, commits a sacrilege by locking up the totem in a box. This exemplifies current threats to ecological heritage. Globalization and Western religion have produced 'Oduche's' or cultural aliens in contemporary society. The belief in totems is considered witchcraft by some critics. Fiona Bowie argues that:

> The Bangwa of South West Cameroon (West Africa) Bangwa, whether living in Cameroon or overseas, conceive of themselves as individuals and as social beings…. Everyone has a spirit animal that lives in his or her stomach, which can be 'sent out' in order to operate in the spirit world…. In many places spirits have been driven away by clearing the bush,

> so people can move more freely. Spirits like the dark so it is dangerous to travel at night. They like bushy places. Water spirits include hippos, crocodiles and water snakes. Land spirits include the elephant, leopard, snakes, porcupines, bush pigs and a type of dear. Owls are air spirits. Not all are spirits but it is believed that all leopards, crocodiles, hippos and owls are spirits. People change into a bush pig or porcupine to eat crops, cocoyams, etc. of others. There is a type of big wilder deer with two horns that is a spirit. Every owl that you see is some individual transformed. You only have one animal spirit. If your spirit animal is shot you will die. The person who owns the animal spirit will fall sick (Bowie 2020, 68-72).

Her picture of magic realism in this Cameroonian clan depicts the reality of eco-spiritualities. Africans relate to nature at a physical and metaphysical level. The latter is more eco-friendly as it hinders certain natural actions that harm the ecosystem, such as deforestation and pollution of water bodies.

These forms of magic realism and practices are deeply rooted in ancient traditions. They are factored into many written texts through literary archaeology. The writers use symbolism, detail, and other narrative forms to encode these archaeological practices. The Oroko clan in Cameroon has similar experiences of magical beliefs to those found in the Bangwa practices mentioned above. The Oroko clan has deer, antelopes, and crocodiles (*ngando*) as totems as well. Snake totems cut across most African tribes as totems. They are not peculiar to a particular people but are used by many.

Having totems, therefore, is an open secret in Africa. The totems could be animals or even trees. Laye even states categorically in his autobiographical narrative that, "I, too had my totem, but I no longer remembered what it was" (62). This archaeological vacuum highlights the need for historical documentation and oral traditions as forms of memory, which is our concern in the last chapter of this study. As time passes, culture evolves but knowing the original state or condition of certain beliefs or practices before their evolution is of great importance.

Laye himself attests that,

> The world rolls on, the world changes, my own world perhaps more rapidly than anyone's; so that it appears as if we were ceasing to be what we were, and that truly we are no longer what we were, and that we are not exactly ourselves even at the time when these miracles took place before our eyes. Yes, the world rolls on, and changes (62).

TOTEMISM AND TABOOISM AS ECO-PRESERVATION STRATEGIES

Manash Pratim Goswami (2018) views totemism as a strong belief held by the people of a certain tribe, who perceive the existence of souls or spirits not only in human form but also in animals, plants, trees, rocks, and all natural elements. One way to protect the environment and natural elements is by enhancing our understanding of totemism and tabooism. Totems often have taboos attached to them, so keeping them would deter humans from abusing natural features, which are most often habitats or incarnations of these totemic spirits.

Goswami further admits that totemic belief is in decline with the advent of modernity, and those who still adhere to ideological, mystical, emotional, reverential, and genealogical relationships with totemic objects keep them at a distance from the self-centric modern world. Apart from Africans, he notes, the totemic belief is an integral part of the social, cultural, religious, and spiritual behavior of peoples in India, Asia, Australia, and other regions. It is also a message of living in coexistence with nature. The more people adhere to totemic beliefs, the more they abuse nature because they become ignorant of nature's role in their given cultures.

Francis Darko and Abdul Karim Issifu (2015) advocate for 'the prohibition of killing and eating of frogs, crocodiles and pythons that are totems by both Sankana and Tongo Tengzuk communities.' They also critically condemn the use of harmful chemicals for fishing because of 'their potential danger to the lives of the totemic animals living in the water bodies and which could cause the wrath of the gods living in them if used.' In this vein, they hold that 'cutting down of forest trees for charcoal and the quarrying of rocks in these areas have also been prevented because of the belief that lesser gods and other spirit beings reside in them' (127).

These, among other things, are believed to have contributed significantly to the promotion of natural resource conservation and management for a long time.

Therefore, taboos, totems, belief systems, and other cultural values of the African have been successfully utilized by these critics to promote the conservation and management of natural resources in the Sankana and Tongo-Tengzuk communities. This chapter shares a similar goal: to demonstrate how our culture is intertwined with archaeology and how a deeper understanding of our culture contributes to preventing environmental degradation.

In the same light of totemic beliefs, Manash Pratim Goswami (2018) views totemism as a strong belief held by the people of a certain tribe, who perceive the existence of souls or spirits not only in human form but also in animals, plants, trees, rocks, and all natural elements. He holds, however, that totemic belief is in decline with the advent of modernity, and those who still adhere to the ideological, mystical, emotional, reverential, and genealogical relationships with totemic objects keep them at arm's length from the self-centric modern world. Apart from Africans, he notes, the totemic belief is an integral part of the social, cultural, religious, and spiritual behavior of peoples in India, Asia, Australia, and other regions. It is also a message of living in coexistence with nature.

There is intercourse between Totemism and Tabooism. Most totems are tied to taboos. There are always cultural restrictions on the use or dealings with totems and even their habitats. Breaking of these cultural principles usually attracts repercussions from the spirit or totemic realm.

In Achebe's *Arrow of God*, Oduche, the son of Ezeulu, who joins the missionaries, locks up the royal or sacred python in his box specially designed by the "mission carpenter" (43). Idemili, the deity, owned this royal python. This act of Oduche's is a taboo – it desecrates the land, given that the sacred python is the totem of the people of Umuaro. It is not an ordinary python; it has been consecrated and given a more profound epistemological and cosmological dimension in the spirit realm. No one was allowed to harm this reptile in any way. Although the culture is limited as it doesn't issue any punishment for one who locks the snake in a box, Oduche's absurd act is still considered a bigger sacrilege that warrants perpetual sacrifice and cleansing. This explains why Ezidemili sends a young emissary to ask Ezeulu, "how you intend to purify your house of the abomination that your son committed" (54). Unfortunately, Ezeulu allows pride to get the better of him as Ezidemili is his enemy among the six tribes. He asks the emissary to tell "Ezidemili to eat shit" (54). This pride and arrogance, as portrayed by Ezeulu on such a serious matter —a taboo subject —bring out his tragic flaw, or "hamartia," in Aristotelian terms, as it marks the beginning of his falling apart with the neighboring deities and his own "chi".

Talking about taboos related to animals in some Ghanaian localities, they hold that, "the prohibition of killing and eating of frogs, crocodiles and pythons that are totems by both Sankana and Tongo Tengzuk communities" (127) coupled with the prohibition of harmful chemicals "used for fishing because of their potential danger to the lives of the totemic animals living in the water bodies and which could cause the wrath of the gods living in them if used" (127) has immensely contributed to the people's cosmological and environmental preservation.

Keeping totems thus enhances environmental preservation, cultural values, and ensures the survival of habitats, which is essential for nature.

In Camara Laye's *The African Child*, most totems have restrictions or taboos attached to them. Laye's mother warns him not to kill a snake he sees in their compound. She says, "My son, this one must not be killed: he is not as other snakes" (15). "This snake," his mother adds, "is your father's guiding spirit" (15). Laye tells us that initially he felt like killing the snake, "but a power greater than myself stayed my hand and prevented me from pursuing him (18). His use of the masculine feminine to refer to the snake instead of it as in ordinary snakes shows that indeed it is a spirit. It is a person, a deity that guides the living.

In Africa, women also had and have totems. It is not solely a masculine affair. In Laye's *The African Child*, water bodies have multiple functions, one of which is serving as a habitat for totems. Laye's mother has an ancestral bond with water. He says:

It was in my mother that the spirit of her caste was most visibly –I was going to say ostensibly manifested. Finally she had naturally inherited from my grandfather his totem, which is the crocodile. This totem allowed all Damans to draw water from the Niger with impunity (61).

It becomes taboo when an outsider draws water from this river. This reduces the rate of abuse or pollution of this water body, thereby preserving it. Laye says among the Damans, the crocodiles "are not to be feared. You can bathe quite freely on the banks of pale sand, and do your washing there. But at the time of the rising of the waters, the volume of the river is increased threefold; everywhere there is deep water and the crocodiles are dangerous" (61). Nevertheless, his mother "continued to draw water from the river" despite such danger. He says, "the crocodiles could do no harm to my mother"; and this privilege is quite understandable: the totem is identified with its processor: this identification is absolute, and of such a nature that its processor has the power to take on the form of the totem itself (62).

The fact that certain persons can transform into animals or have a dual nature as both human and animal symbolizes the eco-critical understanding that humans should be one with their environment.

Having totems, therefore, was an open secret in the African past. It was not taboo. It instead became taboo if the totemic rules were violated. The totems could be animals or even trees. Laye states categorically in his autobiographical narrative that "I, too had my totem, but I no longer remembered what it was" (62). This archaeological vacuum highlights the need for historical documentation and oral traditions as forms of memory, which is our concern in the last chapter of this study. As time passes, culture evolves but knowing the original state or condition of certain beliefs or practices before their evolution is of great importance.

In essence, the more totems exist, the more natural and environmental elements are preserved. Trees would not be cut and exploited by capitalists carelessly. Poachers will not shoot at endangered species as has been the case over the decades. Most importantly, water bodies will not be polluted by fishermen because they will fear and not hurt the spirits or persons that dwell in all these natural and environmental forms.

We must also acknowledge that totemism has contributed to the preservation of certain endangered species. Restricting animals from being killed because of their metaphysical relevance to people has helped most of these animals to survive hunters' and poachers' bullets. A case in point is the elephants at Mount Fako in Cameroon, which are believed to be Totems according to the Bakweri indigenous culture. Killing the elephants would not only be destroying their specie but depriving a traditionalist from preserving his spirit in this ecological habitat.

We can observe the prevalence of the belief that ancestral spirits are likely to inhabit certain African hills, valleys, mountains, and large rocks. The case is similar in Cameroon, where the Bakweri ethnic community believes that "Evasa Moto", their deity, dwells on Mount Fako. Their totems, which are elephants, dwell up the mountain, guiding this precious rock and other spirits that dwell there.

Charles Teke demonstrates the spiritual relevance of the forest using Nathaniel Hawthorne's *Young Goodman Brown*. While in the African sphere, the forest is a habitat for spirituality, totems, and ancestral spirits, it can also be "haunted" (40) and demonized, becoming a meeting ground for cultic encounters. Such a scenario could be likened to the "evil forest" in most African indigenous communities like Umuofia in *Things Fall Apart,* where those who die after committing atrocities, like suicide, are dumped. The forest, therefore, is an archaeological or ecocultural site. This explains why most Cameroonian and African indigenous communities have a sacred forest reserved for the Fon, the Chief, and a few notables. Deforestation has not only environmental and economic damages, but also spiritual consequences. It is against such a backdrop that Lynn White, as quoted by Eunice Fombele observes that, "What people do about their ecology depends on what they think about themselves in relation to things around them" and that "human ecology is deeply conditioned by beliefs about our nature and destiny" (68). Fombele further refers to the spiritual ecosphere as "extraterrestrial worlds" (69). If people believe that animals, forests, rivers, and mountains harbor the living dead and present spirits (besides other natural benefits), they will certainly guard these features jealously and treat them honorably.

CONCLUSION

This chapter argues that African culture is deeply ingrained in nature; they are inseparable. The African environment is under threat, and if value is restored to its belief systems like totemism and tabooism, the exploitation and abuse of its flora and fauna will be curbed. This natural and metaphysical perception of nature is deeply rooted in the African's [precolonial] history, literature and archaeology through symbolic edifices and artefacts as well as via abstract documentations of belief systems and oral traditions. Given that culture and environment are threatened by modernity and the trends of globalization, there is a dire need to preserve these cultural and ecological objects and values, many of which are equally factored into our archaeology. Preserving our archaeological epistemology by reinforcing beliefs in taboos and totems, most of which are natural features such as trees, rivers, and animals, becomes a strategy for ecological heritage. When ancient beliefs, practices, and artifacts carved out of natural resources are valued and given significance, certain trees will not be felled irresponsibly, rivers will not be polluted carelessly, and animal species will not be hunted purposelessly. These artifacts, depicted in texts, serve as literary archaeology and didactic tools that enhance knowledge of eco-cultural heritage. In essence, eco-cultural heritage is anchored in reigniting belief systems, such as totemism and taboos, that surround it.

REFERENCES

Achebe, Chinua. 1974. *Arrow of God*. London: Heinemann.

Alembong, Nol. 2015. "African Philosophy and the Ethics of Ecoculture." In *Ecocultural Perspectives*. Raytown: Ken Scholars Publishing.

Bowie, Fiona. 2020. "Witchcraft and Healing among the Bangwa of Cameroon." In *Indigenous Religion: A Companion*, edited by Graham Harvey. Suffolk: Paston PrePress Ltd, Beccles.

Chinweizu, Onwuchekwa Jemie, and Ihechukwu Madubuike. 1988. "Evaluation of African Literature: Eustace Palmer." *The International Fiction Review* 15 (1).

Darko, Francis, and Abdul Karim Issifu. 2015. "Exploring the African Traditional Belief Systems in Natural Resource Conservation and Management in Ghana." *The Journal of Pan African Studies* 8 (9).

Fondze-Fombele, F. Eunice. 2015. "Shaping Perceptions of Human/Nature Relations: African Ecocultural Identity in Werewere Liking's Ritual/Narrative *Orphée–Dafric*." In *Ecocultural Perspectives*. Raytown: Ken Scholars Publishing.

Goswami, Pratim M. n.d. "Totemism and Tribes: A Study of the

Concept and Practice." Department of Journalism, Media and Mass Communication, Indira Gandhi National Tribal University, Amarkantak (MP). Accessed July 28, 2025. https://www.researchgate.net/publication/326655380_Totemism_and_Tribes_A_Study_of_the_Concept_and_Practice/

Gumo, Sussy, Joseph O. Ouma, and Charles O. Ochieng. 2012. "Communicating African Spirituality through Ecology: Challenges and Prospects for the 21st Century." *Religions* 3 (2): 523–543. https://doi.org/10.3390/rel3020523

Hongie, Godlove, and Divine Ngwa. 2015. "Sustainable Development: A Panacea to the Eco-sustainability." In *Ecocultural Perspectives*. Raytown: Ken Scholars Publishing.

Laye, Camara. 1959. *The African Child*. Glasgow: Fontana.

Mandillah, K. L. Lucy, and Georges-Ivo Ekosse. 2019. "African Totems: Cultural Heritage for Sustainable Environmental Conservation." *Conservation Science in Cultural Heritage* 18 (1): 201–218. https://doi.org/10.6092/issn.1973-9494/9235

Said, Edward. 1994. *Culture and Imperialism*. New York: Vintage.

Soyinka, Wole. 1963. *A Dance of the Forest*. London: Oxford University Press.

Teke, Charles N. 2015. "The Eco-Existential(ist) Dimension of Nol Alembong's *Forest Echoes*." In *Ecocultural Perspectives*. Raytown: Ken Scholars Publishing.

PART FOUR

NEW DIRECTIONS IN AFRICAN ECOCRITICISM: EMPIRICAL & OTHER GESTURES

CHAPTER EIGHTEEN

Experimenting with Empirical Ecocriticism
Author and Ecological Imaginaries beyond the Text

Chinonye C. Ekwueme-Ugwu & Chiamaka Ugoka

INTRODUCTION

Several twenty-first-century African authors and critics have emerged as highly successful ecocritics and environmentalist authors, having engaged with the environment as subjects of inquiry from postcolonial viewpoints. Performing an "advocacy function" for natural ecosystems and imaginary spaces (Huggan and Tiffin 2010, 14) that literature offers, they negotiate Africa's past, present, and possible future environmental experiences. Within the strictures of colonial and postcolonial ambivalences, they theorize, postulating possibilities and offering diverse means of escape from the realities of poverty, wars, squalor, and general insecurity that characterize life in Africa, the African ecosystem, and the African diaspora. These authors and critics, operating from the supposedly more secure and comfortable countries of the Global North, render their voices, all resonating with concern over the endangered continental ecosystems. However, neither imagination nor criticism appears to assuage the continuous assault on nature by culture, with consequences so real and dire as to jolt some authors from their cultural comfort precincts.

Among 21st-century African authors whose environmental instinct has been awakened by the incessant attacks on nature is Aliyu Kamal. For decades (he revealed in an interview), he had directed his creative arsenal against the erosion of his familiar indigenous Hausa and Muslim cultural values. As the environment became increasingly endangered and more and more of a global concern, with observable ecological and sustainability issues of natural resource exploitation, deforestation, leading to desert encroachment, environmental degradation, climate change and shortage of agricultural produce; with resultant hunger and poverty, he has turned toward ecology, producing the novel *Fire in My Backyard* (*Fire* subsequently). With strong evidence of personal attachment to the physical environment in the novel, which won the 2005 ANA/Chevron award, Kamal's concern for his Kano ecosystem is comparable to that of the late Ogoni, Niger Delta, Southern Nigerian creative writer and environmental activist, Ken Saro-Wiwa.

Unlike Saro-Wiwa, however, Kamal apparently avoided politics, militant activism and a direct confrontation with the powers-that-be, remaining within the academe and the borders of language and literature, engaging through characterization and other representative techniques the increasing degradation of social and environmental mores, and proving the capacity of the creative artist for navigating academic boundaries through his choice of botanical and other linguistic elements in an effort to replicate societal and ecological injustices that are at the heart of postcolonial cultural and environmental studies. Demonstrating the efficacy of empirical encounters with the natural environment, beyond the confines of classrooms, libraries, and artistic boundaries, through his representative style and techniques, Kamal reiterates, in an interview, similar possibilities that arose from his personal encounter with the physical environment as instrumental to his ecological consciousness and imagination.

Of particular interest to this chapter is Kamal's encounters with the natural environment of Kano and his imaginative reconstruction of the ecology, as well as the associated problems of depredation, climate change, and sustainability issues that are both African and global in scope. The chapter thus derives its insights primarily from two sources: first, the ecological and sustainability opportunities presented through the narrative actions of Kamal's literary oeuvre, and second, from empirical insights obtained from an interview with the author. Thus, using the interview method, this chapter qualitatively analyzes the author's responses to questions specifically crafted to explore the relationship between imagination and reality in the context of Kano, Northern Nigeria, as depicted in the novel, vis-à-vis the influence of the latter on the former.

Aiming to broaden the horizons of ecocriticism in African literature, the study moves beyond its current library-centric focus and advances toward more pragmatic, empirical endeavors, echoing the fundamental concern of ecocriticism: how to "turn words into something other than more words" (Rueckert 121). Thus, leveraging on the existing understanding of literature's capacity for representing "both lived and imagined experiences" (Okolie and Ukwueze 2023, 207) and the almost infinite scope of imagination and creativity, the chapter underscores the influence of the physical environment on the writer. Drawing on the empirical ecocriticism proposed by Matthew Schneider-Mayerson, Alexa Weik von Mossner, and P.W. Malecki (2020), the chapter extends from literature to an investigation of the author and the replicated factual environment.

Areas traditionally reserved for research and methodology of the social and natural sciences, including psychology, cognitive and behavioral fields, environmental pedagogy, etc., where the researcher is usually equipped with the methodologies and the applications of specialized tools for investigating empirically verifiable problems, are now being opened up through interdisciplinary and collaborative endeavors and approaches. Moreover, recent empirical research reveals that "an environment with natural elements stimulates curiosity and a flexible imagination more than viewing an artificial environment" (Chin-Wen Yeh et al. 2022, 11), buttressing the positive influence of the natural environment on creativity. Therefore, deploying some of the pragmatic investigative values of empirical ecocriticism, proposed by Schneider-Mayerson et al., seemed the most probable option for this examination of imagination and fact, but not without a gloss through mainline ecocriticism as the foundation and precursor of all other variants of the literary environmentalist tenets.

SOME ECOCRITICISM TURNS

Ecocriticism emerged as a literary movement in the 1990s, but its ideological foundations date back even further (Glotfelty 1996, xv). Etymologically, it emerged as a fusion of two Greek terms *oikos* and *kritis*, eco and critic, to bring into the literary artistic domain the environmental notion of eco/ecology as habitation and a network or system of dwellings for all – human and non-human, and the ecocritic as judge – "house judge", according to William Howarth (1996, 69).

William Rueckert in his 1978 essay "Literature and Ecology: An Experiment in Ecocriticism" (Slovic 2010, 4) is believed to have first used the term in the literary discuss, where he explained that ecocriticism is an experiment in his application of "ecological concepts to the reading, teaching, and writing about literature" (Rueckert 1996, 107). Since then, ecocriticism has evolved, developing into divergent yet significant national and ideological typologies and phases over the last four or so decades.

From its earliest American "white movement" (Glotfelty 1996, xxv) to the ethno-regional "other" movements, nature and culture-specific boundaries have been broken, entwined, and reopened, with unimaginably vast explorations of the various experiences of different global regions through literature practiced with an ecologically conscious outlook. With strong alliances, such as the USA Association for the Study of Literature and Environment (ASLE), or the Asian and UK associations of the same kind, ecocriticism has grown, "exceeding the boundaries" (Slovic 2010, 5), beyond the mere revision of the "relationship between literature and the physical environment" (Glotfelty 1996, xviii), and opening diverse environmental imagination possibilities, with theories and essays in every possible direction, diving further afield into regions, cultures, religion, ethnicity, and even medicine, all espousing multidisciplinary ideologies, and accommodating diverse disciplinary viewpoints on the environmental question.

Beginning officially as an organized movement in North American literature, it offered limitless theoretical options with its doctrinal emphasis on the influence of culture on nature and the relationships between human beings and the non-human ecosystem, as well as with others. It has, however, advanced since from a focus, in Western literature, only on the environment, to an all-inclusive overlap of diverse human experiences and limitless ecological spaces and time, including slavery, colonial, and post-colonial incidents, and the animist ideologies of primal cultures expressed in Manes (1996), all of which have helped to alter and continue to alter the way that literature views nature, from its Romantic or Negritudian glorious tributes to its all-encompassing environment: natural and not so natural, with its resources, exploited, depredated and place forsaken as crude for glittering technology.

Lawrence Buell, underscoring the significance of place in ecocriticism, views the former as a "resource of environmental imagination" (Buell 2001, 56) and a source of "great moral and therapeutic power"

(75). Beyond the literary attribute of place as setting, Neil Evernden also observes that "knowing who you are is impossible without knowing where you are from" (Evernden 1996, 101), underscoring the significance of place in ecocriticism and American literature.

Similarly, from post-colonial African contexts, myriads of socio-economic and political challenges, posing what has been described as a "Malthusian nightmare" looming over the continent's seeming inability to manage its teeming population sustainably (Wolputte 2024, 2), ecocriticism has opened up vistas for engaging place as central to the existence of all.

From industrialized West's conception of Africa as a natural resource mine, yet "an out-of-sight … place remote from green activists' terrain of concern" where toxic wastes could be dumped with ease of mind and conscience, ecocriticism has given rise to a more compacted scope dealing with the postcolonial in ecocritical, an ideological shift championed by many African and African-Diaspora ecocritics.

POSTCOLONIAL ECOCRITICISM

Protesting what he perceives as faint, the African response to the then already trending "green approaches to literature and literary criticism" of the West, William Slaymaker (2007, 683) may have inadvertently initiated the postcolonial approach to literature and environment, "a convergence of postcolonialism and ecocriticism" that combines environmental aesthetics with politics (Huggan and Tiffin 2010, 9).

Ignoring the prevailing sentiments in the "Green Studies" about Africa's concern with issues that are "tied to their daily subsistence" (Slaymaker 2007, 684), as contrary to environmentalist activist biases of the West, interested only in the preservation of the aspect of nature that gives pleasure, Slaymaker earns an avalanche of condemnations. Foremost among his critics are his fellow South Africans, Byron Caminero-Santangelo, Rob Nixon, Anthony Vital, and other postcolonial African critics who emerged subsequently.

Caminero-Santangelo, conscious that applying the overtly Western model espoused by Slaymaker would almost entirely erase the environmental ideology from the annals of African literature "literary or critical" (699), proposes an examination of "African literary texts in light of issues raised by ecocriticism and African environmental history" (699). Nixon, on the other hand, cites the case of the Ogoni, Southern Nigerian social activist, Ken Saro-Wiwa and his fight against "the ruinage of his Ogoni people's farmland and fishing waters by European and American oil conglomerates in cahoots with a despotic African regime" (2007, 715), demonstrating vividly the connection of resource politics and social justice with ecocriticism as fundamental to postcolonial ecocriticism discourse.

Building on his postcolonial treatises, Nixon (2011) draws attention to what he terms the "slow violence of ecological degradation" (13), the invisible devastations caused by the West's global environmental politics, which are directed against impoverished and marginalized worlds. Hence, his advice that "writers, filmmakers, and digital activists may play a mediating role in helping to counter the layered invisibility that results from insidious threats" (16) continues the propagation of the postcolonial political and activist ideals that emphasize ecological justice.

From a postcolonial perspective, Iheka (2018) also offers an ecocriticism of African literature that focuses on human-nonhuman relationships, agency, and the struggle against ecological degradation. Stressing that in addressing such challenges as "global warming and climate change, postcolonial studies ought to reassess those actions hitherto applauded for demonstrating the agency of the oppressed to ensure they are cognizant of nonhuman interests" (125).

From ecocriticism's postcolonial, gender, and other ideological shifts, the question of how to navigate from the literary to the non-literary natural or social environments replicated in literature, the possibility of engaging directly with real persons or places as environmentalist subjects in an experiential or empirical way has prompted the study of imagination and fact from the point of view of Aliyu Kamal (teacher, Professor, and author) and his foremost eco-centered novel *Fire*.

ECOLOGICAL IMAGINARIES AND FACTS OF FIRE IN MY BACKYARD

Ecological thoughts and creative manipulations of literary tools suggest a significant influence of factual environmental settings on authors and their writings. This is the assumption that prompted this investigation of fact, from an earlier reading of the novel, as source of data for what we consider a mixed-method approach (explained further in this chapter) that combines information from imaginative text with first-hand data from a real person to conclude African literature of the environment and ecocriticism. Thus, with a focus on the influence of the physical environment on the author, Kamal's imagination and writing, we adopted an interview as a method of data collection. We designed questions and arranged an interview with the author.

The author employs ecological words, natural settings, rural metaphors and characters in the story of the efforts by the protagonist, Umar-Faruq Adam, to curb excessive wood logging, as a means of combating the climate effects of deforestation, desertification, and poverty in the Kano, Northern Nigerian setting of the novel. The choice of Kamal and *Fire* is based on the scant literature on trees as endangered species, unlike imaginaries and criticisms of crude oil exploration in southern countries. Kamal's much later endeavor into ecological literature, as he acknowledged in the interview, is a credit to the Northern Nigerian ecological cause. Towards underscoring the influence of ecological fact on his ecological imaginary, the interviews that went back and forth through emails, mobile phone calls, and WhatsApp conversations were transcribed and presented as an appendix to this chapter, besides the analysis presented below, beginning with the person, Aliyu Kamal himself:

> I was born in Kano city in 1958 and attended Bayero and Edinburgh Universities majoring in Applied Linguistics and have been teaching in the former since 1983 during which time I wrote 21 novels (published 16 and have 5 in manuscript) one (*Fire in My Backyard*) of which won the ANA/Chevron Award in 2005" (See Appendix, question [Q subsequently] 1).

Two external factors—environment and culture—are basic influences that are parallel to the response of his protagonist, Umar-Faruq to climate issues:

> Umar-Faruq himself had realized that his choice of what

to do after getting his degree could not have been opting for anything other than ... what the environment, as it was turned barer, drier, and starker by the minutes had shown as an urgent need for sustainable utilization (*Fire* 4).

Similarly, Kamal's turn around, from Hausa cultural mores, to ecological issues occurs much later as: "All the novels other than *Fire* dwell on Muslim Hausa life set in Kano" (See Q2) and "Fire is experimental in my effort to attract a larger audience the world over since environmentalism is a global issue that affects us all" (Q3).

In line with the view that novelists possess "the kinetic energy necessary for social transition and change" (Achebe 1990, 152), Kamal employs *Fire* as a tool for promoting ecological change in his Kano ecosystem, shifting his focus from a socio-cultural commitment to an environmentalist loyalty.

In response to themes in the novel, Kamal says: "All the themes pertain to pollution and combine to give the reader a full picture of the issues at stake" (Q4). But when asked about his relationship with his protagonist, Umar-Farq, Kamal quips: "it's me in disguise!" (Q6). Irked by the in/actions of the ecologically uninformed commercial wood loggers and farmers, which render "barer and starker" the natural environment, Umar-Faruq embarks on an ecological research, deploying Rumbu peasant farmers as his research subjects, approaching the social and environmental problems of fictional Rumbu from personal observation, as the foundation of his empirical research. The local farmers' "powerlessness and hopelessness to take charge in the effort to end their misery and destitution" (*Fire* 7), is attributed to their lack of knowledge. Correlationally, Kamal reveals:

> I was interested in rural farmers leading lives independently founded on their effort at sufficiency in food production and contributing to the economy through exporting food outside the country and not giving up farming and fleeing to the city looking for odd jobs, raising the urban population and polluting cityscapes (Q5).

Thus, Kamal, deploying narrator and characters as tools, confronts the issue of ecosystem imbalance, precipitated by deforestation and its consequent desertification, which the local farmers and wood loggers are ignorant of, even as poverty and squalor loom large. He disguises himself as the young ecologist, with the narrator as mouthpiece, who reveals that:

> The task for the young scientist was to persuade the local farmer to desist from all the rampant loggings, to let the forests regenerate, to slow down the advancement of the desert of the desert sands and to spare the biosphere of the danger and degradation as to which it had all but succumbed (*Fire* 66).

On the question of his experiences and source of ecologic knowledge Kamal said: "I taught as a teacher-trainee for two years one in rural Jahun and the other in suburban Birnin Kudu in the former Kano state where I came into contact with the ecological issues I raised in the novel" (Q8), indicative of the environmental influence on his creativity. His application of scores of botanical and other ecological terminologies raised the question of validity and source of the exotic registers, to which he responds: "I read them. I got ecological books from the library, read and copied them … I am familiar also with the Hausa names of the plants. I know all those trees from my Kano locality" (Q6c). However, in response to the question of the author's direct encounter with farmers and loggers whose activities are depicted as constituting danger to the novel's ecosystem, replies: "I was aware of rampant logging but I never confronted and tried to stop anybody from indulging in it" (Q19). This is bloated with the question of the extent to which the writer could go in confronting environmental issues. Is the novelist equipped only to observe decaying or decayed ecosystems, make speculations based on those observations, but not confront the situation directly or conduct an actual study of the place, persons, or things? However, here is a changing world order that pays little heed to cognitive or intuitive knowledge. Can the eco-activist writer and critic in Africa survive by keeping away from the real forest, waters, animals, the biosphere, and the real human subjects of extrapolative verbal and articulate absorptions?

Kamal further reveals his source of inspiration saying: "Some of the scientific aspects were sourced from my background reading and the human details from the figments of my imagination" (Q12); thus buttressing his earlier response (to Q6) about reading ecological books to gain knowledge and that the elements – humans, non-humans, and the environment/setting, "were all drawn from [his] life experiences" (Q7) in and around rural and urban Kano, Asked for a percentile quantification of the environmental influence on his imagination, his response of fifty percent, and that the rest to were attributable to reading materials from the science ecological fields is also testament of the connection of imagination and reality. However, beyond observation, reading, and documentation of the knowledge, his job as an eco-activist author comes to an end.

His further response: "Umar-Faruq in my guise conducts research to collect data and write journal articles and me to pen a novel" (Q15) also stamps the finality of the eco-activist's pragmatism in the library. Kamal does not collect data from the villagers. He does not interact physically with wood loggers in his vicinity, even though he is aware of the ecological damage caused by their business activities on the Kano ecosystem. So, of what practical use are his observations, his reading of ecological or social science books, and documentation of many of the botanical and Hausa names of plants and their uses? Besides sentimental consciousness raising, without further action toward amelioration of the problems, say of food shortage, deforestation, and desertification, what real use are the eco-writer and critic's efforts? No wonder our students are paying less and less attention to reading. Can the African ecocritic and writer afford the luxury (like the European and other technologically advanced nations) of just reading and writing, and remain insignificant in her/his social and ecological milieu; a situation Achebe (1990) attributes to Africa's European cultural heritage:

> Because of our largely European education our writers ... [think] that the relationship between European writers and their audience will automatically reproduce itself in Africa. We have learnt from Europe that a writer or an artist lives on the fringe of society—wearing a beard and a peculiar dress and generally behaving in a strange, unpredictable way. He

is in revolt against society, which in turn looks on him with suspicion if not hostility. The last thing society would dream of doing is to put him in charge of anything (42).

Kamal's imagined place, in Kano, Northern Nigeria, is no less endangered than Ogoni land, Southwest of the same country, or any of the other operational bases of natural resource exploitation in Africa. Kamal's portrayed place is a rural ecology endangered by excessive "tree-felling and fire-wood-selling business" (*Fire* 5) for the satisfaction of the city-dwelling population. Moreover, Kamal, the writer, is aware of all these, as are Helon Habila, Kaine Agary, and Tanure Ojaide, probably are, or the late Isidore Okpewho and J.P. Clark were during their lifetime. However, the disciplinary construct of the West forbids imaginative author/writer/critic to have any political or socio-economic plan or practice towards the remediation of the ecological evils within their socio-environmental sphere of influence.

However, the limitations that foreground the literary artist/writer's social and environmental impediments towards a responsibility to the environment they inhabit are currently being contested and renegotiated. From literature to the design and application of social science tools, such as questionnaires or oral interviews, 21st-century eco-conscious readers are invited to transcend the boundaries of the library and venture out to obtain factual information as additional evidence for validating their ecological claims, beyond mere imagination and speculation. Through participant observation of phenomena, they can encounter living organisms—human and non-human—and gain firsthand information about environmental issues. This is the crux of the empirical ecocriticism dialog initiated by Matthew Schneider-Mayerson, Alexa von Mossner Weik and W.P. Maleki (2020).

EMPIRICAL ECOCRITICISM

As an emerging trend within ecocriticism's larger sphere, empirical ecocriticism advocates for the application of practical and experiential methodologies and tools, particularly from the social sciences, to investigate the effect of environmental fiction on the behavior of its audience towards non-human environmental others. Matthew Schneider-Mayerson,

Alexa Weik von Mossner, and W.P. Malecki (2020), foremost empirical ecocriticism advocates, define it as "an empirically grounded, interdisciplinary approach to environmental narrative" that aims at carrying ecocriticism "to its logical conclusion by conducting original empirical research, to learn, for example, whether climate fiction influences the attitudes and behaviors of its readers … or whether narrative empathy can make readers care about the plight of nonhuman species" (2).

Straddling the borders of ecocriticism with those of the social and environmental sciences, empirical ecocriticism seeks a stronger and more pragmatic bond between literature and the environment by including real persons, animals, places, and things in ecocriticism research subjects. Schneider-Mayerson's research application of a qualitative survey method, designing a questionnaire as tool for eliciting responses from "American readers of well-known climate fiction novels [to ascertain the readers'] awareness of climate injustice and the perception of climate migrants" (2020, 4), among other variables, concludes with his stated conviction that the empirical methodology "offers valuable information about the flesh-and-blood people that read environmentally engaged literature, how they come to do so, and what they make of their reading experiences" (4).

By focusing on ecologically relevant creative fiction of various genres "novels, short stories, poetry, children's literature, film, television, video games, music, and theater, among other media", empirical ecocriticism, according to Schneider-Mayerson et al., overlaps ecocriticism and the social sciences environmental communication, but differs from both in some significant ways. They submit that it defers from ecocriticism in that its assumptions are not solely based on discoveries from reading texts, listening to, or viewing audio-visual fictions; and from environmental humanities, in that "it combines social scientific methodologies with the kind of textual analysis that has long been the métier of ecocriticism" (Schneider-Mayerson et al. 2020, 4). With several other instances, they demonstrate empirical approaches as a credible pragmatic model for advancing the ecocriticism frontier beyond the library, and attempting, as it were, to address the misgivings and questions by William Rueckert about ecocriticism in the decades from its proposition:

> Halfway between literature and ecology, the energy pathways

> obscured, the circuits of life broken between words and actions, vision and action, the verbal domain and the non-verbal domain, between literature and the biosphere – because I can't further … how can we apply the energy, the creativity, the knowledge, the vision we know to be in literature to the human-made problems ecology tells us are destroying the biosphere … How can we turn words into something other than more words … how can we do more than recycle WORDS (Rueckert 1996, 121)?

Credible as the empirical ecocriticism option may seem, its endeavor at sensitizing and increasing the urban/cityscapes' environmental sensibilities offers little to post-colonial Africa, currently burdened by the "slow violence" (Nixon 2011) socio-economic yoke surreptitiously imposed on the continent by the West. Empirical ecocriticism's emphasis on consumers of imaginative works – readers of texts, viewers of climate movies and television, its methods and interests exclude the vast non-reading, non-movie or TV viewing African population.

The daily living experiences of Africans are still tied to their physical environment. Fewer still have access to, or the leisure time, for viewing climate or other movies. Very few in both urban and rural communities have access to literary texts for any productive endeavor. Real Africans – farmers, wood loggers, fishermen, and artisans influence their physical environment and are directly influenced by it in their peculiar ways. The indigenous Africans have always been compelled by the harsh socio-economic and political realities of all times to exploit the nature that surrounds them without a thought for the sustainability implications of their actions. Like the research on the subjects of Kamal's protagonist, Umar-Faruq, their lives are adversely influenced by the environmental changes occurring globally. However, they know next to nothing about climate change, its impacts, and ways of mitigating them, except through occasional physical contacts offered by international agencies such as the International Food and Agriculture Development (IFAD) and other UN climate and environment agencies.

In assessing the behavioral attitudes of individuals toward the environment, empirical ecocriticism's exclusion of non-literate members of human communities overlooks Africa's socio-economic, political, cultural, and environmental injustices stemming from colonial and post-colonial antecedents. As such, any meaningful effort to reach indigenous persons with ecocriticism's pragmatic principles must advance from literature to dialoguing and having experiential encounters with persons and their real physical setting, in collaboration with the actual persons already on ground, such as the aforementioned food, agriculture and environmental agencies, issues raised in this study of imagination and fact from literature to its author. With questions such as how imaginative authors' physical encounters with the environment influence their imagination, as seen in this novel, drama text, or poem, the ecocritic is well on the way to understanding and appreciating the environmental problems and peculiarities of different African places better.

The empirical ecocritics' apparent suggestions or advice for advancing ecocriticism from its imaginary and library spaces to actual physical environmental spaces, such as city or urban landscapes, among consumers of climate fiction and films, offer some practical implications for ecocriticism in African literature. Post-colonial Africa's environmental literature exhibits thematic and setting peculiarities, including the depletion of forests for subsistence. Wood is a cheaper and more readily available alternative source of fuel. Examples include its use in developmental projects, solid mineral mining, and crude oil exploitation.

While such issues in African texts have produced an avalanche of ecocriticism, postcolonial ecocriticism, and ecofeminist approaches in the context of African imaginaries, examinations of the influence of environmental fiction on readers' attitudes toward endangered ecosystem species in real social settings are not yet prevalent. Besides meeting academic requirements and promotion criteria, the notion of confronting climate issues in desert-prone areas, as well as the devastating consequences of solid mineral mining on agriculture and crude oil exploitation on fishing communities, concerns ecocritics, who may have to devise peculiar ways of engaging with the natural environment beyond mere words. As such, empirical ecocritical postulations present assumptions that are not altogether to be jettisoned, but accorded further attention towards opening more possibilities, involving, for instance, a mixed-method, and combining data from literature and field/empirical sources, with the latter authenticating information from the former – consisting of imaginative literature and non-fiction (essays, reports, papers, theses and dissertations).

CONCLUSION

Drawing on insights from Aliyu Kamal, Professor, author, and cultural and literary ecological activist, we advocate in this chapter for cross-breeding activities among ecocritics that involve both cognitive awareness of environmental evils and field experiences with the human and non-human elements of the environment. It will proceed from literary activities, such as reading and writing, to practical observation of the natural or social environment, involving information gathering from non-literary fields about specific endangered ecosystems, and ultimately to an actual engagement with these fields. Also, to gain more information with which to validate data from the representative texts, and for creating awareness about climate change consequences – degradation of an imagined place, animals, trees, etc., the ecocritic, by asking informed questions and getting informed answers to the questions, constitutes a more potent force in combating peculiar local ecological challenges.

Kamal's message is clearly addressed to all informed eco-activist authors, critics, teachers, farmers, community leaders, etc. This suggests that ecocriticism in African literature can make more meaningful contributions through a more pragmatic and advocacy approach to endangered African ecologies.

However, advancing from literature into areas of empirical enquiries opens up opportunities for debates about those actual places that are within the ecocritic/activist's sphere of influence. Through the use of a questionnaire or an oral interview, eco-conscious readers would obtain factual information as additional evidence for validating their ecological claims beyond mere imagination.

Kamal's imagined place, in Kano, Northern Nigeria, is no less endangered than Ogoni land, Southwest of the same country, or any of the other operational bases of natural resource exploitation in Africa. Kamal's portrayed place is a rural ecology endangered by excessive "tree-felling and fire-wood-selling business" (*Fire* 5) for the satisfaction of the city-dwelling Adam family. But do such places actually exist outside imagination?

Yes. Such places visited by the author lead him to the conclusion that "Desertification and deforestation have diverse effects on farming and threaten livelihoods" Q11).

On the other hand, aspects of other works, such as Helon Habila's *Oil on Water*, Isidore Okpewho's *Tides*, Kaine Agary's *Yellow-Yellow*, and a host of others set in Nigeria's Niger Delta, challenge crude oil spillage and other hazards of crude oil exploitation. These works, in line with ecocriticism's advocacy for environmental consciousness through literature, have enjoyed endless eco-conscious reading but have hardly been subjected, beyond the library, to an empirical investigation, for example, of the influence of an actual physical environment or organisms on the author's imagination. Investigations into the influence of academic domains outside the arts on imagination are also scarce. Yet, advancing from empirical ecocriticism's utilization of social science tools, these investigations offer possibilities in our study of African literature, as areas awaiting exploration and exploitation by literary experts.

Proceeding from a close reading of *Fire in My Backyard* to an analysis of firsthand information from the author on the contribution of factual settings to shaping his imagination and writing, this study has revealed, moreover, a link among the depredation of African ecosystems, migration, and socio-cultural alienation. Kamal's insights affirm that engaging directly with one's environment and understanding its unique challenges are vital steps toward the remediation of endangered spaces.

The success of our mixed-method approach is also a step toward initiating visits and interactions with the place and its people, experiencing their losses and gains firsthand, and paying close attention to the atmosphere. The author's words, though in denial of direct encounters with local ecosystems and entities, suggest that these experiences are crucial for achieving ecological authenticity in literature.

Furthermore, Kamal's observations reveal that imagination is grounded in real-life experiences from specific locations and is essential for fostering ecological awareness through literature. For the 21st-century African ecocritics, exploring endangered areas is a more effective approach to addressing the detrimental effects of culture on nature than developing concepts detached from these natural settings and their intended beneficiaries.

REFERENCES

Achebe, Chinua. 1990. *Hopes and Impediments: Selected Essays*. New York: Anchor Books.

Buell, Lawrence. 1995. *The Environmental Imagination: Thoreau, Nature Writing, and the Formation of American Culture*. Cambridge: Harvard University Press.

Buell, Lawrence. 2001. *Writing for an Endangered World: Literature, Culture, and Environment in the U.S. and Beyond*. Cambridge: Harvard University Press.

Caminero-Santangelo, Byron. 2007. "Different Shades of Green: Ecocriticism and African Literature." In *African Literature: An Anthology of Criticism and Theory*, edited by Tejumola Olaniyan and Ato Quayson, 698–705. Oxford: Blackwell Publishing.

Evernden, Neil. 1996. "Beyond Ecology: Self, Place, and the Pathetic Fallacy." In *The Ecocriticism Reader: Landmarks in Literary Ecology*, edited by Cheryl Glotfelty and Harold Fromm, 92–104. Athens: University of Georgia Press.

Glotfelty, Cheryll. 1996. "Literary Studies in an Age of Environmental Crisis." Introduction to *The Ecocriticism Reader: Landmarks in Literary Ecology*, edited by Cheryl Glotfelty and Harold Fromm, xv–xxxvii. Athens: University of Georgia Press.

Howarth, William. 1996. "Some Principles of Ecocriticism." In *The Ecocriticism Reader: Landmarks in Literary Ecology*, edited by Cheryl Glotfelty and Harold Fromm, 69–91. Athens: University of Georgia Press.

Huggan, Graham, and Helen Tiffin. 2010. *Postcolonial Ecocriticism: Literature, Animals, Environment*. New York: Routledge.

Iheka, Cajetan. 2018. *Naturalizing Africa: Ecological Violence, Agency, and Postcolonial Resistance in African Literature*. Cambridge: Cambridge University Press.

Kamal, Aliyu. 2004. *Fire in My Backyard*. Kano, Nigeria: Estate of Aliyu Kamal.

Kamal, Aliyu. 2019. Interview with the authors, December 10.

Manes, Christopher. 1996. "Nature and Silence." In *The Ecocriticism Reader: Landmarks in Literary Ecology*, edited by Cheryl Glotfelty and Harold Fromm, 15–29. Athens: University of Georgia Press.

Nixon, Rob. 2011. *Slow Violence and the Environmentalism of the Poor.* Cambridge: Harvard University Press.

Nixon, Rob. 2007. "Environmentalism and Postcolonialism." *ISLE: Interdisciplinary Studies in Literature and Environment* 14 (1): 1–19.

Okolie, Mary J.N., and Ogochukwu Ukwueze. 2023. "Women, Agency, and the Environment in Helon Habila's *Oil on Water* and Kaine Agary's *Yellow-Yellow.*" *Matatu: Journal for African Culture and Society* 54. Brill, Ecobordering.

Rueckert, William. 1996. "Literature and Ecology: An Experiment in Ecocriticism." In *The Ecocriticism Reader: Landmarks in Literary Ecology*, edited by Cheryl Glotfelty and Harold Fromm, 105–123. Athens: University of Georgia Press.

Schneider-Mayerson, Matthew, Alexa Weik von Mossner, and W.P. Malecki. 2020. "Empirical Ecocriticism: Environmental Texts and Empirical Methods." Oxford: Oxford University Press, for *ISLE: Interdisciplinary Studies in Literature and Environment.*

Slaymaker, William. 2007. "Ecoing the Other(s): The Call of Global Green and Black African Responses." In *African Literature: An Anthology of Criticism and Theory*, edited by Tejumola Olaniyan and Ato Quayson, 683–694. Oxford: Wiley-Blackwell.

Slovic, Scott. 2005. "The Third Wave of Ecocriticism: North American Reflections on the Current Phase of the Discipline." *Ecozon@* 1 (1).

Wolputte, Steven van, Michael Thomas Bollig, Martina Gockel, Clemens Greiner, and Noah Kahindi. 2024. "The Aftermath – What Future for African Studies (in Europe?). A View from Behind the Scenes of ECAS9." *Africa Spectrum* 59 (2)

Yeh, Chin-Wen, Shih-Han Hung, and Chun-Yen Chang. 2022. "The Influence of Natural Environments on Creativity." *Frontiers in Psychiatry* 13: 895213. https://doi.org/10.3389/fpsyt.2022.895213. Accessed February 22, 2024.

CHAPTER NINETEEN

Conclusion: Three Cameroonians on the Futures of African Ecocriticisms
Interviews with Nnane Ntube, Ekpe Inyang, and Nji Tem

Nsah Mala

In this brief concluding chapter, Nsah Mala interviews three Cameroonians: poet, writer, editor, and artivist Nnane Ntube; educationist, environmentalist, and poet Ekpe Inyang; and literary scholar Edwin Nji Tem. They discuss the possible and potential futures of African ecocriticisms. This chapter aims to contribute to disrupting what counts as scholarship, thereby underscoring the role of dialogue in scholarship broadly, and African ecocriticisms in particular.

NSAH MALA:
Nnane Ntube, as a bilingual teacher, editor, poet-writer-artivist, and researcher from Cameroon dealing with, among others, climate change and ecological issues, what kind of future do you see for ecocriticism in and about Africa? Are there some evolutions, and which are some emerging new directions and voices in the fields of African eco-writing and ecocriticism? In these different capacities, what would you do differently going forward?

NNANE NTUBE:
In a conversation with one of my students, he said, "Nature is so generous, but we have proven to be selfish." This got me thinking about environmental existentialism. I wondered why "we" (humans) have proven to be selfish. Is it that in our numerous actions for survival, we fail to recognize the existence and central place that Nature occupies in

our lives? In 2019, I set out with what I termed "innovative research" in the domain of environmental discourses during my Master's studies in the Department of Literature and African Civilization at the University of Yaoundé 1 (Cameroon). My focus was on Cameroonian poets whose works embrace nature writing. I was so excited about this research venture as I knew it would permit me to delve further into the idea of "positionality" in environmental studies. The idea itself was good, but what seemed lacking was a wealth of knowledge on the topic from an African perspective.

I can still hear the voice of my supervisor telling me to focus on ecocriticism from an African perspective. Honestly, at that point in time, the only knowledge I had about environmental activism came from a Eurocentric perspective, as championed by the media's hyping of Swedish environmental activist Greta Thunberg's transformative speeches on the need for environmental protection by all for all. My supervisor's advice came as an eye-opener and influenced me to pay particular attention to what African poets and researchers are saying in their writings regarding nature and the environment, as well as the changes occurring in and around Africa.

While I was figuring out where to start, I stumbled on an article online titled "Contemporary Cameroon Poetry in English: Nature and the Politics of Consciousness Raising for the Future" by Eunice Ngongkum, published in the *Journal of African Literature Association* Vol. 11. This inspired my motivation to search further in order to explore innovative ideas on nature writing, ecocriticism, and climate change from the African perspective. I was amazed by the rising interest in the abovementioned domains from not only Cameroonian researchers, poets, and playwrights, but from poets, novelists, playwrights, and researchers from other African nations such as Nigeria, Kenya, and South Africa. This rising concern to focus on ecocritical studies from the African viewpoint can only be likened to the collective awareness of these researchers and writers to the danger Africans faces and would continue to face – culturally, economically and health-wise – if little is done to save the trees, royal animals, medicinal plants, water sources, the soil, etc., from global warming, illegal haunting, slash-and-burn, deforestation, etc.[1]

Interestingly, through my research, I developed a deeper environmental awareness. I understood the central role of the poem "Notre Dame de Paris, Pray for Cyclone Idai's Children!" by Nsah Mala, Joyce Ash, Mbizo Chirasha, et al.[2] The poem is a call for action from the sons and daughters of Africa to exercise self-awareness in identifying environmental problems, creating a supportive system to solve their immediate environmental challenges, and being intentional about it. The poem was published online in 2019 in memory of Cyclone Idai's devastating impact in Mozambique, Malawi, and Zimbabwe on March 14-15, 2019. It highlights the unusual silence and inaction of African leaders to form a collective support system for the victims, while shamelessly rushing to send messages of sympathy to France following the fire accident at the Notre Dame de Paris in the same period.

Research shows that there has been a plurality of voices from Africa in the domains of eco-writing and ecocriticism, responding to Eurocentric ecocriticism. William Slaymaker in "Ecoing the Others: The Green Call of the Global Green and Black African Responses" remarks that "Black African writers take nature seriously in their creative and academic writing, but many have resisted or neglected the paradigms that inform much of global warming" (2001). Although his statement appears to be true, it is essential to note that these African writers address concerns about global warming from a bottom-up approach, which may make their contributions seem less significant. It is only normal for them to identify the signs of global warming from their context, no matter how minimal, to prevent a potential danger.

Such actions are enough reasons for me to think that ecocriticism has a bright future in Africa, especially with innovative voices from

---

1   Think about, for example, recent foresight and futures workshops on the Congo Basin and Royal Animals facilitated by Nsah Mala in Yaoundé, Cameroon, on Saturday 7th September 2024, leading to an edited anthology of futuristic stories entitled *Stories from the Futures of the Congo Basin*, published in 2015.
2   See "Notre Dame de Paris, pray for Cyclone Idai's Children – A Poem," Voice4Thought, 17 May 2019 < https://www.voice4thought.org/notre-dame-de-paris-pray-for-cyclone-idais-children-a-poem/> accessed on 12 November 2024.

Cameroonian writers like Imbolo Mbue whose novel explore oil extraction in Anglophone Cameroon; Eric Ngalle Charles whose eco-poems unveil environmental commitment and awareness from a cultural perspective; John Ngong Kum Ngong's *Blot on the Landscape* and *Tears of the Earth* that fuels environmental activism and raises eyebrows on global warming; Nol Alembong's *Green Call* that gives an active voice to a silent Nature; Ekpe Inyang's *Tastes of Nature*; Nsah Mala's *Chaining Freedom, Bites of Insanity, Constimocrazy, Les Pleurs du mal*, etc. Other eco-writers from across Africa include Tanure Ojaide, Helon Habila, Nnedi Okorafor, and Kofi Anyidoho, among others. Some notable African researchers in this domain include Cajetan Iheka, Sule Egya, Eunice Ngongkum, Kenneth Toah Nsah (also known as Nsah Mala), Ogaga Okuyade, Étienne-Marie Lassi, Blessed E. Ngoe, Emmanuel Adeniyi, and Paul Oyodele Onanuga, among others.

Moving forward, I have engaged my students in practicing environmental stewardship as a means to enhance their commitment towards understanding the silent cry of the environment. Additionally, I have become more involved in eco-writing through poetry. I have poems such as "Life Beneath" and "The Wait". I am poised to maintain this momentum for as long as possible.

NSAH MALA

Ekpe Inyang, you are a seasoned Cameroonian poet-writer, playwright, environmentalist, and researcher dealing with, among others, climate change and ecological issues in your writing and work. For instance, you are one of the writers from the Congo Basin that I examined in my PhD thesis. Your work has been studied by scholars in and beyond Cameroon. What kind of future(s) do you see for ecocriticism in and about Africa? Are there some evolutions, and which are some emerging new directions and voices in the fields of African eco-writing and ecocriticisms? What would you do differently going forward?

EKPE INYANG

I am Ekpe Inyang, a Cameroonian environmentalist, educationist, eco-poet, and playwright. Today, August 29, 2024, I read a post on a WhatsApp platform about a university advertisement focusing on the

Faculty of Arts. The advert was an incredible showcase of the programmes in the various departments of the faculty, highlighting the competencies the students stand to acquire and the career opportunities available to them. Immediately below was this negative comment, translated from Pidgin English: "See the direction our country is taking. While others are talking Science, Technology, Engineering, and Mathematics, we are here celebrating History and Literature. Juju is a bad thing, indeed." What does this comment really mean?

In fact, I have listened to several people condemn the arts in favour of science and technology. To them, all arts programmes in our universities should be suppressed to give room for science and technology. They have been observing or hearing about the level of technological advancement in Japan and China, and do not see why subjects like literature should occupy our high school and university curricula. They do not see the role of the arts in the development of science and technology. I grew up loving science and mathematics, with a demonstrated ability to invent, but I never hated literature, even though I frowned upon the fact that it earned me the lowest marks. I would have really loved to become an engineer. As a child, I was often seen constructing and inventing toys, such as vehicles, guns, and tools for work. However, today, I am not only an environmentalist but also a playwright and poet whose artistic works are utilized in universities for research and teaching. Have I taken the wrong path? No, not at all.

As an eco-writer, I have been utilizing the arts to convey scientific concepts in forms that are more accessible to the general public and local communities. I have worked with some literary minds involved in ecocriticism, and I have seen their level and depth of analysis of natural phenomena that fall in the realm of ecology (e.g., see Kenneth Nsah's or Nsah Mala's eco-writing and ecocritical scholarship). Sometimes I wonder whether they are not already ecologists! From this, I see a future in which ecologists embrace ecocritics in order to expand their scientific boundaries and depths…to give society the scientific ingredients needed to make informed decisions and develop responsible attitudes. I have realized that where science provides the skeleton, the arts provide the flesh needed to give a fuller picture, and that the one inspires the other into higher levels of expression and performance. In fact, I see ecocriticism as a bridge that links the arts with ecological science.

There is a growing but timid number of eco-writers in Cameroon, but the most prominent and committed amongst them are Nol Alembong and Ayang Federick Enoh. Nol Alembong is an eco-poet who has published several collections (e.g., *Forest Echoes, Green Call, The Passing Wind*) and continues to write and share some of his poems with me. Ayang Federick Enoh is best known for his play, *Green Hills*. Eco-writing originated from concerns about species and ecosystems, but it is now expanding to address broader global issues, including climate change and biodiversity decline. Prominent voices in ecocriticism include Nsah Mala, who not only conducted an ecocritical analysis of my play, *The Hill Barbers*, but also completed his PhD in ecocriticism, utilizing a significant number of my works and the works of other eco-writers in the Congo Basin. Nsah Mala himself is a multilingual eco-poet in his own right and is currently editing a bilingual Congo Basin Poetry Anthology.

Personally, my creative output is seen as rich and diverse, but now I must refocus to ensure that the materials others and I have produced are more meaningfully exploited to serve society. I have actually started by discussing with curriculum developers from high schools and universities the need to introduce modules that expose art students to ecological or environmental thinking. In this way, the arts will not be pursued purely for their own sake, but rather to address ecological and other issues confronting society. By the same token, science students should be introduced to modules that expose them to relevant art content, helping them cultivate adequate critical and analytical thinking. Above all, readings on ecocriticism should be used to develop a module that brings together art and science students, even at the university level. This will enable students to see themselves as embarking on a journey with a common purpose of saving the Earth.

NSAH MALA

As a researcher from Cameroon grappling with, among others, climate change and ecological issues, what kind of future(s) do you see for ecocriticism in and about Africa? Are there some evolutions, and which are some of the emerging new directions and voices in the fields of African eco-writing and ecocriticisms? What would you do differently going forward as a scholar?

EDWIN NJI TEM

Ecocriticism in Africa, under the aegis of Postcolonial Ecocriticism, in my view, has only just taken root and is branching out to a vibrant new future in a multiplicity of perspectives. Since William Slaymaker published his article, "Echoing the Other(s): The call of Global Green and Black African Responses", in 2001, there has been a very robust academic response to his views by scholars from Cameroon in particular and Africa in general. Building the case for postcolonial ecocriticism, numerous scholarly voices have underscored the idea that African writers' engagement with the environment dates back to a long history. For example, Elizabeth DeLoughrey and George Handley in their introduction to *Postcolonial Ecologies: Literatures of the Environment* argue that "there are many examples from the mid twentieth century of authors who were grappling with the relationship between landscape and colonization" (2011, 5). Using the case of Chinua Achebe's 1958 novel, *Things Fall Apart*, for example, these scholars further submit that the novel "emphasized the radical ontological shift in understanding place that occurred through the process of European colonialism and Christian missionization" (2011, 6). The early scholarly framing of the African writer's preoccupation with the environment, and the African people writ large, as is the case with *Things Fall Apart* cited above, was in essence to show what Onoriode Philip Aghoghovwia has described as "…the context of African environmentalism or the conditions of the African eco-imagination and critical epistemology" (2014, 33). In many respects, the pioneering work on African ecocriticism focused mainly on African epistemology in relation to environmental lore and ethics.

However, ecocriticism in Africa has evolved greatly and now engages aspects such as environmental justice and eco-cosmopolitanism. Within the context of the extractive industry in Africa, with a focus on resources such as oil, timber and gold, for example, writers and scholars like Ken Saro-Wiwa, Tanure Ojaide, Nnimmo Bassey, Sule Eya, and Nsah Mala have examined aspects of extractive violence in Africa and the devastating effects on human and nonhuman populations. The Niger Delta is a notable example of an area that has garnered significant attention, particularly following the execution of Ken Saro-Wiwa. Sule Egya, writing about the attention this area has received, submits: "Eco-writing is mainly characterized by the creation of protagonists or personas (in the case of poetry) that mobilize the locals to confront institutional powers mainly framed as multinational oil corporations in connivance with the Nigerian government" (2020a, 6). In showing how the poor have been deprived of their right to land and health in the light of ecological despoliation, the views of Rob Nixon on *Slow Violence and the Environmentalism of the Poor* have been particularly instructive. However, the Niger Delta and oil extraction are not the only preoccupations of contemporary scholars of the environment. Kenneth Toah Nsah's award-winning, full-length study on the Congo Basin, for instance, is yet another example of how recent scholarly voices are preoccupied with extractivism and climate change writ large.[3]

It must, however, be said that while the extractive industry and anthropogenic climate change have preoccupied many scholars of African ecocriticism, other scholarly voices contend that African eco-writing, and indeed ecocriticism, has largely been anthropocentric, privileging the human over other aspects of the environment in their rendition of agency. Examples of such scholars are Cajetan Iheka and Eunice Ngongkum. Iheka, for example, offers a critique of postcolonial theory and its influence on postcolonial ecocriticism as one of the reasons why ecocriticism from Africa has largely been anthropocentric. In making the case for what he calls the "aesthetics of proximity," Iheka contends that "accounts of agency are yet to seriously take notice of the nonhuman protagonists in the environment often implicated in their renditions of agency" (2018: 4). These nonhuman protagonists in his view are plants, animals and forests and other abiotic components of the environment like soil and water. This argument animates the idea of African ecocriticism and multispecies existence, survival, and death in the context of "…the neoliberal machine's instrumentalization of bodies" (2018, 5). Ngongkum takes a similar stance in her book *Anglophone Cameroon Poetry in the*

---

3   Nsah, Kenneth Toah. (2022). "Can Literature Save the Congo Basin? Postcolonial Ecocriticism and Environmental Literary Activism." Aarhus University: PhD Thesis.

Environmental Matrix where she dedicates an entire chapter, for example, to the study of "river discourses." While environmental justice criticism, focusing on both human and nonhuman components of the environment, has been highly debated, Sule Egya still cautions that African ecocriticism must never lose sight of the complexities of African environments, which must continue to animate scholarship. In his article, "Out of Africa: Ecocriticism Beyond the Boundary of Environmental Justice," Egya contends that "this emphasis on environmental justice has suppressed the crucial dimension of environmental literature in Africa by failing to foreground natural worlds and their roles in shaping thoughts and ways of living as well as the preservation and conservation of diverse life forms" (2020b, 67). Ngongkum's scholarship above is very much in this direction.

Aspects of eco-cosmopolitanism have also preoccupied recent scholars of eco-writing and ecocriticism in Africa. Kenneth Toah Nsah (also known as Nsah Mala), for example, has examined aspects of urbanization, urban sprawl, and squalor in Congo Basin plays.[4] He shows the effects of urbanization on the urban poor and politics of water (pollution) resulting from inept political leadership, socio-political corruption, and citizens' inattention to aspects of environmental protection. Nsah has studied youth climate activism from a literary prophetic prism, drawing on plays, poems, and novels from the Congo Basin.[5] These, in broad strokes, are some of the new directions that ecocriticism in Africa is taking.

What would I do differently? I believe the issue of extractivism in the global South, and Africa in particular, still requires attention. I would like to build on three broad resource sites: timber, oil, and gold extraction, interpreting their effects on human and nonhuman populations with insights drawn from Achille Mbembe's necropolitics in relation to ecological decline. In another direction, although Iheka has done some work on this, I still think the ecologies of war require further attention, considering the numerous wars across Africa, from Cameroon through

---

4   Nsah, Kenneth Toah (2022). "The Ecopolitics of Water Pollution and Urbanization in Congo-Basin Theatre." *Orbis Litterarum*, 77, 314– 332. <https://doi.org/10.1111/oli.12323>

5   Nsah, Kenneth Toah (2023). "Our Children Will Fight for the Climate: How Congo-Basin Writers Prophesied the Global Youth Climate Movement." *Electronic Green Journal* 48(2023). <https://escholarship.org/uc/item/88n2v0wv>

Mali, Burkina Faso, and Ethiopia to Somalia. In this regard, Nixon's word of caution on slow violence and "the radioactive aftermaths of wars" (2011, 2) still requires attention.

REFERENCES

Achebe, Chinua. 1958. *Things Fall Apart*. London: Heinemann.

Aghoghovwia, Onoriode Philip. 2014. "Ecocriticism and the Oil Encounter: Readings from the Niger Delta." PhD diss., Stellenbosch University.

Alembong, Nol. 2010. *Forest Echoes*. Bamenda: Langaa RPCIG.

Alembong, Nol. 2013. *The Passing Wind*. Kansas City, MO: Miraclaire Publishing LLC.

Alembong, Nol. 2017. *Green Call*. California: Notion Press, Inc.

Ayang, Frederick Enoh. 2012. *Green Hills: A Play on Environmental Protection*. Bamenda: Awah Publishers.

DeLoughrey, Elizabeth, and George B. Handley, eds. 2011. *Postcolonial Ecologies: Literatures of the Environment*. Oxford: Oxford University Press.

Egya, Sule E. 2020a. *Nature, Environment and Activism in Nigerian Literature*. London: Routledge.

Egya, Sule E. 2020b. "Out of Africa: Ecocriticism Beyond the Boundary of Environmental Justice." *Ecozon@* 11 (2): 66–73. https://doi.org/10.37536/ECOZONA.2020.11.2.3495.

Iheka, Cajetan. 2018. *Naturalizing Africa: Ecological Violence, Agency, and Postcolonial Resistance in African Literature*. Cambridge: Cambridge University Press.

Inyang, Ekpe. 2022. *Tastes of Nature: New and Selected Poems*. Colorado: Spears Media Press.

Mbembe, Achille. 2019. *Necropolitics*. Durham, NC: Duke University Press.

Ngong, John Ngong Kum. 2015. *Blot on the Landscape*. Bamenda: Langaa RPCIG.

Ngong, John Ngong Kum. 2018. *Tears of the Earth*. Bamenda: Langaa RPCIG.

Ngongkum, Eunice. 2017. *Anglophone Cameroon Poetry in the Environmental Matrix*. Lausanne: Peter Lang.

Ngongkum, Eunice. 2017. "Contemporary Cameroon Poetry in English, Nature and the Politics of Consciousness Raising for the Future." *Journal of the African Literature Association* 11 (1): 83–98. https://doi.org/10.1080/21674736.2017.1335949.

Nsah, Kenneth Toah. 2022. "Can Literature Save the Congo Basin? Postcolonial Ecocriticism and Environmental Literary Activism." PhD diss., Aarhus University.

Nsah, Kenneth Toah. 2022. "The Ecopolitics of Water Pollution and Urbanization in Congo-Basin Theatre." *Orbis Litterarum* 77: 314–332. https://doi.org/10.1111/oli.12323.

Nsah, Kenneth Toah. 2023. "Our Children Will Fight for the Climate: How Congo-Basin Writers Prophesied the Global Youth Climate Movement." *Electronic Green Journal* 48. https://escholarship.org/uc/item/88n2v0wv.

Nsah Mala. 2012. *Chaining Freedom*. Kansas City, MO: Miraclaire Publishing LLC.

Nsah Mala. 2015. *Bites of Insanity*. Bamenda: Langaa RPCIG.

Nsah Mala. 2017. *Constimocrazy: Malafricanising Democracy*. Lockport, NY: Pski's Porch.

Nsah Mala. 2019. *Les Pleurs du mal*. Denver: Spears Media Press.

Nsah Mala, ed. 2025. *Stories from the Futures of the Congo Basin*. Kent: Next Generation Foresight Practitioner (NGFP) Fellowship. https://nextgenforesight.org/stories-from-the-futures-of-congo-basin/

Nsah Mala, ed. Forthcoming. *Congo Basin Poetry Anthology – Anthologie poétique du Bassin du Congo*. Denver: Spears Books. https://spearsbooks.org/product/congo-basin-poetry-anthology-anthologie-poetique-du-bassin-du-congo/

Nsah Mala et al. 2019. "Notre Dame de Paris, Pray for Cyclone Idai's Children – A Poem." *Voice4Thought*. https://www.voice4thought.org/notre-dame-de-paris-pray-for-cyclone-idais-children-a-poem/

Slaymaker, William. 2001. "Ecoing the Other(s): The Call of Global Green and Black African Responses." *PMLA* 116 (1): 129–144. https://www.jstor.org/stable/463646.

Contributors

ABOI, DOMINIC JAMES. Department of English and Literary Studies, Ahmadu Bello University, Zaria.
Aboi is a Nigerian writer, essayist and editor with degrees from universities in Zaria, Nigeria, and Cambridge, United Kingdom. He is interested in creative writing, literary theory, African and African American literature, and contemporary works that address peace and conflict, social justice, racial equality, history, genocide, minority representation, postcolonial exegesis, and the environment. He currently teaches in the Department of English and Literary Studies, Ahmadu Bello University (ABU), Zaria, Nigeria.

AGBOOLA, OLUBUNMI TAYO. Ajayi Crowther University, Oyo.
AGBOOLA holds a PhD in Oral Literature from Ajayi Crowther University in Oyo, Nigeria. She is a scholar with a focus on gender and environmental studies. Her academic interests are distinguished by an interdisciplinary approach, with a particular focus on literary environmentalism, gender dynamics, and the preservation of landscape and cultural heritage sites. Agboola's scholarly activities are reflected by her vast research involvement and publications, which demonstrate her broad focus on the intersectionality of literature, the environment, and cultural heritage preservation.

AGOFURE, JOYCE ONOROMHENRE, PhD, & EZEKIEL SOLOMON AKUSO. Department of English and Literary Studies, Ahmadu Bello University, Zaria.
AGOFURE is a recipient of many awards and fellowships, including the Fulbright Foreign Student Researcher Fellowship from the University of Idaho, USA; the American Council of Learned Society of the African Humanities Program Postdoctoral Fellow (ACLS/AHP) with a residency at Rhodes University, South Africa; the African Humanities Program

Mentoring and Application-Preparation Workshop Grant Award; and the Social Science Research Council/African Peacebuilding Network Fellowship. Her research interests straddle environmental humanities, postcolonial studies, gender discourse, and African peacebuilding. AKUSO is a Professor of Comparative Literature. He specializes in Caribbean and African literatures. He is also interested in the frontiers of ecocritical and interdisciplinary studies. He has to his credit books and research articles published in both local and international journals.

AMAMCHUKWU, ABUNDANCE. University of Nigeria, Nsukka. Her interests in literary research include ecocriticism, gender studies, border poetics and interdisciplinary research. As a creative writer and storyteller, she has written a few short stories. She is also the Founder of Penswrit Consult, a writing, coaching, and business consulting firm. When she is not writing, researching or mentoring youths, you'll find her reading a nice novel or connecting with new people.

CORNELIUS, BEVERLEY JANE & JEAN ROSSMANN. Department of English Studies, University of KwaZulu-Natal.
CORNELIUS is a Lecturer in English Studies at the University of Kwa-Zulu-Natal, South Africa. Her research interests include postcolonial nostalgia in South African literatures, postcolonial ecocriticism, and narratives of migration. ROSSMANN is a Senior Lecturer in English Studies at the University of KwaZulu-Natal, South Africa. Her research interests lie in contemporary South/African literature, spirituality, and ecopoetics.

DAWODU, SUNDAY OLAOLUWAGBAMILA, PhD. Holy Cross Church, The United Kingdom & GRACIOUS OJEIBUN, PhD; The University of Benin.
DAWODU focuses on ecocatastrophes in Nigerian and Japanese literature. He has extensive teaching experience across Nigeria, Benin, and Liberia. He has published on and continues to research ecocritics, gender and religion dialogics. He is an Associate Professor at William V.S. University, Liberia, and a Youth and Children Minister at Holy Cross Church, UK. OJEIBUN is currently a Senior Lecturer at Edo State College

of Education, Benin, and an Adjunct Lecturer at the University of Benin.

EKWUEME-UGWU, CHINONYE & CHIAMAKA UGOKA. University of Nigeria, Nsukka: EKWUEME-UGWU is a Senior Lecturer in the Department of English and Literary Studies, University of Nigeria, Nsukka. Her research and teaching areas include Comparative, African and American literature; postcolonial, environmental, and border literary studies. UGOKA is a Lecturer in the Department of English and Literary Studies, University of Nigeria, Nsukka. Her research interests include literature and disability studies, and ecocriticism.

JAJI, SULEIMAN A., PHD. Kashim Ibrahim College of Education, Maiduguri.
JAJI taught English literature, literary theory and criticism, literature and language methodology at Kashim Ibrahim College of Education, Maiduguri, Nigeria and Ahmadu Bello University, Zaria, for two decades. In between, he was a public servant for 15 years at both state and federal levels as an education administrator at the National Commission for Mass Education, Abuja and Yobe State Universal Basic Education Board, Damaturu. His research interests include literary theory and criticism, popular culture, and literature in northern Nigeria. Currently, he is lecturing at the Department of English, Yobe State University, Damaturu.

LAWAL, HAMEED OLUTOBA & TIJIME JUSTIN AWUAWUER. Department of Dramatic Arts, Obafemi Awolowo University, Ile-Ife.

LUM, MARY LOUISA, PhD: Department of English and Foreign Languages (ANLE), Douala.
LUM is an English literary scholar and poet with a research focus on romantic and postmodern discourses of emancipation. She facilitates several literary and creative writing courses at the undergraduate and graduate levels. She has published numerous research papers, books and poetry collections. Lum's fascination with poets like Lord Byron and Carol Ann Duffy stems from a passion for emancipation discourses embodied in their poetic visions. Her major hobbies include writing poetry, swimming, and watching football.

NDELEY, NJUME ARTHUR N. University of Buea, Cameroon.
NDELEY holds a PhD in African Literature from the University of Buea, Cameroon. His research interests lie in cultural studies, specifically in literary archaeology. His research engagements and publications demonstrate his keen interdisciplinary focus on literary archaeology, gender relations and gender archaeologies, totemism and tabooism as alternatives to environmental conservation, as well as magic realism and oral traditions. Njume Ndeley has interdisciplinary prospects for the digitization of African folklore, ecocultural, and archaeological heritage via cartoon and game design, digital museology, and galleries. He looks forward to post-doctoral research engagements in these areas.

NSAH MALA. UNESCO-MOST BRIDGES Coalition, University of Cologne (Germany), University of Lille (France).
NSAH MALA, PhD, is a poet, writer, children's author, consultant, editor, translator, journalist, futurist, foresight practitioner, and interdisciplinary scholar of English, French, and Mbessa. His research interests include comparative literature, anglophone and francophone African literatures, public and environmental humanities, sustainability science, literary activism/artivism, creative writing, foresight and futures thinking, long-term governance and future generations; has published widely in these areas; co-editor (with Prof Nicki Hitchcott) of a volume entitled *Ecotexts in the Postcolonial Francosphere* (Liverpool University Press, 2025), his research has been funded by the British Academy, School of International Futures (SOIF), and Cluster of Excellence Seed Funding from the University of Cologne. Nsah earned his PhD in Art, Literature and Cultural Studies from Aarhus University (Denmark) in 2022.

OKPALA, VICTORY; EZINWANYI ADAM (Corresponding Author); & ARINZE THANKGOD OKPALA
VICTORY OKPALA holds a PhD in English Literature from Babcock University, Ilishan-Remo, Ogun. She is an early-career researcher with research and teaching interests in African literature, gender, and interdisciplinary studies. Currently, she is a Lecturer at the Use of English Unit, School of General Studies, University of Nigeria, Nsukka. EZINWANYI ADAM is a lecturer in the Department of Languages and Literary Studies,

Babcock University, Ilishan-Remo, Ogun, while THANKGOD OKPALA is a lecturer in the Social Sciences Unit, School of General Studies, University of Nigeria, Nsukka.

OMONZEJIE, EUNICE. Ambrose Alli University, Ekpoma, Benin. OMONZEJIE, MNAL, completed her undergraduate studies at Grenoble and Ile-Ife, and her postgraduate studies in Benin City. She was a visiting Professor of French Studies and Francophone Literature in the Department of Modern European Languages at Nnamdi Azikiwe University, Awka, during the 2023/2024 academic session. With over three decades of teaching experience, she served as Sub-Dean of the Faculty of Arts, Ag. HoD, Modern Languages, Ambrose Alli University, Ekpoma. Her research interests include ecocriticism, African masculinities, and cultural and migrant studies. She has authored two French-language textbooks, edited Women Novelists in Francophone Black Africa: Views, Reviews & Interviews (2011), and co-edited *The Humanities and the Dynamics of African Culture in the 21st Century* (2017) and *Language Matters in Contemporary West Africa* (2021).

SLOVIC, SCOTT. Oregon Research Institute and the University of Idaho. SLOVIC is a senior scientist at the Oregon Research Institute and a distinguished professor of environmental humanities emeritus at the University of Idaho in the United States. He was the founding president of the Association for the Study of Literature and Environment (ASLE) in the early 1990s and served as Editor-in-Chief of *ISLE: Interdisciplinary Studies in Literature and Environment* from 1995 to 2020. The author, editor, and coeditor of dozens of volumes in the field of ecocriticism, he is especially involved in supporting the development of ecocriticism internationally and in guiding fellow scholars to "go public" with their academic work. He lives in Eugene, Oregon.

USMAN, ABUBAKAR SHEHU. Department of English & Literary Studies, Ahmadu Bello University, Zaria.
USMAN was born in Nassarawa Local Government in Kano State, Nigeria. He is currently pursuing his M.A. in the Department of English and Literary Studies, Ahmadu Bello University, Zaria. He obtained his BA in

English Literature from Usmanu Danfodiyo University, Sokoto. He has some scholarly papers to his credit. His research interests include African literature, postcolonial literature and women's writing.

UZOMA, DEBORAH CHINONYEREM. Federal Polytechnic, Nekede. Uzoma is currently a lecturer in the Department of Humanities, School of General Studies. She is a budding writer and a performance poet who enjoys writing literary essays and other creative genres. In September 2023, she became a Fellow of Ebedi International Writers' Residency. She has won multiple awards both domestically and internationally. Deborah hails from Nenwe, Aninri LGA in Enugu State, Nigeria. She is an ordained Evangelist and practicing Christian.

YUSHAU-WAZIRI, ZULFAA, PhD. Department of English and Literary Studies, Ahmadu Bello University.
YUSHAU-WAZIRI's research interests include pragmatics, discourse analysis, general linguistics, and ecocritical discourses.

ZAURE, FRANKLIN PYOKPUNG. Department of Theatre and Performing Arts, Ahmadu Bello University Zaria.
ZAURE completed an undergraduate degree in Theatre and Performing Arts. Due to his interest in interdisciplinary research, he had his master's in industrial design (Graphics Section). He is currently pursuing his PhD in Eco-Scenography (Theatre Design and Ecology) in the Department of Theatre and Performing Arts. All his studies to date have been conducted at Ahmadu Bello University, Zaria, Nigeria. He is a multi- and transdisciplinary artist, a community and participatory development strategist, a creative arts for development strategist, and a lecturer in scenography and environmental sustainability.

Index

Abacha regime 135
Achebe, Chinua 24, 112, 113, 127, 141, 165, 218, 233, 237, 245, 277, 279, 280, 285, 289, 300, 302, 309, 317, 320
Adejunmobi, Moradewun 7
Adimora-Ezeigbo, Akachi viii, 12, 103, 104, 105, 106, 107, 112, 113
aesthetics 20, 158, 179, 180, 185, 186, 192, 204, 216, 277, 297, 318
aesthetic status 215
African animism 74
African cosmology 21, 279
African cultural values 52, 59
African-Diaspora ecocritics 297
African ecocriticism vii, xv, 1, 4, 7, 8, 9, 11, 19, 20, 21, 24, 27, 28, 29, 31, 33, 68, 158, 166, 237, 317, 318, 319
African ecologists 82
African environmentalism 11, 21, 29, 317
African female poets 112, 113
African holism 22
African Knowledge Systems 82. *See also* indigenous knowledge systems
African literary criticism 4
African literary studies 179
African literatures 4, 5, 6, 7, 9, 10, 11, 13, 324, 326
African media makers 8
African mythology 55
African oral traditions 60
Afrocentric identity 52
Afrophobia 65
Afrophobic 65
Aghoghovwia, Onoriode Philip 317

Ahmadu Bello University 137, 165, 180, 187, 188, 192, 195, 196, 198, 323, 325, 327, 328
air pollution xii, 24, 117, 118, 171, 258. *See also* pollution problems
air quality 117
Alembong, Nol vii, xv, 1, 12, 15, 32, 35, 36, 37, 38, 39, 40, 41, 42, 43, 44, 45, 47, 48, 49, 50, 289, 290, 314, 316, 320
alienation 59, 169, 172, 173, 176, 308
Aliyu, Kamal 217
Amadiume, Ifi 141
Amazon, the xii
ancestors 21, 55, 125, 279
Angles, Jeffrey 93
animal studies 6, 53
Anthropocene 71, 79, 84, 85, 150
anthropocentric beliefs 57
anthropocentric view of nature 53
anthropocentric viewpoint, the 35, 56
Anthropocentrism vii, 35, 256
anthropomorphism 54, 61
Anyidoho, Kofi 314
Anyokwu, Christopher 26
apartheid 27, 70, 77, 81
Arrhenius, Svante 253
Ash, Joyce 313
assimilation 181
Association for the Study of Literature and Environment 89, 219, 220, 296, 327
Australia 75, 99, 133, 184, 284, 285

Bacon, Francis 22
Balewa, Sadiq 194
Barry, Peter 71

INDEX

Bassey, Nnimmo 317
Bate, Walter Jackson 76
belief systems 60, 278, 279, 285, 288, 289
Bhabha, Homi K. 88
biblical dogma 76
biocentric equality 45, 47, 48, 49
biodiversity xiii, 2, 9, 24, 25, 28, 105, 251, 277, 278, 279, 316
biology 155, 167
biosocial destruction 71
biosphere 45, 64, 65, 220, 301, 305
Black African writing 73
black gold 144
Botswana 192
Boym, Svetlana 79
Brecht, Bertolt 194
Brownell, Emily 1, 4
Buckingham, Susan 93
Buell, Lawrence 25, 88, 97, 103, 154, 156, 236, 296
Buhari, Jerry 137, 145, 147, 148
Burkina Faso 320

Cameroon xii, 14, 15, 16, 22, 33, 38, 39, 50, 235, 278, 282, 283, 288, 289, 311, 312, 313, 314, 316, 317, 318, 319, 320, 321, 326
  Bakweri people 278
  Bangwa 282, 283, 289
  Mount Fako 278, 288
  Yaoundé 312, 313
Caminero-Santangelo, Byron xv, 1, 4, 5, 6, 15, 21, 24, 25, 28, 32, 90, 98, 297, 309
cannibalism 61
capitalism 24, 69, 80, 91, 133, 134, 135, 146, 160, 161, 165, 221
  capitalist society 70, 71
Capitalocene 71, 85
Cartesian dualism 29
Central African Republic 138
Central America 133
Charles de Gaulle airport 65

Charles, Eric Ngalle 314
Charon, Pierre 61
Chaudhuri, Una 182
childhood 81, 83, 216
children's theatre 180, 185, 188, 191, 192
Christian attitudes 30
Christian ideology 30
Christianity 30, 91
  Bible 30, 219
  Christian prayer 43
Chthulucene 71, 85
citizenship 137
civilization 28, 61, 89, 142, 161, 220, 221
civil war 105, 111, 167
Civil War Literature 167
Classical Greek Humanism 29
climate action 260, 261, 262, 264, 265, 266
climate change viii, ix, xii, 7, 8, 13, 70, 71, 92, 106, 166, 184, 185, 187, 199, 200, 201, 202, 203, 204, 207, 208, 209, 210, 211, 212, 213, 220, 235, 238, 244, 245, 247, 251, 252, 253, 254, 255, 257, 258, 259, 260, 261, 262, 263, 264, 265, 266, 267, 268, 269, 270, 271, 272, 273, 274, 275, 294, 298, 305, 307, 311, 312, 314, 316, 318
climate crisis 260, 267, 270, 273
climate fiction xv, 304, 306
climate mitigation 9, 263. *See also* climate change
climate-sensitive resources 202
climatologists 253
Coetzee, Carli 7
Coleridge, Samuel Taylor 46
collective consciousness 37
colonial imagination 157
colonialism 9, 10, 14, 22, 26, 27, 69, 70, 74, 77, 79, 81, 103, 105, 113, 132, 133, 139, 146, 157, 159, 317
  British colonialism 79
colonial literatures 5

colonization 19, 133, 157, 159, 192, 317
commodification of nature 70. *See also* capitalism
Commoner, Barry 52
communal life 55, 60
Congo xii, 8, 9, 14, 16, 22, 33, 55, 111, 138, 313, 314, 316, 318, 319, 321
Congo Basin 8, 9, 14, 16, 33, 313, 314, 316, 318, 319, 321
conservation 5, 13, 23, 40, 52, 56, 70, 75, 82, 174, 175, 259, 278, 285, 319, 326
consumerism 19, 30, 31, 219, 223
consumption xii, 29, 60, 91, 107, 139, 162
Côte d'Ivoire xii
Courlander, Harold 236, 238, 239, 240, 241, 246
crime 234
Crowley, Dustin 5
cultural representations of nature 6
cultural studies 20, 71, 326
culture xi, xiii, xvi, 1, 10, 19, 25, 27, 29, 30, 31, 38, 51, 53, 54, 57, 70, 79, 81, 82, 88, 89, 107, 108, 110, 134, 150, 154, 156, 157, 158, 159, 172, 180, 181, 183, 184, 194, 195, 196, 200, 216, 217, 218, 221, 222, 229, 234, 235, 236, 237, 238, 252, 255, 272, 277, 279, 280, 282, 283, 285, 287, 288, 289, 293, 296, 299, 308, 325
customs 31, 37, 65, 108, 124, 126, 237. *See also* culture
Cyclone Idai 313, 321

Darko, Francis 284
deep ecology 13, 35, 36, 37, 38, 41, 42, 43, 49, 74, 75, 81, 82, 83
deforestation xii, xvi, 24, 89, 122, 123, 124, 126, 164, 168, 199, 201, 209, 225, 228, 283, 293, 299, 301, 302, 308, 313
DeLoughrey, Elizabeth 90, 317
Democratic Republic of Congo 22
deportation 65
depression 94
Descartes, René 22
desertification 162, 163, 199, 251, 299, 301, 302
Deval, Bill 35
diaspora 1, 2, 3, 157, 159, 293
disaster 93, 94, 95, 96, 106, 107, 144, 161, 202, 212, 223, 225, 259
Disease 258
dramaturgy 13

Eastern philosophical views 37
eco-activism 12, 87, 89, 92, 97
eco-bio-communalism 22
ecocentric dialectics 51
ecocentric perspective 52, 53
eco-citizens 60
eco-consciousness 88, 89, 277
ecocritical interconnectedness 52
eco-critical studies 112
ecocriticism vii, ix, xi, xiii, xv, 1, 2, 3, 4, 5, 6, 7, 8, 9, 10, 11, 13, 14, 15, 16, 19, 20, 21, 24, 27, 28, 29, 31, 33, 34, 51, 52, 53, 55, 67, 68, 70, 71, 72, 73, 84, 85, 89, 90, 91, 98, 99, 100, 103, 114, 116, 119, 120, 127, 131, 133, 134, 137, 139, 150, 151, 152, 153, 154, 155, 156, 157, 158, 159, 165, 166, 167, 168, 176, 179, 181, 182, 183, 185, 196, 198, 201, 202, 213, 218, 221, 222, 226, 230, 231, 235, 236, 237, 246, 247, 252, 254, 255, 256, 257, 272, 273, 274, 293, 294, 295, 296, 297, 298, 299, 303, 304, 305, 306, 307, 308, 309, 310, 311, 312, 313, 314, 315, 316, 317, 318, 319, 320, 321, 324, 325, 327
ecocriticism in Africa 7, 72, 317, 319.

See also African ecocriticism
Ecocriticism of the Global South xi, 151, 152
eco-cultural heritage 277, 289
eco-feminism 58, 103
Ecofeminists 221. *See also* feminism
Ecolinguistics 255
eco-literature 90, 103
ecological activism 39, 115, 120
ecological alienation 169
ecological consciousness 35, 36, 40, 184, 201, 256, 272, 294
ecological crisis xiii, 30, 36, 39, 169, 201
ecological crusade 45
ecological degradation 89, 90, 91, 115, 149, 167, 298
ecological disasters 201
ecological estrangement 12, 167, 168, 169, 170, 172, 174
ecological ethics 83, 183, 187
ecological identity 59
ecological justice xvi, 13, 66, 298
ecological knowledge 6, 19, 31, 254
ecological metaphors 272
ecological polemic 56
ecological praxis 84
ecological restoration 10, 15
ecological scholarship 10, 14
ecological systems 173, 174, 175, 176, 183, 201
ecologism 157
ecology xv, xvi, 5, 13, 35, 36, 37, 38, 39, 41, 42, 43, 49, 51, 52, 56, 70, 72, 74, 75, 80, 81, 82, 83, 90, 154, 155, 167, 184, 185, 201, 216, 236, 255, 279, 288, 294, 295, 303, 304, 305, 307, 315
ecomedia 51, 52, 53, 54, 56, 60, 66
economic development 115, 133
economic slavery 159, 161
ecophilic cultures 52, 56
eco-philosophy 155
ecophobia 56, 60
ecophobic activities 54
ecopoetics 71, 324

ecopoetry 98
eco-preservation 52
eco-restoration 26
eco-scenography 179, 180, 182, 183, 184, 185, 186, 187, 196
Eco-Socialist 158
eco-theatrical praxis 183
eco-ubuntu 81, 83
Egya, Sule E. xv, 1, 7
Emenyonu, Ernest N. 7, 15, 32, 216, 218, 231
Enekwe, Ossie 141
Enoh, Ayang Federick 316
environmental activism 38, 45, 70, 256, 312, 314
environmental awareness 9, 161, 181, 196, 245, 256, 313
environmental consciousness 3, 12, 13, 24, 31, 39, 61, 179, 182, 183, 196, 237, 252, 308
environmental crises 8, 19, 31, 70, 73, 90, 97, 144, 150, 154, 155, 164, 201, 202, 220, 222
environmental degradation xi, xvi, 6, 8, 13, 87, 88, 92, 97, 117, 119, 120, 122, 123, 125, 126, 134, 135, 139, 146, 150, 162, 164, 168, 169, 172, 200, 201, 204, 205, 207, 208, 209, 211, 236, 244, 256, 259, 264, 268, 282, 285, 294
environmental disasters 87, 88, 89, 93, 259
environmental discourses 9, 14, 31, 233, 272, 312
environmental ethics 103, 155, 240, 241, 245
environmental exploitation 8, 12, 126, 159
environmental health xii, 14
environmental injustice 119, 121, 126
environmentalism xv, 1, 11, 14, 20, 21, 26, 29, 31, 112, 134, 138, 143, 149, 150, 155, 168, 218, 225, 230, 233, 300, 317, 323
environmentalist discourses 52

environmental justice xv, xvi, 6, 7, 10, 11, 14, 31, 69, 84, 116, 139, 150, 168, 169, 201, 236, 237, 269, 271, 317, 319
environmental literacy campaigns 60
environmental literature xi, 2, 6, 90, 112, 156, 254, 306, 319
environmental protection 12, 35, 38, 43, 126, 176, 212, 219, 236, 312, 319
environmental racism 140
environmental sustainability 183, 186, 187, 188, 328
Eritrea 111
erosion 59, 160, 199, 200, 208, 238, 293
Estok, Simon 155
Etherton, Michael 194
ethical perspective 23
Ethiopia 320
European Conference of African Studies 2
Evernden, Neil 297
evolutionary biology 155
exploitation of nature 36, 47, 153, 225
extractive capitalism 24

Fall, Aminata Sow 54, 56, 57, 60
Falola, Toyin 1, 4, 15, 32
famine 42, 123, 124, 241, 244, 245
Fatunde, Tunde 141
feminism 103
Feminist Ecocriticism 157
first law of ecology 52. *See also* Commoner, Barry
folklore 23, 235, 326. *See also* proverbs
folktales 13, 60, 233, 234, 235, 236, 245
food insecurity 13, 199, 201, 202, 203, 239, 262
food production 186, 199, 204, 205, 207, 209, 210, 211, 212, 300
food scarcity 200, 238, 240, 241, 242
food security 199, 200, 201, 202, 203, 204, 207, 211, 212, 239
fossil fuels 91, 201, 253
France 9, 313, 326
Francophone African novels 13
francophone African writers 51
Francophone world 9
French Renaissance 61
freshwater ecosystems 220
Fromm, Harold 71, 158

Galtung, Johan 137
Geertz, Clifford 88, 99
gender 12, 105, 110, 133, 154, 298, 323, 324, 326
Germany 137, 326
Gerrard, Greg 158
Ghana xii, 137, 247, 289
global ecocriticism 11
global environmental politics 11, 298
globalism 146
globalization 20, 21, 29, 71, 98, 112, 125, 139, 165, 275, 282, 289
Global North xi, 73, 131, 133, 134, 138, 139, 140, 149, 150. *See also* Global South
Global South xi, 2, 9, 72, 73, 132, 133, 148, 150, 151, 152
global warming 38, 89, 92, 146, 149, 150, 275, 298, 312, 313, 314
global world order 28
Glotfelty, Cheryll 51, 52, 67, 68, 71, 81, 82, 84, 85, 89, 99, 100, 114, 116, 127, 154, 155, 158, 165, 168, 176, 246, 256, 295, 296, 309, 310
governance 55, 175, 326
grassroots environmental movement 24. *See also* Green Belt Movement
Green Belt Movement xv, 24, 219, 231. *See also* Maathai, Wangari
Green Cultural Studies 154
green culture 54
green energy 139
Greenpeace 42

INDEX

Green Poetry 154
Green Revolution 149
green studies 51, 60, 246, 297

Habila, Helon 168, 177, 218, 303, 308, 310, 314
Haeckel, Ernst 255
Hann, Rachel 182
Haraway, Donna 70
hazardous substances 118
Heads, Dominic 157
health xi, xii, xiii, 14, 31, 40, 58, 67, 81, 87, 107, 116, 117, 121, 137, 156, 203, 226, 239, 241, 258, 259, 262, 264, 270, 271, 312, 318
healthcare infrastructure 258
Hitchcott, Nicki 9
Hobsbawm, Eric 140
Holling, C.S. 174
homophobia 60, 65. *See also* sexism
homophobic 54, 56, 65
Huggan, Graham 157
Hunt, Alex 158
Hutchings, Kevin 70

Ibekwe, Sixtus 161
Iheka, Cajetan xv, 1, 7, 8, 15, 20, 32, 33, 99, 114, 134, 137, 148, 151, 152, 237, 246, 298, 309, 314, 318, 319, 320
immigrants 110
imperialism 132, 135, 139, 140, 146, 158. *See also* colonialism
India 133, 138, 146, 149, 152, 284, 285
indigeneity 157, 159
indigenous African ecosystems 10
indigenous ecology xv
indigenous knowledge systems 23, 70, 82, 254
indigenous peoples 19, 72, 172
indigenous populations 138
industrialization 20, 30, 115, 146, 161, 219, 253, 275. *See also* globalization
Industrial Revolution, the 30, 131, 198, 253
Inglehart, Ronald 144
inhumanism 52
injustice 9, 65, 107, 108, 110, 112, 119, 121, 126, 153, 168, 229, 234, 237, 238, 304
Intergovernmental Panel on Climate Change 203, 253. *See also* climate change
interspecies relationships 73
inter-subjectivity 13, 51
Inyang, Ekpe 14, 314
Issifu, Abdul Karim 284

Japan 87, 89, 93, 137, 315
  Shinto cosmology 96
Johnson, Stella 38, 40
Judeo-Christian 30. *See also* Christian attitudes
justice xv, xvi, 6, 7, 10, 11, 13, 14, 31, 61, 66, 69, 70, 72, 84, 116, 126, 139, 150, 168, 169, 174, 192, 201, 217, 233, 234, 236, 237, 238, 242, 243, 245, 259, 269, 270, 271, 298, 317, 319, 323

Kamal, Aliyu viii, 14, 153, 160, 161, 162, 163, 164, 165, 217, 230, 293, 294, 298, 299, 300, 301, 302, 303, 305, 307, 308, 309
Kenya 24, 25, 104, 219, 278, 279, 312
  Kikuyu 25
Kenyan women 24
kinship 37, 76, 77, 78, 83
Kirksey, Eben 71
Kpade, Sabo 134
Kulcur, Rakibe 93

Labang, Oscar 38

Lassi, Étienne-Marie xv, 1
Laye, Camara 237, 247, 277, 280, 281, 283, 284, 286, 287, 290
Leopold, Aldo 49, 220
Libya 111
literary criticism 4, 53, 71, 72, 116, 139, 297
literary ecology 70
literary studies 53, 155, 179, 221, 325
literary theory 4, 51, 72, 323, 325
local ecological knowledge 6

Maathai, Wangari xv, 24, 25, 26, 31, 33, 82, 85, 134, 219
Mabanckou, Alain 52, 53, 54, 55, 56, 57, 60, 61, 62, 63, 65, 66, 67
Madondo, Manasa 23
Maduka, Chidi 167
magical beliefs 283
magic realism 12, 283, 326
malaria 258, 270
Malawi 313
Malaysia xii
Mali 320
Marxism 103
mass extinction xii, 70, 71, 150
Mbaijiorgu, Greg 201, 204
Mbatha, Sicelo 69
Mda, Zakes 21, 24, 27, 28, 31, 32, 33
media representations 13, 254, 272, 274. *See also* climate change
medicine 22, 54, 55, 58, 83, 296
metaphor 38, 44, 97, 108, 156, 167, 174, 204, 225, 226
Migration 151, 152, 239, 240
modernization of agriculture 271
Molla, F. Fiona 6
Montaigne, Michel de 61
Moolla, F. Fiona 1, 20
moral lessons 60, 61
Mother Earth 21, 144, 239
Mozambique 313
multilingualism 13
multinational corporations 25, 31, 97, 172
multispecies studies 73, 82
Münster, Ursula 71
Museka, Godfrey 23
Mwangi, Evan Maina 1
Myers, Garth 4

Naess, Arne 12, 35
National Aeronautics and Space Agency xii
naturalization 137
natural resources 24, 30, 31, 115, 121, 123, 124, 125, 126, 132, 134, 135, 138, 139, 149, 160, 161, 172, 173, 200, 201, 220, 278, 285, 289
nature writing 72, 103, 113, 201, 219, 236, 237, 312
Nchoujie, Augustine 90
Newell, Stephanie xv, 7, 15, 20, 32, 33
newspaper framing 13
newspapers xi, 251, 252, 253, 255, 257, 272, 273. *See also* Nigerian News
New Zealand 133
Nfa-Abbenyi, Juliana Makuchi 1, 4
Ngezem, Eugene 38
Ngong, John Ngong Kum 314
Ngongkum, Eunice xv, 1, 312, 314, 318
Nigeria xii, xvi, 13, 21, 22, 24, 31, 87, 88, 89, 91, 92, 100, 105, 118, 119, 127, 137, 138, 140, 141, 143, 148, 151, 160, 161, 162, 165, 185, 192, 193, 194, 195, 196, 197, 198, 199, 203, 204, 206, 207, 208, 212, 215, 216, 217, 218, 220, 223, 225, 229, 230, 231, 235, 241, 242, 246, 247, 251, 252, 254, 257, 258, 259, 260, 261, 262, 263, 264, 265, 266, 267, 273, 275, 279, 294, 303, 307, 308, 309, 312, 323, 324, 325, 326, 327, 328

INDEX

Calabar 92
Daily Trust Newspaper 252, 257
Eastern Nigeria 104
Igbo 21, 107, 238, 239, 240, 241, 244, 280
Kaduna Oil Refinery 223
Kaduna State 137, 165
Kwara State 261
Lagos 92, 100, 117, 118, 128, 150, 151, 165, 166, 198, 205, 231
Niger Delta xii, 9, 87, 90, 92, 118, 119, 120, 121, 122, 127, 144, 167, 168, 169, 174, 177, 203, 204, 206, 294, 308, 317, 318, 320
Nigerian eco-literature 90
Nigerian Environmental Protection Agency 92
Nigerian literature 90, 218
Nigerian newspapers 251, 252, 253, 255, 257, 272, 273
Nigerian theatre 179, 187
Ogoni people 135, 168, 294, 298, 303, 307
Punch Newspaper 261
The Guardian Online Newspaper 269
The Nation Online Newspaper 265
The Sun Online Newspaper 267
Tribune Online Newspaper 263
Vanguard 252, 259
Yoruba 21, 26, 32, 148, 233, 234, 235, 236, 237, 238, 245, 246, 247
Nigerian Meteorological Agency 260
Nixon, Robert 1, 4, 88, 168, 297, 318
noise pollution 117, 164
Non-governmental Organizations 164
nonhuman entities xv, 45
nonhuman species 35, 37, 39, 43, 44, 45, 47, 48, 49, 304. *See also* interspecies relationships
Nsah, Kenneth Toah 1, 314
Nsah Mala iii, iv, vii, ix, xvi, 1, 8, 9, 14, 16, 39, 311, 313, 314, 315, 316, 317, 319, 321, 326
Ntube, Nnane 14, 311

Occident, the 131, 140
Ogunade, Raymond 235
Ogungbem, Segun 22
Ohaeto, Ezenwa 141
oil and gas industry xii
oil companies 87, 120, 122, 135, 208
oil exploration 121, 126, 138, 169, 204, 209, 299
oil extraction 92, 167, 168, 314, 318
oil firms 119, 120, 121, 122, 126
oil spills xii, 92, 122, 168
Ojaide, Tanure 99, 100, 127, 134, 144, 146, 151, 156, 169, 177, 218, 254, 275, 303, 314, 317
Okara, Gabriel 134
Okorafor, Nnedi 314
Okuyade, Ogaga xv, 1, 5, 16, 20, 34, 90, 100, 314
Olaniyan, Tejumola 4, 20
Omofonmwan, Samson 88
oppression 27, 108, 111, 134
orality 233, 235
Orientalism 131, 152
Osundare, Niyi vii, 12, 21, 24, 26, 27, 31, 32, 34, 87, 88, 91, 92, 93, 97, 99, 100, 141, 156, 169
Oswald, Alice 35, 39, 49
overconsumption 139
Oyekunle, Segun 193

pastoral escapism 90
patriarchal norms 110. *See also* gender
peasant farmers 207, 212, 300
performing arts 179, 180, 183, 185
phenomenological approaches 76
Phillips, Walter Dana 70
Pidgin English 106, 315
Pitt, Bridget 69
Plantationocene 71, 79, 84, 85
Plumwood, Val 168
poetry 12, 26, 35, 37, 38, 39, 44, 47, 88, 93, 97, 103, 104, 105, 112, 154, 167, 168, 169, 215, 219, 236,

304, 314, 318, 321, 325
Pojma, Louis 29
political ecology 5
polluting industries 140
pollution xii, xiii, 2, 9, 24, 43, 88, 89, 91, 92, 97, 116, 117, 118, 122, 139, 143, 162, 164, 171, 184, 199, 200, 205, 206, 208, 209, 210, 220, 223, 225, 227, 228, 229, 238, 258, 283, 287, 300, 319
pollution problems xii
Postcolonial and Eco-Studies 157
postcolonial crises 73
postcolonial criticism 156, 158
postcolonial ecocriticism 7, 9, 16, 28, 33, 67, 85, 99, 114, 131, 133, 134, 137, 138, 139, 150, 151, 153, 156, 157, 158, 159, 165, 226, 230, 231, 246, 297, 298, 306, 309, 317, 318, 321, 324
postcolonial ecological concerns 156
postcolonial elucidation 11
postcolonial green scholarship 158
post-colonialism 103, 105, 113, 157
postcolonial studies 157, 298, 324
post-colonial theory 37, 159
poverty 74, 118, 127, 139, 228, 244, 263, 293, 294, 299, 301
pre-colonial African ecosystems 3
proverbs 11, 22, 23, 26, 60, 228, 280
Prozesky, Martin 22

Qualitative methods 278
Quayson, Ato 4, 16, 20, 34, 98, 166, 309, 310

racial injustice 112
racism 137, 140, 157, 159
radio drama 185
Rangarajan, Swarnalatha xi
reformist ecology 35
refugees 104, 110, 111
regeneration, environmental 25

religion 37, 79, 91, 157, 180, 220, 234, 235, 282, 296, 324
religious dogma 76. *See also* biblical dogma
Romantic Ecocriticism 157
romantic philosophy 13
Romantic poets 46
Romantic traditions 10
Roos, Bonnie 158
Rothenberg, David 37
Rotimi, Ola 282
Roy, Arundhati 134
Rueckert, William 52, 89, 154, 158, 201, 236, 295
Rwandan genocide 62, 63

Sachs, Wolfgang 132
Saro-Wiwa, Ken xv, xvi, 134, 135, 138, 152, 168, 169, 177, 294, 298, 317, 318
Sarveswaran, Vidya xi
scenography 179, 180, 181, 182, 183, 184, 185, 186, 187, 188, 196, 197, 328
Schneider-Mayerson, Matthew 303
sculpture 8, 157
Sesan, Azeez Akinwumi 206
Sessions, George 12, 35, 36
sexism 157, 159
sexual assault 120
sexual objectification 109
Shales, Melissa 55
Shell Oil 135
Shinto beliefs 95. *See also* religion
Shire, Warsan viii, 12, 103, 104, 105, 109, 111, 112, 113, 114
Sinha, Indra 134
Sixth Mass Extinction 146
slavery 157, 159, 161, 296
Slaymaker, William xv, 1, 4, 20, 34, 72, 73, 103, 114, 155, 156, 166, 297, 310, 313, 317, 321
Slovic, Scott xiii, xv, 132, 151, 152, 155, 256, 275, 295, 296, 310, 327

INDEX

Social-ecological Resilience 172
social injustice 110, 168, 229
social media 210
Somalia 111, 138, 320
Soper, Kate 60
South Africa xii, 22, 24, 28, 31, 75, 79, 81, 275, 278, 279, 312, 323, 324
  Eastern Cape 75, 76
  KwaZulu-Natal 69, 79, 81, 85, 324
  Xhosa community 28
  Xhosa village 27
  Zululand 69, 74, 79, 81
South African literature 69, 70, 84
Sowande, Bode 204
Soyinka, Wole 23, 34, 233, 247, 290
spirituality 21, 40, 60, 192, 238, 279, 282, 288, 324
Sreeter, Hazel 39
Stanley, Brooke 70
stereotypes 104, 107, 109, 113
storytelling 70, 78, 79, 84, 180, 192
Streeter, Hazel 39, 50
subjectivity 13, 51, 53, 74, 272
Sudan 111
Sule, Emmanuel Egya viii, xv, 1, 7, 15, 32, 90, 99, 128, 153, 160, 161, 164, 166, 231, 314, 317, 318, 319, 320
Summers, Lawrence 140
supernatural, the 29, 210
superstition 210, 211
sustainable development 9, 29, 176, 182, 202, 266
sustainable practices xvi, 9, 10, 14, 181, 183, 196, 257, 267
symbolism of nature 41
sympathetic imagination 76, 80, 82

taboo 11, 12, 22, 23, 108, 109, 277, 278, 279, 280, 284, 285, 286, 287, 289. *See also* customs
Tangwa, Godfrey 22
technological industrialism 70, 71
Tem, Edwin Nji 14, 311

terrorism 71, 223, 225, 227
theatre and performance practices 14. *See also* Cameroon
Thoreau, Henry 155
Thunberg, Greta 312
Tiffin, Helen 28, 33, 53, 67, 80, 85, 91, 99, 132, 133, 141, 150, 151, 157, 158, 159, 165, 220, 221, 231, 237, 246, 293, 297, 309
totemic spirits 284
toxic imperialism 140
toxic waste 140, 229. *See also* pollution
toxins 171
Traditional Chinese Medicine Market 74
trauma 30, 79, 110, 111, 167, 206
tree-planting activity 188
tsunami 87, 93, 94, 95, 97
Tutu, Archbishop Desmond 83

ubuntu 23, 81, 83
Udechukwu, Obiora 141
Ukpokolo, Isaac 23
underdevelopment 139
unemployment 57, 223
United Kingdom 104, 113, 212, 323, 324
  London 5, 7, 8, 15, 23, 25, 32, 33, 34, 50, 67, 98, 99, 106, 107, 127, 128, 150, 151, 152, 165, 166, 176, 177, 193, 198, 231, 245, 274, 289, 290, 320
United Nations Framework Convention on Climate Change 251, 275
University of Jos 137, 197, 213
urbanization 24, 28, 30, 31, 125, 219, 319
Usman, Adamu Kyuka 217, 218, 222, 229, 230

Venter, Eben 69, 74, 75, 76, 77, 80, 83, 84, 85, 86

Venter, Maureen 75
visual arts 137, 156
Vital, Anthony 1

waste management 118, 184, 225, 237
Wellek, Rene 44
Western enlightenment discourse 74
White, Lynn 288
White-supremacy-cene 71
wilderness 20, 35, 72, 74, 81, 82, 83, 84, 142, 219, 221, 236
wildlife 23, 25, 28, 29, 55, 122, 123, 135, 220, 224, 278
wildlife preservation 23
Williamson, Judith 221
Williams, Raymond 154
Women's Literature 167
Wordsworth, William 44
World Bank 140
World Health Organization 270
World Meteorological Organization 260
World War II 144, 146
Wu, Chengyi Coral 6

Yoruba belief system 234
Yoruba cosmology 148
youth participation 261
Yukie, Kinno 12

zero-sum game 78
Zimbabwe 22, 313
Zola, Emile 219
zoocriticism 53
zoomedia 51, 52, 60, 61, 62, 65, 66
zoomorphism 61
zoophobia 60
zoophobic 54, 56
zoopoetics 53, 60
Zulu philosophy 82. *See also* ubuntu

www.ingramcontent.com/pod-product-compliance
Lightning Source LLC
Chambersburg PA
CBHW042041240426
43667CB00047B/2933